T0135958

Structural Self-organization
in Multi-Agents and Multi-Robotic Systems

Von der Fakultät Informatik,
Elektrotechnik und Informationstechnik der Universität Stuttgart
zur Erlangung der Würde des akademischen Graden
Doctor rerum naturalium (Dr.rer.nat.)
genehmigte Abhandlung

Vorgelegt von

Serge Kernbach

aus Kislowodsk

Hauptberichter:	Prof. Dr. habil. P. Levi
Mitberichter:	Prof. Dr. Dr. h.c. mult. H. Haken
Tag der mündlichen Prüfung:	25 Oktober 2007

Institut für Parallele und Verteilte Systeme
der Universität Stuttgart

2007

Bibliografische Information der Deutschen Nationalbibliothek

Die Deutsche Nationalbibliothek verzeichnet diese Publikation in der
Deutschen Nationalbibliografie; detaillierte bibliografische Daten sind
im Internet über http://dnb.d-nb.de abrufbar.

D93 (Diss. Universität Stuttgart)

ISBN 978-3-8325-2048-9

Logos Verlag Berlin GmbH
Comeniushof, Gubener Str. 47,
10243 Berlin
Tel.: +49 030 42 85 10 90
Fax: +49 030 42 85 10 92
INTERNET: http://www.logos-verlag.de

Serge Kernbach

Structural Self-organization
in Multi-Agents and Multi-Robotic Systems

D93(Diss. Universität Stuttgart)

Drei Verwandlungen nenne ich euch des Geistes: wie der Geist zum Kamele wird, und zum Löwen das Kamel, und zum Kinde zuletzt der Löwe.

Vieles Schwere gibt es dem Geiste, dem starken, tragsamen Geiste, dem Ehrfurcht innewohnt: nach dem Schweren und Schwersten verlangt seine Stärke.

Was ist schwer? so fragt der tragsame Geist, so kniet er nieder, dem Kamele gleich, und will gut beladen sein...

Aber in der einsamsten Wüste geschieht die zweite Verwandlung: zum Löwen wird hier der Geist, Freiheit will er sich erbeuten und Herr sein in seiner eignen Wüste...

Neue Werte schaffen - das vermag auch der Löwe noch nicht: aber Freiheit sich schaffen zu neuem Schaffen - das vermag die Macht des Löwen...

Aber sagt, meine Brüder, was vermag noch das Kind, das auch der Löwe nicht vermochte? Was muss der raubende Löwe auch noch zum Kinde werden?

Unschuld ist das Kind und Vergessen, ein Neubeginnen, ein Spiel, ein aus sich rollendes Rad, eine erste Bewegung, ein heiliges Ja-Sagen...

Die Sorglichsten fragen heute: "wie bleibt der Mensch erhalten?" Zarathustra aber fragt als der Einzige und Erste: "wie wird der Mensch überwunden?"

[*F. W. Nietzsche, "Also sprach Zarathustra"*]

Contents

CONTENTS

List of Figures

List of Tables

Abbreviations

MAS	multi-agent systems
MA	multi-agent, e.g. MA-mechanisms
PCM	pulse-code modulation
PWM	pulse-width modulation
IR	infra red
OP	order parameter
SO	self-organization
CSP	constraint-satisfaction problem
COP	constraint-optimization problem
CML	coupled map lattice
CA	cellular automata
ODE, PDE	ordinary and partially differential equations
NLD	nonlinear dynamics
φ	the state variable used in normal forms
ξ	the state variable used in mode amplitude equations
q	the state variable used in original systems
λ_u, λ_s	"unstable" and "stable" eigenvalues

Collective, self-organizing, emergent, macroscopic phenomena/systems/behavior are used in this work as synonyms with similar (not the same) meaning.

Agent is used as a common-sense notion of *autonomous unit*. We do not differentiate between hardware, software and biological agents.

Analytic and algorithmic approaches/methodologies/methods are used in the context of *reductive and computational* approaches/methodologies/methods in the investigation of collective phenomena.

Within this work (in the frameworks of corresponding projects) we used the *Delmia^{TM}*, developed by *Delmia Corporation* © for simulating industrial process planning. Agent-based scaling mechanisms as well as the architecture of micro-robots are simulated by using *AnyLogic^{TM}*, developed by *XJ Technologies Company* ©.

Abstract

This thesis deals with a creation of desired self-organizing processes in collective, primarily in multi-agent and multi-robotic, systems. Such processes are called artificial self-organization. It is demonstrated that emergent phenomena can artificially be designed when to treat the corresponding systems on a new structural level. The thesis establishes relations between structural, functional and behavioral levels of collective systems and introduces a systematic approach towards creating artificial self-organization. Among others, it is shown, that analytic (e.g. ordinary/partial differential equations) and algorithmic (e.g. non-differentiable discrete algorithms) models are useful in a supplemental description of collective systems and successful handling of their enormous complexity.

The developed approach is demonstrated by two practical examples of real systems where the artificial self-organization, created on the structural level, leads to the desired emergent behavior. The first one is the multi-agent planning system, used in modern flexible manufacturing. The implemented structural generators make this system adaptive to a wide range of environmental changes. The second example originates from the domain of swarm robotics. The structural rules, programmed in micro-robots Jasmine, enable the robotic swarm to reveal different spatio-temporal and functional effects. Both examples demonstrate how the real restrictions change the emergent properties of collective systems and give a deeper understanding of such a phenomenon as collective artificial intelligence.

Zusammenfassung

Die Doktorarbeit beschäftigt sich mit dem Erschaffen von gezielten Selbstorganisation-pozessen in kollektiven, hauptsächlich Multi-Agenten und Multi-Roboter Systemen. Solche Prozesse sind als künstliche Selforganisation bekannt. Es wurde gezeigt, dass die emergenten Phänomene künstlich erschaffen werden können, wenn man die entsprechenden Systeme auf einem neuen strukturellen Niveau behandelt. Die Arbeit zeigt die Relation zwischen Strukturellen-, Funktionalen- und Verhaltensebenen in kollektiven Systemen und führt ein systematisches Verfahren für das Erschaffen der künstlichen Selbstorganisation ein.

Das erste Kapitel dieser Arbeit widmet sich der formalen Einführung, Problemdefinition, allgemeinen Literaturüberblick, Struktur und Gliederung der vorliegenden Doktorarbeit. Die praktischen Aspekte der Arbeit, wissenschaftliche Projekte und Veröffentlichungen werden betont und kurz aufgelistet.

Das zweite Kapitel befasst sich mit den ursprünglichen Problemen des kollektiven Verhaltens. Es wird zwischen analytischen und algorithmischen Vorgehensweisen unterschieden. In dem ersten analytischen Teil wird das klassische Drei-Körperproblem betrachtet, wobei auf die prinzipielle analytische Unlösbarkeit eines Systems mit n-wechselwirkenden Körpern hingewiesen wird. Hier wird auch die reduktive synergetische Strategie kurz eingeführt. In dem zweiten Teil werden die zentralen, verteilen und selbstorganisierenden Systeme betrachtet. Agenten- und Multi-Agenten-basierte Verfahren und ein entsprechender Formalismus werden dargestellt. Es wird auch das Anwendungsszenario mit Mikroroboterschwarm und die entsprechenden Probleme angesprochen. Am Ende des Kapitels wird die Skalierbarkeit des kollektiven Verhaltens erwähnt.

Das dritte Kapitel beschäftigt sich mit einer grundlegenden Frage: was ist eine künstliche Selbstorganisation? Es wird zuerst ein historischer Überblick verschafft, indem die unterschiedlichen Betrachtungsweisen der Selbstorganisation geschildert werden. Anschliessend werden die Beispiele für eine natürliche und künstliche Selbstorganisation dargestellt. Dabei wird die besondere Rolle der technischen Restriktionen deutlich gemacht. In diesem Kapitel ist eine Unterteilung zwischen funktionalen und strukturellen Teilen der Selbstorganisation eingefügt und anhand der ausgewählten Beispielen erläutert. Anschliessend wird eine Funktion der lokalen Regelen erklärt und zwei Fälle der künstlichen Selbstorganisation mit vertikalen und horizontalen Aufbauprinzipien gezeigt.

Das vierte Kapitel betrachtet eine funktionale Selbstorganisation. Die erste Hälfte dieses Kapitels beschäftigt sich mit einer analytischen Vorgehensweise für eine gezielte funktionale Selbstorganisation. Unterschiedliche Verfahren, u.a. Interaktion mit räumlichen Eigenvektoren, Normalformenverfahren und inertiale Mannigfaltigkeiten sind gezeigt. Die zweite Hälfte dieses Kapitels beschäftigt sich mit den algorithmischen Ansätze für eine gezielte funktionale Selbstorganisation. Hier ist ein Beispiel der modernen selbstorganisierenden Produktion eingefügt. Anhand dieses Beispieles wird die Anwendung der algorithmische Methoden, z.B. constraints-safisfaction Algorithmus oder Multi-Agenten basierte Planerstellung betrachtet. Anschliessend wird die Skalierbarkeit der funktionalen Selbstorganisation noch einmal diskutiert.

Das fünfte Kapitel geht weiter in der Darstellung der künstlichen Selbstorganisation und betrachtet eine strukturelle Selbstorganisation. Dieses Kapitel ist zentral in der gesamten Doktorarbeit, hier werden die theoretischen Begründung und praktischen Anwendungen einer strukturellen Selbstorganisation aufgeführt. Zuerst werden einige ausgewählte Beispiele der horizontalen Emergenz gezeigt, wobei eine entscheidende Rolle der sogenannten Regelgeneratoren, wie z.b. L-Systeme, Selbstreferenz, oder genetische Programmierung, unterstrichen wird. Danach sind diese Regelgeneratoren auf bereits aufgefürten Produktionssystemen und Schwarmroboter angewendet. Die Ergebnisse sowie die technische Einzelheiten und die Experimente werden ausführlich betrachtet. Die Doktorarbeit wird mit einer Zusammenfassung beendet.

Chapter 1

Introduction

1.1 General motivation

What will happen if technical systems become able to change themselves ?
What potential does hide in this ability ?
Where is a limit of self-modification, can it be predicted and controlled ?
Does it lead to a revolution of machines ?
Could they evolve the intellect and civilization like human one ?

These questions represent a new understanding of the dedicated natural phenomenon. This phenomenon occupied the attention of the greatest east and west antic philosophers like Lao Tzu, Platon, Aristotel. This was studied by Galileo, Kepler, Newton, Poincare from the viewpoint of dynamics. Diderot, Lamarck, Darwin considered its biological aspects. Ashby, Wiener, von Neumann developed the first computer models. In the newest time, the discussion broke out with all one's might. "Game of life", "Matrix", "Machine Revolution" are only a few social and technical terms associated with new understanding of this phenomenon. Its name is *evolution*.

Evolution, or a process of changes over time, is one of the basic property of the World. *"In the broadest sense, evolution is merely change, and so is all-pervasive; galaxies, languages, and political systems all evolve. Biological evolution ... is change in the properties of populations of organisms that transcend the lifetime of a single individual"* (Futuyma, 1986). It can be thought as of only simple dynamical changes, complex adaptation or even in the context of creating. It takes specific forms in each system, so there are natural organic evolution, evolution of celestial bodies, evolution of societies and so forth.

Understanding evolutional processes is one of essential tasks of natural and technical science. It helps solving biological problems that impact our lives, as e.g. vaccinations or methods to combat insect pests for crop management. Learning about the evolutionary roots of diseases may provide clues about how to treat them. And considering the basic processes of evolution can help us to understand the origin of genetic diseases. Even the idea that extraterrestrial intelligent beings may inhabit planets in other stellar systems is related with understanding evolutional processes: *"... whether the origin of simple self-replicators is so common a phenomena that they are likely to have arisen on the planets suitable for life. When we know the answer to these questions the final and biological question is whether simple self-replicators on suitable planets will evolve toward complex and intelligent beings"* (Witting, 1997, p.14).

In the light of technological progress in the last two decades, the understanding evolutional processes gets new value: from natural evolution to artificial evolution. *"Recently, however, technology has become available which allows artificial evolution to manipulate the configuration of a silicon chip directly ... But why should one be interested in this? ... The answer is that evolution of reconfigurable hardware need not be just a high speed implementation of what could easily be done in software: evolution is crafting a physical object that exists in real time and space ... For the scientist, all three [opportunities of artificial evolution] are of great interest, as they apply as much to evolution in nature – and attempts to draw inspiration from it – as to electronics"* (Thompson, 1997). It is recognized, that an industrial progress obeys some principles; they have a few analogies to natural evolution. Rise of computational power and new understanding the role of collective systems, like those in internet or in collective robotics, created new questions to researchers of evolution: Could machines be developed by means of some evolutionary process ? Could machines create their own civilization ? Are artificial systems just a part of natural evolution ?

The investigation of main principles of evolution as well as a collection of experimental evidences towards evolution was undertaken a long time ago in many different scientific areas. However, until now, there is no single theory of evolution, but there is a continuing change in our understanding of evolution. We can find many ideas related to evolutional principles in different schools of Greek cosmologists. They first attempted to develop comprehensive and systematic accounts of natural phenomena. Greek thinkers came to recognize the concepts of space, time and motion, which lay at the heart of any view of natural phenomena. *"Aristotle died in 324 B.C. His legacy was a comprehensive cosmological system which, however, he did not pretend to be either complete or final. Many details, e.g., the exact motions of the planets and the details of projectile motion, were either left for other investigators or included in Aristotle's scheme in only a very sketchy sense. Furthermore, Aristotle's system was not the only available scientific world view in ancient times. There was, of course, the Platonic system, the Atomistic point of view, and, with the development of Hellenistic culture, a number of alternative systems based on Stoic and Epicurean principles were developed"* (Bradie & Duncan, 1997, cpt.6).

In ages, after Greek thinkers, we found many evidences towards further development and modifications of Greek systems, like neo-Platonism, neo-Stoicism, different streams of medieval mystical theology and so on. These works reflected evolutionary processes in the light of Christian doctrines almost 12 next centuries. *"The emergence of the Aristotelian system as the embodiment of the scientific world view of Western man prior to the scientific revolution in the 17th century was a long and complex process"* (Bradie & Duncan, 1997, cpt.6). Only in 17-18th centuries, in the stream of Rationalism and Empiricism, evolutionary ideas got their further development. We point here to three fundamental works, among many other, that essentially contributed to a modern view on evolution. These are Descartes's *Principia philosophiae (Principles of Philosophy)*, published in 1644, Newton's *Philosophiae Naturalis Principia Mathematica*, 1687 (*Mathematical Principles of Natural Philosophy*, 1729) and Darwin's *On the Origin of Species by Means of Natural Selection, or the Preservation of Favoured Races in the Struggle for Life*, published in 1859.

These works are of importance, because here we can find the first clear differentiation between earlier philosophical and theological and later scientific treatment of evolutionary processes. Descartes-Newton-Darwin system leaved for scientific community three important points: the scientific methodology, the explicit causality between action and reaction, and understanding the dynamics of evolution as natural and comprehensible process. *"These principles are the laws and conditions of certain motions, and powers or forces, which chiefly have respect to philosophy; but, lest they should have appeared of themselves dry and barren, I have illustrated them here and there with some philosophical scholiums, giving an account of such things as are of more general nature, and which philosophy seems chiefly to be founded on; such as the density and the resistance of bodies, spaces void of all bodies, and the motion of light and sounds. It remains that, from the same principles, I now demonstrate the frame of the System of the World"* (Newton, 1687, b.III).

After Newton and Darwin, discussions and further evolutionary research in the large scientific, social and philosophical context did not finish even today. The rediscovery of Mendelian genetics in 1900, and the initial development of mathematical theory underlying population genetics in 1908 paved the way for deeper understanding biological evolution and the rise of neo-Darwinian theories. In modern time, evolution becomes a focus in a large number of interdisciplinary works. Wiener (Wiener, 1948), Ashby (Ashby, 1962), von Neumann (von Neumann, 1966) proposed principles of cybernetic evolution and so contributed to further computer-based theories of evolution. Synergetics (Haken, 1983a) suggests common principles of self-organization. Biological researchers supplement and expand theories of evolution on ecological, biological, biochemical systems (e.g. (Bonabeau *et al.*, 1999), (Camazine *et al.*, 2003)). Robotics and especially swarm robotics provides experimental results about controlling artificial societies (Nolfi & Floreano, 2004). Even to give on overview of main modern works towards evolutionary processes represents a serious scientific task. However, evolution still remains *terra incognita*. Scientists, even today, are unable to explain exactly how evolution works. Some aspects of evolution are easy to understand, but generally, effects and dynamics of evolution are unknown. *"Today, nearly all biologists acknowledge that evolution is a fact. The term theory is no longer appropriate except when referring to the various models that attempt to explain how life evolves... it is important to understand that the current questions about how life evolves in no way implies any disagreement over the fact of evolution"* (Campbell, 1990, p. 434).

The works of XIX-XX centuries revealed two principal obstacles in understanding evolutional processes. The first of them originates from physics, or more exactly from quantum physics and nonlinear dynamics. The famous *"The more precisely the position is determined, the less precisely the momentum is known in this instant, and vice versa"* [Heisenberg, uncertainty paper, 1927] and *"In the past an equation was only considered solved when one had expressed the solution with the aid of a finite number of known functions; but this is hardly possible one time in a hundred. What we should always try to do, is to solve the qualitative problem, that is to find the general form of the curve representing the unknown function"* [Poincaré, 1889] essentially change our understanding of predictability of evolutional processes. Even having formulated mathematical models of some evolutional process, we often fail to predict arising effects since we cannot solve these models, even in principle.

Another fundamental problem consists in a huge complexity of evolutionary systems. *"At least since the days of Darwin, the idea of evolution has been associated with the increase of complexity: if we go back in time we see originally only simple systems ... while more and more complex systems ... appear in later stages. Traditional evolutionary theory, however, had no methods for analysing complexity, and so this observation remained a purely intuitive impression. The last decades have seen a proliferation of theories offering new concepts and principles for modelling complex systems ... These have led to the awareness that complexity is a much more important aspect of the world than classical, reductionist science would have assumed"* (Heylighen, 1996). A huge complexity obstructs not only analyzing, but also modeling evolutionary systems and processes. In this way a growing computational power of modern computers assists in further understanding the evolution, however cannot principally solve the problem of evolutionary complexity.

Thus, after many centuries of philosophical, theological, scientific and social development, we come closely to the origin of evolutionary processes. However, the latest state of evolutionary research consists in many, more or less independent, streams (like modern genetics, "game of life", cellular robotics) and researchers are looking for new ways to get the most "deepest" insight into evolution and to consolidate these research domains.

Thinking about evolution a few years ago, we once observed how our child played with Lego constructor. We were fascinated how simple stones composed step-by-step more and more complex constructions. However, our attention was attracted to that how he played with created constructions: cars can move; with two additional stones they get flayed; some other changes and so the construction becomes an "universal spaceship-car-submarine". It seems that the kind of game depends on characteristics of construction: wheels allow "moving games", wings - all kinds of flight. Most interesting was a transformation between constructions initiated by their "imagined" behavior: if a car encounters an obstacle, it got wings to fly it round. Observing this game, we suddenly understand that in this "evolution" there are three different dynamical processes: dynamics of structure, dynamics of function and some dynamical process that maps a behavior of Lego construction on the structure of this construction. With this last process the sequence *structure → function → behavior* gets closed and the game becomes evolutional: from unconnected stones to "complex, multi-functional construction".

These three dynamical processes can be found in many evolutionary systems, like biological populations or self-organizing networks. However, the systematic investigation a relation between structure, function and behavior has a quite short history. One of the first remarks on this relation can be found by W.Ross Ashby. He was interested in the relationship between various properties of parts (function of subsystems) and corresponding properties of the whole (structure of system). Here we can refer to his statement about e.g. equilibrium: *"The whole is at a state of equilibrium if and only if each part is at state of equilibrium in the conditions provided by the other parts"* (Ashby, 1957, p.83). The relation between structure and function received an essential attention in cybernetics, e.g. in the famous book of Valentin Turchin (Turchin, 1977). Many useful ideas about hierarchies of structures can be found in works of Herbert Simon (Simon, 1962). Serious attention to structures and functions is paid by researches of biological evolution as those in ecological systems e.g. (Zhang & Wu, 2002), molecular chemistry (Lehn, 2002) and so on. There are some interdisciplinary works aimed to this topic as e.g. the work of Stuart Kauffman: *"We may have begun to understand evolution as the marriage of selection and self-organization"* (Kauffman, 1993, p.78) or the mentioned work of Francis Heylighen (Heylighen, 1996).

Looking for a theory, that could explain a relation between *structures, functions* and *emergent behavior* in a precise/mathematical fashion, we failed to find it. Even nonlinear dynamics, the discipline that delivers the most exact information about evolution, does not treat these processes. Dynamics, from the time of Galileo, Kepler and Newton, considers equations of motion, which model only a functionality of dynamical systems. The equations produce some behavior that is similar to a real behavior of the system. Structural components remain completely outside of the model. *These rules [for the member of biological groups] are often implemented in the form of mathematical model or simulation. The primary goal of such models in not to include in minute detail every aspect of the system's biology, but rather to capture its essence. Therefore a model based upon self-organization will often appear to be an overly simplified caricature of a biological process"* (Camazine et al., 2003, p.91). Thus, mathematical models, explaining evolutional processes, are always focused on the relation *function → behavior*. For instance, let us consider the predators-preys system. It models a specific functionality (behavior) of both species. There are no mathematical models that connect individuals (the structure of population) with the resulting functionality of population and with a behavior of predators-preys coexistence. We believe that structural components are principal in evolutionary processes; they can change the functionality of systems and so provide mechanisms for *self-modification* during evolution. Understanding structural dynamics opens the way to *controllable artificial evolution*.

Thus, the evolution, or more exactly, a gap in our understanding a relation between structure, function and emergent behavior in evolutionary processes represents the main motivation of this thesis. We are interested in this question because of two reasons: it represents some fundamental issue and has a large practical importance. For example, the newest technological development, such as micro-robotics, demonstrated that controlling collective behavior of robotic groups cannot be based on traditional principles. The micro-robots are "too simple" for e.g. behavioral-based controlling; new principles are required. These should be also simple, distributed, emergent, evolutionary - like those in societies of collective insects. We believe that these principles are interdisciplinary: biology, computer science, nonlinear dynamics and other disciplines can compose a basis for a "swarm mathematics" - a discipline that deals with evolution in artificial systems.

1.2 Problem formulation, goals and methodology

As pointed out in the previous section, understanding the role of structures in evolutionary processes represents the main motivation for this work. However, we cannot even think about exploring the whole issue of evolutionary structures because of its high complexity. Therefore in the following consideration we have to restrict ourselves to the type of **systems** and evolutionary **processes**, that we deal with. After that we have to formulate the problem and research goals more precisely.

We start with **systems**. Systems, where we investigate a relation between structures and evolutionary processes, are primarily technical systems. Therefore, evolutionary processes represent the important research point in technical systems: forms, differences to natural evolution and so on. These technical systems are collective systems; they consist of many interacting components without central elements. Examples of them are multi-agent systems of different origin: hardware agents like robots, software agents like those in planning systems or in internet and so on. Lately, collective robotic systems build a separate branch of robotics, known as networked robotics, swarm robotics and so on. However, multi-agent systems (MAS) still allow generalizing collective systems and treating their essential properties; MAS will be often mentioned in this thesis.

Speaking about evolutionary **processes**, we distinguish three main aspects of them:

- *Dynamical aspect.* Here the stability, qualitative and quantitative characteristics of dynamics are in the focus;

- *Self-organizing aspect.* The focus of this aspect lies on the spontaneous emergence of new characteristics;

- *Evolutionary aspect.* This aspect includes many short-term as well as long-term processes, like adaptation, learning and self-learning, purposeful modifications, dealing with information and so on.

All these aspects of evolution are closely related, i.e. evolution includes self-organization, which demonstrates some dynamics. However, these aspects are of different complexity; each following aspect introduces new components and so increases complexity of consideration. In this work we treat the second aspect, namely self-organization, because of two reasons. Firstly, the dynamics of collective systems was already a long time in the focus of many investigations. There are known analytical works, as e.g. Synergetics (Haken, 1977), nonlinear dynamics (Wiggins, 1990), coupled map lattices (Kaneko, 1993), modeling (Helbing, 1997), as well as algorithmic/simulative ones, as e.g. negotiations in multi-agent systems (Sandholm, 1996), dynamics of distributed cooperation (Back & Kurki-Suonio, 1988), generally distributed systems (Coulouris *et al.*, 2001) and so on. In opposite, the self-organization in collective systems, and especially its structural and algorithmic aspects, is relatively weak investigated. For example, an appearance of emergent properties during self-organization is not completely understood. There are no known general mechanisms of self-organization. Finally, there are almost no works, which explain the self-organization in technical systems. Secondly, a further exploration of evolutionary aspects cannot be done without deep understanding the self-organizing processes.

Defining the research topics more precisely, we are interested in how the self-organization can be created artificially, which rules can create a purposeful self-organization and how to generate these rules. We reformulate the problem of structures in evolutionary processes in the following way. We investigate the *relation between structures, functions and emergent behavior of self-organizing processes in collective systems from the viewpoint of local rules which generate these SO-processes.* This point can be summarized as the **structural self-organization in multi-agent and multi-robotic systems** and represents the title of the thesis. This formulation leads to three following important research points:

1. to specify a relation between functional, structural and emergent properties of collective systems;

2. to demonstrate the methodological way of how to deal with a high complexity of emergent phenomena;

3. to investigate structural self-organization in artificial (multi-agent and multi-robotic) systems and to develop an approach to generate local rules.

These three points are **three main goals of this work**. These research goals contain, in turn, the following sub-goals and are expected to be investigated by using the following methodology:

1. Relation between functional, structural and emergent properties of collective systems.
It is expected to answer the following questions about self-organization in artificial/ technical systems:
– main differences between self-organization in natural and technical systems;
– appearance of hierarchies in artificial SO-phenomena;
– relation between functional and structural SO-phenomena.
This point is the first one because it delivers a methodological foundation for the further work. We intend to compare natural and artificial self-organizing phenomena from different viewpoints: analogies, local rules, benefit and so on. Based on this comparison, we expect to come to underlying notions behind self-organization and then to reformulate them for artificial systems in the structural case.

2. Methodological way of treating a high complexity of emergent phenomena.
Treating complexity represents the important methodological point underlying the work. We refer here to Prof. Haken: *"Complex systems are composed of many individual parts,*

elements, or subsystems that quite often interact with each other in a complicated fashion. One classical recipe for coping with such systems is that due to Descartes. According to him one has to decompose a complex system into more and more elementary parts until one arrives at a level at which these parts can be understood. ... On the other hand, by means of the interaction of the elements of a system, new qualitative features are brought about at a macroscopic level. Thus undoubtedly there remains an enormous gap in our understanding of the relations between the microscopic and the macroscopic level. It is the goal of synergetics to bridge this gap ..." (Haken, 1996, p.9).

As mentioned by Prof. Haken, there are two methodological ways to deal with a high complexity of collective phenomena. The first one is the decomposing approach. It is more known as a reductive methodology and it suggests to reduce complexity to only several characteristics that can be understood. We denote this way sometimes also as an analytic treatment of collective phenomena, because it is closely related to nonlinear dynamics. Another way states that emergent phenomena arise exactly due to a high complexity and proposes to consider it as a non-reductive value. Instead of decomposition, the simulation becomes the focus of investigation. This methodology is often denoted as the computational (or algorithmic) treatment of collective phenomena. In this work we apply and compare both methodological ways.

3. Investigation of structural self-organization in artificial (multi-agent and multi-robotic) systems and generation of local rules.

Derivation of local rules, which can generate the desired emergence, represents one of the main points of this work. We consider two cases: functional self-organization, where the focus of consideration lies on specific mechanisms of coordination and structural case, where we are primarily interested in a generation of local rules. For this research point we use a few different methodological approaches: horizontal mechanisms of coordination, top-down rules derivation and so on. In each section the underlying methodological schema is represented.

1.3   Structure of the thesis

This work is divided into five chapters by following the logic:

- *understanding collective phenomena (Chapter 2, 3)*;

- *functional self-organization (Chapter 4)*;

- *structural self-organization (Chapter 5)*.

The structure of this work is shown in Figure 1.1. We make an overview of literature, already existing approaches (state of the art) at the beginning of each chapter. This form is chosen because the chapters are thematically very different and to collect overviews into one chapter is hardly possible.

In the first **chapter** we introduce the general motivation, formulate the problem and sketch the solution suggested by the work. Especial attention is paid to the applications.

Chapters 2 and 3 are devoted to understanding collective phenomena. Chapter 2 demonstrates the general origin of problems encountered by investigating SO-systems. We consider first the "classical" analytical viewpoint on collective phenomena, originated from the problem of three interacting bodies. Then, we introduce algorithmic methodology on the example of multi-agent systems. Here we discuss several analogies with analytical

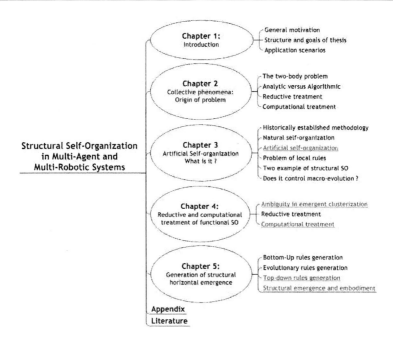

Figure 1.1: *Structure of the thesis. Underlined sections contain practical examples.*

case. Based on "analytic" and "algorithmic" we introduce the reductive and computational methodologies.

Chapter 3 considers the important methodological question: which form does take a self-organization in artificial, primarily technical, systems ? The need of this chapter is formulated in Chapter 2, where we consider the following paradox: *emergent behavior appears without being preprogrammed, however, technical systems cannot work without being programmed.* In Chapter 3 we consider a large background of natural self-organization and establish several analogies for the artificial case. The important result of this chapter is a separation between functional and structural SO-phenomena and introduction to the problem of local rules. Two next chapters treat the functional and structural self-organization, whose consideration is started here.

In Chapter 4 we return to the reductive and computational methodologies and apply them to autonomous systems undergoing the *functional* self-organization. The chapter is started by an example of emergent clusterization. This examples is intended to demonstrate the ambiguity in collective phenomena. Then we consider the reductive methodology on several independent examples. Computational methodology is demonstrated on one practical example originating from manufacturing environment.

Chapter 5 prolongs the consideration, started in the previous chapter, for the case when a collective system undergoes the *structural* self-organization. The main point lies on the generation of local rules. We give an overview of bottom-up and evolutionary generation and introduce the top-down technique. For that we consider the decomposition approach, and then, based on this, the generation of local rules. In this chapter we apply the rule-generation technique to real robotic system and for that introduce a few concepts dealing with real systems. One of them is the embodiment concept introduced in Section 5.9. Finally, we describe the micro-robotic test platform "Jasmine" and illustrate the derived emergent behavior in real experiments with swarm robots.

Appendix
In appendix we give an overview of electrical schemes of the micro-robot "Jasmine".

1.4 Application scenarios

The works have been performed within tree big research projects:

- **SFB 467** (Sonderforschungsbereich 467) "Transformable Business Structures for Multiple-Variant Series Production", supported by the German Research Foundation (Deutsche Forschungsgemeinschaft, DFG);

- **I-Swarm** Project: Intelligent Small World Autonomous Robots for Micro - manipulation, supported by European Union (I-Swarm, 2003-2007);

- **Collective Micro-Robotics**: IPVS project dealing with swarm robotics (see more in www.swarmrobot.org).

The main point of SFB467 is intended to develop flexible decentralized structures in information technologies, planning, production, assembling and so on, applied to a new type of modern manufacturing. The part, which we contributed to, is related to autonomous planning systems. The goal of these systems to perform quick and flexible replanning as a reaction on different disturbances arising in modern small-series and multiple-variant production. Within this part we developed one scenario with several transformable processing machines. Description of the scenario as well as some variations is done in Sections 4.4.4 and 5.7.5.

I-Swarm project deals with developing new micro-robots. Because of many limitations (communication, computation, sensors and so on), these micro-robots can be controlled only by specific swarm-like mechanisms. The goal was to develop these mechanisms. Within this project we worked on one scenario of micro-cleaning described in Section 2.5. The robots in this scenario have to perform many collective tasks: exploration, collective sensing, coordination etc. and represent a perfect example of artificial swarm.

Collective micro-robotics is an internal project, motivated by development of the open-source (open-hardware) micro-robotic platform "Jasmine. It started in 2004.

All projects, at least in the parts, which we contributed to, treat the same problem: how to control collective systems, consisting of many planning agents or micro-robots. The problem of these projects can be narrowed down to one essential question: *which local rules have to be introduced into the each agent/robot so that common system emerges the desired collective activity ?* This question can be considered in the light of structural/functional self-organization and exactly this issue represents a practical field for this works. The results are published (among others) in (Kornienko *et al.*, 2003a), (Kornienko *et al.*, 2003b), (Kornienko *et al.*, 2003c), (Kornienko *et al.*, 2004a), (Kornienko *et al.*, 2004b), (Kornienko *et al.*, 2004c), (Kornienko *et al.*, 2004d), (Kornienko *et al.*, 2004e), (Constantinescu *et al.*, 2004). In several parts, primarily definitions of scenarios, these works have been done in cooperation with other project partners, especially with Olga Kernbach. In each case, all these cooperative parts are noted separately and I give a reference to a common source. Especial thank to my students, who, in their master theses, performed experiments with Jasmine platform and confirmed many ideas from this work.

Chapter 2

Collective behavior: origin of problem

A scientific theory should be as simple as possible, but not simpler.

[Albert Einstein]

2.1 Motivation

In this work we intend to investigate the emergent properties of collective systems from different viewpoints. However, before starting, we have to answer several important questions. Firstly, why does the collective behavior generally need to be investigated? What is an origin of this problem ? What is a specificity of collective behavior, why does it differ from other behavioral types?

Secondly, we have to outline the framework, where we perform the investigation. As mentioned in Chapter 1, we intend to study the artificial emergent phenomena on the base of collective autonomous systems. The corresponding questions are whether their collective behavior possesses its own features, which have to be taken into account. What are accompanying problems of the "big emergence problem" in autonomous systems? Here, we have also to sketch the scenarios, which exemplify our approach.

Thus, the goal of this chapter is to give an insight into the problem of collective behavior, to sketch its origin. We intend to do it in the following way. Firstly, we consider several analytical problems from classical mechanics and dynamics, because the problem of collective behavior arose first in celestial mechanics. We give also a brief look at the synergetic approach, which deals with collective phenomena. Then, we switch to collective phenomena in autonomous systems in trying to find algorithmic equivalents to analytical notions from mechanics. We expect to achieve here a clear understanding of main difficulties and to draw a way to get them round. Finally, we describe the scenarios as well as some research points needed further.

2.2 Analytic versus Algorithmic ?

In this work we often oppose "analytic" to "algorithmic". In this way we intend to achieve three goals. Firstly, to demonstrate a difference between "analytic" and "algorithmic", which lies primarily in the way of how to treat a complexity of collective phenomena. Secondly, to show that although both methodological ways are different, they are complimentary in describing emergent phenomena. Finally, to point to some issues behind both concepts, which could be denoted as "swarm mathematics".

Speaking about "analytic" and "algorithmic", we basically have in mind the following points:

- modeling of collective phenomena;

- approaches towards analyzing and forecasting the emergent properties;

- representation of information;

- general methodology applied to self-organization and effects of self-organization in collective systems.

We collected in Table 2.1 several distinctive features of "analytic" and "algorithmic" approaches.

Feature	"Analytic"	"Algorithmic"
Modelling	ODE, PDE, maps, CML	hybrid systems, Petri (Bayes, Markov) Nets, CA, Agent-based modelling
Analyzing and forecasting	reductive approaches (CM, NF approaches) statistical forecasting	simulation
Information	numeric form	symbolic form
Methodology	NLD, synergetics, dissipative systems	distributed and MA systems

Table 2.1: *Several differences between analytical and algorithmic approaches towards collective phenomena (see explanation of abbreviations at the begin of the work).*

Modeling of collective phenomena:

From our point of view, modeling is the most important issue (see e.g. (Thompson, 1989)), because a form of modeling essentially determines/restricts analyzing the derived models and forecasting a collective behavior. Analytical models are represented in the form of differential (Arnold, 1983) or discrete ((Sandefur, 1990), (Kelley & Peterson, 1991)) dynamical systems. Known are also hybrid discrete-differential (e.g. (Thompson, 1999)), integro-differential (Lakshmikantham & Rao, 1995) and some other models. Analytic models can generally be separated into microscopic and macroscopic ones.

Macroscopic models deals with some global characteristic, like temperature, pressure (in physical models (Ebeling & Feistel, 1986)), global pheromone, number of individuals (in biological models (Murray, 1977)), fuel consumption, down time (in traffic models (Helbing, 1997)), total consumed energy, number of sent communication packages (in robotic swarms (Kornienko *et al.*, 2004b)) and so on. Macroscopic models are the most commonly used models because of two reasons. Firstly, biological and chemical collective phenomena, that the investigation of emergent systems was started on, are described by reaction-diffusion systems (see overview in (Prigogine & Nicolis, 1977)). A good experience with these models is transferred also to other systems and models. The second reason is that these models reduce a complexity of collective phenomena and, in this way, essentially simplifies a treatment of these models. The reduced macroscopic representation contains, from another side, a disadvantage because we cannot work on the level of individuals. Analytical microscopic models work on the level of individuals, they are often modeled as coupled map lattices (Kaneko, 1993). Microscopic models allows representing individual behavior, however, they are of high complexity. In order to analyze these models the complexity has first to be reduced (see the next section).

Almost all algorithmic models are of microscopic nature (except computer simulation of analytical macroscopic models). In the algorithmic modeling paradigm we have essentially more instruments to describe the individual behavior. There are known several modeling approaches, like Petri/Bayes/Markov/neural nets (Russell, 1995), cellular automata (Codd, 1968), agent-based modeling (Luna & Stefannson, 2000) and so on. The choice of modeling techniques depends on the aspect of behavior, which we take into account, environmental conditions etc. The main difference between analytic and algorithmic modeling consists in different representation of underlying dynamics. Analytic models use an infinitesimal representation of dynamics (integral and differential calculation, maps are obtained as Poincaré section of corresponding differential systems, see (Wiggins, 1990)), whereas algorithmic models use different forms of a non-infinitesimal representation of dynamics (see e.g. (Prigogine & Stengers, 1984).

Analyzing and forecasting the emergent properties:

Infinitesimal and non-infinitesimal as well as microscopic and macroscopic representation of dynamics determines a further treatment of these models. Macroscopic analytical models can often be solved directly (or at least directly analyzed, e.g. stationary states, bifurcation and chaotic dynamics etc. (Guckenheimer & Holmes, 1983)). Microscopic models with more than two interacting components, in the case of resonances, cannot be directly solved (as followed from examples of celestial mechanics). Even very simple models have to be reduced (e.g. dimension) in order to perform an analysis (see e.g. examples with coupled logistic maps (Kornienko, 2007, p.91) or Hénon map (Levi et al., 1999)). Microscopic models are often treated statistically (Girko, 1974) (these approaches have some thermodynamic origin). There are known several numerical methods, allowing us to analyze infinitesimal dynamics, like numerical stability analysis, reconstruction of attractors form time series, symbolic dynamics and so on (e.g. (Thompson, 1992)).

Non-infinitesimal representation of dynamics essentially restricts further analyzing (even numerical one). Therefore, the main approach towards analyzing and forecasting algorithmic models remains only a direct simulation. There are several approaches to estimate e.g. running time, consumption of resources, even several aspects of stability, some graph-based approaches (e.g. (Sedgewick & Flajolet, 1996)), however, there is still no breakthrough in analyzing algorithmic models. We believe that non-infinitesimal character of these models does not allow such an analysis in principle. Thus, reduction/statistical ways and the direct simulation are the main differences in analyzing analytic/algorithmic models.

Representation of information and general methodology:

Difference between analytic and algorithmic models appears also in some other issues like representation and treatment of information. Analytic models treat information in a numeric form. This restricts possibilities to deal with information content and context. Although information in Shannon sense (Shannon, 1948), or more generally in sense of thermodynamic entropy (Klimontovich, 1995), is characteristic for both types of models, we correlate quantitative or statistical information primarily with analytic models (e.g. (Haken, 1983b, p.41)). There is only one exception, where we can associate a fuzzy decision (e.g. "I'm currently being 60% sure to vote for some collective decision") with some simple "pre-semantics", see more in Chapter 4. Generally, semantic information can be treated only in algorithmic models, which represent information in a symbolic form and offer more instruments to process the content of information (see overview in (Ebeling *et al.*, 1998)).

More generally, this historically established difference between analytical and algorithmic representation of cooperative phenomena appears also in the methodology of how to work with collective phenomena. Analytical domain traditionally offers a methodology from nonlinear dynamics, theory of dissipative systems, in several cases - thermodynamics. There is an attempt to summarize and generalize this methodology in the field of synergetics (Haken, 1983a). Algorithmic domain considers the collective phenomena in a context of distributed and multi-agent systems, autonomous (e.g. robotic) systems (Weiss, 1999). Here, the corresponding fields offer their own methodologies. It is sometimes difficult to compare research results (e.g. in swarm robotics) because one team is motivated by macroscopic approach from the theory of dissipative system, whereas another one is guided by an experience from the field of distributed systems. The problem of different methodology becomes more complicated because the emergent behavior seems to be different from analytic and algorithmic viewpoints. We also discuss this more in Chapter 4.

Our intension:

Looking again at Table 2.1, we see that "algorithmic" and "analytic" describes the same phenomenon, but from two different viewpoints. Moreover, these viewpoints are complementary. The next chapters of this work are so composed that to demonstrate this point. "Analytic" and "algorithmic" can work very useful together e.g. in a framework of hybrid agent. In the hybrid agent, analytical models can be applied to collective decision making and algorithmic models to a behavioral part of an agent.

Another important point concerns the mentioned notion of "swarm mathematics". As shown by experiments in I-SWARM (I-Swarm, 2003-2007) and other projects, to achieve complex collective behavioral patterns, we need approaches from different scientific domains. These domains, with their specific approaches, in fact contribute to one goal - obtaining the desired emergence. However, we fail sometimes to find a common methodology, which unifies the application of these approaches. In many cases, such a common methodology can be delivered by concepts of synergetics ((Haken, 1983a)). We return to the issue of "swarm mathematics" and a relation to "analytic" and "algorithmic" in the last chapter again.

2.3 Reductive treatment

2.3.1 Mechanics and thermodynamics

Emergent properties of collective systems are closely related with macroscopic behavior that becomes ordered during self-organization. This ordered behavior is a result of nonlinear interactions. These interactions are produced by local rules incorporated into each participant of a collective system. This basic scheme describes an appearance of collective phenomena, that this work deals with.

The principal problem of collective behavior lies in a high degree of complexity. The first scientific domain that confronted with a complexity of collective phenomena was physics (we do not consider here social science). However, in physics, the understanding and treating of this problem was historically developed in two different ways. Today, we can denote these two ways as mechanics and thermodynamics. Exactly mechanics and thermodynamics give birth to computational and reductive paradigms of treating collective phenomena that we often mentioned. In further discussion we follow in several points the work of Prigogine and Stengers (Prigogine & Stengers, 1984).

Mechanical viewpoint on collective phenomena traditionally attributes to Newton. This represents a synthesis of the developed physical (Kepler's celestial mechanics and Galileo's laws) and mathematical (infinitesimal or differential calculation) instruments and techniques. Newton mechanics establishes a dependence between forces affecting on a system and a motion (or generally dynamics) of this system. This motion can be calculated as a sum of infinity large number of infinity small "parts of motion", i.e. by integration. Infinitesimal representation of dynamics is an essential point, because it allows a calculation of displacement, velocity and acceleration in each arbitrary time point. In this way, knowing an initial condition (initial position, velocity and acceleration) and corresponding forces, we can write a differential equation. This process corresponds to modeling a dynamical system. Integration of this equation delivers a solution. To solve differential equation means to calculate an explicit trajectory of motion.

Newton dynamics is reversible, i.e. by $t = -t$ the dynamical process can be returned from actual to initial state. Newton dynamics is also deterministic, i.e. once the initial state of the system is known, it is possible to predict its further evolution as well as to reconstruct its evolutional history (the famous Laplace's demon). We skip a physical discussion about irreversible processes, as well as quantum fluctuation and deterministic chaos (Haken, 1983a, p.21) and focus on the issue of how Newton dynamics deals with complexity of collective phenomena. We would assume, that knowing the model of interacting systems, we would be able to solve it, i.e. to calculate the explicit trajectories of motion (we skip also a discussion about technical possibility to do it). However, the main problem consists in interactions between components of collective systems. In Newton dynamics (or more exactly in theory developed by Hamilton) by means of corresponding coordinate transformation (by so-called canonical transformation) we can exclude a term being in charge of potential energy, i.e. in charge of interactions between components. In this case we can solve the system in cyclical variables. Periodical character of this solution appears in the notion of *resonance*, i.e. when corresponding frequencies are commensurable. However, in trying to exclude interactions, these resonances lead to the problem of "small denominators", i.e. the corresponding potential series diverge and lead to infinite values. Poincaré in 1889 proved that the problem of "small denominators" belong to the *principal problem of nonlinear dynamics*. It means that most of the interacting systems is non-integrable. The developed later KAM theorem (Kolmogorov, Arnold, Moser) classified the cases caused by resonances (e.g. (Haken, 1983a, p.317)), see Section 2.3.3. Non-integrable systems can still be solved numerically, by methods of perturbation theory, approximated by the "closest" integrable system and so on. However, no one of these methods can give an exact and complete solution of original non-integrable system (even for a simple non-integrable system).

Another way was suggested by thermodynamics. The developed in 1811 by Fourier mathematical theory of a heat propagation in solid bodies contained principles that are not directly related with Newton dynamics. Entropy, introduced by Clausius (Clausius, 1865) in 1865 and being the central notion in thermodynamics, is a function of system's state (pressure, temperature, volume) and also not connected with kinematical equations of motion of e.g. gas molecules. Thermodynamic laws describe the properties of interacting systems on the macroscopic level. In opposite to mechanics, thermodynamics is not reversible and not deterministic. We also skip here a discussion about equilibrium and non-equilibrium, stable and unstable states (that can be found in the book of Prigogine and Stengers) and focus on how the thermodynamics treats a complexity of collective phenomena. Firstly, in several practical cases, the behavior of gas molecules is not of interest, more important is to know a dependence between e.g. temperature and volume in heat machines. Therefore, thermodynamics models have a macroscopic or mezoscopic character. Secondly, in order to return to microscopic level, Boltzmann introduced a probabilistic description. It means that we can calculate a probability to find n particles with a velocity v' between v and $v + dv$ if

29

we know macroscopic state of the systems.

Comparing Newton dynamics (denoted as mechanical point of view) and thermodynamics we can find in them an origin of diverse microscopic and macroscopic approaches. The systems, from Kepler's celestial mechanics, Newton'a apple, Boltzmnan' ideal gas, are changed to software agents or mobile micro-systems. However, the main problem of collective systems still remains the same: *we cannot exactly predict a behavior of nonlinearly interacted collective systems.* On the microscopic level we obtain non-integrable systems, on the macroscopic level we can describe a behavior of interacting components only in probabilistic way. In other words, *we do not know exactly which interactions/local rules can produce the desired self-organizations/emergent properties.* We will come to this conclusion many times in this work.

Returning to mechanics and thermodynamics, we encounter primarily two ways of how to deal with a complexity of collective systems. The first one originates from a numerical solution of differential equations. More generally, it means a simulation of microscopic models. Simulation has two main disadvantages: problem of parameters and different simulation-specific errors (e.g. rounding error, in algorithmic models it corresponds to an inadequacy of simulation model and so on). The second way consists in applying diverse reduction approaches, like a formulation of macroscopic models, reduction of microscopic models, approximating approaches and so on. *The reductive and computational approaches represent two main techniques to deal with a complexity of collective phenomena.* In the following next sections we describe the mechanical point of view as well as reductive synergetic methodology more exactly because we can transfer several useful notions from analytical to algorithmic models.

2.3.2 Mechanical point of view

Reviewing literature on a history of science (e.g. (Wall, 2002)), we encounter that each scientific field has its own origin in one or a few philosophical concepts. We believe that mechanical point of view (except astronomical and astrological origin) find some background in the problem of *many and one*, known from Ancient Greek (Cohen *et al.*, 2000). Discussion about a difference between individual and collective has a long history and continues even now. However, a quantitative understanding of differences between *many and one* took place in the scientific field only in XIX century. Classical mechanics was the first discipline, which expresses different characters of individual and collective behavior. This estimation is of essence for our treatment, because it allows us to draw several conclusions about solvability and principal restrictions of collective systems. Therefore we briefly sketch the mechanical approach to collective phenomena.

Classical mechanics is directly related to a behavior in terms of motion. In study of collective phenomena we distinguish between three important notions: *participant or agent* that takes a part in a phenomenon, this agent shows a *behavior* and, finally, *rules* that govern this behavior. All these notions have a set of descriptors, like roles, activities, abilities and so on. We show that mechanics has equivalent notions to all them. In the further description we follow (Arnold(Ed.), 1988).

Mechanics uses *point s* instead *participant* and *motion* instead *behavior*. Motion takes place in Euclidian (or three-dimensional) oriented *space* E^3. Motion implies that the point s has a *position (radius) vector* $\underline{r}$ and this position changes with time t. Position can be also described by coordinates $\underline{q}$ in E^3. This space is known as the configuration space. There are some characteristics both of motion and point. Motion can be characterized by the *velocity* $\underline{v}$ defined by $\dfrac{d\underline{r}}{dt} = \underline{\dot{r}}$ and the *acceleration* a defined by $\dfrac{d\underline{v}}{dt} = \underline{\dot{v}}$. The point can be characterized by the mass m. The pair $(\underline{r}, m)$ is called a material point (or mass-point, or particle) of mass m. Finally, instead *rules* mechanics operates with *forces* $\underline{F}$. Newton's second law determines the relation between forces, characteristics of motion and characteristics of a point (relations between agent, rules and behavior)

$$m\ddot{\underline{r}} = \underline{F}(t, \underline{r}, \dot{\underline{r}}). \tag{2.1}$$

If there are several forces, they are additive $\underline{F} = \sum_i \underline{F}_i$, e.g. interaction of n point-masses

$(\underline{r}_1, m_1), ..., (\underline{r}_n, m_n)$ in space acts as a force on the i-point as $\underline{F}_i = \sum_{i \neq j} \underline{F}_{ij}$, where $\underline{F}_{ij} = \frac{\gamma m_1 m_2}{|\underline{r}_{ij}|^3} \underline{r}_{ij}$ and $\underline{r}_{ij} = \underline{r}_i - \underline{r}_j$, $\gamma = const > 0$. *Additivity of forces means that they are of similar nature.*

To solve a mechanical problem means to find a function of time $\underline{r}(t)$ that describes a motion of a point mass s driven by the force $\underline{F}$. Inverse problem can be defined as to find the force $\underline{F}$ that cause a motion with a defined trajectory $\underline{r}(t)$. We can affirm that in this work we try to solve the inverse problem of mechanics, applied to multi-agent systems - to find such rules, that produce the desired collective behavior of agents.

Mechanics introduces several quantities that connect force, motion and point. These are:

- the moment of point-mass $\underline{p} = m\underline{v}$,

- the moment of the force $\underline{M} = \underline{r} \times \underline{f}$,

- the moment of inertia $\underline{I} = m\underline{r}^2$,

- the angular moment $\underline{k} = \underline{r} \times \underline{p} = m(\underline{r} \times \underline{v})$,

- kinetic energy $T = \dfrac{m||\underline{v}||^2}{2}$.

Existence of these cross-notions is also important for algorithmic systems, because they allow describing the corresponding processes more precisely. Examples are e.g. a number of collective decisions per steps in collective robotics, consumed energy per a number of useful activities and so on.

If the system consists of n point-masses, the corresponding dynamical quantities are additive functions $P = \sum p_i$, $F = \sum F_i$, $T = \sum \frac{m_i v_i^2}{2}$ and the point $\xi = \frac{m_i q_i}{\sum m_i}$ is center of mass of the system. The potential energy of the interaction of point-masses m_i and m_j is $\sum_{i<j} U_{ij}$, $U_{ij} = \int f_{ij}(|r_{ij}|)d|r_{ij}|$. The notion of energy allow us to consider a dynamics of the system from the viewpoint of energy conservation. So, e.g. *if the forces are conservative, then for every motion the total energy $T + U$ is constant.*

There is an observation that the fundamental law of force balance (2.1) is based on some variational principles. If we introduce a function of coordinates q_i and velocities $\dot{q}_i$ $L(q_i, \dot{q}_i, t)$, the motion at the moment t_1 and t_2 between the positions given by $q^{(1)}$ and $q^{(2)}$ can be expressed in such a way that the integral

$$S = \int_{t_1}^{t_2} L(q_i, \dot{q}_i, t)dt \tag{2.2}$$

takes a minimal possible value. The function L is called the *Lagrangian* of the system and the integral (2.2) is known as the *action* of a system. For a system of n moving particles in E^3 the L often has a form of kinetic minus potential energy

$$L(q_i, \dot{q}_i, t) = \frac{1}{2} \sum_{i=1}^{n} m_i ||m_i||^2 - V(q_i). \tag{2.3}$$

If the Lagrangian of a system is known, the equation (the Euler-Lagrange equation)

$$\frac{d}{dt}\left(\frac{dL}{d\dot{q}_i}\right) - \frac{dL}{dq_i} = 0, (i = 1, 2, ..., n) \tag{2.4}$$

forms the relationship between the acceleration, velocities and coordinates, i.e. it is the equation of motion. This is a system of n differential equations of the second order of n unknown function $q_i(t)$. The general solution contains $2n$ arbitrary constants. To determine them, it is necessary to know the initial condition, i.e. initial values of coordinates and velocities.

To pass to Hamiltonian formalism, we introduce the conjugate momenta

$$p_i = \frac{dL}{d\dot{q}_i}, i = 1, 2, ..., n, \tag{2.5}$$

make the change of variables $(q_i, \dot{q}_i) \to (q_i, p_i)$ and introduce the Hamiltonian

$$H(q_i, p_i, t) = \sum_{j=1}^{n} p_j \dot{q}^j - L(q_i, \dot{q}_i, t). \tag{2.6}$$

Since the coordinate functions $p_1, ..., p_n, q_1, ..., q_n$ form a complete set of independent functions, equations

$$\frac{dq_i}{dt} = \frac{\partial H}{\partial p_i} \tag{2.7}$$

$$\frac{dp_i}{dt} = -\frac{\partial H}{\partial q_i}, \qquad i = 1, 2, ..., n \tag{2.8}$$

form a closed system. They are called Hamilton's canonical equations.

Mechanics has two main points of view, Lagrangian mechanics and Hamiltonian mechanics. In one sense, Lagrangian mechanics is more fundamental since it is based on variational principles and it is what generalizes most directly to the general relativistic context. In another sense, Hamiltonian mechanics is more fundamental, since it is based directly on the energy concept and it is what is more closely tied to quantum mechanics. Fortunately, in many cases these branches are equivalent ...

2.3.3 The three-body Problem

The three-body problem is one of the most famous and fundamental problems of dynamical systems. This led Poincaré to make his observations of chaos. The three-body problem represents not only general approaches of nonlinear dynamics, but also demonstrates main difficulties, like nonintegrability and appearance of small denominators. In full generality this problem is still too complicated for a systematic analysis, therefore there are various simplifications or restrictions of it.

In this section we originally intended to consider the problem of three interacting bodies by following George D. Birkhoff's work (Birkhoff, 1927a, p.260) in the manner, demonstrated in the previous section. However, we was confused by the used 18th (and later 12th) dimensional vector notion and very awkward expressions. Analyzing numerous literature on the object (see overview in (Marchal, 1990)), we came to conclusion that to demonstrate even a part of this problem essentially oversteps the framework not only of this section, but also of complete thesis. Therefore we decide to discuss this important point more generally in the focus of appearance of small denominators for the cases $N = 2$ and $N > 2$. In this discussion we follow (Zaslavsky & Sagdeev, 1988).

We start from a Hamiltonian system with N degrees of freedom

$$H(p, q) \equiv H(p_1, q_1; ...; p_n, q_n), \tag{2.9}$$

and introduce the motion integral (or the first integral) F

$$F(p, q) \equiv H(p_1, q_1; ...; p_n, q_n), \tag{2.10}$$

so that

$$[H, F] \equiv 0, \tag{2.11}$$

where $[H, F]$ is a commutator or Poisson brackets

$$[A, B] \equiv \sum_{i=1}^{n} \left(\frac{\partial A}{\partial p_i} \frac{\partial B}{\partial q_i} - \frac{\partial A}{\partial q_i} \frac{\partial B}{\partial p_i} \right). \tag{2.12}$$

It is known that a system of differential equation of order $2N$ can be solved if there are $M = 2N$ first integrals of it. Hamiltonian systems can be solved if there are only $M = N$ first integrals. We can make more strong statement that if $M < N$ the system can not be solved. Integrability of the system (2.9) with N linear independent ($[F_i, F_j] \equiv 0$, i,j=1,...,n) first integrals is established by Liouville-Arnold theorem (see more in (Zaslavsky & Sagdeev, 1988)). This theorem states that motion trajectories of this system lies on N-dimensional torus and this motion is quasi-periodical with N-frequencies

$$\omega_i = \omega_i(F_1, ..., F_N), \quad i = 1, 2, ..., N \tag{2.13}$$

with corresponding angular variables ϑ

$$\dot{\vartheta}_i = \omega_i(F_1, ..., F_N), \quad i = 1, 2, ..., N, \tag{2.14}$$

where

$$\vartheta_i = \omega_i t + const, \quad i = 1, 2, ..., N. \tag{2.15}$$

Since the motion trajectory lies completely on a torus, we can speak about invariant torus. Changing the first integral F_i, we obtain a family of invariant torus. At $N = 2$ the tori, corresponding to different values of integral (F_1, F_2), do not overlap, whereas for $N > 2$ they overlap. A character of motion on a torus depends on the relation between frequencies ω_i. For instance at $N = 2$ any trajectory is closed if $\omega_2 : \omega_1$ is rational (e.g. 3:2). For irrational $\omega_2 : \omega_1$ (e.g. π : 1) the trajectory is not closed, it fills up the whole torus (or in other words it comes arbitrary close to any given point). A good illustrative example of motion on two-dimensional torus is given in (Haken, 1983a, p.28). The rational relation between $\omega_2 : \omega_1$ (or generally between $\omega_1, \omega_2, ..., \omega_N$) calls *resonance*.

Resonances are very important in understanding the dynamics of motion. To demonstrate it, consider a motion of a particle that is perturbed by a small periodical force

$$\ddot{x} = \varepsilon F(x, t), \tag{2.16}$$

33

where
$$F(x,t) = F(x, t+T). \tag{2.17}$$

The expression (2.17) means that $F(x,t)$ can be expanded into Fourier series

$$F(x,t) = \sum_{n=-\infty}^{\infty} F_n(x) e^{in\Omega t}, \quad \Omega = 2\pi/T. \tag{2.18}$$

Since $\varepsilon \ll 1$ is very small, we can write in the first approximation

$$\ddot{x}^{(0)} = 0, \tag{2.19}$$

with
$$x^{(0)} = v^{(0)} t + const. \tag{2.20}$$

The second term can then be written

$$\ddot{x}^{(1)} = \varepsilon F(x^{(0)}, t) = \varepsilon \sum_n F_n(x^{(0)}) e^{in\Omega t}, \tag{2.21}$$

and more generally
$$\ddot{x}^{(m+1)} = \varepsilon \sum_n F_n(x^{(m)}) e^{in\Omega t}. \tag{2.22}$$

It seems that the expression (2.22) gives us the method to calculate the motion of a particle driven by a small force εF. However, we have several difficulties on this way. Let be $F_n(x) \sim x^2$. Then we have $x^{(1)} \sim exp(in\Omega t)$, whereas in $x^{(2)}$ we can encounter

$$x^{(2)} \sim exp[i(n_1 + n_2 + n_3)\Omega t], \tag{2.23}$$

where n_i are positive and negative integer numbers. At the resonance condition $n_1 + n_2 + n_3 = 0$ the term $x^{(3)}$ diverges

$$x^{(3)} \sim \varepsilon t^2. \tag{2.24}$$

Consequently for times t
$$t > t_\varepsilon = const/\sqrt{\varepsilon} \tag{2.25}$$

the series
$$x = x^{(0)} + \varepsilon x^{(1)} + ... \tag{2.26}$$

will diverge. Here we encountered the simple form of resonance. We can demonstrate that the resonances between the system and external force as well as resonances between degrees of freedom are fundamental property of nonlinear dynamics.

Consider a periodical perturbation of a Hamiltonian system

$$H = H_0(\underline{I}) + \varepsilon V(\underline{I}, \underline{\vartheta}; t), \qquad V(\underline{I}, \underline{\vartheta}; t) = V(\underline{I}, \underline{\vartheta}; t+T), \tag{2.27}$$

where $\underline{I}$ and $\underline{\vartheta}$ are N-dimensional vectors. Non-perturbed motion is integrable and lies on a torus. The perturbation V can be written as

$$V(\underline{I}, \underline{\vartheta}; t) = \sum_{n,m} V_{nm}(\underline{I}) exp[i(\underline{n}\,\underline{\vartheta} - m\Omega t)], \tag{2.28}$$

where $\underline{n}$ is a vector with integer positive and negative components. We consider Hamiltonian equations of motion (2.27) with series expansion (2.28)

$$\dot{I}_j = -\frac{\partial H}{\partial \vartheta_j} = -i\varepsilon \sum_{n,m} n_j V_{nm} exp[i(\underline{n}\ \underline{\vartheta} - m\Omega t)], \tag{2.29a}$$

$$\dot{\vartheta}_j = -\frac{\partial H}{\partial I_j} = \omega_j(I) + \varepsilon \sum_{n,m} \frac{\partial V_{nm}}{\partial I_j} exp[i(\underline{n}\ \underline{\vartheta} - m\Omega t)], \quad (j = 1, 2, ..., N) \tag{2.29b}$$

where $\omega_j(I) = \frac{\partial H(I)}{\partial I_j}$ $(j = 1, 2, ..., N)$. Expanding, we can write

$$I_j = I_j^{(0)} + \varepsilon I_j^{(1)} + ..., \quad \vartheta_j = \vartheta_j^{(0)} + \varepsilon\vartheta_j^{(1)} + ... \quad (j = 1, ...N), \tag{2.30}$$

where for the first terms

$$I_j^{(0)} = const, \quad \vartheta_j^{(0)} = \omega_i^{(0)}t + const, \quad (j = 1, ...N). \tag{2.31}$$

Substituting (2.31) into (2.29) we derive the second term

$$I_j^{(1)} = -\sum_{n,m} \frac{n_j \tilde{V}_{nm}^{(0)}}{\underline{n}\ \underline{\omega} - m\Omega} exp[i(\underline{n}\ \underline{\omega} - m\Omega)t]. \tag{2.32}$$

The expression (2.32) contains the denominator that can be equal to zero at the following resonance condition

$$\underline{n}\ \underline{\omega} - m\Omega = 0. \tag{2.33}$$

This condition means that ω and Ω (system's own frequency and external force) are commensurable. If there is no external force, resonances are possible between internal degrees of freedom ($N \geq 2$). In this case we set $\Omega = 0$ in (2.28), (2.29), (2.32). The resonance condition (2.33) yields the following form

$$\underline{n}\ \underline{\omega} = n_1\omega_1 + ...n_N\omega_N = 0 \tag{2.34}$$

Thus, an existence of resonances is a characteristic feature of nonlinear systems. If the resonances do not appear in low-order terms of the expansion (2.29), it can appear in some high-order terms. This is the problem of small denominators that prevents an analytical solution of the system (2.27).

To finish this section, we need to mention a principal difference between the case $N = 2$ and $N > 2$ stated by the KAM theorem. As already shown, *the main problem of nonlinear dynamics is to estimate a character of quasi-periodical behavior perturbed by small disturbance.* This definition originated from Poincaré. The essence of this problem is that even a very small disturbance can fundamentally change a dynamics of nonlinear system. *There are no approximative approaches that enable us to know which changes are potentially possible.* Serious investigation of this problem has been undertaken by Poincaré. However, the first success was done by Kolmogorov in 1954 that formulates the conditions, when invariant tori do not get destroyed by a disturbance. Arnold in 1961 and Moser in 1963 proved this theorem for different conditions. The KAM (Kolmogorov-Arnold-Moser) theorem states that for non-degenerate Hamiltonian systems the invariant tori do not completely disappear at a disturbance, only a small neighborhood of them is destroyed by a disturbance. Moreover, a configuration of destroyed area can be estimated. However, a behavior of a system depends on a topology of phase space and is different in the case of $N = 2$ and $N > 2$.

At $N = 2$ invariant tori share the phase space, therefore the destroyed tori lie between invariant tori. The behavior of nonlinear system occurs between invariant tori and a deviation from a non-perturbed motion converges to zero at $\varepsilon \to 0$. At $N > 2$ invariant tori do not share the phase space and the destroyed tori exists everywhere in the phase space. Therefore trajectories of motion can have an arbitrary large deviation from a non-perturbed motion. This effect calls Arnold diffusion.

Finally, we try to summarize the three-body problem. The main difficulty is an appearance of small denominators, which make the corresponding series expansions divergent. These denominators appear at the resonance, i.e. a relation between frequencies of quasi-periodical motion is rational. This resonance can be external (between the system and external forces) or internal (between internal degrees of freedom). Poincaré has demonstrated that this problem is of fundamental nature, i.e. although we can formulate a model as a system of nonlinear differential equations, this system is non-integrable and we cannot derive a behavior of this model (in the analytical way). The Liouville-Arnold theorem points to conditions when a system is integrable. Here there exist two principal cases of two and more then two degrees of freedom. At $N = 2$ the invariant tori (the trajectories that can be described by corresponding Fourier series) do not overlap and share the phase space, whereas $N > 2$ they overlap. The consequence is that for $N > 2$ the phase space (independent of the value of distortion) is covered by a "stochastic web" (see more in (Zaslavsky & Sagdeev, 1988, p.153)), where a dynamics becomes chaotic.

What is the main issue behind the case of $N > 2$? The point is that the nonlinear interactions between internal/external degrees of freedom (many interacting components) causes irregular (e.g. chaotic) behavior. There are many explanations of this irregularity, from the topological viewpoint - destroyed invariant tori, from the viewpoint of correlations - increasing flow of correlations and so on. This irregular behavior is too complex to be described completely analytically (see Arnold's remark (Arnold(Ed.), 1988, p.212) given in Section 3.6). A consequence is that *we cannot proceed directly from microscopic to macroscopic level, i.e. from individual models to emergent collective behavior. If we need some specific collective behavior, we do not know which individual models can produce it.* Even if we cannot derive a continuous model of interacting systems (and use algorithmic models) the irregularity of behavior and its complexity is the main characteristics of nonlinearly interacting systems. By analogy, we assume, that in algorithmic models we cannot also establish a direct relation between individual and collective behavior. We do not think that this assumption can ever be proved in the strong way (like analytical one), however, the problem of three bodies gives us some analogies that can later be used in a treatment of similar algorithmic problems.

2.3.4 Reductive strategy of synergetics

As demonstrated in the previous section, nonlinearly interacting systems can be non-integrable in the case of resonances. Many authors point out that most of the interacting dynamical systems possesses internal resonances (e.g. (Prigogine & Stengers, 1984)). Therefore instead a direct solution, we need some other approaches that can tell us, at least, qualitative characteristics of a considered nonlinear system, i.e. they perform reduction of complexity. There are many approaches, like symbolic dynamics, stability analysis, bifurcation theory and so on, that describe a system from particular viewpoints. However, investigating collective phenomena, we need a methodological concept, which can provide some global picture about emergent phenomena. Such a methodology has to explain the processes of self-organization and to unify an application of different approaches in a research of SO phenomena.

Moreover, self-organization is observed in many systems of completely different nature: hydrodynamic, chemical, biological and many others, even it is assumed to occur in human brain (Haken, 1996). The principles of self-organizing processes are expected to be of similar nature. Therefore, the chosen methodology has to explain these principles independently of a nature of system, where collective phenomena are emerged. In other words, we need a methodology which makes possible interdisciplinary investigation of collective phenomena. The synergetics (Haken, 1977) gives us this methodology.

Origin of synergetics lies in nonlinear dynamics, or more generally, in theoretical physics. Therefore, synergetics treats collective phenomena from *reductive* point of view. We refer to Prof. Haken:

There is still another difficulty with what we might call Descartes' approach. In order to describe the individual parts, an enormous amount of information is needed, but nobody can handle it. Therefore, we have to develop adequate methods to compress information. A simple example of how this goal can be reached is provided by our temperature sense. As we know, a gas, such as air, is composed of myriads of individual molecules, but we do not notice their individual motion. Rather, we somehow integrate over their motion and feel only a certain temperature. ...

Can we develop a general theory that allows us to adequately compress information quite automatically? As we shall see, such information compression takes place in situations where a system changes its macroscopic state qualitatively. In the inanimate world, there are a number of such abrupt changes, called phase transitions. Examples are provided by freezing, where liquid water goes over into the state of solid ice, or the onset of magnetism, or the onset of superconductivity. As we shall see, biology abounds with similar qualitative changes, though at a far more sophisticated level (Haken, 1996, p.9).

So, synergetics reduces collective phenomena to macroscopic changes. The value, which describes such qualitative changes, calls the order parameter. The general approach of synergetics towards the order parameter is already described many times (by Prof. Haken in a brief form e.g. in (Haken, 1983a, p.35) or in the application to several test systems (Levi *et al.*, 1999)). Two technical points in a derivation of the order parameter are also demonstrated in the next sections. However, the question is whether the order parameter, or any other reductive values, can bridge the gap between microscopic and macroscopic description, mentioned by Prof. Haken (see Chapter 1) ?

This question is of especial importance for collective autonomous systems. Considering a collective behavior of e.g. soccer playing or swarming robots, we can encounter many elements of self-organization. There are elements of macroscopic nature, as e.g. collective decisions, which allow reducing a complexity. However, there are many elements, as e.g. collective motion, which cannot be reduced at all. The reductive approach cannot generally be applied to these self-organizing processes. Perhaps, the gap between "microscopic" and "macroscopic" can be bridged by fusing computational and reductive approaches. As pointed out by Prof. Haken (Haken, 1988, p.14), many principles of synergetics wait to be explored:

"Synergetics is very much an open-ended field in which we have made only the very first steps. In the past one or two decades it has been shown that the behavior of numerous systems is governed by the general laws of synergetics, and I am convinced that many more examples will be found in the future. On the other hand we must be aware of the possibility that still more laws and possibly still more general laws can be found."

In the given work, we investigate both approaches in hoping to find a receipt of such a "mixture".

2.3.4.1 Separation into slow and fast components

In this and in the next sections we briefly demonstrate two most important points in deriving the order parameter. The first of them is a separation of dynamics into "slow" and "fast" components, whereas the second one consists in "uncoupling" these components. The uncoupled slow components represent a basis for the order parameter (OP).

Macroscopic changes occur at critical values of control parameters. From the viewpoint of mathematical models, the linear parts exert the most intense influence on the local dynamics in the vicinity of these critical points. By means of coordinate transformation, which diagonalizes the Jacobian of the considered model (see e.g. in (Wiggins, 1990, p.200),(Levi et al., 1999)), we can "exfoliate" the models into the components with independent linear parts. As a result, we find such components that cause instability and lead to changes in behavior. These components are denoted as correspondingly stable and unstable (amplitude) modes. Stable and unstable models are "fast" and "slow", because in the vicinity of local instability stable modes vary much faster than unstable ones. Since both modes are linearly uncoupled, but still coupled in nonlinear parts, the fast modes are forced to follow the slow modes. These different time scales allow neglecting (or expressing by slow modes) the stable modes. In the synergetic terminology this time hierarchy calls the slaving principle and allows uncoupling nonlinear parts. The separation of low-dimensional unstable modes can be thought of as a final goal of the performed local analysis (e.g. (Guckenheimer & Holmes, 1983, p.118)). The reduced uncoupled equations of unstable modes calls the order parameters equations and can be applied for description and controlling the macroscopic phenomena. For instance, stabilizing unstable modes we can shift or even avoid an instability, that several control techniques are based on (Alvarenz-Ramírez, 1993), (Basso et al., 1998). Generally, there are many different control strategies (e.g. (Levi et al., 1999)) based on OP, that can modify the collective behavior of distributed systems (Kornienko, 2007).

Now we introduce the required formalism[1]. Transformation starts from the nonlinear equations of motion, written for general case in the tensor-like notation[2]

$$\underline{\mathbf{q}}_{n+1} = \Gamma_{(1)} + \Gamma_{(2)}(:\underline{\mathbf{q}}_n) + \Gamma_{(3)}(:\underline{\mathbf{q}}_n)^2 + \ldots = \sum_{r=0}^{p} \Gamma_{(r+1)}(:\underline{\mathbf{q}}_n)^r. \tag{2.35}$$

Next, the following coordinate transformation is performed

$$\Delta \underline{\mathbf{q}}_n = \sum_k \xi_n^k \underline{\mathbf{v}}_k = \Gamma_{(2)}^V(:\underline{\boldsymbol{\xi}}_n), \tag{2.36}$$

where $\Delta\underline{\mathbf{q}}_n = \underline{\mathbf{q}}_n - \underline{\mathbf{q}}_{st}$, $\underline{\mathbf{v}}$ are the eigenvectors of the Jacobian of the system (2.35) evaluated at $\underline{\mathbf{q}}_n = \underline{\mathbf{q}}_{st}$ ($\Gamma_{(2)}^V$ is the corresponding tensor) and $\underline{\boldsymbol{\xi}}_n$ are so-called mode amplitudes. As a result, the following nonlinear equation of motion is obtained

$$\Gamma_{(2)}^V(:\underline{\boldsymbol{\xi}}_{n+1}) = \Gamma_{(2)}^L \Gamma_{(2)}^V(:\underline{\boldsymbol{\xi}}_n) + \sum_{r=2}^{p} \Gamma_{(r+1)}^N (\Gamma_{(2)}^V(:\underline{\boldsymbol{\xi}}_n))^r, \tag{2.37}$$

where Γ^L and Γ^N are the tensors, presenting the linear and nonlinear parts respectively. Multiplying from the left side with the inverse tensor $\Gamma_{(2)}^{V-1}$, the mode amplitude equations get the following form

---

[1] see for details (Kornienko, 2007).
[2] This notation is useful to reduce indexing of multi-variable expressions, see more about used tensor notion in the work of Uhl, Friedrich and Haken (Uhl et al., 1995)

$$\underline{\boldsymbol{\xi}}_{n+1}^{u} = \Gamma_{(2)}^{\Lambda_u}(: \underline{\boldsymbol{\xi}}_n^u) + \sum_{r=2}^{p} \Gamma_{(r+1)}^{\tilde{N}_u}(: \underline{\boldsymbol{\xi}}_n)^r = \underline{\tilde{N}}_u(\underline{\boldsymbol{\xi}}_n), \tag{2.38a}$$

$$\underline{\boldsymbol{\xi}}_{n+1}^{s} = \Gamma_{(2)}^{\Lambda_s}(: \underline{\boldsymbol{\xi}}_n^s) + \sum_{r=2}^{p} \Gamma_{(r+1)}^{\tilde{N}_s}(: \underline{\boldsymbol{\xi}}_n)^r = \underline{\tilde{N}}_s(\underline{\boldsymbol{\xi}}_n). \tag{2.38b}$$

Here $\Gamma_{(2)}^{V^{-1}} \Gamma_{(2)}^{L} \Gamma_{(2)}^{V} = \Gamma_{(2)}^{\Lambda}$ is the tensor of the eigenvalues of the Jacobian of system (2.35), $\Gamma^{\tilde{N}}$ presents the nonlinear part of the mode amplitude equations (2.38) and the following identity was used

$$(\Gamma_{(2)}^{V^{-1}} \Gamma_{(2)}^{V})_{ij} = \delta_{ij}, \tag{2.39}$$

where δ_{ij} is the well-known Kronecker symbol. In general the tensor $\Gamma_{(2)}^{\Lambda}$ presents the eigenvalues in Jordan normal form, see (Haken, 1983a, p.76). The mode amplitude equations Eqs. (2.38) have the decoupled linear parts given by $\Gamma_{(2)}^{\Lambda_{u,s}}$. From the conditions $|\lambda| \geq 1$ and $|\lambda| < 1$ the eigenvalues and corresponding mode amplitudes are denoted as unstable u and correspondingly as stable s ($\underline{\boldsymbol{\xi}}^s, \underline{\boldsymbol{\xi}}^u$).

Remark that by means of transformation (2.36)-(2.39) only linear parts of mode equations (2.38) become uncoupled, whereas nonlinear parts still remains depended on stable as well as unstable amplitudes $\underline{\boldsymbol{\xi}}$. Further steps will be addressed to uncouple the nonlinear parts and to derive in this way the OP equations.

2.3.4.2   Derivation of order parameter

With the transformation (2.36)-(2.39) we can proceed further. For simplification the system (2.38) is rewritten in the following form

$$\underline{\boldsymbol{\xi}}_{n+1}^{u} = \underline{\underline{\Lambda}}_u(\alpha)\underline{\boldsymbol{\xi}}_n^u + \underline{\tilde{N}}_u(\underline{\boldsymbol{\xi}}_n^u, \underline{\boldsymbol{\xi}}_n^s, \alpha), \tag{2.40a}$$

$$\underline{\boldsymbol{\xi}}_{n+1}^{s} = \underline{\underline{\Lambda}}_s(\alpha)\underline{\boldsymbol{\xi}}_n^s + \underline{\tilde{N}}_s(\underline{\boldsymbol{\xi}}_n^u, \underline{\boldsymbol{\xi}}_n^s, \alpha), \tag{2.40b}$$

where $\underline{\underline{\Lambda}}_u, \underline{\underline{\Lambda}}_s$ are the eigenvalues matrices of the corresponding Jacobian, evaluated at the stationary state q_{st} and $\tilde{N}_s$, $\tilde{N}_u$ are nonlinear function of amplitudes $\underline{\boldsymbol{\xi}}_n^u, \underline{\boldsymbol{\xi}}_n^s$. Now, the following time scale hierarchy

$$|\lambda_s| < 1, |\lambda_u| > 1, \tag{2.41a}$$

$$1 - |\lambda_s| \gg 1 - |\lambda_u|, \tag{2.41b}$$

imposes the condition when the stable modes $\underline{\boldsymbol{\xi}}^s$ varies very fast and is forced to follow the unstable modes $\underline{\boldsymbol{\xi}}_n^u$ which vary slowly. This behavior is denoted as the slaving principle (Haken, 1983a, p.187) and as result we get

$$\underline{\boldsymbol{\xi}}_n^s = \underline{\mathbf{h}}(\underline{\boldsymbol{\xi}}_n^u). \tag{2.42}$$

Substituting the functions (2.42) into the unstable mode equations (2.40a), the desired reduced equations can be finally written as

$$\underline{\boldsymbol{\xi}}_{n+1}^{u} = \underline{\underline{\Lambda}}_u(\alpha)\underline{\boldsymbol{\xi}}_n^u + \tilde{N}_u(\underline{\boldsymbol{\xi}}_n^u, \underline{\mathbf{h}}(\underline{\boldsymbol{\xi}}_n^u), \alpha). \tag{2.43}$$

These low-dimensional equations, called as the order parameter equations, depend only upon $\underline{\boldsymbol{\xi}}_n^u$ and describe completely the behavior of the original system in the neighborhood of the instability. Finally, note that the exact form of the order parameter equations (2.43) is not unique defined (Arrowsmith, 1990). The reason is that the expression (2.42) has approximate nature and can be calculated in many different ways. Here we show the main ideas of three following methods: the center manifold reduction, the adiabatic elimination procedure and normal form reduction.

The **center manifold approach** belongs now to "standard" techniques of reduction, explained in fact in all classical textbooks of nonlinear dynamics (e.g. (Guckenheimer & Holmes, 1983), (Wiggins, 1990), (Kuznetsov, 1995)). There are elegant geometrical explanations of this approach (e.g. (Arrowsmith, 1990)), we show primarily the calculation side of the method originated from the work of Carr (Carr, 1981, p.7). First, the following substitution $\alpha = \alpha_{cr} + \varepsilon$ is performed, where ε is the smallness parameter and α_{cr} is the critical value of the control parameter α. Substituting it into (2.40), we expand then all ε-dependent terms into a Taylor series with respect to ε up to the order r (e.g. $\lambda_u^{(0)} + \lambda_u^{(1)}\varepsilon + \lambda_u^{(2)}\varepsilon^2 + \ldots$). Now, as suggested by Carr, the smallness parameter ε can be included as a new dependent variable ε_n

$$\xi_{n+1}^u = \lambda_u^{(0)}\xi_n^u + \hat{N}_u^{(r-1)}(\xi_n^u, \xi_n^s, \varepsilon_n) + O(r), \tag{2.44a}$$

$$\xi_{n+1}^s = \lambda_s^{(0)}\xi_n^s + \hat{N}_s^{(r-1)}(\xi_n^u, \xi_n^s, \varepsilon_n) + O(r), \tag{2.44b}$$

$$\varepsilon_{n+1} = \lambda_\varepsilon \varepsilon_n, \tag{2.44c}$$

where $\hat{N}_u, \hat{N}_s$ are the nonlinear parts of these equations with respect to $\xi_n^u, \xi_n^s, \varepsilon_n$ up to the order r and λ_ε is constant such as $\lambda_\varepsilon = 1$ or $\lambda_\varepsilon = -1$. As a consequence of this transformation the system (2.44) will have the two-dimensional center manifold $h(\xi_n^u, \varepsilon_n)$, that can be expressed as the following polynomial up to order r with respect to ξ_n^u and ε_n

$$\xi_n^s = h(\xi_n^u, \varepsilon_n) = A(\xi_n^u)^2 + B\xi_n^u\varepsilon_n + C\varepsilon_n^2 + \ldots + O(r). \tag{2.45}$$

Now substituting this expression into the stable mode equation (2.44b) and collecting the terms up to the order r with respect to ε_n and ξ_n^u, the coefficients $A, B, C, \ldots$ and accordingly the center manifold $h(\xi_n^u, \varepsilon_n)$ can be determined.

For the center manifold other polynomials can also be chosen, but here there are several remarks that should be taken into account. Considering a bifurcation dynamics of the order parameter equations (2.43), we can make one relevant observation that the asymptotical dynamics of the unstable mode $\underline{\xi}^u$ immediately after bifurcation is a function of the smallness parameter ε. Indeed, finding the stationary states of the OP and expanding it into a Taylor series with respect to ε we would ascertain that

$$\xi^u = \beta_1\varepsilon^\gamma + \beta_2\varepsilon^{2\gamma} + O(\varepsilon^{3\gamma}) = f(\{\beta\}, \gamma, \varepsilon) , \tag{2.46}$$

where β_1, β_2 and γ are some constants. From this point of view, the expression (2.45) represents in fact different degrees of smallness parameter. Therefore choosing this polynomial (and collecting coefficients), we should take into account equal degrees of the parameter ε, otherwise the function (2.42) will not represent the real dependence between amplitude modes $\underline{\xi}_n^u$ and $\underline{\xi}_n^s$.

The low-order approximation of the CM approach can be obtained by the **adiabatic approximation procedure**, described by Haken in (Haken, 1983b, p.202). The adiabatic approximation uses the assumption that the variations of stable mode can be neglected (see e.g. (Levi *et al.*, 1999))

$$\xi_{n+1}^s = \xi_n^s. \tag{2.47}$$

The assumption (2.47) allows to carry out the simple calculation of the functions $h(\xi_n^u, \varepsilon_n)$ which consists in solving the algebraic equations given by (2.40b)

$$(\underline{\Lambda}_s(\alpha) - 1)\underline{\xi}_n^s + \tilde{\underline{N}}_s(\underline{\xi}_n^s, \underline{\xi}_n^s, \alpha) = 0. \tag{2.48}$$

The approach based on (2.47) gives a good approximation of the function (2.47) in the small neighborhood of the bifurcation point. Obviously, the further away from a bifurcation point the control parameter a is, the less the solutions of CM approach and adiabatic approximation will coincide.

Investigating behavior of the order parameter equation, we can remark that not all nonlinear terms in these equations influence a local behavior of the Eq. (2.43) (Golubitsky & Schaeffer, 1985), (Golubitsky *et al.*, 1988). There are so-called resonant and non-resonant nonlinear terms. Resonant terms determine nonlinear structure of the OP (2.43), whereas non-resonant terms can be removed from these equations. Resonant and nonresonant conditions are completely defined by linear parts of the OP equations, i.e. by eigenvalues. The remained nonlinear structure has some minimal structure that is characteristic (normal) for each type of bifurcation (include such notions as e.g. unfolding and codimension of local bifurcation (also (Arnold, 1983)), therefore this form is denoted as normal form and corresponding reduction method as the **methods of normal form** (Nayfeh, 1993).

The methods of normal form has a long history that dates back to Poincaré (e.g. (Poincaré, 1899)) and Birkhoff (e.g. (Birkhoff, 1927b)). This concept involves a coordinate transformation in order to rewrite the original system in the "simplest possible" form. This consecutive coordinate transformation is local and near-identity because it is generated in a neighborhood of known solution, moreover for nonlinear systems this transformation is also nonlinear.

Deriving the order parameter by the normal form reduction, the mode equations (2.38) should be rewritten in the following form

$$\underline{\xi}_{n+1} = \underline{\underline{\Lambda}} \, \underline{\xi}_n + \underline{\tilde{N}}^{(2)}(\underline{\xi}_n) + \underline{\tilde{N}}^{(3)}(\underline{\xi}_n) + O(4). \tag{2.49}$$

Here, $\underline{\tilde{N}}^{(l)}$ are the nonlinear functions of the order l, $\underline{\xi} = \begin{pmatrix} \xi^u \\ \xi^s \end{pmatrix}$ (as an example in the two-dimensional case) and $\underline{\underline{\Lambda}}$ is the Jacobian. We perform all transformations and calculations up to the fourth order with respect to $\underline{\xi}$.

Now using the following near-identity transformation for *rhs* and *lhs* of (2.49)

$$\underline{\xi}_n = \underline{\varphi}_n + \underline{g}^{(2)}(\underline{\varphi}_n) + \underline{g}^{(3)}(\underline{\varphi}_n) + O(4) \tag{2.50a}$$

$$\underline{\xi}_{n+1} = \underline{\varphi}_{n+1} + \underline{g}^{(2)}(\underline{\varphi}_{n+1}) + \underline{g}^{(3)}(\underline{\varphi}_{n+1}) + O(4) \tag{2.50b}$$

, where $\underline{g}^{(l)}$ is a polynomial function of order l, $\underline{\varphi} = \begin{pmatrix} \varphi_1 \\ \varphi_2 \end{pmatrix}$, we choose the function $\underline{g}$ so that it takes the simplest possible form for small $\underline{\varphi}$

$$\underline{\varphi}_{n+1} = \underline{\underline{\Lambda}} \, \underline{\varphi}_n + \underline{\tilde{g}}^{(2)}(\underline{\varphi}_n) + \underline{\tilde{g}}^{(3)}(\underline{\varphi}_n) + O(4), \tag{2.51}$$

where the $\underline{\tilde{g}}^{(l)}$ are the resonance terms of order l. This equation is said to be in normal form (e.g. (Wiggins, 1990, p.216), (Kuznetsov, 1995)). For simplification we will further call it normal form equation of the corresponding local bifurcation and it describes behavior of the original system in the vicinity of instability. Comparing with order parameter (2.43), derived by the center manifold approach (adiabatic elimination), one can see that OP (2.43) contains all nonlinear terms up to the order (l) unlike the system (2.51) that contains only resonant terms. These resonant terms can be obtained by substituting (2.50) and into (2.49)

$$\underline{\varphi}_{n+1} + \underline{g}^{(2)}(\underline{\varphi}_{n+1}) + \underline{g}^{(3)}(\underline{\varphi}_{n+1}) + O(4) = \underline{\underline{\Lambda}}(\underline{\varphi}_n + \underline{g}^{(2)}(\underline{\varphi}_n) + \underline{g}^{(3)}(\underline{\varphi}_n)) +$$
$$\underline{\tilde{N}}^{(2)}(\underline{\varphi}_n + \underline{g}^{(2)}(\underline{\varphi}_n) + \underline{g}^{(3)}(\underline{\varphi}_n)) + \underline{\tilde{N}}^{(3)}(\underline{\varphi}_n + \underline{g}^{(2)}(\underline{\varphi}_n) + \underline{g}^{(3)}(\underline{\varphi}_n)) + O(4) \tag{2.52}$$

and collecting the coefficients with the same powers of φ

$$\varphi_{n+1} = \underline{\Lambda}\,(\underline{\varphi}_n) + [\underline{\Lambda}\,\underline{g}^{(2)}(\underline{\varphi}_n) - \underline{g}^{(2)}(\underline{\varphi}_{n+1}) + \underline{F}^{(2)}(\underline{\varphi}_n)] +$$
$$[\underline{\Lambda}\,\underline{g}^{(3)}(\underline{\varphi}_n) - \underline{g}^{(3)}(\underline{\varphi}_{n+1}) + \underline{F}^{(3)}(\underline{\varphi}_n)] + O(4). \tag{2.53}$$

The function $\underline{F}^{(l)}(\underline{\varphi}_n)$ collects the terms of only order l that are remained after simplification of $\tilde{\underline{N}}^{(l)}(\underline{g}^{(l)}(\underline{\varphi}_n))$. The terms $\underline{g}^{(2)}(\underline{\varphi}_{n+1})$ and $\underline{g}^{(3)}(\underline{\varphi}_{n+1})$ can be eliminated by using either the method of operators shown for example in (Nayfeh, 1993) by following Wiggins (Wiggins, 1990, p.225). The last method is more suitable for the time-discrete systems, it can be performed by involving the normal form (2.51) (take into account the consecutive transformations up to the order $O(4)$)

$$\underline{g}^{(2)}(\underline{\varphi}_{n+1}) = \underline{g}^{(2)}(\underline{\Lambda}\,\underline{\varphi}_n + \tilde{\underline{g}}^{(2)}(\underline{\varphi}_n)) + O(4) \tag{2.54a}$$

$$\underline{g}^{(3)}(\underline{\varphi}_{n+1}) = \underline{g}^{(3)}(\underline{\Lambda}\,\underline{\varphi}_n) + O(4). \tag{2.54b}$$

As a result of the specified transforms (2.54) the Eq. (2.53) yields

$$\varphi_{n+1} = \underline{\Lambda}\,(\underline{\varphi}_n) + [\underline{\Lambda}\,\underline{g}^{(2)}(\underline{\varphi}_n) - \underline{g}^{(2)}(\underline{\Lambda}\,\underline{\varphi}_n) + \underline{F}^{(2)}(\underline{\varphi}_n)] +$$
$$[\underline{\Lambda}\,\underline{g}^{(3)}(\underline{\varphi}_n) - \underline{g}^{(3)}(\underline{\Lambda}\,\underline{\varphi}_n)) + \underline{F}^{(3)}(\underline{\varphi}_n) - \underline{g}^{(2)\to O(3)}(\underline{\Lambda}\,\underline{\varphi}_n + \tilde{\underline{g}}^{(2)}(\underline{\varphi}_n))] + O(4), \tag{2.55}$$

where $\underline{g}^{(2)\to O(3)}(\underline{\Lambda}\,\underline{\varphi}_n + \tilde{\underline{g}}^{(2)}(\underline{\varphi}_n))$ are nonlinear functions of order $O(3)$ defined by expression (2.54a). From the Eq. (2.55) the terms of order $O(2)$ can be selected and, if it is possible, eliminated

$$O(2) \to \underline{\Lambda}\,\underline{g}^{(2)}(\underline{\varphi}_n) - \underline{g}^{(2)}(\underline{\Lambda}\,\underline{\varphi}_n) + \underline{F}^{(2)}(\underline{\varphi}_n) = 0. \tag{2.56}$$

As a consequence of this calculation, the resonance terms $\tilde{\underline{g}}^{(2)}$ (2.55) are already determined and one can continue the calculation of cubical terms

$$O(3) \to \underline{\Lambda}\,\underline{g}^{(3)}(\underline{\varphi}_n) - \underline{g}^{(3)}(\underline{\Lambda}\,\underline{\varphi}_n)) + [\underline{F}^{(3)}(\underline{\varphi}_n) - \underline{g}^{(2)\to O(3)}(\underline{\Lambda}\,\underline{\varphi}_n + \tilde{\underline{g}}^{(2)}(\underline{\varphi}_n))] = 0. \tag{2.57}$$

The main difference of the calculation of the cubical terms's coefficients in contrast to quadratic ones is that the cubical nonlinearity contains the terms of quadratic nonlinearity which must be first calculated. This mathematical subtlety has a dominant influence on the coefficients of high-order terms.

Details and examples of the normal form as well as the center manifold and adiabatic elimination approaches applied to the time-discrete systems can be found in (Levi et al., 1999), (Kornienko & Kornienko, 1999), (Kornienko & Kornienko, 2000), (Kornienko & Kornienko, 2002). The reduced OP equation (2.43) can be also obtained by other techniques (e.g. by multiple scaling technique (Grigorieva et al., 1999), by reduction of differential equations to algebraic system (Kuzmina, 2001)), their details can be read in the corresponding papers. Now we finish the brief introduction into the reduction methods.

2.4 Computational treatment

After representing main ideas of a few reductive approaches, we switch to computational methods. In several next sections we introduce an autonomous agent and discuss some problems arising at programming a separate agent as well as a group of agents. Finally, we demonstrate the scenario, that collective phenomena are studied on, and some preliminary ideas about a scalability of emergent behavior.

2.4.1   *Centralized* versus *Distributed* versus *Self-organized*

We start a discussion about computational side of collective phenomena from one important methodological point, namely, from differences between centralized, distributed and self-organized systems. To demonstrate these differences, we introduce a small example. There is a group of units (agents). Each of these units has individual initial value (e.g. randomly chosen numerical ID) can perform simple operations and can communicate with local neighbors. No one of them knows the number of agents in the group or can globally communicate. The whole group has to perform one collective operation, e.g. to calculate arithmetical mean value from individual initial values (we can choose any other collective operation, it does not change the meaning of this example). We demonstrate how to solve this problem by using different methodology:

- **Centralized.** In this case we introduce a coordinator that knows a number of participating elements and can communicate with each of them. It collects all initial values, calculates mean arithmetical value and sends it backwards to all elements.

- **Distributed.** Solving this problem in a distributed way, it is naturally to introduce, firstly, a communication protocol and, secondly, to unify data, circulating in a network. In the protocol we can define needed collective information processing, i.e. type and order of operations, communication and so on. In the most simple case we can insert a table that will be circulated in the network. Each agent has to insert own initial value into this table and send it to neighbors. As soon as an agent gets this table at the second time, all initial values will be collected in the table and agent can calculate arithmetical mean value. After the second round all agents finish the calculation.

- **Self-organized.** "Organizing a self-organizing calculation" of mean arithmetical value, we cannot preprogram a collective behavior of the whole group, like those in centralized or distributed case. The result has to emerge "spontaneously". However, we expect some exact type of this result the mean arithmetical value. **This contradiction - "spontaneous emergence" and an exactly required result of collective behavior - represents a serious methodological problem.** We devote the complete third chapter to this problem. At least describing a self-organizing solution, instead of coordinator or distributed protocol, we have to define local rules that govern a behavior of separate agents. These local rules do not restrict collective degrees of freedom, so that the systems can demonstrate different types of emergent behavior. However, these local rules have to bind the individual degrees of freedom so, that the system can achieve the result (calculation of arithmetical mean value) in finite time.

The systems with central elements are "simple" for controlling, their advantage is a wide range of developed methods. However, if the number of participating elements becomes large, the central coordinating element gets overloaded. It means that the coordinator has to be more complex (for information processing) than other elements. This correspondingly increases the cost of such a system, and plays a negative role for reliability of the whole system. Moreover, if the coordinator fails, the complete system fails too. The central elements often became an object of external "attacks", like hackers attack.

The distributed case does not use the centralized architectures and is free of disadvantages typical for centralized systems. This increases reliability of a system and reduces its cost. The collective behavior of distributed (as well as centralized) systems is preprogrammed and so well-optimized for forecasted situations, e.g. information traffic in cellular network. Due to fixed behavior, these systems cannot react in non-forecasted situations, e.g. some changes in environment, they are not flexible (adaptable, agile, transformable and so on).

In the case of self-organization, the systems do not contain central elements and collective behavior is not preprogrammed. The desired ordered behavior is a result of negotiations (or more generally - interactions), that are produced by specific local rules. The self-organizing behavior (if it is obtained as optimization of e.g. energy) can also be optimal for given conditions, but this optimization is performed over the time, i.e. it is not optimal at beginning $t = 0$. More generally, we assume that distributed systems can produce more optimal behavior, because developers can make it optimal in advance, whereas the self-organizing systems generate the behavior just on demand during the running time. The main problem of the Self-Organizing (SO) systems consists in local rules: they are not always easy to find. This problem is also known in distributed systems, however in the self-organizing case it gets really hard. In the following we consider self-organizing systems on the base of autonomous agents, explained in the next sections.

2.4.2 Autonomous agents

Distributed systems are currently one of most rapidly growing branches in computer science. It has an enormous number of applications. In the last ten years, a new scientific direction was born within the domain of distributed system. It is known as theory of autonomous agents (Weiss, 1999). There are two reasons for that. From the viewpoint of computer languages, the autonomous agent is a further developing of object-oriented programming. This is a part of the strategy - to make the program structures more reliable and independent from one another. So, *Objective C* prolongs this tendency of *C++*, that in turn, of *Pascal* and so forth. Agent, at least in principle, does not differ from an object, which has a "control" over its own behavior.

Another side in the agent technology represents physics, which investigates collective phenomena from the viewpoint of complexity. Agent in this case is a model of a corresponding participant of natural collective phenomena. The notion of agent successfully enters in the modern science and uses recently in many other, non-compute science and non-physical, areas. However, the agent technology still remains driven by two different forces. We can recognize a tendency to separate intelligent autonomous agent and multi-agent systems. The first from them is equipped with high-computational abilities, semantics, learning and intended to make its own job autonomously from human. The main application area are different assistant systems in internet, in robotics and so on. The point of multi-agent systems focus on the ability of cooperative working, the effect of their synergy. However, this separation is not fixed, e.g. agents in internet build also the multi-agent system. The difference between them lies mainly in a systematical consideration and in the architecture.

Agent technology differs from other branches of distributed systems, primarily, by the way of how they solve arisen problems. As mentioned, the classical distributed systems work on the basis of preprogrammed algorithms. These algorithms describe the exact sequences of activities targeted to the problem to be solved. In opposite, the algorithm governing the behavior of an agent does not describe how to solve one particular problem. This algorithm describes how to cooperate with other agents so that to solve it. Agents are self-motivated, like human, and act being driven by their own motivations. This approach has several advantages and lacks that specifies the application area of agent-based technology.

If a process has a regular nature and does not undergoes any deviations and disturbances, we can describe this process by several rules. These rules (in centralized or in distributed form) can be used for programming. The more irregular and disturbed this process becomes, the more rules are required to describe it. There is some limit, where the further growth of rules does not deliver the expected solution. They make the systems so complex, that it becomes even less reliable. The idea here is to involve some "evolutionary" approaches, which can generate these rules on demand. These "evolutionary" approaches are the negotiation-based solutions. In this way, the main application area of MAS is irregular processes. Now we consider an autonomous agent and multi-agent systems more in details.

2.4.3 Hybrid agent

The most common definition of a rational elementary agent points to the abilities of perceiving, acting and interacting in the environment (Russell, 1995) as well as to autonomous behavior (Weiss, 1999). The agent cyclically iterates some steps such as collecting the sensors information, communication, planning the next state, actions and so on. This cyclical iteration is called *autonomy cycle* (Levi, 1989) of an agent, as shown in Figure 2.1. In this context, an *autonomy* implies that an agent has a closed internal cycle, i.e. it determines activities on the base of own knowledge (rules) and interactions with other agents.

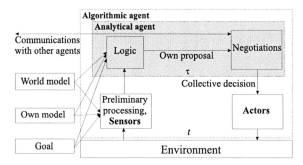

Figure 2.1: *Autonomy cycle of a rational elementary agent, t is the environmental time, τ is the internal time.*

As pointed out by many authors, an agent is a finite state automaton (FSA) (e.g. (Green, 1994), (Bertelle *et al.*, 2001)) and its behavior can be represented in a formal way e.g. by Petri net, see Figures 2.2, 2.3 (e.g. (Kornienko *et al.*, 2004c), (Muscholl, 2001)). In this representation an agent has a set of activities, whose execution depends on some conditions. These conditions can be represented by one "branching" point, as shown in Figure 2.2. Coordination of collective activity is based on synchronization of branching points between different agents.

In the suggested approach such synchronization is performed by the *analytical agent*. It is in charge of collective activities (e.g. collective decisions making). The output states of an analytical agent (e.g. decisions) can be encoded by numerical values.

The *algorithmic agent* has sensors, actions, supports communications and provides the concrete realization of made decisions. It can e.g. associate numerical values provided by the analytical agent with the concrete actions performed in environment. The algorithmic agent has a nature of computer program. On the high abstraction level, this program is either absent or possesses the simplest structure. But the more real and complex environment is, the more complex this program i.e. an algorithmic agent becomes. In contrast, the analytical agent is not changed on different abstraction levels.

45

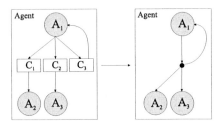

Figure 2.2: *Fragment of agent's activity in the form of Petri network (left), transformed form with the "branching point" (right).*

2.4.4 Programming of algorithmic agent

In programming an algorithmic agent, we use a notion of a role. A role $r \in R$ (R is a set of all roles) is described by a triple $r = (D_r, \underline{z}, a)$, where $D_r \subseteq D$ is a set of services used by a role, $\underline{z}$ is a state vector, and a is an activity, that by D_r changes $\underline{z}$. Services can be understood in a sense of specific abilities that an agent has to possess in order to play a role. These abilities are connected with hardware or middleware, therefore not each agent can have them. For example, in the presented planning approach two kinds of services are required, *object-service* based on resources of operation system and *planning-service* based on e.g. CORBA resources. "Object-service" has primitives "initialize", "find" and has the aim to manipulate other objects. "Planning-service" has primitives *"send"*, *"receive"* *"calculate"* and is used for the propagation approach. Evidently, an activity, described by a role, is based on the required services. Moreover, there are so-called *resource-objects* that possess technological information, number of processing machines, etc., i.e. they have specific resources. These "resource-objects" can be represented by corresponding agents as well as by intelligent databases or a human-computer interface.

A role marking is a triple $p = (r, ag, v)$, where $r \in R$, $ag \in A$ is an agent, $v : D_r \rightarrow ag$ operator that assigns an activity of a role to the ability of an agent. This operator is used by matching between an available agent in pool and a role that is needed to be played. An interaction pattern describes how to solve a problem by means of interacting roles. This interaction consists of a sequence of phases. A phase $p \in P$ is a step of interactions with the set of roles γ_p in this phase. For example, let there be two phases with $\gamma_1 = \{r_1, r_2\}$ and $\gamma_2 = \{r_1', r_2'\}$ that are described by the mark $M(1) = \{(D_{r_1}, \underline{z}_{r_1}, a_{r_1}), ag_1, v_1), (D_{r_2}, \underline{z}_{r_2}, a_{r_2}), ag_2, v_2)\}$, shown in Figure 2.3.

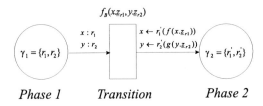

Phase 1   *Transition*   *Phase 2*

Figure 2.3: *Example of two-phases Petri Net with transitions and corresponding roles.*

In the first phase two agents are playing these roles, where the abilities of the agent and activities of roles are ordered by v_1 and v_2. For a transition we define the variable x of the type *role* r_1 and the variable y of the type *role* r_2. Then, the transition is defined by the boolean function $f_B = (x.\underline{z}_{r_1}, y.\underline{z}_{r_2})$. After the transition, the x-connected mark loses the role r_1 and gets the role r_1', where the information transfers from r_1 to r_1' is defined by f. The same applies also to the y-connected mark, where g describes the corresponding information transfer. After the transition we have $M(2) = \{(D_{r_1}, f(\underline{z}_{r_1}), a_{r_1'}), ag_1, v_{1,r_1'}), (D_{r_2'}, g(\underline{z}_{r_2}), a_{r_2'}), ag_{2,r_2'}, v_{2,r_2'})\}$. In this case, it is a priori known, the role r_1' requires the same services as r_1, therefore ag_1 can play it further.

An interaction network is defined by the following tuple $PN = (P, T, F, \sigma_i, \sigma_t, \sigma_o, M_0)$, where P is a set of places, T is a set of transitions, $P \cup T \neq 0$, $P \cap T = 0$, $F \subseteq (P \times T) \cup (P \times T)$ is the flow-relation, $\sigma_i : (P \times P) \rightarrow N$ is an input function, defining the directed arc from places to transitions, $\sigma_o : (P \times P) \rightarrow N$ is an output function, defining the directed arc from transitions to places, $\sigma_t : T \rightarrow N$ is the guard of transitions, M_0 is the initial marking. In this way the interaction pattern is described by the modified Petri net, details can be found in (Muscholl, 2001).

2.4.5 About programming of multi-agent systems

As mentioned in the previous section, an autonomous agent is a finite state automaton, described by Petri Net. It can be distributed, intelligent, include semantic information processing etc., however it still remains a computer program. What will happen when these automata are coupled into a network ? Reviewing literature on the object, we encountered three different viewpoints. There are authors who argue such a network is also a FSA, however, with a large number of states (e.g. (Green, 1994)), other authors point to essential differences in behavior of automaton and a system of automata (cellular automata) (e.g. (Darley, 1994)). There is a third group that even develops languages to describe and to control a collective activity in such systems (e.g. (Bertelle *et al.*, 2001), (Muscholl, 2001)).

Before supplementing this discussion, we have to pay attention to the way of how the agents are integrated into a network (multi-agent system). Following the idea of autonomy, we require the integration keeps autonomy of all agents. It means, each agent makes decisions and executes activities, being driven only by its own rules. It is a very important issue because there is no central instance, which controls a collective activity of multi-agent system. If the MAS consists of n agents, each of them exhibits m states and the history (t-steps) affects the dynamics, then MAS is able to react in $(m^n)^t$ possible ways. For instance, the state space of a very simple system of 10 agents, each from them has 10 states, consists of 10^{100} configurations for 10 time steps. Generally, this behavior is not bound in time and space. This is the point that attracts attention to multi-agent systems. *They are able to react in much more various ways, than any designer can describe in advance.* This emergent flexibility of MAS causes a wide application field.

However, this flexibility has its own price, consisting in an exponential growth of system's complexity. As pointed out by many authors (e.g. (Wolfram, 1985)), in such complex systems the behavior is computationally irreducible, it can be obtained only by direct simulation, no shortcut and no prediction is possible. In this way we encounter an interesting paradox. Following Green (Green, 1994), we postulate that "any array of finite state automata is itself an automaton". Thus, in order to obtain a transfer function of such a "big automaton", we compare it with some another FSA by using the well-known "black box approach". Investigation of input/output relation, unbound in time and space, involves an irreducible computation of arbitrary long time. Therefore, the question about equivalence of FSA and MAS is formally undecidable and so we arrive at contradiction with the original postulation. As pointed out by Wolfram (Wolfram, 1985), it may be undecidable, whether two finite specifications yield equivalent configurations. Although it has been said in context of cellular automata, it is also valid for multi-agent systems. In this way, *though any agent still remains an automaton, the multi-agent system gets new properties which automata do not possess.* It may sound paradoxically and there is no common opinion on this point, but we suppose the MAS is not an automaton and belongs to the class of emergent systems.

The explanation is that on the microscopic level the agent behaves like a FSA, no matter whether it is connected into a system or not. Each agent contributes into a collective effect, that even for very simple 10 agents can have a degree of freedom of 10^{100} states. This collective effect appears on the macroscopic level as emergent behavior. Emergent behavior is a new property of MAS on the macroscopic level, and it makes MAS distinct from agent and so from FSA. These emergent properties are often denoted as *combinatorial emergence*.

Emergent behavior is the second important issue and has a direct consequence for a practical implementation of MAS. On the one hand, the technical systems are expected to behave in a predetermined way specified by a designer. It concerns also the collective activity of multi-agent systems. Indeed, we need to program the collective behavior of agents in a deterministic way, where MAS becomes a FSA and no emergent behavior is possible. On the other hand, the flexibility (emergent behavior) of MAS is required to deal with the irregular processes, for which there are either no predetermined solutions or too many possible solutions (see e.g. (Kornienko *et al.*, 2004e). For these processes the MAS are expected to "find" such a reaction that solves the problem. Therefore a "trick" in the programming of MAS is *to provide such a mechanism that guarantees an emergent behavior with predetermined properties.*

In the language of cooperative processes we call the predetermined activity as the *primary activity*. It is a type of activity, being executed most of time and representing a goal of system. Additional activity, intended to adapt the system to changes so that to prolong executing a primary activity, we call the *secondary activity*. There is a third type of activity, directed to self-modification, but we leave it aside this work. Not all combinations of the emerged agent's states are of interest, only primary and secondary activities are technically useful. This represents a way of how to deal with enormous complexity of MAS, i.e. to restrict the macroscopic behavior only to the determined primary and emerged secondary activities.

Which mechanism can satisfy these conflicting requirements ? As usually, we look for an example in nature. Let us consider a building of a house. There are a building tower crane, bulldozer, excavator, construction personnel of different professions and so forth that are usually needed for such a enterprize. We can say this group is able to build different buildings, traffic roads or even other constructions. However, it is not able to do another kind of occupation, e.g. to construct a car or an airplane. The considered group is specialized in one cluster of activities, i.e. restricted in the emergent behavior. But it still remains flexible in the cluster, where it can emerge different macroscopic behaviors. Mapping this example into an agent group, we point primarily to rules that govern a behavior. We require these rules are "compatible" with each other. For example, a bulldozer and a car's assembling robot are hardly able to emerge any kind of reasonable collective activity. The rules have to provide a compatible types of agent's separated activities, so that different group-behavior can emerge.

Let us return to the example with a building. How does arise exactly this particular house ? The tower crane takes a lading only when it is prepared by corresponding ground personal. They, in turn, can start to do it only when trucks have brought a lading and so on. We can say the separated activity of all participants is coordinated in a specific way, so that to allow a particular type of emergent behavior. If another type of coordination is used in the group, another result is expected to emerge. Indeed, plan of a building, in its final form, represents a coordination pattern between participants. It allows building exactly this construction.

But this coordination pattern is "soft". If there is a deviation from the plan, the common "building" system reacts so that to absorb this deviation and to repair a broken plan. For example, if the lading is not prepared or brought, the corresponding personal try to solve this problem, whereas a crane takes another lading. By analogy from physics, a coordination pattern looks like an energetic minimum in a state space and the system is attracted to this minimum. If there are any "obstacles", the system finds by gravity a bypass. In this way the attractor, as energetic minimum, is a primary activity and a bypass is a secondary activity. We call this type of coordination as the "attracting" coordination.

Summarizing, we state three important points of the primary and secondary activities.

1. The rules, determining behavior of an agent, should be "compatible" with each other, so that a partial behavior of agents supplements each other.

2. The agent's coalition should possess a mechanism that coordinates partial behaviors of all agents. Speaking more precisely, the branching points in the agents rules should be coordinated in a specific "soft" manner.

3. Finally, agents have to make one's contribution into a common business observable on the macroscopic level.

Therefore, the specific rules and their coordination allow appearing specialized emergent behavior. *In order to create the emergent behavior with predetermined properties, the branching points should be "attracted" to corresponding macroscopic states, representing distributed activities.* The attracting mechanism can be implemented in different algorithmic as well as analytic ways. One of them is e.g. an algorithm of symbolic task decomposition (ASTD) (Kornienko et al., 2004e), discussed in Chapter 5. Several analytical approaches are discussed in (Kornienko, 2007).

Finishing the section about the algorithmic treatment of collective phenomena, we point once again to the simulative character of approaches from this domain. This causes specific difficulties, well-known in the "simulative" domain: the problem of parameters, a relation between microscopic and macroscopic levels and so on. The main attention here is paid to programming individual behavior. General origin of collective behavior lies on combinatorial emergence (e.g. (Cariani, 1997)) and a non-reductive complexity. We return to these notions in the next Chapter again.

As mentioned in Introduction, the examples of collective phenomena are taken from micro-robotic systems of the I-Swarm project (I-Swarm, 2003-2007). This kind of agents does not possesses complex computational, communicating, sensor and actor abilities. Therefore, a swarm of micro-robots (or more generally micro-agents) is an ideal example to consider artificial self-organization with desired emergent properties. In the next section we introduce the scenario, where we investigate cooperative phenomena as well as discuss capabilities of micro-robots and a swarm of micro-robots.

2.5 Collective behavior in the surface micro-cleaning scenario

We investigate a swarm behavior based on several examples, collected into some useful scenario. We took this scenario from the I-Swarm project. After some discussions, we decided to use the *surface micro-cleaning scenario*. The surface micro-cleaning includes many different coordinated activities that have to be emerged by a group of micro-robots. These activities can be connected into a more complex behavioral pattern according to functional capabilities of robots. In this way we can compare individual capabilities of robots and emergent capabilities of a whole group.

In the following, we consider three cases of interest: basic, average and extended. In the basic case the micro-robots are assumed to be really simple and very limited: no recognition, no distance measurement and so on. This is really hard case, where we are going to test the limit of possible hardware that still allows emergent behavior. In the average case the robots are assumed to have capabilities like those of the robot Jasmine (see Figure 2.4(d)). In the extended case, capabilities of robots are expected to be equal to Robocup robots (see Figure 2.4(c)). The assumed capabilities of robots for the micro-cleaning scenario are collected in Table 2.2. These three different cases are indented to study the relation between sensor/actor/comutational/communication capabilities and the emergent behavior that the robots can demonstrate.

(a) (b)

(c) (d)

Figure 2.4: **(a)** *The robot Alice developed in EPFL, ASL/LSA, image taken from (Caprari & Siegwart, 2003);* **(b)** *The robot MiCRoN, developed by the MiCRoN consortium.* **(c)** *The RoboCup robot of Stuttgart's team;* **(d)** *The 'Jasmine' micro-robot.*

The tasks and sub-scenarios in the surface micro-cleaning

Corresponding to three cases of hardware capabilities, we developed three sub-scenarios: basic, averaged and extended. In all these sub-scenarios robots have to perform the following activities:

1. To explore a surface;

2. To detect a dirtiness (or something else need to be cleaned);

3. To build a cluster in specific formation (e.g. a ring) around dirtiness;

4. To perform functional activities of cleaning (in some simple, but not predefined, sequence of functional activities).

In basic sub-scenario, there is only one position and one kind of dirtiness and no need of collective agreement. In this most simple and observable case the collective behavior can be demonstrated by forming spatial groups. In average sub-scenario, there are several kinds of dirtiness in different positions and there exists a need of collective agreement. Robots have not only to form the groups, but also to perform several coordinated operations in these groups. In the extended sub-scenario we expect that robots will perform an active form of cooperative activities (e.g. active exploration with scouts), dynamical exchange of information between clusters and so on. These three sub-scenarios are briefly summarized in the Table 2.3. These sub-scenarios allow us to find a relation between possible "swarm-tasks" and hardware capabilities of robots (e.g. the worst case of communication allows executing only the basic scenario and so on).

Comparison between individual and collective capabilities

Within the surface micro-cleaning scenario the swarm of micro-robots uses several types of collective activities. As already mentioned, we can compare individual capabilities of robots and collective capabilities of a whole swarm. We can find 10 different swarm capabilities that can be divided into three following clusters:

- *Spatio-temporal cluster, associated with collective movement and spatial formation;*
- *Information-based cluster, associated with collective information processing;*
- *Activity-based cluster, associated with collective planning, tasks decomposition, building functional structures and so on.*

The swarm capabilities related to the above mentioned sub-scenarios are collected in Table 2.4. Tables 2.2 and 2.4 demonstrate the relation between individual and collective capability of micro-robots. In the next three section we treat these three clusters of capabilities and specific problems arose in each cluster more in details.

2.5.1 Spatio-temporal capabilities of collective behavior

The spatio-temporal capabilities of collective behavior are the most basic features that the swarm has to demonstrate. Primarily they mean collective movement and building different spatial formation.

Collective movement is closely related with coordination and synchronization in spatially distributed groups. For example, exploring a surface, robots can move randomly without any coordination. However, if the group sends firstly several scouts performing reconnaissance and only then the small groups into the explored areas, this strategy allows increasing the effectiveness of exploring large areas.

Building different spatial formation is especially important for executing coordinated functional activities. In the surface micro-cleaning scenario these are structural and mechanical cleaning, consisting in creating sequences of dedicated activities in defined temporal and spatial order. One of the main problem in building spatial formation concerns regularity and irregularity of emergent patterns. We return to this issue many times in the following chapters.

Individual capability	Level of complexity		
	The basic case	*The average case*	*The extended case*
Sensors	1. Agents can detect and recognize an object		
	no recognition	*between robot and object*	*btw. diff. robots and objects*
	2. Agent can measure a distance $Dist$ (angle α) to an object:		
	no distances	*binary distance, angle*	*short-range distance, α*
	no angles	*(e.g.Dist, α >, <, = Tresh)*	*(within R. of 3 robot bodies)*

3. Agent can perceive and classify a touch (some discrete angle of a touch)

4. Agent can perceive some "virtual" pheromone. It could be:
   - of optical kind (gradient light)
   - sound (like in experiments with crickets by Barbara Webb in Stirling)
   - of chemical nature
   - of electromagnetic nature

5. Agent can estimate own connectivity degree (CD):

	no estimation	*CD of physically connected robots*	*CD of robots within R. of 3 robot body*

6. Agent can have an ID number (its role) and can transmit it to other:

	no ID	*fixed ID*	*dynamical ID*
Actors	1. Agent can move, at least, in 8 different directions with small velocity		

2. Agent can do something with dirtiness:
   - chemical cleaning
   - mechanical cleaning (collection and transportation)
   - structural cleaning (mechanical destroying the structure of dirtiness)

3. Heterogeneous robots are equipped by different actuators, they have to build functional sequences:

	no sequences	*2-3 diff. actuators*	*3-5 diff. actuators*

4. Agent can monitor the result of own activities:

	no monitoring	*binary monitoring*	*qualitative monitoring*
Communi- cation	1. Agent can send binary values (analog signals):		
	a few bits to contacted robot	*a few bits to closest robots*	*a few bits to all within R. of 3 robot bodies*
	2. Agent can communicate by means of pheromone. Pheromone can contain:		
	binary value	*analog value*	*a few bits*
Computa- tion	1. Agent has internal coordinate system (world model):		
	no coord. system	*coord. of a few objects*	*complete visible environment*
	2. Agent has a data memory, being able to store:		
	a few bits	*a few bytes*	*a few kbytes*

3. Agent can perform simple logical/arithmetic operations

4. Agent can create and manage sensor/actor couplings (local rules).
   The rules memory and system's architecture can manage:

	a few rules	*a few dozens of rules*	*create rules dynamically*

Table 2.2: *Different hardware capabilities of micro-robots in the surface micro-cleaning scenario.*

Scenarios	Individual contribution	Collective contribution
Basic	1. *explore a surface*	
	2. *detect a dirtiness*	
	3. *build a cluster in specific formation*	3. *agreement about spatial formation*
	4. *perform functional activities of cleaning*	
Average	1. *explore a surface*	
	2. *detect a position and kind of dirtiness*	2. *agreement about type of dirtiness*
	3. *build a cluster in specific formation*	3. *agreement about spatial formation*
	4. *perform functional activities of cleaning*	4. *cooperative executing*
Extended	1. *explore a surface*	1. *active exploration*
	2. *detect a position and kind of dirtiness*	2. *agreement about type of dirtiness, information exchange btw. clusters*
	3. *build a cluster in specific formation*	3. *agreement about spatial formation*
	4. *perform functional activities of cleaning*	4. *cooperative executing, feedback-based collective adaptation, collecitive decision making*

Table 2.3: *Different sub-scenarios in the surface micro-cleaning scenario.*

The general problem of spatio-temporal capabilities is that the robots do not know where they are. They possess only local coordinate system (e.g. "I see something behind me"). There is an open discussion about necessity of the global navigation in the micro-robotic domain. We think that to know global positions is generally not necessary in the cleaning scenario, neither for exploring a surface nor for building spatial patterns. Other known problems consist in the insufficiency of coordination mechanisms, e.g. initial coalition formation (see more in (Sandholm, 1999)), and the general problem of relation between desired and undesired emergence.

This compromise is the especial point of interest, because here we have to define how many robots will do useful job and how many robots will do something useless. The "usefulness" degree is closely related with a spatial and functional distribution of robots and ability to detect dirtiness. This problem we encounter in simulation. It can happen, that because of non-homogeneous distribution on a plane robots cannot discover a dirtiness. This point concerns the number of I-Swarm robots needed to perform the cleaning successfully (in some (mm^2) surface).

2.5.2 Information-based capabilities of collective behavior

Information-based capabilities of collective behavior concern two main points: collective information processing (incl. collective decision making) as well as collective perception.

Two basic problems of swarm communication. After describing software and hardware aspects of robot-robot communication, we treat more "general" topic about communication and coordination (Weiss, 1999) in a swarm. The swarm communication has two essential problems that can not be solved on the technological level, and therefore requires specific behavior-based mechanisms for their solution. The first problem is a routing of

N	Swarm Capabilities	Subscenario		
		Basic	*Averaged*	*Extended*
	ST			
1	*Collective movement*	*non-coordinated*	*coordinated*	*coordinated*
2	*Building spatial structures*	*regular patterns (grid, circle, etc.)*	*irregular patterns*	*dynamic irregular patterns*
	IB			
3	*Building informational structures*	—	*propagation of information*	*"swarm network"*
4	*Collective decision making*	*simple coordination*	*coordination and synchronization*	*multiple decisions network*
5	*Collective information processing*	—	—	*simple distributed processing*
6	*Collective perception/ recognition*	—	*collective classification*	*collective recognition*
	AB			
7	*Building functional structures*	—	*dynamic sequences of activities*	*adaptive functional behavior*
8	*Collective tasks decomposition/allocation*	—	*simple decomp. and allocation*	*dynamic decomp. and allocation*
9	*Collective planning*	—	—	*simple planning based on tasks dec.*
10	*Group-based specialization of behavior*	*and clusterization*	—	*simple functional*

Table 2.4: *Swarm capabilities in dependence of subscenario complexity, ST - spatio-temporal cluster, IB - information-based cluster, AB - activity-based cluster.*

information packages in a swarm. In the routed package-based communication each package consists of a header with IDs of sender and receiver, routing information and the package content. The package ID is coded by 10 bits, IDs of sender/receiver by 12 bits (6 bit each), so the header is of 22 bits (+1 parity bit), the package content is only of 8 bits. For recording the package history each robot needs about 900 bytes RAM only for routing 300-600 packages within a few minutes however has only 1Kb RAM on board. In this way pure package routing is not suitable for propagating information through a swarm (however package-based communication is used for local communication between neighbor robots).

The second problem of swarm communication is so-called clusterization. This phenomenon appears when robots fall to groups so that any communication between groups is broken down, see Fig. 2.7. When the detached group is small, these robots usually lose "orientation" and are "lost" for swarm. When this group consists of 1/3-1/2 of all robots, it starts "parallel" processes: building a communication street, looking for resources and so on. When the number of robots is not sufficient, both groups, primary and secondary, fail in their activities. The strategies for solving both problems consist in specific information exchange mechanisms - robots receive some message, change it and send further as their own messages. During receiving, sending and waiting they behave in a specific way. Before we discuss these communication and behavioral mechanisms, we have to mention the following essential point.

Common knowledge and collective connectivity. The basics of the swarm communication is the notion of "common knowledge", well-known in the domain of distributed systems, see e.g. (Halpern & Mosesi, 1990). The "common knowledge" describes the degree of collective awareness in a swarm, how the robots are informed about the global and particular states of other robots. We can say, that the more cooperatively the swarm should operate, the more "common knowledge" it needs. Therefore in the domain of distributed systems different degrees of "common knowledge" are distinguished (e.g. "all know it", "I know that you know" and so on). The "lowest" degree of common knowledge can easily be achieved (e.g. "I know something about neighbors"), whereas the "highest" degree is very "expensive" from the viewpoint of the resources, required to achieve it. It means, that for the cooperative behavior we pay the price of communication effort, computational resources and, finally, the running time and energy. The more "intelligence" of the swarm system is required, the more advanced cooperation (and so communication and computation) should be involved. This conclusion is done even for distributed economic agents (Malone, 1987). To exemplify this postulation, we collect in Table 2.4 some "swarm activities", that microrobots can collectively perform. To express different degrees of information transfer in a swarm, we use the notion of *collective connectivity*. Collective connectivity means the mechanism that makes a robot aware about other robots and their intentions.

1. Local connectivity. Those swarm approaches, which originate from biological or physical systems, use mostly the *local collective connectivity*. Each robot is aware only about its local neighborhood. It is done by means of proximity sensing or by simple robot-robot communication without messages propagation. In the nature a similar mechanism names stigmergy (Bonabeau *et al.*, 1999). Particular robot does not receive any feedback about its own intention, i.e. **collective behavior of the robots is regulated through physical constraints imposed on a swarm and swarm capabilities are primarily defined by swarm density.** To exemplify this case, we refer to experiments with aggregation around the low-gradient light, see Fig. 2.5(a) (see for details (Kornienko *et al.*, n.d.)).

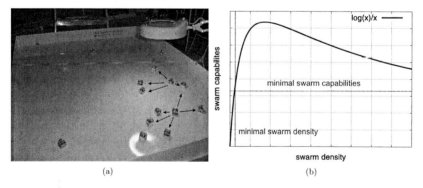

(a)   (b)

Figure 2.5: **(a)** *Local collective connectivity in experiments with aggregations. Arrows show proximity sensing of two robots. There is no communication in this experiment;* **(b)** *Qualitative dependency between swarm capabilities and principal factor for the case of local connectivity.*

In this experiments, robots are equipped with one light sensor, so that they cannot find any gradient in the light. The idea of the algorithm is that a robot, when encountering another robot, should stop and wait some time. In this case, the more brighter the light is, the more longer robots are staying and the more robots will be collected under the lamp. When there is some number of robots under a lamp, they are blocked by new coming robots and are continuously staying, so that we observe growing a cluster. When there are only a few robots, no aggregation is observed, i.e. it is typically collective behavior. When the light is moved in another position, robots, after some time, follow the light. We see from this example, that collective aggregation behavior appears without global propagation of information, however due to local physical interaction (collisions). The parameters of collective aggregation are defined by collision avoiding behavior, i.e. by physical constraints.

The swarm capabilities in this case are primarily defined by the swarm density, see Fig. 2.5(b). Increasing the number of robots leads rapidly to growing collective capabilities. However, there is some minimal threshold imposed on the number of robots (for experiments in (Kornienko *et al.*, n.d.) it is 9 robots), where no collective behavior is observed at all. Moreover, there is the growing maximum, after that the swarm capabilities are merely decreasing. As shown in (Kornienko *et al.*, n.d.), we estimate a character of this curve as $log(N)/N$. Since there is no propagation of information in this case, the routing and clusterization problems are avoided.

2. Global connectivity. Based on experiments, we can say that approaches with the local collective connectivity can produce stable and scalable, but relatively simple and mostly only *mono-functional* collective behavior. As observed from Table 2.4, almost no

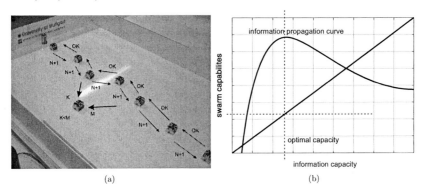

(a)   (b)

Figure 2.6: **(a)** *Global collective connectivity in experiments with the creation of communication street. The messages are globally propagated during this "street". The collective behavior is regulated through circulation of these messages, e.g. the robot is navigating along the "street" based on the "gradient" of messages;* **(b)** *Qualitative dependency between swarm capabilities and principal factor for the case of global connectivity.*

information-based and no functionality-based types of swarm behavior are possible with this mechanism. To achieve more advanced cooperation, robots should propagate their own information over a swarm. Each robot, when getting a message, has to propagate this message further. Thus we can denote this as *global collective connectivity*.

The collective capabilities are primarily defined in this case by information capacity of the swarm. The more messages of different type can be propagated through the swarm, the more diverse is the resulting collective behavior. We estimate this dependency as linear or closely-linear, see Fig. 2.6(b). However, the information propagation depends, in turn, on the information capacity (among other factors) and has typical one-maximum curves, that we observed in Fig. 2.5(b). Therefore there is optimal information capacity that maximizes propagation of information. **The collective behavior is regulated through circulated messages and swarm capabilities are primarily defined by information capacity of the swarm.** This mechanism allows even a multi-functional behavior of robotic group.

3. Feedback connectivity. The global collective connectivity provides messages transfer over the swarm, however this is not enough when robots have to receive the feedbacks on their own messages. It can be e.g. the request for specific resources or team building of robots with specific capabilities (robots are heterogeneous), asking for collective state and so on. The communication mechanisms, when the robots are able to receive answers to their own messages, we call the *global feedback connectivity*. To give an example of this communication case, we consider the experiment with a team building for cooperative actuation, see Fig. 2.7. In this experiment, the robots-scout, equipped with the color sensor, found the

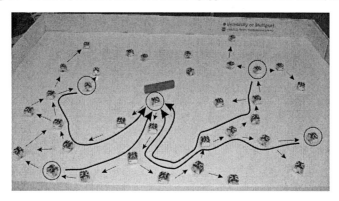

Figure 2.7: *Global feedback connectivity in experiments with the cooperative actuation. Robots, equipped with color sensors, are marked by circles. Thin arrow points to a global propagation of messages, thick arrow points to feedback messages. Behinds are robots that do not have any connections to the rest of the robots - this cluster is disconnected from the swarm.*

blue object (object in the middle of arena). It sends request to the swarm and ask about support it looks for robots with a specific functionality (in this case also equipped with color sensor). The behavior of robot-scout (and also the swarm) depends on the feedback signals of other robots with color sensors: when there are no such robots available, scout will look further; when at least two other robots give the feedback, the scout will wait them. The mechanism of the feedback sending is much more complex: the robots should know when they have to stop sending, know the recipience and so on.

We do not have now enough experimental material to estimate the primary factor influencing the collective capabilities. We assume that in the case of "individual-to-individual" cooperation, this is defined by a functional diversity of robots, the more different types of robots are in swarm, the more different activities swarm can demonstrate. This relation has combinatorial character and therefore seems to be exponential (Kornienko *et al.*, 2004e). **The collective behavior is regulated in this case by a cooperation between individual robots and swarm capabilities are expected to be primarily defined by functional diversity of robots.**

We summarized these three cases of information transfer in Fig. 2.8. It seems now that they have completely different character not only of underlying algorithms, but also in

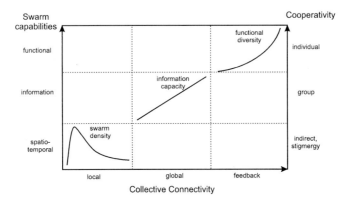

Figure 2.8: *Summarization of different cases of information transfer in a swarm and, as a result, different cases of cooperativity and swarm capabilities.*

scalability, principal factors, allowed coordination mechanisms and, the most important, in a degree of collective knowledge. In this way, we assume that these three cases of information transfer lead to qualitatively different swarm capabilities. Thus, we can expect the type of communication is a primary factor defining the phenomenon of "swarm intelligence".

2.5.3 Activity-based capabilities of collective behavior

Activity-based capabilities of collective behavior are closely related with plans and plan making in swarm. Considering pre-made and dynamically generated plans, we point out, that pre-made plans have a huge disadvantage - they do not work at any, even very small, disturbance (except belief-based plans, like partially observable Markov decision process). Therefore pre-made plans do not work in real situations, and we do not consider them at all. The robots, and correspondingly swarm of robots, is controlled by local rules. Controlled is not an appropriate term, because we create in this way the purposeful self-organization. Derivation of local rules represents the main problem.

We followed several last years the biological researches of cooperative phenomena in nature (e.g. cockroaches by Jean-Louis Deneubourg in Brussel, crickets by Barbara Webb in Stirling, cooperative neural patterns by Scott Kelso in Florida and other researchers). After many discussions in conferences and workshops, we came to the conclusion that biological researches give us very important insight about natural emergent phenomena, e.g. the pheromone- and trophallaxis-based mechanisms, audio- and visual navigation, pattern-forming mechanisms and so on. For example, for exploration and detection of dirtiness in cleaning scenario we can apply the mechanisms of signal pAMP in Dictyostelium discoideum. However, there are two problems.

Firstly, how to extract the local rules from the collective behavior of e.g. social insects ? Observing the colony of cockroaches, we can construct the model of individual behavior and then to test it in experiments. However, the real local rules, governing behavior of each cockroach, still remain unknown. In several cases these models are very good, in other cases it is very difficult to extract all rules to build really adequate model. Secondly, the natural emergent phenomena and technically useful emergent phenomena are quite different. In our opinion, the main difference consists in many restrictions (constraints) that technical systems deal with. These constraints can completely change the local rules of similar emergence but without constraints. For example, if we try to consider the feedback of cleaning (success of cleaning), we have drastically (more than in three times) to increase the number of local rules.

Another example, demonstrating influence of constraints, can be given by the transition from macroscopic to microscopic levels of description. The well-known predator-prey model, formulated as the macroscopic reaction-diffusion equation of two variables, demonstrates characteristic relation between both species. Now we rewrite this model on the microscopic level as the system of n-interacting agents ($n \gg 2$). In the behavioral routines of agents we take into account different restrictions existing there: collisions, probabilities of "own death", individual adaptability, different kinds of noise and so on. The behavior of macroscopic and microscopic (with constraints) models coincides only in a small range of parameters and only qualitatively. Instead, we got a large spectra of "unexpected" and sometimes "undesired" emergent phenomena, which are not contained in the macroscopic model: overflow of population area, "quick death" of prey-population and so on. It is enormously difficult (or even impossible) to estimate influence of such low-level constraints on emergent behavior, without using complex computational approaches.

The question is how to derive (to obtain, to calculate) the local rules, being able to generate the desired (technically useful) emergent behavior ? Can we directly apply the biologically obtained rules to technical systems ? As said by Jean-Louis Deneubourg, there is still no "biological receipt-book" for this case. We believe that discovered biological mechanisms and non-biological (synergetics, computer science, physics, chemistry, etc.) researches of collective phenomena are complementary.

2.6 The scalability problem of collective behavior

We devote the last section of this chapter to one of most important problems, which we encounter in collective behavior. This problem concerns a scalability. Scalability is obviously a desirable feature of collective systems, meaning economical functioning in a wide range of sizes and configurations. However, we fail to find a useful and rigorous definition of it. Several authors often define scalability in terms of productivity and performance (Jogalekar & Woodside, 2000). Connie Smith (Smith, 1990) first used the term "performance engineering" to bring together performance evaluation and systems design. In the domain of multi-agent systems, scalability can be also stated in terms of co-ordination policies as e.g. total number of message exchanges necessary to converge on a solution (Rana & Stout, 2000).

Metrics	Examples
Productivity-based metrics (Jogalekar & Woodside, 2000)	speedup, efficiency
Coordination-based metrics (Rana & Stout, 2000)	coordination policy
Capacity-based metrics (Brataas & Hughes, 2004):	
- processing capacity	rate of messages
- information capacity	amount of storage
- connectivity	N of connections

Table 2.5: *Different scalability metrics.*

To treat scalability, we need to establish a relation between types of scaling and the produced by them effect on the collective systems. For this relation we have first to introduce metrics of scalability. The need of scalability metrics has been pointed out many times in the domain of massively parallel computation as well as distributed systems (e.g. (Jogalekar & Woodside, 2000)). Reviewing the vast literature on the object, we encounter basically three kinds of metrics, collected in Table 2.5. We refer to (Woodside, 2000) for details of scalability metrics. If the metrics can be expressed as formal expressions (with corresponding numeric values), the types of scalability can be hardly defined in the formal way. We distinguish the following types of scalability (see e.g. (Bondi, 2000)), collected in Table 2.6. The presented metrics and types of scalability allow us to consider three cases of systems

Type	Description
Load scalability	functioning at different loads
Structural scalability	growing number of subsystems
Diversity Scalability	growing heterogeneity degree
Dynamic Scalability	shifting to short-term dynamics

Table 2.6: *Different types of scalability.*

scalability (Carrillo *et al.*, 2003), listed in Table 2.7.

Systems	Appearance
Unscalable	bottle necks, scaling limit
Scalable	smooth decreasing of performance
Superscalable	constant performance

Table 2.7: *Different types of systems in relation to scalability.*

Returning to collective information systems, we remark that scalability here differs in several ways from scalability in other, like multiprocessor, systems. Firstly, scalability in collective information systems means primarily structural scalability of two types: growing amount of identical components as well as a growing diversity of components, i.e. *structural and diversity scalability*. Almost all collective systems reveal this property. Secondly, a growing number of components increases the load on the system. Therefore, the *load and dynamic scalability* are also typical for collective information systems. There are several challenges we have to face in each case of the above mentioned scalability types. The *structural scalability* induces the increase of coordination effort to solve a problem, the overload of communication, the explosion of communication costs and the fail of communication channels. The *diversity scalability* has impact on the flexibility with the need of adaptations for the new components and on the functional adaptation of collective procedures to new components. The *load and dynamic scalability* influences the appearance of overloads and bottle necks, the growing of probability for partial failure's and the need of activities monitoring.

We briefly present several approaches and mechanisms being useful in solving these problems. The first way consists in predicting a performance (bottle necks and overloads) by several modeling techniques. Some authors (e.g. (Rana & Stout, 2000)) suggest applying for this goal the multi-agent systems, based on Petri nets, temporal logics, coordination languages, category theory and others. Besides prediction of performance, agents can monitor the activities and predicts possible failures, based on e.g. POMDP (Partially Observable Markov Decision Process, see e.g. (Williams & Nayak, 1996)) approach. Agents can not only monitor activities, but also suggest several alternatives, for instance alternative routes, to avoid bottle necks and overloads. Several approaches have recently been suggested for this purpose (e.g. decomposition approaches, see (Kornienko *et al.*, 2004e)).

The second way consists in the increase of flexibility to get round the diversity problem. The flexibility and adaption are very complex issues. Several authors suggest utilizing different biological mechanisms to guarantee the flexibility (Bonabeau *et al.*, 1999). The problem of flexibility is often treated in the context of multi-agent systems (Kornienko *et al.*, 2004c). At least, for collective information systems and data propagation, the flexibility can be reduced to the question of flexible adaptors and mechanisms of dynamics generation of dependencies (Rantzau *et al.*, 2002). In this case, the providing of flexibility can successfully be performed by agents, as suggested in (Kornienko *et al.*, 2004c).

The mentioned two ways can potentially absorb the most of problems arising at the *diversity* as well as the *load and dynamic scalability*. However, the problems arising at the *structural scalability* are hard to solve. We think that the possible solutions consist in creating either scale-independents or adaptive mechanisms. The scale-independents are specific mechanisms of coordination and communication that do not depend on the scaling factors. Examples are "deadlock-free" marking in Petri-nets or "T,P-invariant" tokens (Rana & Stout, 2000). Generally, there are many efficient coordination and communication mechanisms, which provide such a scale-independence. The mechanisms of adaptation allow changing one part of the systems so that to compensate other changes caused by scaling. Although both approaches are useful in creating structural scalability, they can not guarantee a solution for e.g. the case of new scale-dependent constraints. Generally, the structural scalability in collective systems still remains an open research point. We return to scalability in the context of functional self-organization in Section 4.4.5.

2.7 Summary

The main point of this section was to introduce several main notions towards reductive and computational approaches and to demonstrate an origin of "collective problem". As shown in both parts of this chapter, the origin of the problem lies in a huge complexity of collective phenomena. This complexity can be either reduced or treated by simulation. We denote these reductive and computational approaches also as analytical and algorithmic ones, because the first of them is "located" in the domain of nonlinear dynamics and, whereas the second one in the domain of "algorithmic" (e.g. multi-agent) systems. We have also considered the scenario, where the collective phenomena are studied as well as the question about scalability of collective systems.

Chapter 3

Artificial self-organization: what is it ?

> The individual is going to be universalized,
> the universal is going to be individualized,
> and thus from both directions
> the whole is going to be enriched.
>
> *[Jan Smuts, "Holism and Evolution"]*

3.1 Motivation

The main focus of this chapter can be covered by the simple question: what is a self-organization in artificial (technical) systems ? Variety of natural self-organization phenomena emerged in physical, chemical, biological systems demonstrates that in a visible absence of control center, these systems work in completely ordered way. Considering these phenomena more closely, it gets visible that the control center is replaced by its invisible distributed analog, i.e. by local rules determining behavior of each subsystem and subelements. Nature of these rules is given by the corresponding physical laws, thereby any modification of natural self-organization phenomena seems impossible. In contrast to natural systems, the artificial systems possess more degrees of freedom, choice and determination of rules are under a supervision of developers. Therefore the ordered behavior of such systems can easily be "programmed" by accordingly chosen rules. The arisen questions, which are expected to be answered here, are whether we can refer this "programming" also to self-organization phenomena or self-organization is something more ? Which methodological tools can be applied to the "programming" of self-organization and what practical importance of obtained results should be expected ?

3.2 Introduction

Artificially created systems play an important role in a neoteric human life. If a pair hundred years ago natural systems completely surrounded human habitation and it was a big challenge to investigate, to systematize and to control them, now artificial systems substantially occupy this position. In everyday life we deal more with computers, networks, automation systems, embedded systems and autos than with animals, insects and other objects and phenomena of natural origin. We inhabit artificial eco-systems and no longer natural eco-systems. Although these still fascinate by diversity, complexity and "originality", artificial systems are becoming more and more complex and numerous. In this way there arises an interesting paradox. Though artificial systems have been designed by humans and we know all about their functions and constructions, due to interactions, they start to demonstrate such properties that were not provided at designing. Very famous example is traffic jams (Helbing, 2001). It is known all about a car, it is being permanently improved, however, this undesired collective effect (traffic jams) cannot still be avoided. Thus, if earlier only natural systems are in focus of investigations, now artificial systems require similar efforts of researchers.

Nonlinear interactions, arising in a conglomerate of modern artificial systems, lead to several effects of interest. One of them is a phenomenon of self-organization, which is widely studied in hydrodynamic fluids (Ebeling & Feistel, 1986), social insects (Pasteels *et al.*, 1987), molecular biology (Eigen *et al.*, 1988), lately in computer networks (Dorogovtsev & Mendes, 2001), robotics (Chantemargue & Hirsbrunner, 1999), networks of citations (Barabási & Albert, 1999), of binary strings (Banzhaf *et al.*, 1999), traffics (Helbing, 2001) and several other systems. Considering the self-organization more closely, all authors, in fact, agree that the origin of self-organization lies in specific rules, that govern behavior of each "collective" participant. In natural systems these rules are determined by the corresponding physical laws and can hardly be changed. In contrast to them, the rules in artificial systems are primarily determined by a designer, though the physical laws are also of significance, especially in devices of micro- and nano-scales.

The self-organization, emerged by one of the pathways in natural systems (Haken, 1983a, p. 56) manifests if some control parameters overstep the critical value and all components start to behave in the ordered way without a visible "commander". Actually, exactly this phenomenon fascinates researchers in hoping to find a key to Pandora's box, namely, to obtain a desired behavior without efforts of programming it ... The ordered behavior of artificial systems can easily be programmed and so a "fascination" of such a self-organization is lost. This system behaves in ordered way without a visible "commander", but it is preprogrammed. The question is whether these preprogrammed phenomena belong to self-organization, even to artificially created, or self-organization in artificial systems is something more, something that is really *SELF-organized* ? Results obtained in the last years by a research of emergent behavior are impressive, however, there is only a limited number of quantitative principles that can be directly applied in creating the self-organization (Helbing & Vicsek, 1999) and they cannot also answer the question about practical value of self-organization.

The meaning of self-organization for artificial systems is another and not less interesting question. Natural collective phenomena underlie an emission of laser light, in many cases a thermodynamic heat-transfer, in social systems various forms of swarm behavior, like a collective attack and defense by insects and so on. However what is the self-organization in artificial systems ? What can be achieved by self-organization and cannot be done in another way ? This is the difficult question because there is only a limited number of works in this domain. At least, as remarked by investigations in autonomous robotics, e.g. (Fukuda & Ueyama, 1994), modular space constructions (Sedwick *et al.*, 1999), it is much cheaper to produce many small robots and to put them to perform one cooperative activity, than to make one big robot that does the same. One interesting point, that attracts a huge attention, is an attempt to reproduce the self-replicating systems (Sipper *et al.*, 1997a). The self-organization can be made as invariant to the number of participants and can serve as a basis for developing very reliable self-replicating systems. Another reason, already mentioned by many today's researchers, is related to a behavior of mobile robotic systems that becomes too complex to be directly programmed. The artificial self-organizing is expected to be used as coordination mechanisms that, among other utilizations, allow avoiding a programming of behavioral details in each robots.

These questions are addressed primarily to communities that deal with a cooperation in multi-robot and multi-agent systems, as well as develop collective activities in molecular and nano/micro-scales devices. We manage this on the most common level by applying concepts related to those from nonlinear dynamics (Wiggins, 1990) and theory of autonomous agents (Weiss, 1999). In this way we are going to show that *analytic as well as algorithmic methods (in sense of the previous chapter) are well applicable to the problem of emergent behavior.*

The remained of this chapter is organized in the following form. Sections 3.3, 3.4 are devoted to a brief overview of historically established methodology in a research of self-organizing phenomena. Section 3.5 deals with artificial self-organization, where we consider the problem of artificial emergence 3.5.1, emergent patterns 3.5.2 and a general benefit of SO phenomena in Section 3.5.4. Section 3.6 faces some aspects of the central problem - the problem of local rules. We demonstrate the mentioned principles on two examples of artificial SO, based on the vertical (Section 3.7.1) and the horizontal (Section 3.7.2) operational principles. The relation between artificial self-organization and artificial evolution is briefly discussed in Section 3.8, the main results are summarized in Section 3.9.

3.3 Historically established methodology

The phenomenon of self-organization appears on two different levels (Haken, 1983a, p.18). Macroscopically, the self-organization does not differ from the classical black box systems, where at a change of control parameters the system changes its output. For example, increasing a pumping energy, a laser emits the laser light. From this point of view, the self-organizing system has a *transfer function* defined by input/output and a set of control parameters. However, from the microscopic viewpoint, the self-organization seems to be completely different. Firstly, there are a great number of participants without visible coordinator. The behavior is governed by local rules establishing nonlinear interactions among elements. Secondly, a macroscopically visible result of self-organization is not observable on this level. For instance, the laser light is not observable on the atomic level.

It is of especial importance to make a clear difference between these levels at a designing of self-organization. For example, the control strategy, being guided by the macroscopic approach, has, most probably, a form of centralized/distributed automatic regulator (Vinter, 2000). In contrast, a control, based on the microscopic approach, utilizes a strategy, which modifies local rules. In the work (Kornienko, 2007) both methodological approaches as well as their implementations are compared. As followed from that work, both approaches perform a control, however, they are completely different from the viewpoint of collective behavior. Therefore, the main goal of this section is briefly to sketch the historically established dominant methodology (this methodology can be thought of as thinking way, e.g. eastern and western thinking way (Reese, 1996), (Kishine, 1997)). This dominant methodology, applied unconsciously, influences the result and researchers should be at least aware about a nature of obtained results. The need of this section arose after numerous discussions in conferences on autonomous robotics and multi-agent systems.

Effect of ordered and reasonable behavior of natural systems fascinated humans perhaps from an origin of human being. These systems are well observable, like animals in a hunting region of a tribe, or weather phenomena, later more abstract notions like the well and the evil. A dominant idea in those ages consisted in existing a causal dependency between action and reaction, that appeared in the form of an "organizer" that manages these phenomena.

Being interested in a manipulation of them, humans tried to "communicate" with this "organizer", that process remained in sacral rituals and myths (Hodson, 1990). Staying in the framework of the work, remark two interesting ideas, that can be found also now: ideas of manipulation and an existence of central element being able to control these phenomena. In this way, the natural elements were assumed to be hierarchically ordered with strong vertical coupling and a weak horizontal coupling. Moreover, there always was a direct causal connection between changing on one level of hierarchy and an effect of this changing on the level below. This approach can be noted as the vertical (hierarchical) methodology. In modern literature such a notion is often called an operational principle, therefore in this case it will be the *vertical operational principle*.

An origin of another operational principle is difficult to find out. Many archeological finds point to ancient polytheistic religions such as those of the Greeks, Romans, Egyptians, Mayans, Norse, and others (Wilkinson & Charing, 2004). However, first, the development and decentralization of Mediterranean states allowed understanding that a wide range of phenomena is of decentralized nature and much more complex than it was assumed before. In this epoch one important notion arose, namely a concept of a system (Aristotle, 1989) - "*The system is more than simply a sum of parts*". Within this system the role of central hierarchical element is lowered, and instead there exists a lot of connected horizontal elements. Moreover, elements can be coupled on different levels of hierarchy, building a kind of multidimensional matrix. Modification of this system should be either performed very carefully or even avoided, because changing one element, other elements will be also changed; common result can be unpredictable. This approach can be noted as the horizontal methodology, or the horizontal operational principle. Many authors are convinced that origin of empirical analysis and horizontal operational principle lies in ancient Greece (see e.g. (Greuter, 2002)). We can find some reflections of the horizontal operational principle in the School of Atomism (Leucippus, Democritus (460-370 BCE.)) that postulated all things consist of *atoms*. In opposite, the Eleatic School (Parmenides (b. 510 BCE.), Zeno (b. 488 BCE.) stated that "all" is continuous and indivisible, there is a *roof* of all elements (Empedocles 450 BCE.). This school we can associate with the vertical operational principle.

The discussion, started in the Ancient Greek, continued during the following historical epochs in the west world. In Europe and North America, both operational principles are coexisted, however hierarchical approach (e.g. in the form of monotheistic religion) still remained dominant. This principle has been applied overall, from the royal state organization, till instrumental tools applied to investigation of natural phenomena.

"*Thus Desaguliers transposed the meaning of the new natural order into a political lesson: a constitutional monarchy is the best possible system of government, since the King, like the Son, has his power limited by it .... Although he (Newton) himself did not encroach upon the domain of the moral science, Newton had no hesitation regarding the universal nature od the laws set out in his* **Principia***. Nature is "very consonant and comfortable to herself," he asserts in the celebrated Question 31 of his* **Optiks** *- and his strong and elliptical statement conceals a vast claim: combustion, fermentation, heat, cohesion, magnetism ... there is no natural process, which would not be produced by these active forces - attracting and repulsions - that govern both the motion the stars and that of freely falling bodies*" (Prigogine & Stengers, 1984, p.27).

In fact all basic scientific tools of 15th - 19th centuries was developed with the underlying vertical operational principle - a set of laws being able to explain all natural phenomena. The residual "unexplained stuff" was absorbed by introducing the theory of stochastic processes. For example thermodynamics:

"*Actually, the problem of the transition from the microscopic to the macroscopic level were to prove exceptionally fruitful for the development of physics as a whole. Boltzmann was the first to take up the challenge. He felt that new concept had to be developed to extend the physics of trajectories to cover the situation described by thermodynamics. Following in Maxwell's footsteps, Boltzmann sought this conceptual innovation in the theory of probability"* (Prigogine & Stengers, 1984, p.122).

The probabilistic approach was criticized many times, especially in the areas, where it "does not work", e.g. in psychology (see e.g. the discussion between Wolfgang Pauli and Carl Gustav Jung (Meier *et al.*, 2001)). However, the first time, when the vertical principle was "seriously injured", occurs in 1889 by Poincare. Trying to solve the three-body problem, Poincare showed that in the case of interactions between bodies this system is non-integrable. It means that even knowing all physical laws, governing behavior of each particle, is not enough to know the collective behavior of these particles. We can think about this year as the birthday of the science of collective phenomena. However, this discovery does not attract a proper attention of scientists - many of them believe, this is only a computational difficulties that can later be solved.

The established position of vertical operational principle was first earnestly shaken by a change of geopolitical positions in the world after the Second World War. It became clear that in complex systems there are many horizontal elements coupling on different hierarchical levels. Modification of the system became much more complicated problem than guessed heretofore. The scientific community was ready to accept the horizontal principle. The first modern development occurred in two fields: nonlinear dynamics and cybernetics.

In the field of nonlinear dynamics it appeared in an elaboration of principles of dissipative systems (Prigogine & Nicolis, 1977) and Synergetics (Haken, 1977).

"One of the most interesting aspects of dissipative structure is their coherence. The system behaves as a whole, as if it were the site of long-range forces. In spite of the fact that interactions among moleculs do not exceed a range of some 10^{-8} cm., the system is structured as though each molecule were "informed" about the overall state of the system"(Prigogine & Stengers, 1984, p. 171).

"Synergetics deals with systems composed of many subsystems, which may be of quite different nature, such as electrons, atoms, molecules, cells, neurons, mechanical elements, photons, organs, animals or even human. ... we wish to study how the cooperation of these subsystems brings about spatial, temporal or functional structures on macroscopic scales. In particular, attention will be focused on those situations in which these structures arise in self-organized fashion, and we shall search for principles which govern these processes of self-organization irrespective of the nature of the subsystems" (Haken, 1983a, p.1).

Cybernetics considers the horizontal principle from the viewpoint of how to control (and later how to create) complex systems.

"Here I need only mention the fact that cybernetics is likely to reveal a great number of interesting and suggestive parallelisms between machine and brain and society. And it can provide the common language by which discoveries in one branch can readily be made use of in the others. ... Cybernetics offers the hope of providing effective methods for the study, and control, of systems that are intrinsically extremely complex. It will do this by first marking out what is achievable (for probably many of the investigations of the past attempted the impossible), and then providing generalized strategies, of demonstrable value, that can be used uniformly in a variety of special cases" (Ashby, 1957, p.5).

In the modern history the vertical operational approach became "classical" and horizontal one is called as "modern". In the 80th one of the first steps towards the horizontal operational principle was made by the "science of complexity" that investigated a connection between complexity and organization. After that, a lot of "horizontal" fields appeared:

neuronal networks, evolutionary computation, cellular automata and so on. In computer science there arise distributed systems and multi-agent systems that got high acceptance because of the last technological developments (mobile phone, robotics and so on). Just in this latest period the wide spectra of self-organization phenomena became in focus of separated investigations.

In this way there are two operational principles and the vertical operational principle is traditionally the most prevailing type. Many researches point out that the vertical operational principle is the most economic mode of operation in computational systems, and therefore a human brain widely uses it in own analytical processes (Minsky, 1985). And here the following paradox arises: phenomena with basically horizontal operational principle are investigated by scientific tools based on the vertical operational principle. Speaking about self-organization, this vertical principle means basically the macroscopic point of view, mentioned at begin of this section. For an analysis the question about utilization of one or another principle is secondary. However, for a designing of artificial self-organization it is of decisive importance. For example, a control of self-organized systems is performed as

- an automatic regulator in case of vertical operational principle;

- a distributed rules-modifier in case of horizontal ones.

The question is of which from both principles should be applied (and why) to self-organization phenomena in artificial systems ?

This is important because even the definition of self-organization depends on operational principle used by researcher (this can at least partially explain the fact that there is no mutually accepted definition of self-organization although this phenomenon was being investigated more than 100 years). Many aspects of this question still remain unclear, it is difficult directly to answer on this question. We discuss later advantages and disadvantages of both principles, applied to artificial self-organization. However, we again point it out, researchers should be aware about nature of applied principles and obtained results.

3.4 Natural self-organization: energy, structure, invariance

Speaking about self-organization, it makes sense first to look at self-organization in nature. In the given overview we are not going to repeat already known results and conclusions explicated in many popular books (e.g. (Camazine *et al.*, 2003), (Nicolis & Prigogine, 1977), (Bushev, 1994)). Actually the goal is to treat these phenomena so, that the drown conclusions can be applicable to the undertaken investigation of artificial self-organization.

Accordingly to thermodynamics, the self-organization phenomena can be thought of as equilibrium and nonequilibrium phase transitions. In equilibrium phase transitions all phases share equal external conditions (parameters) like temperature, pressure, chemical concentration, whereas nonequilibrium phase transitions are far away from such an equilibrium.

I. **Equilibrium phase transitions**

- **Physical system**
  - liquids (liquid-gas transition)
  - ferromagnet (ferromagnet-paramagnet-antiferromagnet)
  - metals (normal metal-superconductor)

II. **Nonequilibrium phase transitions**

- **Physical system**
  - the Bènar effect
  - Taylor instability
  - Laser
  - Nonstationary Josephson effect
  - Gunn effect
- **Chemical system**
  - Chemical oscillations (the Belousov-Zhabotinsky reaction)
- **Biological system**
  - Biorithms
  - Autocatalysis and hypercycles
- **Social/Ecological system**
  - Social revolutions
  - Ecological catastrophes (catastrophes theory e.g. in (Ebeling & Feistel, 1986, p. 110))

Now we can start defining a notion of self-organization. First, the difference between organization and self-organization could be best explained by the example in ordinary life given by H. Haken in (Haken, 1983b, p.191):

"Organization. Consider, for example, a group of workers. We then speak of organization or, more exactly, of organized behavior if each worker acts in well-defined way on given external orders, i.e. by the boss. It is understood that the thus-regulated behavior results in a joint action to produce some product.

Self-organization. We would call the same process as being self-organized if there are no external orders given but the workers work together by some kind of mutual understanding, each one doing his job so as to produce a product".

The system, undergoing self-organization, behaves autonomously, it is disconnected organizationally from environment. However, from informational or energetic viewpoint, this system is still coupled with environment, this can be thought of as sensors, perceiving each change from outside. In a relation to this the influence from outside, *"the self-organization is a process by which global external influence stimulate the start of internal for the system mechanisms, which bring forth the origin of specific structures in it"* (Bushev, 1994, p. 24)). Moreover, on the previous pages of this book, the self-organization is associated with an organization of complex systems, thereby this organization is being created, reproduced or improved.

Accordingly to many authors (e.g. (Conant, 1974), (Bushev, 1994)) the term "self-organizing system" was first used by W.R. Ashby in 1947 (Ashby, 1962), in the field of cybernetics. In this case the notion of self-organization was applied just for technical systems and was mainly connected with a control. Generalizing, we can draw five main features of natural self-organization, that are useful for the next steps of this consideration.

1. *The elements of self-organizing systems are autonomous in the sense of autonomy cycle.* It means these elements are functionally complete, they are able to work in absence of external control. The influence from outside is represented by control parameters. Correspondingly there is an important difference of how to control these systems. If the control is incorporated from outside, the whole system ceases to be the self-organized system.

2. *Natural self-organization phenomena appear in macroscopical forms.* In fact, we decide whether this is a self-organization or not just on the base of the observable qualitative change of spatial, temporal or spatio-temporal macroscopic structures (the observer problem, e.g. (Hejl, 1981)). From the mathematical viewpoint this change is connected with the notion of structural stability (e.g (Robinson, 1995)) that is discussed further.

3. *Interactions among elements in natural self-organizing systems are fixed* (for example, interactions among liquid molecules in hydrodynamical systems, atoms in laser, bacteriums or cells in biological systems, etc.).

4. *In the most natural self-organizing systems the control parameters are represented by energy (matter) flow, change of control parameters are given by a change of these quantities* (the heat energy in the Bénard effect; the control parameter in the Taylor effect is dimensionless, but it is a function of rotation speed, that is coupled with kinetic energy; pump power in laser; concentration of the starting reagents or light in chemical reactions; e.g. food supply in ecological systems; money or goods in economy and so on). This energy (matter) flow determines interactions among elements in these systems.

5. *Most natural self-organizing systems are size-invariant, the self-organization phenomena, taking place there, are independent from a number of participating elements* (number of molecules in hydrodynamical phenomena; number of species/cells in biology). Correspondingly, exceptions are such systems, where the number of components is a control parameter (pathway of self-organization though number of components (Haken, 1983a, p.57)).

3.5 Artificial (technically useful) self-organization

Now we switch from natural to artificial self-organization. What is it ? Is it the same phenomenon or is it something different ? Let us remember that self-organization is a process. Result of this process is the emergence of different (behavioral, functional and other) patterns. Therefore, the issue about artificial self-organization consists of four independent points: the phenomenon of "technical" emergence, construction (evolution) of behavioral patterns, a self-organizing generation of behavioral patterns and, finally, a scalability of behavioral patterns as well as the self-organizing generation. We consider separately in the next sections the difference between natural and artificial SO based on these points.

3.5.1 Emergence in technical system

"Emergence is a process by which new structures and functions come into being" (Cariani, 1997). There are several kinds of emergence, e.g. "combinatorial", "creative", "thermodynamic" and so on. Generally, we refer the emergent property of a system to arising of something, being not explicitly programmed. We assume that this arising "new" possesses some useful properties, otherwise the phenomenon of emergence would not attract so much attention to itself.

Almost all examples of emergence originate from natural systems. Swarm behavior in flocks, insect colonies and shoals is fascinating. However, how much this behavior can be applied to precise technological systems of robots, software and mobile agents ? Natural and technical systems are quite different and the questions is whether the swarm behavior in these systems is also different ?

We consider this problem on a maximally simplified example of micro-object assembling. Let we have two different kinds of agents (these are "micro-agents" from the I-Swarm project) with different abilities and two kinds of objects with different geometry (see Figure 3.1). The common task, to assemble them into a construction, can be solved only by a cooperation between agents. This cooperation can be determined by e.g. corresponding scheduling, performed in advance. However, we do not predetermine this cooperation, therefore an appearance of cooperative behavior can be thought as an emergent property of this system.

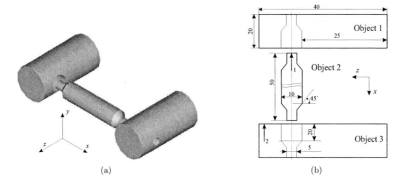

| (a) | (b) |

Figure 3.1: *The workpiece to be assembled by micro-agents;* **(a)** *3D Representation;* **(b)** *The x-z section of objects.*

An assembling of the workpiece should be performed in some specified order, otherwise we do not obtain the desired detail. *Independently of the assembling method, classical or swarm-based, the assembling order should be preserved.* The assembling plan is represented as the Petri net, shown in Figure 3.2. The plan consists of 7 steps, shown as the phases p_1-p_7 with the corresponding positions and rotation angles. The order of assembling is following: the phases p_1, p_3 and p_6 can be started in parallel. However, other phases have to be proceeded sequentially. The phase p_7 can be started only if p_5, p_6 are finished. For the phase p_5 we have two cases. The objects Ob^1 and Ob^2 can be assembled if either the object Ob^1 or the object Ob^2 are placed in the required position, $t_5 = \{p_4, p_2\}$ for the first case, $t_5 = \{p_4\}$ for the second one. The restrictions on the order of operations are the global restrictions C_g.

There are two kinds of agents. The first one Ag^1 can rotate an object, where as the second one Ag^2 can transport an object. Both agents have a "position" (x, y) in the agent's local coordinate system and have a simple 8-directional movement system. Objects also have "position" (x, y), "rotation angle" α and "geometry" (h, l). Each agent observes neighbors in some radius R_{vis}. It can also measure a distance to target and a rotational angle of target (closely to object). In order to simplify the problem, we do not consider collisions between agents and an agent takes an object by placing itself in the geometric origin of an object (x_0, y_0). Each agent reads from the plan only relative distances between objects (position of assembling place is marked by a mark). If an agent starts some activity with an object, it marks this object by putting a number of current phase on the mark (e.g. in electromagnetic way).

An agent can start transportation or rotation only if its position coincides with the

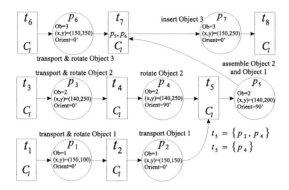

Figure 3.2: *The Petri net-based assembling plan of the workpiece, shown in Figure 3.1. P_i are phases, where t_i are transitions with the shown conditions (e.g., conditions for t_7 are the satisfaction of local constraints C_l from Figure 3.3, and the finished phases p_5, p_6).*

position of an object. Moreover, before starting an activity, an agent has to be sure that the object is not currently processed by another agent or a current activity is not already done by other agents (these problems can be solved by marking). We denote these restrictions as the local restrictions C_l. Activity of each agent can also be represented in the form of Petri net (see Figure 3.3). Agents start from random initial positions. Objects are also initially

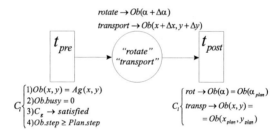

Figure 3.3: *Activity "transport" and "rotate" with local constraints C_l. Activity "move" is called automatically if a position of agent does not coincide with a position of target.*

placed in random positions with random angles, but without intersections between objects.

Emergence of cooperation. In simulation (see Figure 3.4), each agent looks for objects in its own neighborhood. For the found object, the agent reads the mark and calls the required activities from the locally stored plan. If the local and global restrictions are satisfied, the agent executes the required activities. The local rules of an agent have the following form:

```
Ob=look for (visible objects); read mark (Ob);
if (constraints(Ob)) do(Activity);
```

As already mentioned, agents can start assembling from different initial phases of the plan. In Figure 3.5 we compare the possible initial phases with the average length (time steps)

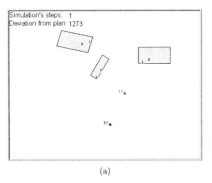
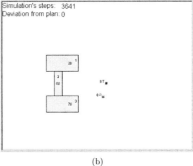

(a)   (b)

Figure 3.4: *Simulation of micro-assembling the workpiece shown in Figure 3.1.* (a) *The initial state of simulation.* (b) *The final state of simulation.*

of assembling. Two generated agent-agent cooperation's patterns are shown in Figure 3.6. We see, the initial order of phases causes completely different cooperation between agents. Therefore we can choose more short assembling by putting additional rules as e.g.

```
at choice -> choice phase with smaller number;
```

Discussion. On this example we can discuss the question why do we need the emergence in technical systems ? *The first advantage of emergent behavior is a simplicity of generating local rules.* They can be implemented even in a very restricted hardware. Simplicity of local rules represents important issue for micro-systems. *The second advantage consists in a flexibility of generated behavior.* Flexibility means that if some elements of agent's system or a plan itself will be perturbed, agents can absorb this disturbance and are still able to accomplish their common business. We do not need to reprogram the system every time (we discuss this point more in Section 3.5.4). To demonstrate it, we perturb positions and rotation angles of all objects. In this way we simulate micro-vibration of mechanical origin. Comparison between unperturbed and perturbed assembling is shown in Figure 3.7. As followed from this figure, agents can still finish assembling even at very strong positional noise. However, they are sensitive to positional-angle noise.

We see, that the cooperation, even in this simple example, emerges without being *pre-programmed*. Emergence arises because of *interactions* between agents. These interactions, in turn, are determined by *local rules* that govern a behavior of each agent. However, this kind of emergence differs from natural emergence, observed e.g. in biological systems.

Firstly, in technical systems we needed more or less specific spatial or functional emergent behavior. "Specific" means that the behavior should meet predefined requirements. We denote these requirements as "irregularities", because they introduce into normal ("regular") behavioral course irregular components. In the assembling example, they are local and global constraints. We could denote this emergence as constrained or irregular emergence.

Special kind of irregularities is represented by parameters. In the assembling, each operation is *parameterized* by data from the plan. Without knowing these parameters, agent cannot accomplish assembling. There is still open discursion about how many parameters have to be involved in the emergent behavior ? Should the agents e.g. know own neighbors ? Where is a limit of parametrization, after that the behavior is less emergent and more predetermined ? One possible way to answer these questions is to define a compromise

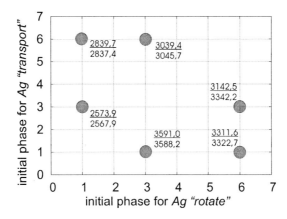

Figure 3.5: *Phases diagram of the Petri net shown in Figure 3.2. In the fraction near each initial point, the numerator shows an average length of an assembling with $t_5 = \{p_4\}$, the denominator shows an average length of an assembling with $t_5 = \{p_4, p_2\}$. Agents start from random initial conditions, 100×100 square, $R_{vis} = 400$, shown is the average result of 10000 simulation's cycles.*

between "useful" and "useless" emergent behavior. We can "sacrifice" a "useless" part of collective system, so that to minimize a parametrization of a "useful" part. Generally, a parametrization still remains an open research point.

Secondly, as observed from the simple assembling example, the emergent behavior can be of different efficiency. In contrast to natural systems, which have to be foremost *reliably*, the technical emergence has to be also *optimal*. Thus, we have to derive such local rules that not only generate the desired emergence, but also optimize it.

3.5.2 Construction of emergent patterns

Speaking about emergent behavior, we mean primarily emergent behavioral patterns. This issue, in turn, consists of two following points: construction of desired patterns and generation of desired patterns.

Construction of emergent patterns. This point concerns regularity and irregularity of patterns to be emerged. We can intuitively assume that regular patterns are more "ordered", than irregular patterns. The "order"-degree of a pattern can be associated with the number of rules, required to construct it. Thus, if a pattern is regular we need less rules to construct it, than in the case of irregular pattern. The number of required rules we can estimate by calculating Kolmogorov complexity (Kolmogorov, 1963) of corresponding symbolic sequences. To exemplify this idea, let us consider two simple patterns, shown in Figure 3.8.

We write a pair of distance D_k (between neighbors j and i) and neighbors i, j as $[D_k, (j, i)]$. For the shape in Figure 3.8(a), (b) we have correspondingly the sequences $S_1 = [D_1, (1, 2)], [D_1, (2, 3)], [D_1, (1, 3)], ...$ and $S_2 = [D_2, (1, 2)], [D_2, (2, 3)], [D_3, (1, 3)], ...$ Now we find the rules that can generate S_1 and S_2. For that we use the well-known LZ77 approach (Ziv & Lempel, 1977). The schematic output of LZ77 algorithm in the form $(O, L)C$ (O-offset from current position, L-length, C-chairs) is shown in Figure 3.9.

We see, that irregularity of the pattern in Figure 3.9(b) occurs in two ways: **appearance**

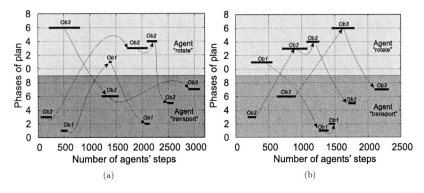

Figure 3.6: *Two examples of emergent "agent-agent" cooperation, generated by the local rules.* (a) *Initial phases are* $(Ag_1)_{init} = p_6$ *and* $(Ag_2)_{init} = p_3$; (b) *Initial phases are* $(Ag_1)_{init} = p_1$ *and* $(Ag_2)_{init} = p_3$.

of additional rules (the 1st and 2nd cycles) and **parametrization of these rules**. As known, the regular behavior (and in this way local rules) can be derived by optimizing some quantities (e.g. energy consumed by a system) or by some simple principles. Can the local rules in Figure 3.9 be obtained in this way ? We can write such a principle without difficulties for the first sequence S_1:

keep up equal distance to all agents;

As a result we get an equilateral triangle. If we have to obtain a specific equilateral triangle we have to specify the desired distance. However, how to obtain the rules for S_2 in Figure 3.9(b), especially their parametrization ? In Figure 3.10 we show more complex irregular pattern. Obviously, this pattern requires essentially more rules and parameters. Can it be generated by some compact evolutional process ? We think it is possible, but the Kolmogorov complexity of generating grammar is much higher, than the irregular generated pattern itself. For the pattern in Figure 3.10 we know only one evolutional process that can generate it, namely, evolution of human civilization ! Therefore for generating irregular patterns, the irregularities (primarily parametrization) have to be explicitly introduced into the rules. Unfortunately, most of the technically useful behavioral patterns are irregular.

The question is whether we can generalize this conclusion for other kinds of behavioral patterns (e.g. functional patterns, like the assembling's plan, shown in Figure 3.2) ? Here we refer to the genetic programming, namely, to the evolving of computer program capable of emergent collective behavior, discussed in the Koza's work (Koza, 1992, p. 340), shown briefly in Section 5.6. He considers a group of independent agents with one common goal to consolidate widely dispersed pellets of food into one pile. Agents have behavioral and transportation rules, but initially there is no composition of these rules that allows accomplishing the common task. Koza introduces the fitness function "to minimize the sum of distances between food pellets". This fitness is similar to the evolutional rule that generates the sequence S_1. Performing the GP procedure with this fitness, agents collect the food pellets into one pile. This behavior corresponds to the regular behavioral pattern. However, if agents have to collect the food in some specific way, or the pile should have some specific form (e.g. a storehouse) we have to introduce parameters, which will describe irregularities (to create the desired emergence). These parameters cannot arise evolutionary, they have to

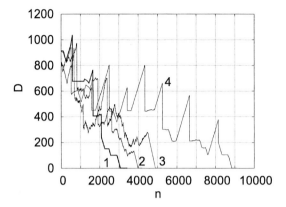

Figure 3.7: *Perturbation of micro-assembling by "vibration", D - difference between the plan and real assembling's state ($\sum$ of all positions and angles), n- number of steps; 1- unperturbed assembling, 2- with perturbed positions of objects (± 1 per simulation's tact); 3- with perturbed positions of objects (± 2 per simulation's tact); 4- perturbed positions and rotation angles of objects (± 1 per 50 simulation's tacts).*

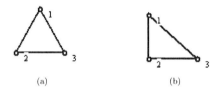

Figure 3.8: *Examples of regular (a) and irregular (b) spatial patterns.*

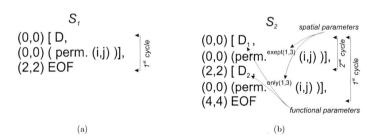

Figure 3.9: *The schematic output of LZ77 algorithm, applied to the symbolic sequences S_1 (a) and S_2 (b), describing corresponding spatial patterns from Figure 3.8.*

Figure 3.10: *Example of complex irregular spatial pattern.*

be defined in advance. In this way, the conclusion about parametrization can be expanded to other kinds of behavioral patterns.

3.5.3 Generation of emergent patterns

Emergent behavior arises as a result of self-organization. Therefore the generation of desired emergence consists in creating purposeful self-organization. However, such a self-organization that takes place in technical systems. Are there differences between "artificial" and "natural" self-organization ?

Self-organization is defined by the emergence of ordered macroscopic structure in absence of central control. But if we apply this notion to technical systems, many systems will be matched up with this definition. For example, consider organization's local network. Data, e-mails and news are accurately delivered from senders to receivers, printers print different documents, servers operate with clients and so on. All elements of this network remain autonomous, there is no central element, finally, at some control parameters, this system demonstrates either ordered or chaotic behavior. *But this behavior is not a result of self-organization, the order in this system arises in a preprogrammed way.* Therefore, here we face the problem of how the artificially created self-organization differs from similar natural/technical phenomena. This is a confusing task because of high complexity of natural as well as artificial systems, moreover, because of a still open discussion about general origin of self-organization.

Can we refer the process of assembling, discussed in Section 3.5.1, to self-organization phenomena ? Let us compare this system with natural systems. Firstly, this is the open system influenced from environment. Secondly, modifying control parameters (e.g. the visibility radius R_{vis}), a cooperation between agents becomes ordered. There is no central element, which would tell each agent what is to do. The cooperation is not preprogrammed, it arises due to interactions between agents. Therefore, from the general viewpoint, the assembling occurs in the self-organizing way. However, this group of agents has remarkable differences with natural systems.

- This technical system is designed to behave in ordered way. This is, perhaps, the main contradictory point in developing self-organizing systems. Although the ordered behavior is an objective of designing, it does not mean, that the system cannot be self-organized. *The self-organization is a way to achieve the desired ordered behavior.*

- Collective phenomena appear not only in macroscopic form, but also in the form of different functional, informational, structural configuration, modification of structure and couplings, information flow and so on.

- In the most natural self-organizing systems the control parameters are represented by energy (matter) flow, a change of control parameter is given by a change of these quantities. This energy (matter) flow determines interactions among elements in these systems. *Information is disconnected from energy (matter) flow in artificial systems.*

- Interactions among elements in natural self-organizing systems are fixed by chemical, physical or other laws. *However, the interactions as well as structure of artificial systems can be changed.*

- In opposite to natural systems, where invariance (scalability) was developed evolutionary, the artificial systems do not possess this property "automatically". The invariance has to be developed and tested for each new system.

In natural systems a dependence between interactions, structure, function, information and control parameters is determined by physical laws introduced into a system by energy flow. This dependence determines effects that we denote as natural self-organization. In artificial systems an energy flow (matter) does not influence the system so strongly as in natural systems. Therefore, in order to create a purposeful artificial self-organization, this dependence has to be defined anew. In general, artificial collective phenomena have essentially more degree of freedom, it is directly connected with a growth of complexity.

Now backwards to the question of what is self-organization in artificial systems. As said above, the artificial self-organization has more degrees of freedom, than the natural self-organization. These additional degrees are the structure, rules, transfer functions, information processing, number of elements, control parameters, initial conditions and so on. We represent the structure of these systems in Figure 3.11.

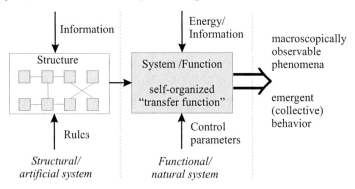

Figure 3.11: *The structure of artificial self-organizing systems.*

We see, that the emergent behavior is the macroscopically observable phenomenon, generated by a "transfer function" of system. Arising of this "transfer function" represents a self-organizing process, which is controlled by control parameters. Changing control parameters changes "transfer function" and, in turn, macroscopic phenomena. Such a kind of self-organization on the level of functions can be denoted as the **functional (or natural) self-organization.** *In functional SO interactions among elements are predefined, so that the self-organized "transfer function" is fixed.*

Additional degrees of freedoms in artificial systems appears on the level of structures. Changes of structures modify the "transfer functions", which, in turn, change macroscopic phenomena. The structures, that we are interested in, consist of interacting basic elements (agents). Interactions are created by local rules governing basic elements. If there is a mechanism, which can systematically change the structure, *interactions among elements are no longer preprogrammed, they, as well as the self-organized "transfer function", are generated dynamically.* The self-organization created on the level of structures by these "structure-generating-mechanisms" can be denoted as the **structural self-organization.**

To exemplify a relation between structures and functions, let us consider the following example, motivated by evolvable hardware (e.g. (Sanchez & Tomassin, 1996)). We define some simple mathematical operators like addition, sine, square root and squaring. These operators can be thought of as hardware modules placed inside a silicon chip. Coupling

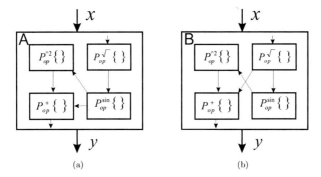

(a)   (b)

Figure 3.12: *Example of flexible structure motivated by evolvable hardware. Change of this structure (from (a) to (b)) results in the transfer function $y = f(x)$.*

different operators-modules, we obtain different functions. In Figure 3.12 two such functions (different combinations of basic operators) are shown. The message of this example is that a function of distributed system is an attribute of its structure and, primarily, such a structure that can be modified by couplings. Changing these local couplings, we can influence global structure of whole system. This, in turn, affects the transfer function, i.e. this modifies a functionality of system. The changed transfer function, in turn, changes macroscopic phenomena.

Functional and structural SO-phenomena generate emergent behavior. However, there is a big difference between them. *The functional SO creates only one emergent behavioral pattern, where as the structural SO generates a cluster of such patterns.*

Now we try to answer the question of what is self-organization in artificial system. Primarily, the natural and technically useful self-organizations coincide in many points. Thus, the definitions, quoted in Section 3.4, can be applied to both. However, there are two main differences. Firstly, the artificial self-organization is designed to demonstrate the desired emergence. As demonstrated by real projects, e.g. the project DSS (Distributed Satellite System, see the next section) in the Space Systems Laboratory, MIT, or the already mentioned I-Swarm project, resources and computational efforts are required to be invested in the development of artificial SO phenomena. Developers know a priori, analytically and in numerous simulations, the behavior of their systems. *From the viewpoint of designer, the artificial SO is not really self-organized.* However, from the viewpoint of external observer, a SO-behavioral pattern appears in the emergent way. It is created by interactions among subsystems and is not explicitly preprogrammed. *External observer cannot differentiate between natural and artificial self-organization.* Introduction of the external observer allows us to avoid the problem of *"self"* and *"not-self"*.

Secondly, the self-organization in artificial systems can appear on the level of functions and structures, where as the *known* natural phenomena appear only on the functional level. Considering functional and structural self-organization in artificial systems, we can remark that they are also completely different. Which kind of self-organization is of interests for artificial systems ? What is a general benefit of artificial self-organization ? These questions are in the focus of our consideration in the next section.

3.5.4 Benefit of artificial self-organization

The need of this section arises because a position of self-organization and the attitude of researchers to self-organization is dramatically changed in last years. The previously established viewpoint refers the self-organization to natural "phenomena" that need to be investigated. Correspondingly, the treatment of self-organization was related to a pure theoretical business, being not applicable to technical systems, because of e.g. their high complexity.

However, in the last years, the complexity of technical systems and especially treatment of irregular processes as well as developing micro-systems stimulate a growth of new concepts in technical controlling. From this viewpoint, the **self-organization represents an instrument of creation and controlling distributed autonomous technical systems**, like genetic programming, Fourier transformation or the control theory. It allows designing the collective activity without central control, central synchronization, central knowledge, huge computational and communication resources and so on. We try to show a benefit of self-organization based on examples from several application domains.

(I) Economical benefit.

This point of view has been many times said in self-organization communities, namely, it is much cheaper to produce many small elements and to make them self-organized, than to produce one huge mono-block/single-unit device of the same functionality. We carefully consider this point, taking into account costs of products, consisting of:

1. R&D (research & development);

2. Manufacturing;

3. Maintenance;

4. Repair;

5. Some unaccounted factors, that are individual for each system.

Let us consider the first four factors separately.

Production cost. It depends of device's complexity and a number of manufactured elements. The simpler and more numerous these elements are, the cheaper their production is. Therefore, from this point of view, collective systems are more favorable, than the corresponding centralized analog.

An example can be given by comparison between grid computing and parallel computing by supercomputers. By the rating of the top500[1] in June 2003, the ASCI (Accelerated Strategic Computing Initiative) Red, installed in Sandia National Laboratories, USA is ranked as the 17th fastest supercomputer in the world (see Figure 3.13). This is a parallel

---

[1]www.top500.org

MIMD (Multiple Instruction, Multiple Data) supercomputer, containing 9298 Pentium II Xeon processors and 1212 GB RAM, with computational power 2,38 teraflops (in 1997 with 7264 processors it brought 1,3 teraflops). Cost of this project is about 55 millions US-dollars.

Figure 3.13: *Supercomputer ASCI RED installed in Sandia National Laboratories (Courtesy of Sandia National Laboratories, USA.)*

Now let us consider the grid computing.

"Grid Computing can be defined as applying resources from many computers in a network to a single problem, usually one that requires a large number of processing cycles or access to large amounts of data...

A company with slightly fewer than 2,000 desktop computers can harvest nearly 1 teraflop (one trillion floating-point operations per second) of computing capacity. Even better, the company can capture that power from computers it already owns that sit idle at night and work at less than full capacity during the day" (Pinto, 2003).

It is not difficult to estimate that the cost of this system is about 1-2 millions US-dollars. Therefore, from the viewpoint of manufacturing cost, distributed systems are more "thrifty". As followed from the analysis of the top500, the cluster and grid computing encounters more and more often on the market of supercomputers.

Costs of maintenance and repair. From the viewpoint of maintenance and repairs, there is the following argument in favor of collective systems. Remember that self-organization is invariant to the number of aggregated/composed elements. Thus, we can imagine that if some number of these elements will be out of order (or even destroyed), this accident does not affect the functioning of common collective system. As known, the cost of repair and maintenance depends highly on the conditions, where this labor is performed. It is natural to assume that in the space, at great depths, in hazardous (e.g. radioactive) conditions these works will very expansive. And now, instead of repairs, we make some reserve of these elements, so that these elements automatically replace the damaged ones.

The project DSS (Distributed Satellite System) (MIT, 2004a) developed in the Space Systems Laboratory of MIT, USA has been motivated by these thoughts. The idea behind this project is that a group of small and cheap satellites is able to perform the same functions as one big and essentially more expensive mono-block satellite. As experimental implementation of DSS the SPHERES (Synchronized Position Hold Engage and Reorient

Experimental Satellites) (MIT, 2004b) satellite of the size 0,2x0,2x0,2 m. and the weight of 3,1 kg. has been developed (Miller, 2002) (see Figure 3.14). This small satellite possesses a

Figure 3.14: *Experimental satellite SPHERES developed in Space Systems Laboratory, MIT (Courtesy of Prof. David W. Miller, MIT SSL, USA.)*

microprocessor control system, diverse sensors, can communicate with other satellites, has a small jet engine and so on. This project is not yet finished, therefore it is too early to draw any conclusions. But anyway, the MIT's experimental realisation of SPHERES as well as DSS points that ideas behind an artificial self-organization are correct.

R&D costs. The project SPHERES has brought an additional argument towards artificial self-organization, namely the R&D cost of collective systems can be very high. As followed from the experience of MIT's colleagues, the development of SPHERES is very expensive. This point of view can be generalized for other projects, e.g. "I Swarm" (I-Swarm, 2003-2007) or "Collective micro-robotic", namely it is cheaper to produce and to maintain collective systems, but it does not concern the development of them. The hoping is that after understanding and developing the main principles of collective activity, the R&D costs will decrease.

(II) Benefit of swarm intelligence.

The self-organization can create complex systems from elements of simple and very restricted functionality. This point concerns the collective phenomenon denoted as the *swarm intelligence*. The coordinated activities and collective information processing, emerged in a swarm of simple elements, allow them to behave like one complex system. Despite the simple subsystems, the whole system is able to emerge different spatial functional, and other structures and capabilities.

One example of such a collective functional activity is described in the book "synergetics, introduction" by Prof. H. Haken (Haken, 1983b). The fungi Dictyostelium disciodeum exist originally in the form of unicellular organisms. However, after the growing phase they aggregate into multicellular organism (see Figure 3.15). The mechanism of this aggregation

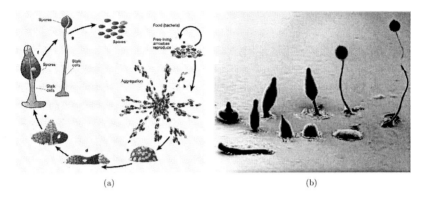

(a)   (b)

Figure 3.15: *Aggregation's phases of fungi Dictyostelium disciodeum (Images and montage are made by L. Blanton and M. Grinson)*

is of interest. Separated cells are able to emit some signal substance (so-called pAMP). Other cells, perceiving these signal molecules, can emit new portion of pAMP, i.e. they, in fact, amplify the signal, emitted by the first cell. The concentric waves arise as a result of this strategy. The gradient shows an origin of these waves and points to the direction, that all cells should move to. The similar strategy can be applied to a search of resources (like food) in other collective systems. The probability, that one element (micro-robot or microorganism) searching randomly will find a food, is small, whereas a whole group find it definitely. In this way the element all alone will perish, whereas a whole group will survive.

Similar effect is used by ants if they are moving from the nest to a food source. They leave a specific chemical substance, called pheromone, on the route, that they move on. The shorter is the route, the more ants will follow this route over a time, the more pheromone will be accumulated on this route. After some transient time, ants only by a concentration of the pheromone can decide which of two routes is shorter. As a result of this strategy, a route from the nest to a food source will be optimized (see Figure 3.16). This approach, after successful experiments of Goss and colleague (Goss *et al.*, 1989), has found an application in the distributed optimization, called later as the ant colony optimization (ACO). Other examples of the SWARM intelligence can be found in the beautiful book of Eric Bonabeau and colleagues "Swarm intelligence: from Natural to Artificial Systems" (Bonabeau *et al.*, 1999).

This and other examples have shown, a group possesses essentially larger functionality, than an individual. This is an important factor for the construction of such systems that are limited e.g. by their own size, like micro-robots. Micro-robotic systems represent new trend not only in robotics, but also in distributed artificial intelligence. Developments in the projects MINIMAN, MiCRoN, I-Swarm (MINIMAN *et al.*, n.d.) and some others (see Figure 3.17) have shown, that at extreme miniaturization, not only hardware questions, but also typical "software" concepts of controlling, perceptions and planning get completely different forms. Because of very small size (prototypes of I-Swarm robots are only of a few mm^3), these robots have only an extremely limited microcontroller and possess very tiny communication bandwidth and range. However, despite these limited abilities, the robots' group has collectively to solve a broad spectra of tasks, as e.g. cleaning, micro-assembling, transportation of micro-objects, collective perception and so on.

(a)

Figure 3.16: *Optimized route from ant's colony to food source (with permission of Dr. J. Utermann, Bundesanstalt für Geo-wissenschaften und Rohstoffe, Germany.)*

Figure 3.17: *Micro-robots "MINIMAN" (with permission of the Institute for Process Control and Robotics, University of Karlsruhe, Germany).*

A way to achieve the desired collective behavior in a group of micro-robots consists in creating specific swarm-like-behavior (see e.g. (Mataric, 1992)), known from the insect world. As shown by natural examples, this emergent kind of behavior is very efficient, flexible and is closely related to collective (or swarm-) intelligence. Moreover it does not require complex control systems and allows a large number of independent units to accomplish collectively the common goal.

(III) Flexibility, adaptability and invariance.

Flexibility, adaptability and invariance are ones of the most important notions of natural and technical science. These notions belong to one domain, namely, they characterize the reaction on changes. We give some definition from Webster's Online Dictionary:

- *Flexibility:*

  1. The property of being flexible.

  2. The quality of being adaptable or variable; "he enjoyed the flexibility of his working arrangement".

  3. The trait of being easily persuaded.

- *Adaptability:*

  1. The ability to change or be changed to fit changed circumstances

- *Invariance:*

  1. The quality of being resistant to variation.

To make the relationship between these notions more clearly, we introduce the concept of *homeostasis*.

"Homeostasis in layman's terms means balance or equilibrium. It is the property of an open system to regulate its internal environment so as to maintain a stable condition, by means of multiple dynamic equilibrium adjustments controlled by interrelated regulation mechanisms" [Wikipedia, the free Encyclopedia, *www.websters-online-dictionary.org*].

Homeostasis is the maintained equilibrium of some values (structure, function, behavior and so on). If these values do not depend on external environment, we call them as being invariant or *invariance*. Invariance means a system is generally insensitive to one or several variations. This property allows reducing the dimension of systems. Considering the problem of scalability, discussed in Section 2.6, we indicate that the simplest form of scalability is the invariance to size.

If the homeostasis's values depend of external environment, we call the mechanisms, maintaining the equilibrium, as *adaptability*. Adaptability means a system is able to absorb (or to fit) one change by some other change(s). This notion assumes an existence of some internal mechanisms of adaptation. Returning to the problem of scalability, we think that the scalability can also be achieved if the collective system has the mechanism, adapting it to the changes of size.

Finally, the general ability to change these values (structure, function, behavior and so on) can be denoted as *flexibility*. Flexibility is very important basic mechanism allowing a plurality of structures, functions, behaviors that the system can demonstrate.

How the artificial self-organization is connected with these notions ? The point is that *the most of known self-organizing systems possess mechanisms supporting homeostasis*. These mechanisms are of different nature. Several physical and chemical SO-systems, e.g. Bénard cells (Ebeling & Feistel, 1986, p.43), Belousov-Zhabotinsky-Reaction (Zhabotinsky & Zaikin, 1973), are size invariant. Some artificial collective systems, like Internet, networks of citations and collaborations possess specific relations between different invariances, like the *degree of distributing*. Investigation of these, so-called, scaling-free systems became recently very popular in physical journals (e.g. (Dorogovtsev & Mendes, 2001)). Other known example of invariance is the time invariance and invariance manifolds, so-called attractors (Guckenheimer & Holmes, 1983, p.256). In opposite to physical systems, biological collective systems demonstrate homeostasis provided by wide spectra of adaptation based on different mechanisms (e.g. (Bonabeau *et al.*, 1999)).

Invariance, adaptation and flexibility are very important for technical systems. This issue is directly connected with scalability, self-replication self-reparation, fault-tolerance and other desired technical properties of e.g. such systems as modern flexible manufacturing or autonomous systems. Even in the software community, for systems, like operational systems or computational networks, the importance of these properties has been recognized (e.g. (Liebherr, 1995)). The understanding of homeostasis's mechanisms in natural SO-systems and their adaptation to artificial ones, allow achieving, as we hope, these properties.

(IV) Reliability, fault-tolerance and security of systems.

This point concerns the general problem of centralized/distributed systems. The central elements represent a weak point of every system; often they are such elements as either coordinators or controllers or they collect common-system information. These elements, e.g. a server, are more complex than other elements, moreover their failure means failure of overall system. These elements often became an object of external "attacks", like hackers attack.

Collective systems are, per definition, distributed, i.e. without central elements. Absence of central element increases reliability of a system and reduces its cost. Characteristic feature of SO-systems is that local communications among elements serve to synchronize them and do not describe the internal states of elements themselves (Kornienko *et al.*, 2001). Therefore, one or more communication channels of SO systems, being "hacked", cannot describe the whole system. This contributes to security and reliability of such a system.

Another point, representing practical interest, originates from the domain of nonlinear dynamics. We means primarily some nonlinear effects that accompany self-organization (but not the SO phenomenon itself). Several of them are synchronization of coupled oscillators (e.g. (Hu *et al.*, 1997)), widely applied to secured communication (Kocarev & Parlitz, 1995), effect of clusterization (e.g. (Kaneko, 1994)), applications of nonlinear oscillators for control (e.g. (Williamson, 1998)) and for some collective strategies (e.g. (Mobus & Fisher, 1999)).

(V). The self-organization, perhaps, allows developing the complex system in "evolutionary" way.

This point belongs to so-called "great visions" or "big challenges". As pointed out by Prof. H. Haken (Haken, 1988, p.1), the development of complex systems is more an art than a profession. Today's development of e.g. such complex systems as a car represents a circular approach. Firstly, the sample model is produced and tested. Then, the improved model will be produced until some defects will again be encountered. After next improvements and tests, the model is produced further, until ... Often the model becomes outdated, still remaining incomplete from the technical/technological viewpoint. The great vision consists in the following idea. If we would collect some simple rules and some simple elements and make them self-organizing, the evolutions of such a system is similar to a growth of a plant. The development process of complex system will be similar to put a seed in earth and observe how a plant grows ... It is completely clear that this vision of science-fiction-nature, but such visions are useful (like a concept-car), because they stimulate a growth of new ideas.

3.6 Problems of local rules

As pointed out in the previous section, the self-organization is very beneficial from different points of view. In this section we consider some preliminary questions of how to create an artificial self-organization. In Chapters 4 and 5 we consider practical aspects of creating self-organizing systems. The context of this consideration lies on problems of local rules, and especially the relation between local rules and structural SO-phenomena, introduced in Section 3.5.3.

As already mentioned, the functional and structural SO can be created in many different ways. Since we consider autonomous systems, the most often discussed way here consists in deriving a set of rules, that govern the behavior of an SO-agent. These rules can be of local or global nature, they determine specific interactions among elements and cause collective effects. Further we consider only local rules. Therefore, **we think about derivation of local rules as the primarily mains of creating and controlling artificial self-organization.** There are two strategies to derive such rules.

At the bottom-up strategy, the local rules are first programmed into each agent. This rule-based programming (Roma *et al.*, 1993), originates from the domain of parallel and distributed computing. Generation of these rules is mostly considered in a context of refining sequential program into concurrent one (Back & Sere, 1991). For these action systems the required cooperation and coordination can formally be defined (Back & Kurki-Suonio, 1988).

The general problem of bottom-up approach is that we cannot say in advance, which emergent behavior will be generated by the chosen rules. As pointed out by some authors (e.g. (Darley, 1994)) *"A true emergent phenomenon is one for which the optimal means of prediction is simulation"*. The origin of this problem lies in enormous complexity of non-linearly interacting system. From the analytical viewpoint, that historically referred to the well-known "three-body problem" from nonlinear dynamics (Arnold(Ed.), 1988)), it faces the problem of integrability discussed in Charter 2. We refer here to Arnold (Arnold(Ed.), 1988, p.212).

"A common feature of the various approaches to the problem if integration of Hamiltonian systems ... is the existence of a sufficiently large number of independent first integrals, or "conservation laws". Unfortunately, in typical situation, not only do we fail to find such integrals, but they simple do not exist, since the trajectories of Hamiltonian systems, generally speaking, do not lie on low-dimensional invariant manifolds. We have in mind, of course, integrals which exist on the entire phase space: a complete set of independent first integrals always exist in a small neighborhood of a nonsingular point."

As pointed out by Arnold, the solutions (in our case - local rules) exist, but we fail to find them. Some authors (e.g. Prigogine, Landau) explained this problem by a growing flow of correlations. If one object (physical body or particle) interacts with another one, they become correlated. If these objects, in turn, interact with other correlated objects, there arises the second-order correlation, after that, the third-order correlation and so on. The flow of correlation grows, while the system interacts ((Prigogine & Stengers, 1984), (Prigogine, 1996), (Landau & Lifshitz, 1976), (Landau & Lifshitz, 1981)). Hence we fail to calculate this correlation's flow analytically, we fail to find analytical solutions (however we are still able to do it numerically).

There exists another way to derive the desired behavior and to get round the bottom-up problem. It consists in the top-down strategy, shown in Figure 3.18. Using this strategy, the derivation of local rules starts from a definition of the macroscopic pattern Ω. This is a desired collective phenomenon, that the system has to demonstrate. Examples of these patterns are shown in Figures 3.2, 3.8, 3.10. The most of macroscopic patterns can be created without any difficulties. Assume, we have an algorithm, that can decompose an achievement of Ω into n-subtasks Ω_i. We also have a set of agents $\{Ag\}$ with corresponding elementary activities, however so, that they can collectively solve each of Ω_i. The decomposition algorithm splits up each of Ω_i further, up to elementary agent's activities. Thus, we have $\{\Omega_{i=1...n}^{j=1...m}\}$ sequences of activities, where an agent Ag_k needs m steps to solve Ω_i. Since this algorithm decomposes systematically, we can assume that all agents can solve Ω by executing $\{\Omega_i^j\}$. Remark, that a cooperation between agents arises naturally as the top-down decomposition of common task.

From agent's viewpoint, each agent Ag_k has a sequence of activities $S_k = \{\Omega_1, \Omega_2, ..., \Omega_m\}$. Now, calculating Kolmogorov complexity of the sequence S_k (finding the smallest grammar (Charikar *et al.*, 2002)), we can derive local rules R_k that can generate S_k. The set of these rules $\{R\}$ defines a cooperation between agents that allows the agents' group jointly to solve the common task Ω. Such a decomposition approach (algorithm of symbolic task decomposition - ASTD) is described in (Kornienko *et al.*, 2004e) and the whole rule-derivation procedure in (Kornienko *et al.*, 2004d). The top-down approach does not try to find any solutions from knowing (or determining) all interactions. Instead we utilize **computational approach** to approximate such a solution.

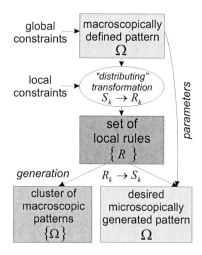

Figure 3.18: *Top-down strategy of derivation of local rules.*

Remark, that the set of local rules $\{R\}$ generates not only one desired pattern. For example, the assembling rules, shown in Section 3.5.1, can generate an arbitrary assembling process of this type. The specific assembling of the workpiece in Figure 3.1 arises by parametrization of these rules by data from the plan in Figure 3.2. Therefore, we associate the top-down strategy of a rule derivation with the structural self-organization. In turn, the structural SO phenomenon can be separated into rule-, parameter- and information-based approaches. Generally, the investigation of structural self-organization represent also the point of further investigation.

3.6.1 Rules and processes: information, function, structure

In the previous sections we discussed local rules and the structure of self-organizing technical systems. Within this structure we estimated an appearance of new structural level. Reformulating this structure in the context of classical "signal-response" approach, we obtain the schema, shown in Figure 3.19. Here, the global structure, determined by local rules (by interactions), forms a transfer function in a self-organized way. This transfer function processes input information and generates output information. Within this basic schema we can connect information, functions, structures and, finally, local rules.

The system can change its own structure (and so the transfer function) by changing interactions (i.e. local rules). These changes, in turn, can be initiated by change of information. The most important fact is that these changes occur not due to a change of information's amount, but due to a change of information's content, i.e. **semantics of information.**

There are several consequences that can be drawn from this schema.

1. The structure of self-organizing system, shown in Figure 3.19 can underlie the investigation of semantic aspects of information.

2. The self-modifying systems still remain "terra incognita" in the field of distributed

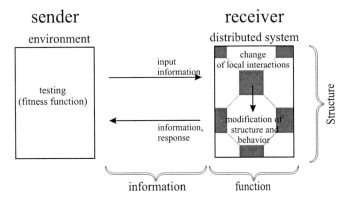

Figure 3.19: *Dependencies between structure, function and information in self-organizing systems.*

artificial intelligence. Investigation of artificial self-organization can assist in understanding the phenomenon of self-modifying systems.

3. The transfer function of SO-system is an attribute of its structure. However, many aspects of this dependence remain unclear, e.g., the influence of basic systems and interactions on the transfer function. Where is a limit of modifications that can be achieved by modifying only interactions (or only basic systems) ?

4. Evolution of self-organizing systems. The purposeful changing of interaction can be used as a mechanism of continuous modification in self-organizing system. The processes of learning, and generally evolution, can utilize this mechanism. This point will be treated in the last section of this chapter.

3.6.2   Rules and methods: control, selection, evolution

The structure of artificial self-organizing system, shown in Figure 3.11, is not a simple combination of two different (structural and functional) distributed subsystems. There subsystems are connected in the hierarchical way. The system, placed above in the hierarchy, generates (changes) under-level system by modifying rules or basic components.

The systems placed on the lowest level of hierarchy are so-called the first level systems. They represent in fact a program, decision, function etc. that are destined to solve a particular problem. They are just "constructed" for this goal. In SO-systems specific local rules are in charge of this behavior on the first-level. The emergence appeared here can be controlled by means of control parameters, but only in some range. For example, changing temperature in Bénar effect, it is possible to switch between the states: "pattern", "no pattern". However, there is no value of temperature that allows creating a new pattern, e.g. triangle cells. As mentioned, the main difficulty here consists in defining local rules and basic systems, which can emerge a macroscopic order.

The so-called 2nd-level systems, placed above in this hierarchy, influence local rules and basic components. The self-organization, emerged in the first level systems can completely be changed by the 2nd-level systems, even new collective phenomena can be constructed. For example genetic programming (Koza, 1992), structures in evolvable hardware (Sanchez & Tomassin, 1996), compilers and so on, represent these systems, denoted sometimes as generators. In some cases (e.g. compilers, evolvable hardware) the generators possess input and control parameters, in other cases (e.g. genetic programming) they have only rules and basic components. Especially interesting case is given when the ordered behavior of these generators is also a result of self-organization, see Figure 3.20.

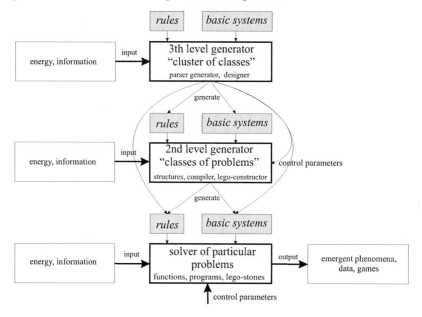

Figure 3.20: *The hierarchical structure of artificial collective systems.*

Why do we need such a three-levels hierarchical structure? Remembering that the 1st level systems solves a particular problem (e.g. finding an optimal path), the 2nd-level-generator can expand this "solver" for some classes of problems (e.g. optimal path with other criterion, finding of minimum/maximum, optimization of monetary values, etc.).

In turn, the 2nd-level generator can be influenced (or even generated) by the 3rd-level generator. This is a pretty rare case, but there exists a pair of examples of such a kind. Parser generator (lexer and parser: Lex and Yacc (Levine *et al.*, 1992)) is destined to generate a compiler, compiler, in turn, generates a working program, and, finally, this working program treats the data. One can imagine that the 3rd-level generator can influence not only the 2nd-level generator, but also directly the 1st-level modules. In this case there are two SO processes that compete with one another and control low-level process. In the classification "particular problems" and "classes of problems" for the 1st- and the 2nd-level systems, the 3rd-level generator corresponds to the "cluster of classes". Following the methodological basis of synergetics, the 1st-level systems are often denoted as functions and the 2nd- and 3rd-level systems as structures and macro-structures. The mentioned kind of architecture is represented in Figure 3.20, several examples of such systems are collected in Table 3.1.

Considering Figure 3.20, we can remark, that the system with three levels architecture possesses many *structural and functional* degrees of freedom. The corresponding question is how to drive such a system from a current state to the desired one, i.e. how to control it?

Level		Input	Basic components	Rules
Programming				
3rd level	parser gen.	—	alphabet	grammar
2nd level	compiler	source	operators	progr. rules
1st level	program	data	operators	progr. rules
Evolvable hardware				
3rd level	—	—	—	—
2nd level	structure	—	basic modules	electrotechnics
1st level	function	signals	basic modules	interconnections
Collective decision making (CDM)				
3rd level	—	—	—	—
2nd level	decis. criteria	—	negotiation types	fitness
1st level	CDM	information	ind. proposals	negotiations
Biology				
3rd level	aminoacid	—	chem.elem.	chem. interactions
2nd level	cell	energy	proteins	DNA
1st level	organism	energy/inf.	organs	homeostasis
Internet				
3rd level	local services	requests	programs	specifications
2nd level	network	information	computers	network topology
1st level	"cyber space"	information	networks	yet unknown rules
Lego constructor				
3rd level	"lego-designer"	ideas	plastic	physics, mechanics
2nd level	player	intensions	game patterns	phantasy
1st level	construction	game strategy	lego stones	stones connection
Collective robotics				
3rd level	human	desires,needs	declar. knowledge	proced. knowlegde
2nd level	robot	sensor inform.	components	electronics
1st level	swarm	collect. inform.	robots	"social laws"
Social systems				
3rd level	ind. behavior	sensor feedback	basic patterns	behavioral fitness
2nd level	individuum	ind. inform.	components	individual laws
1st level	society	collect. inform.	individuums	"social laws"

Table 3.1: *Empirical representation of several collective systems on different levels of hierarchy.*

However, first, the term "control" needs to be specified more exactly. In the most cases the "control parameter" and correspondingly "control" is primarily understood as a modification of parameters. For example, in the function $y = ax + b$ the values a and b are parameters, which allow changing a sloop and can shifting a straight line. There are no values of these parameters, which can make from straight line e.g. a curve or a plane. However, we can change the form of this function, e.g. $y = ax^2 + b$, and so achieve a curve. This is also a control, but more "radical" control, that completely change the given object. In the further consideration we distinguish between these "controls". The functional control by control parameters remains in its accepted sense and the mentioned "radical" control will be denoted as "structural" control by analogy with functional and structural self-organization.

The function (and correspondingly an algorithm and a state of a system) is denoted as structurally known (in the context of structural self-organization), if there is information about a construction, dependencies, structural relations, etc. of this function. For example, the selections algorithms (Sedgewick, 1998) is structurally known, however we don't know anything about the output of this algorithms. The output state depends on the input states, fitness and so on, therefore we assume this to be structurally unknown.

Which general methodology can underlie the structural control of artificial self-organization ? Actually, there are many ways to do it, we can group most of them into three clusters, schematically represented in Figure 3.21.

1. The driving algorithm and output states are structurally known. They depend on several control parameters, so that the system can adapt itself to small variation of environment in the range allowed by control parameters. This strategy is traditionally related to control theory and several other approaches, which drive the system from one state to another one, whereas these states are structurally known. We denote this strategy as the *control strategy*.

2. Only the driving algorithm is structurally known. The output states are structurally unknown and represent a result of some approach, e.g. selection or optimization algorithms. The driving algorithm is in this case of some generating nature, that produces the output states. We denote this strategy as the *generating strategy*.

3. The driving algorithm as well as output states are structurally unknown. This is extremely complex and interesting case. If in two previous cases there is a pattern of how to deal with a system, here, such a pattern is generated "on demand". Example of this approach is e.g. a LISP-program that modifies itself in trying to achieve some fitness or the already mentioned genetic programming (Koza, 1992). We denote this strategy as the *evolutionary strategy*.

As shown in (Kornienko, 2007), an appropriate way to build artificial self-organization consists in creating specific social laws in the group. These social laws can be created by changing interactions among elements (agents). This way corresponds to the generating strategy, that we will follow further. In Section 3.6.3 we show how the mentioned strategies correlate with horizontal and vertical operational principles.

3.6.3 Rules and operational principles

After defining the structure of self-organizing system, we try to express the discussed driving strategies in more precise form. To do this, we need to remember that the self-organization can be constructed by using vertical and horizontal operational principles. They lend to the system completely different forms. However, these operational principles are connected

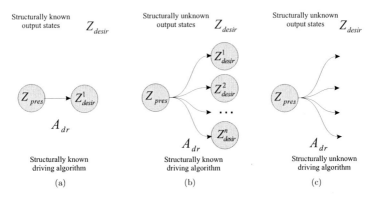

Figure 3.21: *Schematic representation of three different strategies to "control" the self-organizing system.* a) *The control strategy;* b) *The generating strategy;* c) *The evolutionary strategy.*

in one interesting way. To demonstrate this, we show one observation, made on examples of natural phenomena. The point is that natural phenomena possess *one-functional character*. For example, the mentioned Bènard cells, Belousov-Zhabotinsky reaction, Taylor instabilities, laser and so forth demonstrate only one type of collective behavior. The control parameter change only parameters of these effects. For instance, the change of the Taylor-Number influences the critical transitions of Taylor rolls from laminar to turbulent flow (Ebeling & Feistel, 1986, p.47). In several cases control parameters only "turns" it *on* or *off*. There are almost no phenomena, where the control parameter switches different types of collective activity.

We assume it happens because there is a limit of complexity for self-organizing phenomena. As known, the simplest centralized problem, like calculation of mean arithmetical value, becomes highly nontrivial in the distributed formulation. Some authors suggest that instead of further growth of complexity in one layer, the system starts to build hierarchical structures.

"The scheme we have outlined leads one to think that any complex system which has arisen by the method of trial and error in the process of evolution should have a hierarchical organization. In fact, nature–unable to sort through all conceivable combinations of a large number of elements–selects combinations from a few elements. When it finds a useful combination, nature reproduces it and uses it (the whole of it) as an element to be tentatively connected with a small number of other similar elements. This is how the hierarchy arises. This concept plays an enormous role in cybernetics. In fact, any complex system, whether it has arisen naturally or been created by human beings, can be considered organized only if it is based on some kind of hierarchy or interweaving of several hierarchies. At least we do not yet know any organized systems that are arranged differently" (Turchin, 1977, p.37).

In this way, further system's complication increases the number of hierarchies, but a complexity of the lowest level in the hierarchy remains further non-changed. Mono-functional behavior of natural self-organizing phenomena can be explained, at least in principle, by analogy with the mentioned complexity limit. Also by analogy, multi-functional behavior is expected to be obtained by hierarchical coupling of many mono-functional self-organizations. Anyway, until now we can neither prove nor controvert this postulate.

The technical systems require more complex, and first of all, multi-functional behavior.

In order to involve additional functionality in a collective phenomenon, we need to create some kind of hierarchies in it. We are not "happy" to do it, but until now we did not encounter simple rules providing different kinds of emergent behavior ! One possible hierarchical way to achieve it consists in connecting mono-functional horizontal SO-patterns in a sequence by means of collective decision making, as shown in Figure 3.22. The creating

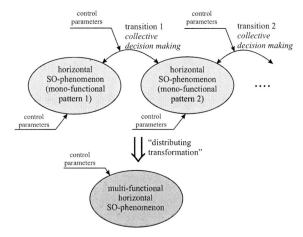

Figure 3.22: *Sequence of mono-functional horizontal SO-patterns connected by collective decision making in one multi-functional pattern.*

of mono-functional patterns is possible, the procedure of collective decision making is also well investigated. Therefore the structure, shown in Figure 3.22 can represent a practical way to create the desired self-organization.

However, by practical reasons, we prefer to build only horizontal collective phenomena without any hierarchies. Here we have achieved the evident contradiction that can be resolved in different ways. Several collective phenomena, e.g. from the insect world, demonstrate diverse self-organizing patterns with a minimal number of hierarchies (see e.g. (Donabeau et al., 1999). These phenomena can be investigated in hoping to apply the obtained principles for artificial systems. However, the biological way cannot always provide the "receipts" for technical systems.

Another way is to find some transformation that allows converting vertical structures into horizontal ones. However, which transformation is suitable for this purpose ? This is a difficult point because there is no standard approach being able to do it. We try to find such a transformation by analogy with an analysis of nonlinear dynamical systems. As known, the order parameter, as a controlling and ordering structure, is nowhere contained in initial systems. The initial systems just consist of a "mixture" of different components. During coordinate transformation we reorganize these components so that to obtain mode amplitudes. These modes are independent from each other in linear parts, they represent "pure" fast and slow components in linear approximation. After some transformation steps, the slowest mode delivers finally the order parameter. This order parameter "enslaves" other fast modes, however by the principle of circular causality, the fast modes "elect" the order parameter (i.e. via the center manifold). This analytical approach can give us some ideas how to perform similar transformation in the algorithmic way.

To illustrate the approach we take the example of the Henon system from (Levi *et al.*, 1999). The initial system is defined by the following set of equations

$$x_{n+1} = 1 + y_n - ax_n^2, \tag{3.1a}$$

$$y_{n+1} = bx_n, \tag{3.1b}$$

where x, y are state variables and a, b are parameters. Applying the coordinate transformation $\begin{pmatrix} x \\ y \end{pmatrix} = \underline{\underline{V}} \begin{pmatrix} \xi^s \\ \xi^u \end{pmatrix}$ where the columns of the matrix $\underline{\underline{V}}$ are given by the eigenvectors of the Jacobian of the system (3.1), i.e., $\underline{\underline{V}} = (\underline{v}^1, \underline{v}^2)$ and ξ_n^s, ξ_n^u are new state variables, this system can be transformed into a form of mode amplitude equations with uncoupled linear parts

$$\xi_{n+1}^s = \lambda_s \xi_n^s - \frac{a(\lambda_s \xi_n^s + \lambda_u \xi_n^u)^2}{b(\lambda_s - \lambda_u)}, \tag{3.2a}$$

$$\xi_{n+1}^u = \lambda_u \xi_n^u + \frac{a(\lambda_s \xi_n^s + \lambda_u \xi_n^u)^2}{b(\lambda_s - \lambda_u)}, \tag{3.2b}$$

where λ_u, λ_s are the corresponding eigenvalues. If the equation (3.2a) can be uncoupled from (3.2a) we derive the order parameter equation.

$$\xi_{n+1}^u = \lambda_u \xi_n^u + \frac{a(\lambda_s h(\xi_n^u) + \lambda_u \xi_n^u)^2}{b(\lambda_s - \lambda_u)}, \tag{3.3}$$

where $h(\xi_n^u)$ is the "slaving" function, that can be obtained by different techniques, see e.g. (Levi *et al.*, 1999).

This example contains two important messages. Firstly, the systems (3.1) and (3.2) represent the same system, though they look differently. In different coordinate bases, they will have different forms. Secondly, the order parameter (3.3) is a top of this hierarchy, it describes the corresponding local behavior. However, this order parameter is already contained in the original system (3.1), but in a "distributed" form. There are different techniques of how to control original systems by modifying the order parameter equation (see e.g. (Kornienko, 2007)). *Modification of the "vertical" order parameter (e.g. controlling) with the corresponding transformation procedure builds the horizontal control structure in original system.*

By analogy we can perform this procedure in the algorithmic way: i.e. to define first the required components and vertical control mechanisms and then to make a mixture of these components in horizontal systems, see Figure 3.23. By analogy, we can denote the coordinate transformation in analytical systems as the "distributing transformation" in algorithmic systems.

The approach, sketched in Figures 3.22 and 3.23 has the following advantages:

1. The control strategies, goals and other designing-oriented points can easily be determined in terms of vertical hierarchies. Human mental processes are familiar with this kind of structures, because our environment is mainly of vertical nature.

2. The horizontal structures (in contrast to vertical structures) are very reliable, scalable, allow flexible executing and so on. On the level of real SO-systems we prefer primarily these structures.

3. The distributing transformation allows to combine the vertical design of artificial SO-phenomena, but horizontal executing of these systems.

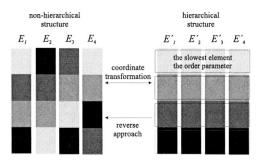

Figure 3.23: *A way to create horizontal SO-phenomena.*

Further in the work, we primarily follow this strategy. The detailed description as well as an example of the distributing transformation are shown in Chapter 5.

In Sections 3.7.1 and 3.7.2 we briefly consider two simple examples of artificial vertical and horizontal SO to exemplify the made here propositions.

3.6.4 Rules and invariance: scalability and self-replication

The issue of scalability and invariance in collective systems is already discussed in Sections 2.6 and 3.5.4. Here we return to this point again, however from the viewpoint of self-replication.

As mentioned in Section 3.4, the most natural self-organizing phenomena are size-invariant (see Figure 3.24) The size-invariance, and more generally scalability, is closely

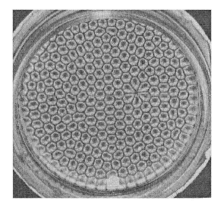

Figure 3.24: *Example of scalable natural SO-phenomena. Hexagonal structures in Bènard experiment (from presentation E. Laurien, Rayleigh-Bènard-Konvektion, University of Stuttgart, Germany).*

related to such an important property of collective systems as self-reproduction. Except biological systems, elements of natural collective systems cannot replicate themselves. Most artificial collective systems also do not have the capability of self-replication. Only a few from them (at least presently, cellular automata, software agents and, in near future, nanotechnology (Balzani *et al.*, 2003), self-reproducing factories, etc) are able to make copies of themselves.

Studying the self-reproduction was started in 50s by the work of von Neumann (von Neumann, 1966). Currently, this study is focused mainly in the field of cellular automata in hoping to derive the specific information processing and algorithms used in natural systems (e.g. (Codd, 1968), (Chou & Reggia, 1997), (Stauffer & Sipper, 1998)). Moreover, several authors distinguish between self-replication and self-reproduction (Sipper *et al.*, 1997b). From this viewpoint the replication is an ontogenetic process, resulting in duplicating a parent element. The reproduction, in contrast, is a phylogenetic process resulting in evolution (Sipper *et al.*, 1997a). In further steps we will use the term "replication" as more generic notion for the process of "duplication and modification".

Self-replication is of interest for artificial SO because of two reasons. Firstly, SO and self-replication are two main mechanisms widely used in natural evolution. Both mechanisms influence one another. Self-replication can control self-organization in the "quantitative" pathway (Haken, 1983a, p. 56). However, the question of how self-organization influences self-replication still remains open. We could imagine that self-organization also controls self-replications. For example, after wars (statistical data concerns the World War I and II) the number of born boys exceeds the number of born girls (Jongbloet *et al.*, 2001), whereas during "normal" time they are almost equal. Thus, this population dynamics is obviously controlled in self-organized way, but the mechanisms of this regulation is yet unclear.

Secondly, controlling the artificial SO by changing the number of elements, we encounter a pure mathematical problem. Usually, on the microscopic level, each element of self-organizing systems is represented by one or a few equations. If the system replicates itself, its dimension grows, e.g. before replication n, after replication $n + m$. However, in both cases we have completely different systems of dimension n and $n + m$. These systems can differ in the number of eigenvalues, stable and unstable mode amplitudes, center manifold, normal forms, order parameters and so on. Moreover it is now unclear, how to investigate the scaling mechanisms, which change the dimension n to $n + m$. In this way the self-replication and self-organization represent very interesting and very promising research field.

3.7   Two examples of structural self-organization

In this section we illustrate the structural self-organization by two simple examples with underlying vertical and horizontal operational principles. In both examples the generating control strategy is utilized. These examples also contain another message: SO-phenomena can be derived in analytical as well as in algorithmic ways. Therefore, the first example is of analytical and the second one is of algorithmic nature. Although both examples are simple and a bit idealized, they are suitable to illustrate the considered points.

As mentioned in the previous sections, the system, undergoing structural self-organization, consists of two parts. Firstly, this is the "functional part" that reproduces the needed transfer function(s). This part includes some control parameters. Modifying these parameter, the system demonstrates macroscopic phenomena. In the distributed case, that we are interested in, SO systems emerge macroscopic phenomena in a visible absence of central control, i.e. elements remain organizationally autonomous. Hence this "functional part" is expected to be invariant to the number of elements. Secondly, this is the "structural part", which forms the transfer function(s). Elements of this "part" are also organizationally autonomous. Interactions among them are determined by local rules. In both example we focus on these parts.

3.7.1 Structural SO with vertical operational principle

The idea behind the first example originates from the theory of normal forms (see e.g. (Nayfeh, 1993)). "Typical" one-dimensional normal form can be represented as the following nonlinear dynamical system (in the time-discrete case):

$$\varphi_{n+1} = F_{tr} = \alpha\varphi_n + F(\varphi_n) + F^m(\varphi_n), \tag{3.4}$$

where F_{tr} is a "transfer function", φ_n is the state variable, α is the control parameter, $F(\varphi_n)$ and $F^m(\varphi_n)$ are nonlinear functions of φ_n. The function $F^m(\varphi_n)$ determines the maximal order of nonlinear terms in this equation (m is so-called determinacy order). The equation (3.4) can be applied to forming groups (the idea to apply normal forms of local bifurcation to building spatial formation for e.g. mobile robots is quite old, we knew first about it from Prof. T. Fukuda (Fukuda, 1997)). For example, the following pitchfork bifurcation (Guckenheimer & Holmes, 1983), (Kuznetsov, 1995)

$$\varphi_{n+1} = \alpha\varphi_n - \varphi_n^3 \tag{3.5}$$

states the system starting from positive initial conditions will be landed on the "positive" attractor or correspondingly from negative initial conditions on the "negative" attractor, as shown in Figure 3.25.

This behavior can be adapted for spatial self-organization in mobile agents. In this case the control parameter α corresponds to some external parameter like temperature or light intensity, and the equation (3.5) is directly incorporated into a motion control of each agent. In this experiment half of all agents starts from positive initial conditions (dark agents), another part starts from negative initial conditions (bright agents). Moreover, small random values are added to all spatial states of agents. At the pre-bifurcation value of α all agents are distributed randomly, but as soon as the value of α jumps to post-bifurcation value, all agents became separated into two groups (correspondingly to positive and negative initial conditions).

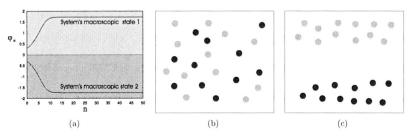

Figure 3.25: **a)** *Post-bifurcation macroscopic dynamics of Eq. (3.5);* **b)** *Random spatial distribution of moving agents, the control parameter α is set up on the pre-bifurcation value;* **c)** *Agents are spatially distributed into two groups accordingly to the behavior of pitchfork bifurcation, control parameter α is set up on the post-bifurcation value.*

By choosing nonlinear terms $F^m(\varphi_n)$ of different order, the dynamical system in functional part can demonstrate different spatio-temporal patterns. Moreover, as pointed out by M. Golubitsky and D.G. Schaeffer in (Golubitsky & Schaeffer, 1985), the normal form can be perturbed by corresponding nonlinear terms $F(\varphi_n)$. The terms $F(\varphi_n)$ represent a combination of different nonlinear terms of the order $\leq m$. In this way, $F^m(\varphi_n)$ represents the basics terms (e,g, $(\varphi_n)^2$, $(\overline{\varphi}_n)^2$, $(\varphi_n)^3$, $(\overline{\varphi}_n)^3$ $(\varphi_n)^4$ etc.), whereas $F(\varphi_n)$ is a combination of them (e.g. $(\varphi_n)^2(\overline{\varphi}_n)^2$). By combination of basic nonlinear terms we can perturb the normal form of corresponding local bifurcations in many different ways.

Structural part. Specific usage of structural part consists in creating the transfer function F_{tr}. Looking for the most simple case for the generating control strategy, we choose the simple dictionary-based generator. This means, there is a finite set of functions and structural part chooses a combination of them in dependence of some external conditions. The motivation for this kind of structural process is that the collective choosing of appropriate functions is very similar to the collective decision making (see e.g. (Sandholm, 1999)).

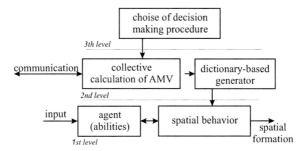

Figure 3.26: *Vertical structure of self-organization allowing to form different spatial groups (AVM - arithmetical mean value).*

This problem, being formulated in the way shown in (Kornienko *et al.*, 2002a), (Kornienko, 2007), assumes there are local numerical values the agent can perceive. The goal is to estimate arithmetical mean value from these initial numerical inputs in a distributed way (all elements are autonomous without central element, there is no global information about all elements) and then, using some numerical threshold, to make an output decision (see for details the mentioned references). The entire approach is sketched in Figure 3.26.

The following dynamical system

$$q_{n+1}^i = aq_n^i + a(q_n^{i-1} + q_n^{i+1}), \quad i = 1, ..., m, \tag{3.6}$$

at $a = 1/3$ can calculate the arithmetical mean value from initial numerical value q_0^i (numerical input) of each i-agent. The dictionary-based generator maps the arithmetical mean value q_n to one of the functions from the dictionary, $q_n \rightarrow F_i$, see Figure 3.27. This generator is implemented in each agent. Since, after calculation, all q_n^i are equal (achieved without central elements), all agents choose consistently the functions from the dictionary.

In the simplest binary case, the output function F_{tr} can be chosen as

$$Output\ Function = \begin{cases} q_n > Threshold : F_1 \\ q_n \leq Threshold : F_2 \end{cases} \tag{3.7}$$

The basic nonlinear terms $F^m(\varphi_n)$, their perturbations as well as the arising bifurcation behavior can be found in details in (Golubitsky & Schaeffer, 1985), and (Golubitsky *et al.*, 1988).

Functional part. We adopt for the functional part the example shown in Figure 3.25. The elements of this system are autonomous, moreover the implemented transfer function allows emergence of different spatial formation. For the functional part we choose the SO

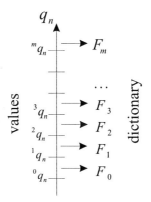

Figure 3.27: *The dictionary based generator, the value of j in $^{j}q_n$ represents different clusters with increasing values of q_n.*

through mutual control parameter (Haken, 1983a, p.57)), whereas the dictionary-based functions are given by the normal form of Hopf and pitchfork bifurcations (e.g. (Wiggins, 1990)):

$$Function_1 \rightarrow x_{n+1}^i = \alpha x_n^i - (x_n^i)^2, \tag{3.8a}$$

$$Function_2 \rightarrow x_{n+1}^i = \alpha x_n^i - (\overline{x}_n^i)(x_n^i)^2, \tag{3.8b}$$

where x_n^i denotes spatial x-position of i-agent at the time step n, $\overline{x}_n^i$ is the complex-conjugate value $(x, y$ coordinates), and α is a mutual control parameter.

Control parameters. This system has one mutual control parameter α and set $\{q_0^i\}$ that represents initial numerical values perceived by each i-agent. The parameter α represents global parameters, like pressure or temperature, which change causes macroscopic self-organization. Interpretation of the set $\{q_0^i\}$ is defined not so unique and can represent connectivity, compactness, degree of "being under attack" and so on. Generally, every change of control parameters in the structural part causes a generation of a new transfer function (in this case change of a transfer function), therefore these parameters have to be treated very carefully. For example, if $\{q_0^i\}$ are connected with the number of local neighbors (local connectivity), the whole system can react on its own size (that refers to self-reproduction). For simplification we assume $\{q_0^i\}$ represents some external influence, i.e. local temperature.

Self-replication. The system is invariant to the number of components in the functional as well as in the structural parts. It means, if the systems elements will be reproduced, this does not modify qualitative behavior of the system. But the system becomes sensitive to size, if the structural parameters $\{q_0^i\}$ will be coupled to size-related values, i.e. the number of local neighbors.

Summary. The common system implemented in each agent consists of two equations:

$$q_{n+1}^i = aq_n^i + a(q_n^{i-1} + q_n^{i+1}), \tag{3.9a}$$

$$\varphi_{n+1}^i = F_{tr}(x_n) = \alpha x_n^i + (q_n^i \rightarrow^{gen} F(x_n)), \quad i = 1, ..., m, \tag{3.9b}$$

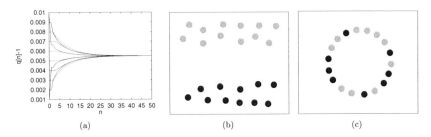

(a)   (b)   (c)

Figure 3.28: **a)** *The behavior of the system (3.9a) - calculation of mean arithmetical value;* **b)** *Spatial distribution of moving agent, corresponding to the pitchfork bifurcation;* **c)** *Spatial distribution of moving agent, corresponding to the Hopf bifurcation.*

where $(q_n^i \rightarrow^{gen} F(x_n))$ is the corresponding generator. The behavior of this system is shown in Figure 3.28. The advantages of this construction is its clearness. Each equation is in charge of corresponding activity and the relation between these equations is similar to "chief-dependent" relation. If we are going to change the agent-agent relation (e.g. collective decisions), we work with the equation (3.9a). If we are going to change the behavioral components of each agent we have to work with the equation (3.9b). This clear distribution of roles is very important for the design of collective phenomena. However, at the executing phase it is a huge disadvantage. **The system (3.9) is not reliable.** Any perturbations of the equation (3.9a) do not destroy the behavior of the decision making part (see Figure 3.29), but dramatically influence the behavioral part (3.9b). There are many real examples (e.g.

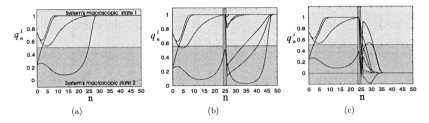

(a)   (b)   (c)

Figure 3.29: *Change of a behavior of dynamic system by a small perturbation.* **(a)** *Microscopic dynamics of seven coupled systems (3.5);* **(c, d)** *Perturbed microscopic dynamics of the coupled system m = 7. Shadowed rectangle represents the perturbation.*

from soccer-playing robots in the Robocup scenario) when small disturbances in the critical part (like the equation (3.9a) interrupt the behavior of the entire system. Therefore, in our Research, we try to avoid vertical construction of self-organizing system and prefer to utilize the horizontal self-organization considered in the next section.

3.7.2   Structural SO with horizontal operational principle

For the structural self-organization with horizontal operational principle we consider an algorithmic example from the domain of multi-agent systems. The problem, that we try to solve by means of self-organization, represents the agent-based solution finding, formulated in the following way.

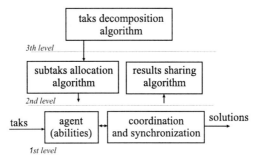

Figure 3.30: *The structure of the solution finding approach.*

Given are a task Ω and a lot of agents with abilities (activities) A_i. We assume that this task can be solved in finite time, there are enough agents to solve it, there are no restrictions (constraints) bounding the solution and so on. The goal is to find such a sequence of agent's activities $\{A_i\}$ that can solve Ω. There are two ways to do it: either to choose the most typical tasks and to preprogram these solutions or to make this system self-organizing so that the agents are able to solve the required tasks without being preprogrammed.

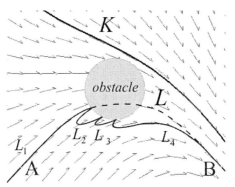

Figure 3.31: *Motion in a vector field with (L) and without (K) obstacle.*

The problem of solution finding can intuitively be divided into three subproblems: to decompose the problem into elementary activities, to allocate these activities so that to start partial solving of the task Ω and to guarantee that a sequence of activities $\{A_i\}$ can solve the task Ω completely[2]. The obvious vertical structure of this approach is shown in Figure 3.30. It has 3 levels of hierarchy: the level of problem's decompositions, the level of subtasks allocation and, finally, the level of executing. In this example we try to reformulate this vertical structure into horizontal one, where the decomposition, allocation and executing will be performed on the same level.

As mentioned in Section 3.6.3, to transform vertical structure into horizontal one, we need some additional elements organized in a process. The specific dynamics of this process

---

[2]The suggested approach is formally introduced in Chapter 5.

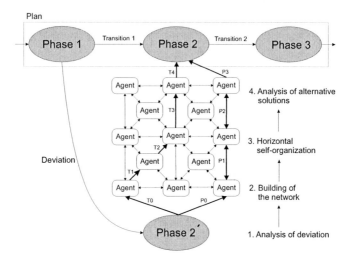

Figure 3.32: *The structure of tasks decomposition approach and the network allowing propagation of deviation. T0 − T4 and P0 − P3 represent two alternative ways to absorb the deviation.*

allows replacing vertical hierarchies. Our idea of a self-organizing solution finding originates from nonlinear dynamics and synergetics (see e.g. (Haken, 1983a)). It is known that a motion of a system is defined by a vector field and if this field contains an attracting manifold, the system from arbitrary initial state (in attracting area) will land on this attractor. Among many applications in bifurcation analysis, in systems's control, there are applications to robot navigation and agent coordination (e.g. (Levi *et al.*, 1999), (Kornienko *et al.*, 2001)). Performing experiments, we have encountered one interesting effect, shown in Figure 3.31.

If we perturb nonlinear field by putting some obstacle (that represents the problem Ω) on a motion trajectory, a system finds a bypass by all alone (here we idealize all physical forces). This is especially evident in time-discrete systems, e.g. the way L from the point "A" to "B" will be automatically decomposed on small parts L_1, L_2, L_3, L_4 approximating a bypass. The way $L_1 − L_4$ represents the "solution" of the problem of how to get from "A" to "B". The question is whether this analytical "approach" can be applied by analogy to algorithmic problems?

To use this analogy for algorithmic problems we need firstly to create similar elements, like field or obstacle in algorithmic system. Firstly, the field (as well as attracting manifolds) determines the motion, i.e. gradient. For algorithmic problem a plan undertakes a similar role; it determines a sequence of activities for the system. To estimate a gradient we calculate a deviation between an actual state and the desired one, i.e. we have to know this desired state and a deviation. Secondly, we need to *express this deviation in terms of activities that the systems (or some element of this system) can perform.*

To express the deviation in terms of agents activities we build the specific network, then propagate a deviation though this network (see Figure 3.32). During the propagation process each agent executes such activities that allow the system to absorb, at least partially, a deviation. These activities are similar to the bypass $L_1 − L_4$ from the above discussed example. Collecting these activities, we can absorb the deviation, i.e. we can solve the

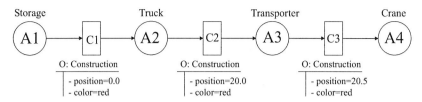

Figure 3.33: *Fragment of a building process in form of simple Petri Net. The circles represent the corresponding activities, conditions for transition are shown below the corresponding rectangles.*

problem Ω. During this phase agents "simultaneously" decompose, allocate and execute, so that we have the horizontal self-organization.

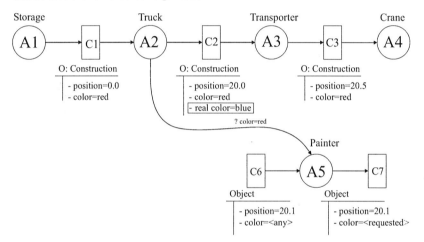

Figure 3.34: *The first step of problem solving.*

To illustrate this horizontal SO, we consider briefly a fragment of some process, e.g. a building of a house. In this fragment a building construction has to be delivered from a storehouse and brought up with a crane. The needed activities, represented as a simple Petri Net, are shown in Figure 3.33.

In the building process a red kind of construction is expected to be delivered. This is the desired state of the plan. However, instead of this red construction, a blue construction is delivered. This is an actual state. The difference between actual and desired state gives us the deviation, representing the problem Ω. We know that this deviation consists in color, therefore we need somebody (an agent "Painter") who can change a color. In the same time the agent "Track", that caused this deviation, asks about additional red construction in the storehouse as well as the next agents (in the plan sequence) to accept the blue construction. This gives several alternatives to choice the most effective one, see Figure 3.34. This is the first step of decomposition.

Now we iterate the procedure recursively. The deviation between the step, when the agent "Painter" can work and an actual step consists in a disposition of this construction. The agent "Painter" works in finishing plant, whereas the construction is placed at a building. To change a location of this object, we need the agent "Transporter". This is the second step of decomposition, see the Figure 3.35. Proceeding decomposition by this scheme further, we receive a sequence of steps, that can resolve the initial deviation. More

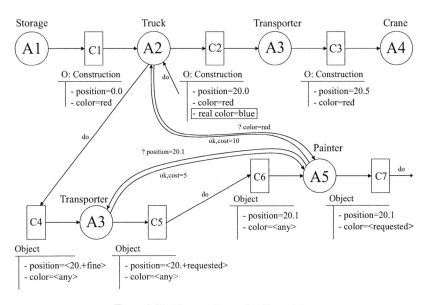

Figure 3.35: *The second step of problem solving.*

formal description of this approach will be done later.

How we consider the collective activity in this approach from the viewpoint of self-organization. A macroscopic result is the sequence of generated steps $\{A_i\}$. This sequence of steps allows solving the problem Ω of wrong color in the delivered construction. There is no central instance that control this process and it is not preprogrammed. The functional part of this system has dynamical structure and consists in functional connections between e.g. global transporter, local transporter and painter. This system (the specific configuration between these elements) is the collective system on the first level. However, this system is generated by the rules of structural part on the second level. These rules are e.g. "find a deviation between actual and desired state" or "find somebody who can eliminate this partial deviation" and so on.

As shown by this example, the structural rules as well as functional connections are of the same level of system's hierarchy. It can easily be tested. If we destroy the structural rules in several elements of this system, the overall system still works. For example, if the agent "Transporter" is out of work and cannot start out decomposing, a tower crane starts the decomposing process. There are many conditions that have to be satisfied by this network as well as by the common process, we consider them in Chapter 5.

3.8   Does the structural SO control a macro-evolution ?

Before starting to deal with evolutionary processes, we should clarify several points. The first point is *how to compare two evolutionary systems ?* In order to do it, we need some kind of evolution's measurement or "metrics of evolution". The meaning of this measure is to estimate and to normalize the changes made during evolutionary process. There are several known measures, e.g. informational capacity achieved during evolution. For distributed system this measure can be formulated in more specific form, namely by a number of connections (couplings) between elements. The more diverse connections the system possesses, the more different functions this system may have.

Secondly, there are two completely different evolutionary processes - individual and collective evolutions. They use different approaches and result in different forms. The individual evolution (in technical systems it corresponds to the evolvable hardware) makes the basis elements (subsystems) more complex. It results in a changed structure and functions of basic systems. In contrary, the collective evolution makes the whole collective system more complex. The changes made by the collective evolution are resulted in changes of interactions, see Figure 3.36. These changed interactions are completely useless for one sys-

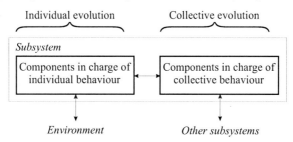

Figure 3.36: *The individual and collective evolution.*

tem. Therefore we state that modifications made by collective evolution are accumulated in an "intersystem space".

We exemplify this statement by the following example. Let us consider the well-known logistic map (e.g. (Gu *et al.*, 1984), (Maistrenko *et al.*, 1998))

$$x_{n+1} = ax_n(1 - x_n), \tag{3.10}$$

where $x_n \in \mathbb{R}$ is the state variable and a is the control parameter. The behavior of the logistic map is well investigated. As followed from Figure 3.36, this map can represent the components that is in charge of individual behavior. Now we couple of pair of logistic maps in order to investigate collective aspects of this system

$$x_{n+1} = cy_n + ax_n(1 - x_n), \tag{3.11a}$$
$$y_{n+1} = cx_n + bx_ny_n(1 - y_n), \tag{3.11b}$$

where $x_n \in \mathbb{R}$, $y_n \in \mathbb{R}$, c is the coefficient of the linear coupling, b is the coefficient of the nonlinear coupling, a is the general bifurcation parameter. The behavior of the system (3.11) is investigated in (Kornienko, 2007) (the OLL map).

How to measure the difference between the systems (3.10) and (3.11) ? We have to find such values that can qualitatively and quantitatively express the differences in behavior. In

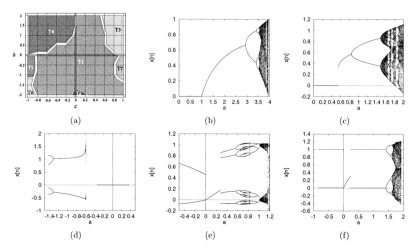

(a) (b) (c)

(d) (e) (f)

Figure 3.37: *Different types of behavior shown by OLL map (taken from (Kornienko, 2007)).* **(a)** *The approx. regions of qualitatively different behaviour of system (3.11) as a function of the parameters b,c. The behaviour types T1, T2 correspond to the bifurcation diagrams shown in Figure 3.37 (b), types T3,T4 - Figure 3.37 (c),(d) and finally T5,T6,(T7) - Figure 3.37 (e),(f);* **(b)** *The bifurcation diagram of the OLL map (3.11) at parameters $b = 1$, $c = 0.1$, $x_0 = 0.1$;* **(c)** $b = 2$, $c = 0.6$, $x_0 = 0.4$; **(d)** $b = 0.5$, $c = -0.8$, $x_0 = 0.01$; **(e)** $b = -1.5$, $c = -1$, $x_0 = 0.1$; **(f)** $b = -0.5$, $c = -1$, $x_0 = 0.1$.

the work (Kornienko & Kornienko, 2002) for such a measurement the dimension and codimension of local instabilities (expressed as the corresponding normal forms) is suggested (see e.g. (Wiggins, 1990), (Golubitsky & Schaeffer, 1985)). The normal form of the transcritical bifurcation in the system (3.10) is

$$\varphi_{n+1} = \lambda_1 \varphi_n - \mu \varphi_n^2, \tag{3.12}$$

whereas the NF of the same bifurcation in the system (3.11) is

$$\varphi_{n+1}^u = \lambda_1 \varphi_n^u + \mu_{12}(\varphi_n^u)^2 + \mu_{13}(\varphi_n^u)^3 + \mu_{14}(\varphi_n^u)^4 + \mu_{15}(\varphi_n^u)^5 + O(6), \tag{3.13}$$

where λ_1 is the unstable eigenvalue and μ_{12} are coefficients at the nonlinear terms. The coupling method of OLL map changes the codimension of local bifurcation ($\lambda_u = 1$) from 1 (transcritical bifurcation contained in the logistic map) to 4. Several bifurcation diagrams of the systems (3.10) and (3.11) are shown in Figure 3.37. Similarly, the codimension as well as the dimension of other local bifurcations is also increased by coupling.

Which message is contained in this example ? Connecting more or less equal subsystems into one system, we can achieve such a behavior of each subsystem that can never be demonstrated by this subsystem alone. This new behavior is essentially more complex than in the not-connected case. It means that each subsystem in the group becomes more complex, although each subsystem itself is not changed. If we consider the differences between the systems (3.10) and (3.11), we see that *the basis part (that is in charge of individual behavior) is in fact not changed. This growth of complexity is caused by couplings (part that is in charge of collective behavior) !* Couplings are also in charge of appearance of new dynamics behavior, that the system (3.11) emerges. This can be proved by comparing the normal forms. Couplings increase the dimension, codimension and the determinancy order of the original normal form (3.12) so that the resulting normal form (3.13) allows emerging more rich behavior. We can denote this kind of emergence as the *revealing emergence*, because the nonlinear terms of (3.13) are also contained in the (3.12). However, they are "inactive", non-resonant, therefore we do not consider they originally. The couplings obviously change some resonant conditions of the original NF and in this way "reveal" the NF (3.13) from other potentially possible normal forms.

What is the use of collective evolution ? We argue it in the following way. The elements of collective systems are physical objects limited by different physical restrictions. For example, on-board computers for micro-robots. We would make them as strong as possible, but there are limitations on the size and on the energy consumed by these devices. There restrictions allow developers of micro-robots to make the on-board computer only easy and small. Even the human brain is limited by the same restrictions: weight and energy consumption. If the brain will more "powerful", it will weight more and this destroys e.g. the dynamics of human body (Minsky, 1985). The "evolutionary obtained" human brain represents a compromise between weight (energy consumption) and "computational power".

However, these physical restrictions limit only individual evolution. *During the evolution, each individual cannot make own organization so complex as it wish.* In contrast, *the collective evolution does not change the physical objects and therefore is not limited by physical restriction.* In principle, the collective evolution is able to make the collective organization arbitrary complex, it is primarily bounded by available time. Example can be given by human society. An individual human, as element of this society, is not changed over last 50.000 years, but human society has been changed well. The still open question is which internal dynamics does allow the collective system to progress or not to regress ?

From the macroscopic point of view, the collective evolution is a chain of structural self-organizations that result in the form of self-modifications, see Figure 3.38. The self-

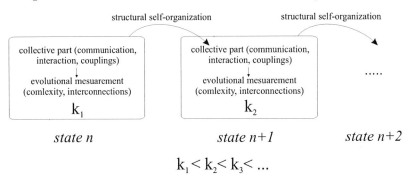

$$k_1 < k_2 < k_3 < \ldots$$

Figure 3.38: *The collective evolution as a sequence of structural self-organizations.*

organization changes the collective part of the system. The changed system interacts with other systems and they emerge a collective behavior. If we can find the corresponding collective fitness function, we can direct the process of collective changes, see Figure 3.39. This can be applied to collective learning or even to desired collective evolution. Therefore it is of importance to understand the several following points. What is the relation between macroscopic behavior and microscopic rules ? Which microscopic rules enable the collective evolution ? How to make the system that can evolve collectively by continuous changing

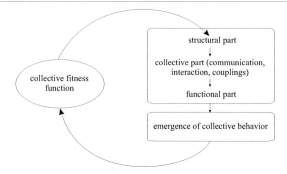

Figure 3.39: *Direction of the collective evolution on the basis of fitness function.*

the rules ? What is a collective fitness ? These points are open and represent the further works.

3.9 Summary

Now finishing this chapter, we can draw some conclusions about artificial self-organization. Speaking about artificial SO phenomena, we primarily refer to self-organization on the level of structures. The structural SO meets all definitions and prerequisites that we usually mean speaking about natural SO. However, between them there are several differences.

Firstly, the structural self-organization arises in distributed systems consisting of interacting autonomous elements, which are driven by local rules. These systems possess hierarchical, at least with 2 levels, organization. Moreover, each next level of this organization generates (controls) the previous level. Speaking about these systems, we have in mind primarily artificially created, technical systems. Secondly, there is a difference between functional and structural self-organization: macroscopically observable phenomena are the result of functional self-organization, whereas an emergence of self-organization itself is the result of structural self-organization.

Finally, structural self-organization can be based on two operational principles: vertical and horizontal. The operational principle does not change the result of self-organization. It primarily influences the working basis of the system. The self-organization generally, and the structural self-organization partially, is beneficial over traditional working principles from different viewpoint: economical, functional, reliability, flexibility and so on. Flexibility is an especially important point. The self-organizing systems can adapt their own behavior to changes of external conditions. Moreover, this adaptation has several levels: level of particular problem, level of problems classes, level of cluster of classes and so on. In this case we can speak about the system that can be completely configured by its own environment.

The self-organization of structures is closely connected with self-modification and, in turn, with collective learning and collective evolution. Generally, the self-modification is highly promising research point. However, here we have more open questions than answers and we hope that further research can answer some of them.

Chapter 4

Reductive and computational treatment of functional SO-phenomena

4.1 Motivation

As pointed out in the previous chapter, local rules are primarily in charge of collective phenomena. These local rules compose a hierarchy of controlling mechanisms with underlying vertical or horizontal operational principles. However, deriving these rules practically, we encounter a few problems. The first problem is that we fail to find a general approach allowing us to derive SO mechanisms in a systematic way. Without such a systematic procedure, a derivation of desired emergence is performed mostly "by trial and error". We focus on this problem in the next chapter.

The second problem consists in an ambiguity of the derivation procedure. As known, there is a variety of different mechanisms: physical (synergetics (Haken, 1983a), nonlinear dynamics (Wiggins, 1990), statistical, e.g. Bolzmann machine (Cooper, 1990), (Ackley et al., 1985)) approaches, different biological mechanisms (pheromone, trophallaxis (Bonabeau et al., 1999)), computational approaches (genetic programming (Koza, 1992), rule-based programming (Roma et al., 1993)) and so on. The same desired swarm behavior can be obtained by using different mechanisms. These mechanisms possess also different emergent properties, like effectiveness, consumed energy required to achieve the goal, a relation between the number of agents doing "useful" and "useless" job and so on. A variety of different approaches towards emergence is a typical characteristics of functional SO-phenomena. It can be explained by structural parts that are not defined on this step. The ambiguity arises exactly because the same functionality can be generated by different structures. Because of "absent" structural parts, functional SO-phenomena possess many degrees of freedom. They represent one of the fundamental problems in developing artificial emergence.

The main goal of this chapter is to consider the mechanisms and approaches, which can be applied to deriving artificial functional self-organization. These approaches originate from scientific domains that face the problem of artificial emergent behavior and contribute to new "swarm mathematics". As mentioned in Chapter 2, the functional mechanisms can be correlated with two main methodologies, reductive and computational ones. Therefore, in the following consideration, we also separate reductive and computational approaches.

This chapter is structured as follows. In Section 4.2 we introduce an example of deriving a simple swarm behavior. This example gives an outlook on the mentioned ambiguity problem.

In Sections 4.3 and 4.4 we represent several mechanisms and approaches from domains of analytic and algorithmic computation. In Summary 4.5 we conclude the obtained results.

4.2 Example of ambiguity in emergent clusterization

In this section we intend to demonstrate the ambiguity problem in deriving an artificial functional emergence. For this purpose we choice a simple swarm behavior obtained in the computational way. The general top-down methodology of this example is described in Section 3.6.

The behavioral pattern Ω, chosen in the example, is the spatial clusterization. The specific feature of this clusterization, that prevent an accident obtaining of this behavior, consists in one-cluster-building character, e.i. agents have *to build only one cluster*, see Figure 4.1. As known from biological examples, clustering is often encountered as a building

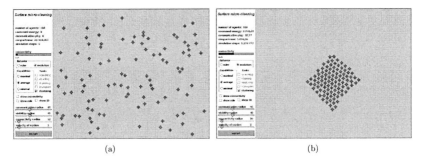

(a)   (b)

Figure 4.1: *Example of emergent behavior in the form of building one spatial cluster.* **(a)** *Random initial condition;* **(b)** *Final spatial one-cluster-formation, obtained by evolutionary algorithm, optimizing global compactness* Φ.

block in more complex types of swarm behavior. This is the main motivation for choosing this kind of emergence. We define the behavioral pattern Ω in evolutional way. For that we introduce, firstly, a few global values and develop an evolutionary algorithm that optimizes them. After that, we analyze the obtained behavior and replace these global values by equivalent local mechanisms. Since there are several such mechanisms, we compare effectiveness of obtained algorithms.

We introduce the local connectivity degree L_{cd} as the number of neighbor agents within the visibility radius R_{vis}. L_{cd}^i demonstrates how many other agents does the agent i "see". Global connectivity degree can be defined as:

$$G_{cd} = \sum_{i=1}^{N} L_{cd}^i,$$ (4.1)

where N is the total number of agents, is the sum of all local L_{cd}^i. Another important value, describing clusterization, is the global compactness Φ, defined as

$$\Phi = \sum_{i}^{N} \sum_{j}^{N} D_{ij},$$ (4.2)

where D_{ij} is a distance between agent i and agent j. The evolutionary algorithm, optimizing Φ can have the following form:

```
do { one step in all directions;
     calculate global compactness;}
choose the step getting min. compactness.
```

This algorithm demonstrates building one cluster, shown in Figure 4.1(b). Since this algorithm uses global values, its performance, like running time or consumed by agents energy, is expected to be the best one. The performance of other algorithms will be calculated in the terms of this evolutionary algorithm.

Now we intend to derive the same behavior, but without using Φ. For that we analyze the behavior of the whole swarm as well as of each agent produced by this algorithm. In Figure 4.2 we show the global connectivity, compactness and the command of robot motion controller (we use 8-directional sensors and motion control, see motivation in the next chapter). As followed from Figure 4.2, the behavior of the whole swarm consists

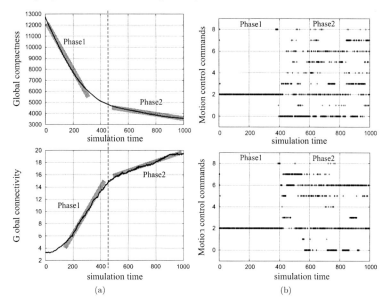

Figure 4.2: *Analyze of collective behavior obtained by optimizing the global compactness* Φ. **(a)** *Global compactness and global connectivity as the function of time;* **(b)** *Motion commands of two neighbor agents in the same time range.*

of two phases, that are characterized by different slopes of both dependencies. In the first phase the global connectivity rapidly increases (global compactness decreases). All neighbor agents during the first phase move in the same direction. In the second phase, the rate of building decreases and robots move no longer homogeneously. In Figure 4.3 we plot in parallel and parallel hierarchical coordinates (Yang *et al.*, 2003) the dependency between information delivered by local sensors (local connectivity degree L_{cd} in each direction) and moving commands (two examples when moving directions equal "5" and "6"). As shown

111

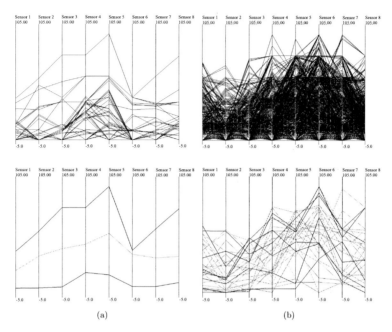

(a)   (b)

Figure 4.3: **(a)** *Sensor information (local connectivity degree L_{cd} in each direction) represented in parallel coordinates (above) and in parallel hierarchical coordinates (below) when an agent decides to move in the direction "5"*; **(b)** *Sensor information in the same representation when an agent decides to move in direction "6"*;

in this Figure, an agent decides to move in the corresponding direction if the L_{cd} has the maximal value in this direction.

Now we analyze the dynamics produced by the evolutionary algorithm. In the first phase all robots in the local neighborhood have the same motion vector. In this way they build small clusters with a homogeneous direction of motion. Gradually, a size of such clusters grows, whereas the number of them decreases. This behavior explains the change of slope shown in Figure 4.2(a). In the second phase agents primarily decrease distances between each other in clusters. They start avoiding collisions and the whole motion dynamics gets chaotic. In both phases robots decide to move in a direction with the most local connectivity degree.

In trying to reproduce this behavior (without using Φ), we faced the question of how to replace the gradient (introduced by global compactness Φ). We can imagine employing the following mechanisms:

- Computational mechanism: degree of local connectivity L_{cd};

- Biological mechanisms: biologically motivated mechanism based on pAMP-gradient waves, emitted by the fungi *Dictyostelium discoideum* during aggregation phase (Haken, 1983b, p.9);

In the experiments we used two values: degree of local connectivity L_{cd} and biologically motivated mechanism based on pAMP-gradient waves, represented by the value k_n:

$$k_{n+1} = log(\sum_{i=1}^{all\ neighbors} k_n^i), \quad k_0 = L_{cd}, \tag{4.3}$$

where n is the simulation step. In the performed experiments, if in some direction there are no neighbors, an agent subtracts from k_n a small constant P. The value k_n grows the more rapidly, the more larger the cluster is. Based on the values L_{cd} or k_n robots can decide about a more larger cluster and move in this direction.

The algorithm, reproducing the one-cluster-building behavior, has the following form (D-direction of motion, nR - neighbor robots with highest Lcd or k_n, Dist - distance to nR):

```
if (Lcd==0) D=random; else D=(D of nR);
if (Dist(nR)>CP) D=(D to nR).
```

The parameter CP as well as the parameter P depends on implementation details (in our experiments $CP = 27$ and $P = 0.5$). This simple algorithm implements the mentioned two phases of motion (D=(D of nR) and D=(D to nR)), the swarm behavior, produced by this algorithm is shown in Figure 4.4. We compare the global compactness, that characterizes

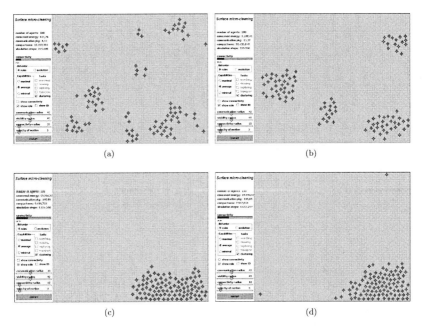

(a) (b)

(c) (d)

Figure 4.4: *Swarm behavior, produced by the two-phases-clustering algorithm.* (**a**) *The first phase, building of small clusters and synchronous motion in the cluster;* (**b**) *The second phase, growing of clusters;* (**c**) *Final cluster;* (**d**) *Situation when cluster is formed, but several agents are "lost".*

clusterization, for the cases of one-phase (only the second phase) motion, two-phases motion based on L_{cd} and k_n in Figure 4.5. As followed from this Figure, the one-phase motion,

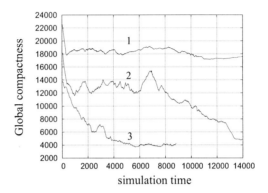

simulation time

Figure 4.5: *Comparison of the global compactness for the cases of: (1) one-phase motion (without homogeneous motion, only the second phase), (2) two-phases motion based on L_{cd} and (3) two-phases motion based on k_n on. All curves represent typical cases of behavior.*

that is intuitively the most evident one, builds only small local clusters without bringing them into the bigger one. Both two-phases mechanisms perform building the common cluster. However, the efficiency of L_{cd} and k_n based mechanisms is different. The biologically motivated mechanism requires less time to converge.

4.3 Reductive treatment of self-organization

As shown by the previous example, swarm algorithms can be based on different mechanisms. In this section we consider several analytical approaches, which can be useful in describing and generating collective behavior in the functional SO-phenomena. Most of these approaches originate from the domain of nonlinear dynamics and synergetics. Before considering them, we discuss once again the local rules from the viewpoint of modeling of interaction.

Interactions, or more exactly dynamics of interactions and dynamics of interacting systems, are central point in the problem of "local rules". Generally, interactions can be separated into spatial and information[1] ones. Spatial interactions define the neighbors that are intended for information exchange. They can be understood in a sense of physical connections, channels between participants (like a network) or a physical graze (at rolling balls). The interacting neighborhood can be of local (only interacting neighbors) or of global (everyone can interact with everyone) nature, moreover spatial interactions may have static or dynamic (e.g. random couplings in CML (Jost & Joy, 2002)) character.

A content, transferred via a communication channel or a pear-to-pear connection, is defined by interactions, where the systems transfer some information. Content interactions represent difficult issue, because we tough here a semantics of content. As it will be shown further, we restrict ourselves only to a dynamics of pre-semantic content, e.g. in collective decision making. It is important to remark that the mentioned separation between spatial and content interactions, as well as dynamics of interaction, is only an useful abstraction. For example, in the case of billiard balls is difficult to separate spatial and information components, because they are proceeded in one *horizontal system*. In the next sections we

---

[1] or content interactions

discuss these problems more in details.

4.3.1 Spatial interactions

Without loss of generality one can assume all subsystems-participants are placed on the two-dimensional plane, where everyone can interact with everyone. This kind of interaction can be represented by the following matrix $\underline{\underline{A}}$:

$$\underline{\underline{A}} = \begin{pmatrix} a_1 & a_{12} & a_{13} & \dots \\ a_{21} & a_2 & a_{23} & \dots \\ a_{31} & a_{32} & a_3 & \dots \\ \dots & \dots & \dots & \dots \end{pmatrix}, \tag{4.4}$$

where each element a_{ij} is a "place holder" for an "interaction channel". For example, the element a_{12} "holds a channel" between the elements 1 and 2. This matrix notation remains very useful in 2D case, but if interactions occur in 3D space, this notation becomes awkward and will be replaced by the tensor notation. The second rank tensor $\Gamma^A_{(2)}$ is equivalent to the matrix $\underline{\underline{A}}$, e.i. $\underline{\underline{A}}_{ij} = (\Gamma^A_{(2)})_{ij}$. The tensor of the third rank $\Gamma^A_{(3)}$ represents "place holders" in 3D case, e.g. $(\Gamma^A_{(3)})_{123}$ "holds a channel" between elements 1, 2 and 3. In order to make some ideas and calculations more clear, we use further the matrix notation.

The matrix $\underline{\underline{A}}$ represents the global interactions. In the case of local interactions, the matrix $\underline{\underline{A}}$ gets specific form:

$$\underline{\underline{A}} = \begin{pmatrix} a_1 & a_{12} & 0 & \dots & a_{n1} \\ a_{21} & a_2 & a_{23} & \dots & 0 \\ 0 & a_{32} & a_3 & \dots & 0 \\ \dots & \dots & \dots & \ddots & \dots \\ a_{1n} & 0 & 0 & a_{n-1n} & a_n \end{pmatrix}, \underline{\underline{B}} = \begin{pmatrix} a & a_{right} & 0 & \dots & a_{left} \\ a_{left} & a & a_{right} & \dots & 0 \\ 0 & a_{left} & a & \dots & 0 \\ \dots & \dots & \dots & \ddots & \dots \\ a_{right} & 0 & 0 & a_{left} & a \end{pmatrix}. \tag{4.5}$$

If the elements of the system are identical (homogeneous system) it is expected that the "place holders" are also equal to each other (the matrix $\underline{\underline{B}}$). The matrix $\underline{\underline{B}}$ calls *circulant matrix* and has some interesting properties. The circulant n*n matrix has only n distinct elements, the elements of each row are identical to those of the previous row, but are moved one position to the right and wrapped around. Therefore the whole circulant matrix is defined by the first row (or column) (Davis, 1979, p.66)

$$\underline{\underline{C}} = circ(c_1, c_2, c_3, c_4, \dots, c_n). \tag{4.6}$$

Spatial interactions between boundary elements represent the next question of interest. Let us consider again the "left-right" neighbors, but for the first element. It is evident that the right element (the element 2) is a local neighbor, but a "locality" or a "globality" of the left neighbor depends on the "closeness" of the whole group. If the group represents a closed 1D-chain (or closed 2D-grid), the left neighbor for the first element is a local one. But if the group is not closed in the mentioned sense, the left neighbor for the first element is not defined and we get the third kind of matrices:

$$\underline{\underline{B}} = \begin{pmatrix} a & a_{right} & 0 & \dots & 0 \\ a_{left} & a & a_{right} & \dots & 0 \\ 0 & a_{left} & a & \dots & 0 \\ \dots & \dots & \dots & \ddots & \dots \\ 0 & 0 & 0 & a_{left} & a \end{pmatrix}. \tag{4.7}$$

This matrix is an example of *Toeplitz matrices* (Böttcher & Silbermann, 1999). The square matrix $A = (a_{ij})$ of the order n is said to be Toeplitz if

$$a_{ij} = a_{i+1,j+1}, \quad i,j = 1,2,3...,n-1. \tag{4.8}$$

Thus, Toeplitz matrices are those that are constant along all diagonals parallel to the principal diagonal (Davis, 1979, p.70). A circulant matrix is a Toeplitz matrix, but not necessarily conversely. In fact, most local spatial interactions in homogeneous systems can be described either by circulant or by Toeplitz matrices. In the vast literature on the object, the mentioned types of interactions are often denoted as one or two way coupled ring with open or closed boundary (see e.g. (Konishi & Kokame, 1999), (Grigoriev *et al.*, 1997)). Considering circulant and Toeplitz matrices, we are primarily interested in calculating *eigenvalues* and *eigenvectors* for large matrices.

A circulant matrix can be diagonalized by the Fourier matrix:

$$\underline{\underline{F}} = \frac{1}{\sqrt{n}} \begin{pmatrix} 1 & 1 & 1 & ... & 1 \\ 1 & w & w^2 & ... & w^{n-1} \\ 1 & w^2 & w^4 & ... & w^{2(n-1)} \\ ... & ... & ... & \ddots & ... \\ 1 & w^{n-1} & w^{2(n-1)} & ... & w^{(n-1)^2} \end{pmatrix} = \frac{1}{\sqrt{n}} \begin{pmatrix} 1 & 1 & 1 & ... & 1 \\ 1 & w & w^2 & ... & w^{n-1} \\ 1 & w^2 & w^4 & ... & w^{n-2} \\ ... & ... & ... & \ddots & ... \\ 1 & w^{n-1} & w^{n-2} & ... & w \end{pmatrix},$$
$$\tag{4.9}$$

where $w = \exp\left(\frac{2\pi i}{n}\right) = \cos\left(\frac{2\pi}{n}\right) + i\sin\left(\frac{2\pi}{n}\right)$ and $n \geq 1$ with the eigenvalues

$$\lambda_j = c_1 + c_2(w^{j-1}) + c_3(w^{j-1})^2 + ... + c_n(w^{j-1})^{n-1} = \sum_{i=1}^{n} c_i(w^{j-1})^{i-1}, \tag{4.10}$$

and $c_1, ..., c_n$ are as in Eq. (4.6). It is evident that if $\underline{\underline{\Lambda}} = diag(\lambda_1, \lambda_2, ..., \lambda_n)$ is the diagonal matrix of eigenvalues, the corresponding circulant matrix can easy be reconstructed by

$$\underline{\underline{C}} = \underline{\underline{F}}^{-1} \underline{\underline{\Lambda}} \underline{\underline{F}}. \tag{4.11}$$

For all $c_i > 0$ or for all $c_i < 0$ the maximal eigenvalue (in magnitude) will be given by the first eigenvalue in expression (4.10), i.e. by

$$\lambda_{max} = \lambda_1 = \sum_{i=1}^{n} c_i. \tag{4.12}$$

Toeplitz matrices represent more difficult issues than circulant matrices, especially for large systems. Many works are devoted to this topic (Berg, 1986), (Grenander & Szegö, 1958), (Hirschman & Hughes, 1977), (Boutet de Monvel & Guillemin, 1981) or the textbook (Böttcher & Silbermann, 1990). Characteristic values of these matrices (e.g. distribution of eigenvalues, determinants) are given by their *symbol*. From the viewpoint of local interactions, we are primarily interested in *Toeplitz band matrices*. A matrix calls the band matrix if $a_n = 0$ for $|n| < N$,

$$\begin{pmatrix} ... & ... & ... & ... & ... \\ ... & a_0 & a_1 & a_2 & ... \\ ... & a_{-1} & a_0 & a_1 & ... \\ ... & a_2 & a_{-1} & a_0 & ... \\ ... & ... & ... & ... & ... \end{pmatrix}, \tag{4.13}$$

where its symbol is determined by the following trigonometric polynomial (Böttcher & Silbermann, 1999, p. 5)

$$a(t) = \sum_{n=-N}^{N} a_n e^{i\Theta} \qquad (4.14)$$

In particular case, if the value on the main diagonal $a_0 = \alpha$ and on two next diagonals $a_1 = a_{-1} = \beta$ all eigenvalues can be calculated by the following formula

$$\lambda_i = \alpha + 2\beta \cos\left(I\frac{i\pi}{N+1}\right) \qquad i = 1, ..., N. \qquad (4.15)$$

This matrix corresponds to local interactions between two neighbors, where the chain, built by agents, remains unclosed. This case often occurs in large systems, where new agent can be incorporated into a system without changing a structure of already existed interactions.

4.3.2 Content interactions

Content interactions define, firstly, information that has to be sent and, secondly, determine how it should be proceeded. Generally, information interaction includes the following important issues:

- information content, i.e. semantics of information;

- dynamics of information interaction in quantitative and qualitative sense;

- modelling of information interaction.

Semantic aspects of information are a long time in the focus of many investigations (e.g. (Morris, 1938)). This problem was primarily considered from the viewpoint of natural (Schaff, 1968) and artificial languages (Salomaa, 1973). There are several research works that deal with information in sense of Shannon (Shannon, 1948) as well as Kolmogorov-Sinai entropy (Kolmogorov, 1963). Many authors consider the dependence between information and self-organization (e.g. (Haken, 1988), (Ebeling *et al.*, 1998)). Since we deal with content interactions in a context of analytical approaches, we restrict ourselves only to simple pre-semantic information. As already mentioned in Chapter 2, pre-semantics can be understood in sense of fuzzy decisions. They, represented in numeric form, allow applying different analytic models and approaches to investigate an underlying dynamics of these decisions. This methodology is very useful for analyzing and designing collective decision making.

The dynamics of content interactions is the second point, that we are interested in. This dynamics has two different aspects: dynamics of information exchange via communication channels and dynamics in sense of information mining. The first aspect represents the focus of several scientific disciplines dealing with communication and information transfer. We do not touch this aspect. The second aspect of content dynamics is relatively weak investigated and focuses in the following question: how the system has to deal with information so that to achieve some goal (to fulfill some criterion, to solve some problem and so no) ?

The modeling of information interaction depends on the chosen representation and information aspects that we work with. Investigating local rules, we are primarily interested in controlling the emergent behavior, i.e. in a dynamics of interactions. From the viewpoint of dynamics, the information content (semantics) still remains of interest, but more important becomes the information changes. Therefore we can introduce the reductive model of information interaction, that allows us to focus only on dynamical aspects. The reduction models are often criticized because of their idealized nature. Indeed, the reduced complexity of these models does not allow performing "realistic" modeling. However, these models offer a possibility to work analytically (by means of evolution equations) with information and local rules, moreover they make investigations more evident and clear.

In this model we can reduce information content from symbols to numbers. This allows modeling a content interaction by dynamical equations of motion. Analyzing these equation, we can understand the dynamics of content interactions. Using numbers for representations of interactions, we need further some approach that reconstructs a complexity of representation. Such an approach is discussed in (Kornienko, 2007, p.170). We can think about numbers in the range 0..1 as of e.g. fuzzy decisions, where 0 corresponds to "negative" and 1 to "positive" decisions. For a representation of this decision the state variable q needs to be introduced. Since decisions changes in time, this variable depends also on time, i.e. $q(t)$ or for the discrete time periods q_n, where n is a time step. If there are several decisions, the corresponding variables are collected in the decision vector $\underline{q}_n = \{q_n^1, q_n^2, ..., q_n^k\}^T$, where k is a number of all decisions (the dimension of the system). It is assumed, that the state vector $\underline{q}_n$ satisfies the following time discrete nonlinear autonomous equation of motion

$$\underline{q}_{n+1} = \underline{N}(\underline{q}_n, \{\alpha\}), \tag{4.16}$$

where $\underline{N}$ is a nonlinear vector function, and $\{\alpha\}$ a set of control parameters. The equation (4.16) can be rewritten in the following tensor-like notation (see more in (Kornienko, 2007, p.41) and (Levi *et al.*, 1999))

$$\underline{q}_{n+1} = \underline{N}(\underline{q}_n, \{\alpha\}) = \Gamma_{(1)} + \Gamma_{(2)}(:\underline{q}_n) + \Gamma_{(3)}(:\underline{q}_n)^2 + ... = \sum_{r=0}^{p} \Gamma_{(r+1)}(:\underline{q}_n)^r, \tag{4.17}$$

where $\underline{q}_n \in \mathbb{R}^k$ is the state vector in the k-dimensional state space and the indices in lower brackets denote the rank of the corresponding tensors and p is the maximal order of this equation. The k-dimensional equation (4.17) represents a separate system (e.g. one agent taking a decision). Coupling m such equations by means of nonlinear functions $\underline{F}$, that consist of multiplicative $\underline{F}^M$ and additive $\underline{F}^A$ components, we get the following coupled system of dimension m

$$\underline{q}_{n+1} = \underline{N}(\underline{q}_n, \{\alpha\})\underline{F}_n^M(\underline{q}_n, \{\beta_M\}) + \underline{F}_n^A(\underline{q}_n, \{\beta_A\}), \tag{4.18}$$

where $\underline{q}_n = (q_n^1, q_n^2, ...q_n^m)^T \in \mathbb{R}^m$ is a state vector in the m-dimensional space, $\underline{N}$, $\underline{F}$ are in general nonlinear functions of $\underline{q}_n$, and $\{\alpha\}$, $(\{\beta_M\}, \{\beta_A\} \in \{\beta\})$ are the sets of control parameters. Evolution of the coupling functions $\underline{F}^M$, $\underline{F}^A$ is written as follows

$$\underline{F}_{n+1}^M(\underline{q}_n, \{\beta_M\}) = \underline{F}_n^M(\underline{q}_n, \{\beta_M\}) + \tilde{\underline{F}}_n^M(\underline{q}_n, \{\beta_M\}), \tag{4.19a}$$

$$\underline{F}_{n+1}^A(\underline{q}_n, \{\beta_A\}) = \underline{F}_n^A(\underline{q}_n, \{\beta_A\}) + \tilde{\underline{F}}_n^A(\underline{q}_n, \{\beta_A\}), \tag{4.19b}$$

where $\tilde{\underline{F}}$ denotes the part that determines modifications of coupling functions; $\tilde{\underline{F}}$ plays the role of a "program" governing an evolution of the system (4.18). For instance, in (Kataoka & Kaneko, 2000) the self-referenced term $\tilde{\underline{F}}_n = \underline{F}_n \circ \underline{F}_n$ has been suggested and investigated. Complete dynamics of the system (4.18) is determined by its own dynamics at fixed couplings and by the functional dynamics (4.19) of couplings. We can consider the systems (4.18) and (4.19) from another viewpoint. The terms $\underline{F}$ in (4.18) represent the interaction, whereas the system (4.19) describes a dynamics of interactions ! This representation offers the way to analyze this dynamics. And the question is how to express, to measure and to control the dynamics of interactions ?

From the viewpoint of synergetics (Haken, 1983a) a collective behavior can be expressed in the form of the macroscopic order parameters (OP). Generally, OPs are reduced low-dimensional equations, obtained by means of reduction procedures, which describe local behavior of original system nearly instability (at critical values of control parameters). Therefore being guided by the synergetic concept, we concentrate on the question of how the dynamics of couplings $\underline{F}$ between initial systems (4.16) influence the qualitative behavior of the system (4.18)[2]. For that we can express the qualitative behavior of the system (4.19) by the normal forms (NF) (Nayfeh, 1993) of the appropriate local bifurcations

$$\underline{\varphi}_{n+1} = \underline{\underline{\Lambda}}_u(\{\alpha\},\{\beta\})\underline{\varphi}_n + \mathbf{g}^{(2)}(\underline{\varphi}_n,\{\alpha\},\{\beta\}) + \dots + O(\mathbf{g}^{(r+1)}). \tag{4.20}$$

In (4.20) the term $\underline{\underline{\Lambda}}_u$ presents the diagonal matrix of eigenvalues, $\mathbf{g}$ are the resonance terms, dependent on both $\{\alpha\}$ and $\{\beta\}$ and r is the determinancy order of this NF. This methods has been already explained in (Kornienko & Kornienko, 2002) and (Kornienko, 2007), therefore here we show only the main points.

The idea consists in the following. The initial systems (4.16), being uncoupled, demonstrate local behavior described by "initial" NF. Local behavior of the coupled system (4.18) differs from the behavior of the initial systems (4.16), that can be viewed as a perturbation of this initial NF caused by the coupling $\underline{F}$. This perturbation, in turn, is controlled by the system (4.19). Although this coupling mechanism simultaneously influences all elements of NF, one can at least distinguish between four main components of such an influence:

- change of the unstable eigenvalue $\underline{\underline{\Lambda}}_u$. Generally speaking the derived in this case normal form completely differs from the initial one;

- appearance of multiple unstable eigenvalues that increase the dimension of normal form (4.20). Forasmuch as there are two critical values ± 1 of unstable eigenvalues, the derived multidimensional normal forms possess specific properties;

- change of the determinacy order r. This includes into consideration additional high-order terms that often lead to an appearance of non-local solutions of bifurcation problem (4.20);

- perturbation of different resonance terms $\mathbf{g}$ of NF and an unfolding of the normal form.

These four points primarily contributes to changing of collective behavior, i.e. to self-organization. The system (4.19) controls these changes. *Analyzing and controlling the system (4.20), we create the structural self-organization in the system* (4.16). For this purpose we can apply approaches suggested in the work (Kornienko, 2007).

What is the meaning of Eq.(4.20) for content interactions ? Remember that the terms $\underline{F}$ in (4.18) represent interactions, whereas the system (4.19) describes a dynamics of interactions. Under this dynamics we understand not only spatial dynamics, but also some information processing that is performed by coupling functions. These coupling functions can radically change the behavior of dynamical system, as shown in Section 3.8. Therefore information processing in $\underline{F}$ has a deep impact on the system (4.16). The system (4.19) describes how the content of information, represented in numerical form, influences information processing by $\underline{F}$. A good example of such a "dynamics over dynamics" is given in already mentioned work (Kataoka & Kaneko, 2000). We suggest here more flexible approach towards controlling such double-dynamical systems: instead of self-referenced terms, we suggest to use the order parameter (4.20). In the next section we discuss more about a relation between the derived order parameter and collective phenomena in interacting systems.

---

[2]see for details (Kornienko, 2007)

4.3.3 Top-Down and bottom-up approaches

The top-down and bottom-up strategies are already considered from the viewpoint of rule deriving procedure in Section 3.6. Here, we discuss these approaches in the analytical framework, that means primarily two different methodological viewpoints. Bottom-up approach can be associated with an analysis (control) of system, where starting from initial equations (or other models), we try to derive some values or parameters that gives us the needed description. Derivation of the order parameter belongs to this approach. OP equation (e.g. equation (4.19) from Section 4.3.2), being once derived, allows understanding the underlying dynamics of the considering system. Moreover, using this equation, we can develop different mechanisms being able to control collective behavior (Levi *et al.*, 1999), (Kornienko & Kornienko, 1999).

Top-down approach is usually associated with system's development. In this case the order parameter is a start point for new system. In the context of self-organization, it means that specific collective properties, determined by OP, are expected to be incorporated into the output system. Since the OP describes collective activity (e.g. emergence of laser light (Haken, 1984), collective decision making (Kornienko *et al.*, 2001) and so on), any changes of this OP correspond to some change of collective activity. However, here there are two questions needed to be answered: firstly, how the macroscopic phenomena do correspond to the order parameter and how to propagate the change from OP to output system ? Two next sections are intended to answer both questions.

4.3.4 Correspondence between collective phenomena and the order parameter

On the high levels of abstraction a correspondence between collective phenomena and the order parameter is evident: the order parameter describes macroscopic changes. However which changes? Do analytical notions (e.g. resonant nonlinear terms) relate to practical examples (e.g. collective defense in ants colony)? *In order to create and to control a collective activity by means of the order parameter, it is necessary to define the OP in terms of this collective activity.* The next points are devoted to clarify this relation.

1. *The most important issue is that the order parameter does not describe the collective activity.* It describes only qualitative changes in this collective activity. Defining difference between qualitative and quantitative changes, we follow Haken (Haken, 1983a, p. 32). He defines as quantitative such a change that can be made by means of some transformation, whereas the object itself remains structural stable; otherwise the change is qualitative. Therefore OP cannot describe how an ants colony performs a collective defense or how cellular automata build a specific pattern. However, the OP is useful if we try to know why one type of collective behavior is changed by another type, e.g. ants colony changes a defensive behavior by assaulter one. This point can be considered from the view point of complexity. The original (or output) system possesses the highest degree of complexity. The OP reduces this complexity, describing only most "interesting" sides of system in a "compact" form. Correspondingly, it is not expected that OP can reproduce the complexity of an original system.

We should remark, that, in several cases, OP describes also a collective activity itself. These cases belong basically to physical systems, where equations model e.g. a behavior of physical particles, so-called kinetic models. If the OP equation demonstrates the Hopf-bifurcation, particles really show a limit cycle in their own behavior (see e.g. (Hassard *et al.*, 1981). In this way we encounter again the problem of modeling. Modeling of real system, and especially mathematical modeling, is a complex issue involving such aspects as the adequacy of model, complexity, restrictions of dynamics and so on. Only a list of related books on the subject could take several pages. We restrict ourselves only to one side of this problem; this can be called as a direct and indirect modeling. For instance, the well-known wagon with a spring intending to demonstrate Newtonian laws can be modeled by differential equation of the first order (Stöcker(Ed.), 1997). This model does not take into account e.g. a windage or adhesion in pillow-block of wheels, however behavior of this equation shows (approximately) a motion of the real wagon. This is a direct model of the considered physical phenomenon. We can change one of parameters in this equation and predict what will happen if a real force (corresponding to this parameter) is changed.

Another example can be given by the Kelso experiment (Haken, 1996, p. 19) with synchronization of finger tapping. In this case nobody (at least now) exactly knows how the finger is moving, which parts of brain and which neurons are participating, there is no model that describes it. There is a model that describe a change from one type of behavior to another. This model can not predict the behavior itself (e.g. amplitude or spontaneous self-motion), it describes merely a "decision" to start a movement of different types (see also a discursion in e.g. (Haken, 1996, p. 87)). *Modeling of decisions (binary or fuzzy) is the most universal indirect modeling.* For instance, strategy of a robot team (Oswald *et al.*, 2000) depends on dozen reasons, a complete model, even algorithmic, is too complex to be constructed. Therefore, instead of direct robot's modeling, only an indirect decision to play defensively or offensively is modeled. Indirect models can not predict a behavior itself, but they are useful to predict a change in behavior. In this context the meaning of order parameter depends on the kind of models; it can describe a "decision" or a real behavior near instability.

2. *The order parameter describes a dynamics of macroscopic changes.* Macroscopic changes possess also their own dynamics (see e.g. the system (4.19)), that can be viewed as a dynamics over a dynamics of separate elements (*structural dynamics*). This idea can be illustrated by the surface micro-cleaning example introduced in Section 2.5.

Simplifying, we assume that each agent can move in N ($N = 4, 8$) directions on the plane, can determine the distance between neighbor agents and perceives some local external influence. We also assume this influence is of binary nature. This can be interpreted as e.g. "I see a dirtiness" or correspondingly "I don't see a dirtiness" and represents an agent's initial proposal for negotiation. According to the number of simultaneously "activated" agents, the whole group has to decide in which spatial formation it will behave, e.g. in the round formation (Figure 4.6(a)) or in the chain-like formation (Figure 4.6(b)). Thus, the agents have to communicate in order to reach a mutual agreement (collective decision) about the spatial structure, that they will behave in. This example can be found in (Kornienko, 2007). Each agent in this group has a dynamics defining its spatial motion, relation to neighbor agents, sensor-actor couplings etc. Each agent possesses also the secondary dynamics that transforms the behavior of the first type into the second one. This macroscopic dynamics can be represented by the "IF" condition: *"IF" number of informed agents < 3 "THEN" the behavior of type 1, "ELSE" the behavior of type 2.*

This point can also exemplify the mentioned idea about direct and indirect modeling. Using direct modeling, we should take into account the local sensor information, neighbors, obstacles. The obtained model describes the structure of the first and the second formations as well as a transition between them. In the indirect model we neglect these details and focus on a transition between formations. In this case the structure of groups can not be described; we need external models describing it. Remark that both models are on the same level of abstraction, they cannot be differentiated into macro- and microscopic models.

A dynamics of a transition from the first to the second group behavior (and correspond-

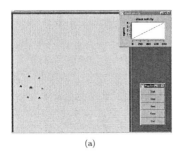
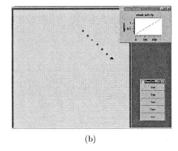

(a) (b)

Figure 4.6: *Macroscopic change of the collective behavior in a group of mobile agents;* (a) *Control parameter is under the critical value;* (b) *Control parameter is above the critical value. This Figure is taken from (Kornienko, 2007).*

ingly the algorithmic "IF...THEN" or "WHICH...CASE" structures) can be represented by the order parameter. For that, let us consider the normal form of transcritical and pitchfork bifurcations (Wiggins, 1990, p.362,366)

$$\varphi_{n+1} = \alpha\varphi_n - \varphi_n^2, \qquad (4.21a)$$
$$\varphi_{n+1} = \alpha\varphi_n - \varphi_n^3, \qquad (4.21b)$$

where $\varphi_n \in \mathbb{R}$ is a state variable and $\alpha > -1$ is the bifurcation parameter with the critical value $\alpha_{cr} = 1$. Making this example more evident, we rescale variable φ and substitute $\varphi_n = \tilde{\varphi}_n(a - 1)$ into the Eqs. (4.21)

$$\tilde{\varphi}_{n+1} = \alpha(\tilde{\varphi}_n - \tilde{\varphi}_n^2) + \tilde{\varphi}_n^2, \qquad (4.22a)$$
$$\tilde{\varphi}_{n+1} = \alpha(\tilde{\varphi}_n - \tilde{\varphi}_n^3) + \tilde{\varphi}_n^3. \qquad (4.22b)$$

Bifurcation diagram of the system (4.21) and (4.22) is shown in Figure 4.7. The equations (4.22a) and (4.22b) execute dynamically algorithmic "IF...THEN" and "WHICH...CASE" operations

$$IF\ (\alpha > 1)\ THEN\ 1\ ELSE\ 0, \qquad (4.23a)$$
$$WHICH\ (\alpha)$$
$$CASE\ < 1:\ \ 0;$$
$$CASE\ > 1:\ \ IF\ (\tilde{\varphi}_0 < 0)\ THEN\ -1;$$
$$CASE\ > 1:\ \ IF\ (\tilde{\varphi}_0 > 0)\ THEN\ 1; \qquad (4.23b)$$

where $\alpha \in (-1,...,0) \cup (0,...,1)$. "Dynamically executed" means that the state variable φ in the equations (4.22) needs several iterations in order to reach the value "0" or "1". (to define the value n is one of practical tasks). The macroscopic dynamics is correspondingly not restricted by the cases of transcritical, pitchfork bifurcations and by the algorithmic construction (4.23). There are other normal forms that give different types of periodical "FOR" or "WHILE" structures. These normal forms can be found in (Golubitsky & Schaeffer, 1985), (Golubitsky *et al.*, 1988). Combining them into one complex order parameter, we can "program" macroscopic dynamics. These "programs" can take into account parameters from environment so as to adapt collective dynamics of a system to changes of these parameters.

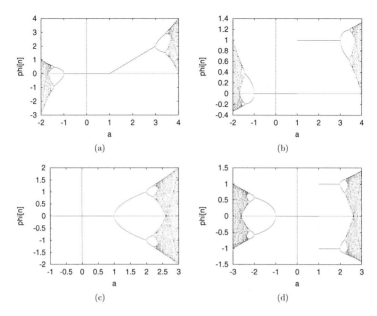

Figure 4.7: *The bifurcation diagrams of:* **(a)** *the transcritical bifurcation (4.21a),* $\varphi_0 = 0.3$ *;* **(b)** *the pitchfork bifurcation (4.21b),* $\varphi_0 = 0.3$ *and* $\varphi_0 = -0.3$*;* **(c)** *the perturbed transcritical bifurcation (4.22a),* $\varphi_0 = 0.3$*;* **(d)** *the perturbed pitchfork bifurcation (4.22b),* $\varphi_0 = 0.3$ *and* $\varphi_0 = -0.3$*;*

Advantage of analytical representation of macroscopic dynamics does not consist only in dynamical emulation of algorithmic structures like "IF" or "FOR". Order parameter is able to demonstrate such types of behavior that are inefficiently or even hardly to implement by algorithmic structures. Let us consider the following dynamical system (Eigen & Schuster, 1978)

$$\varphi_{n+1}^i = \varphi_n^i(\alpha_i\varphi_n^i + 1 - c_0 \sum_j \alpha_j(\varphi_n^j)^2), \quad i = 1, ..., m, \quad \alpha_i > 0 \ \forall i \in N, \quad (4.24)$$

where m is a dimension of this system, α^i are parameters. Behavior of the state variables of this system is shown in Figure 4.8. This is so-called selection process, where the state variables φ_n^i compete and only one from them "wins" this competition, rest becomes equal to zero.

3. *The order parameter activates unstable eigenvectors.* Order parameter is in charge of self-organization, it describes the corresponding macroscopic changes. However, the order parameter itself demonstrates only a dynamics of changes and not the changing structures. What are these structures ? This question may be answered if to rewrite the expression (2.36) in the following form

$$\Delta\underline{q}_n = \sum_k \underline{\xi}_n^k \underline{v}_k = \sum_u \underline{\xi}_n^u \underline{v}_u + \sum_s \underline{\xi}_n^s \underline{v}_s, \quad (4.25)$$

where u and s mean **u**nstable and **s**table, and $s + u = m$. Moreover, the number of stable modes is usually larger than the number of unstable modes. Both amplitudes are multiplied

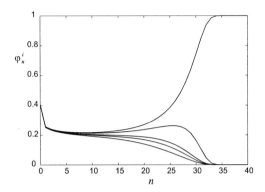

Figure 4.8: *Behavior of the state variables φ_n^i of the system (4.24), where $m = 5$, $c_0 = 1$, $\alpha_i = \alpha$ $\forall i$ and $\alpha = 0.9$ with the following initial conditions $\varphi_0^i = 0.4 + 0.01i$.*

by the corresponding eigenvectors and the changing structures that we see are built by these eigenvectors. They build a transformation basis, i.e. a "final" representation of a system undergoing a self-organization. Eigenvectors are given in a numerical form, but their interpretation is different. For example, in the synergetic computer the eigenvectors represent the stored images, that compete by means of selections dynamics. An image, that appears at the end of recognition, is the corresponding eigenvector of the winning amplitude (Haken, 1991, p.36).

As known from Chapter 2, unstable amplitudes undergo changes in the dynamics. Therefore, the corresponding eigenvectors are expected to be dominant in the collective phenomena. However, this is not completely correct. In the expression (4.25) there exist two amplitudes. Although they are separated from one another, there is a dependence between them. The equations of corresponding amplitudes:

- can be coupled in nonlinear parts;

- can depend on common control parameters in linear part;

- are not coupled at all.

These three cases determine a joint dynamics of amplitudes and this dynamics builds an observable effect of self-organization. In creating artificial self-organization all these cases can be utilized.

Linear parts, i.e. eigenvalues can be thought of as a "switcher" that "switch on" or "off" an instability. Type of instability, dimension, critical value of control parameters is determined by them. Moreover a bifurcation can be eliminated (shifted) by a specific modification of eigenvalues, that is used by many control techniques. The stable and unstable eigenvalues can depend on common control parameters. This mechanism can be used in generating a cascade of fixed point bifurcations, where different amplitudes become unstable at different values of control parameters. It does not concern non-fixed point bifurcations, like period-doubling or Hopf bifurcations. These types of instabilities required such techniques, that modify stationary states.

Unstable eigenvalues at supercritical values of control parameters lead to an infinite increasing of corresponding amplitudes, i.e. they expand a dynamics after a bifurcation.

However, it does not happen because the nonlinear part "stabilizes" an expanding linear dynamics. Nonlinear part determines a behavior of amplitudes after instability. It is important point because in practical applications the behavior of a system is of relevance before a bifurcation as well as after it. Although the stable eigenvalues does not cause changes in behavior, these changes are introduced by nonlinear coupling. In turn, due to nonlinear coupling the stable amplitudes influence unstable amplitudes and so stabilize them. This dependence between both amplitudes is often called as circular causality (Haken, 1996, p.43) (expressed sometimes also as a relation between order parameter and slaved modes via center manifold). Since here both amplitudes are involved into a change, visible macroscopic structures are determined also by stable and unstable eigenvectors. This is the most difficult case.

Generally, a treatment of self-organization can be essentially simplified if to assume that the equations of both amplitudes are uncoupled. In this way a desired dynamics of unstable amplitudes is determined directly by the order parameter. Long-time dynamics of stable amplitudes is either becoming zero or used for a cascade of instabilities, mentioned above. In this case only the order parameter determines a collective macroscopic dynamics, whereas corresponding eigenvectors are in charge of appearing structures. This is a focus of the next section.

4.3.5 Collective phenomena determined by coordinate transformation

As mentioned in the previous section, the order parameter equation determines dynamics of changes, whereas the corresponding eigenvectors determine a structure that undergoes a macroscopic change. As followed from this definition, *a collective dynamics is invariant to final form of a system that demonstrates a collective activity. This invariance can be utilized to transform a system into such a form, where the collective dynamics will have some desired properties.* For example, a macroscopic activity of a system is determined only by one unstable mode that can be viewed a central coordination. By corresponding coordinate transformation the system can be "rewritten" in such a form, where collective dynamics is determined only by interaction between elementary subsystems, i.e. a central coordination will be removed.

This transformation starts from the mode amplitude equations (2.38). These equations are obtained by the linear transformation (2.36), where eigenvectors are derived from the corresponding Jacobian. Performing this transformation backwards, the eigenvectors can (arbitrary) be so chosen that to obtain an output system with some desired properties. It can be interpreted in the following way: interactions among subsystems have different form in different coordinate basis though the subsystems perform the same (more exactly similar) operations. Therefore, we can first choose a coordinate basis with most simple interactions in order to define a form of collective activity and then to transform them into such a basis where interactions will have a desired nature (e.g. local or global, 2-4-8 neighbors etc.).

We start with linear systems intended to illustrate the main notion about this linear transformations. Despite a simplicity of linear systems, an application of them can be very useful in distributed environment. As mentioned above, the transformation is started from the mode equations which are uncoupled in this case

$$\begin{cases} \xi^u_{n+1} = \lambda_u \xi^u_n, \\ \xi^{s_i}_{n+1} = \lambda_{s_i} \xi^{s_i}_n, \end{cases} \qquad \begin{cases} \xi^u_n = \xi^u_0, \\ \xi^{s_i}_n = 0. \end{cases} \tag{4.26}$$

In (4.26) the dynamical system (left) and its solution (right) are shown. Here λ_{u,s_i} are the corresponding unstable and stable eigenvalues with the condition $0 \leq \lambda_{s_i} < \lambda_u$ and $\lambda_u = 1$.

The unstable amplitude represents in this case the simplest form of the order parameter. The system (4.26) can be rewritten in the following matrix form

$$\underline{\xi}_{n+1} = \underline{\underline{A}}\ \underline{\xi}_n \qquad\qquad \underline{\xi}_n = \underline{\underline{B}}\ \underline{\xi}_0 \qquad\qquad (4.27)$$

that can be transformed into another basis by performing

$$\underline{q}_{n+1} = \underline{\underline{V}}\ \underline{\underline{\Lambda}}\ \underline{\underline{V}}^{-1}\ \underline{q}_n \qquad\qquad \underline{q}_n = \underline{\underline{V}}\ \underline{\underline{B}}\ \underline{\underline{V}}^{-1}\ \underline{q}_0 \qquad\qquad (4.28)$$

where $\underline{\underline{V}}$ is a square matrix of eigenvectors. As already mentioned, the eigenvectors $\underline{\underline{V}}$ can be so chosen that to transform the system (4.26) into a desired form. As the first case, the subsystems have to build a closed chain, known also as two-way coupled ring lattice (Kaneko, 1993). Spatial interactions have a local nature and correspond to the circulant matrix, that can be constructed by the Fourier matrix (4.9). Developing a contrary example with a global nature of interactions, we use the following matrix

$$\underline{\underline{V}} = \begin{pmatrix} 1 & 1 & 1 & \dots & 1 \\ 1 & 0 & 1 & \dots & 1 \\ 1 & 1 & 0 & \dots & 1 \\ \dots & \dots & \dots & \ddots & \dots \\ 1 & 1 & 1 & \dots & 0 \end{pmatrix}, \quad \underline{\underline{V}}^{-1} = \begin{pmatrix} 2-N & 1 & 1 & \dots & 1 \\ 1 & -1 & 0 & \dots & 0 \\ 1 & 0 & -1 & \dots & 0 \\ \dots & \dots & \dots & \ddots & \dots \\ 1 & 0 & 0 & \dots & -1 \end{pmatrix}, \qquad (4.29)$$

where $\underline{\underline{V}}^{-1}$ is an inverse matrix to $\underline{\underline{V}}$. The system (4.26) yields then the component form for both cases

$$q^i_{n+1} = 1/3q^i_n + 1/3(q^{i+1}_n + q^{i-1}_n), \qquad\qquad (4.30a)$$

$$q^i_{n+1} = -(N-2)q^1_n + \sum_{i=2}^{N} q^i_n, \qquad\qquad (4.30b)$$

with the following expressions for q^i_n

$$q^i_n = \sum_{i=1}^{N} q^i_0 = \frac{1}{N}q^1_0 + \frac{1}{N}\sum_{i=2}^{N} q^i_0, \quad q^1_0=0 \longrightarrow \frac{1}{N}\sum_{i=2}^{N} q^i_0 \qquad (4.31a)$$

$$q^i_n = -(N-2)q^1_0 + \sum_{i=2}^{N} q^i_0, \quad q^1_0=0 \longrightarrow \sum_{i=2}^{N} q^i_0 \qquad (4.31b)$$

In (4.30) and (4.31) the expressions (a) correspond to the system transformed with the Fourier matrix and all (b) to the system transformed with the matrix (4.29). The system (4.30a) possesses the local nature of interaction, whereas (4.30b) is the globally coupled system. The systems (4.30) calculate a sum of initial values. In this sense the coordinate transformation can be thought of as an operator of distribution, that "spread" the characteristic behavior of order parameter on all equations and variables of output system. Moreover, the transformation basis (4.29) is so chosen that to calculate an arithmetical sum in contradistinction to (4.31a) that calculates mean arithmetical value from all initial values. The idea is that each agent (that models corresponding equation) can determine a common number of participating agents if simple to perform both calculations and compare results. Although the system (4.31b) use a centralized information given by coefficient N at the first term, the corresponding first agent is excluded from the calculation by the condition $q^1_0 = 0$. Therefore for all other agents this calculation remains distributed. Behavior of the systems (4.30) is shown in Figure 4.9.

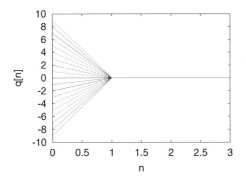

Figure 4.9: *Behavior of the equations (4.30), where $N = 20$ and q_0^i are distributed in the range of [-9...9].*

4.3.6   Coordinate transformation with spatial eigenvectors

In Section 4.3.5 eigenvectors are determined by the Fourier matrix (4.9). In this case the mode equations (4.27) are transformed so that to obtain a system with some desired functionality. Therefore, such a transformation basis has a "functional nature". The transformation basis can also have another "meaning", e.g. spatial one.

To exemplify the self-organization with spatial eigenvectors we refer to the I-Swarm project, mentioned in Section 2.5. As a part of surface micro-cleaning scenario, micro-robots have collective to recognize (primarily to classify) the kind and position of objects that they encounter. This task is often denoted as the collective perception (see more about self-organizing processes in collective perception in Section 5.9.6). The collective perception is highly non-trivial problem. To illustrate it we show in Figure 4.10 an example, where several robots have collectively to recognize a few details distributed on the surface.

Firstly, the same detail, observed from different positions, looks completely different. Therefore, the robots have to convince about the detail that all they currently see. Secondly, a robot can see only a part of a detail. In this case the problem of collective perception is even harder (the well-known Elephant fable from Indian philosophy (Ye *et al.*, 2002), see Figure 4.11). In some cases the problem of collective perception can be narrowed down to a classification problem, where there are several suggested approaches towards solution of this problem (e.g.(Mann *et al.*, 1997)). An elegant analytical approach allowed collective perception/classification in self-organizing way can be demonstrated by the synergetic computer (Haken, 1991).

Considering Figure 4.10, we can remark that there are only four details. These details (the corresponding images) represent the coordinate basis for classification, i.e. spatial eigenvectors, as shown in Figure 4.12. Each image consists of 512×512 (262144) pixels. We can think of the grey values of every pixel as a linear sequence of the length 262144. In this way we have in mind the spatial structure of this sequence (512×512), but consider it as one dimensional array. These four arrays represent the four eigenvectors (p=4), each of the length m=262144. Thus, we have the eigenvectors matrix $\underline{V}$ of the size (m,p)=(262144,4). The needed for transformation inverse matrix $\underline{V}^{-1}$ can be obtained in the way described in (Haken, 1991, p.51). Here the "pseudo-inverse" adjoint vectors are represented as a

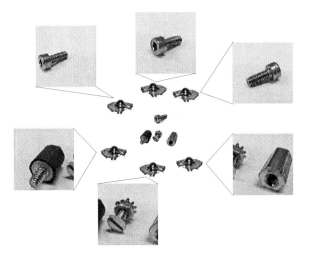

Figure 4.10: *Collective perception performed by a group of micro-robots. In the center there are four details, the particular view on these details from each robots is shown along the border.*

superposition of the transposed vectors $\underline{\underline{V}}^T$

$$\underline{\underline{V}}^{-1} = \underline{\underline{A}} \, \underline{\underline{V}}^T, \tag{4.32}$$

where $\underline{\underline{A}}$ is a matrix of coefficients. Taking into account that $\underline{\underline{V}}^{-1}\underline{\underline{V}} = \underline{\underline{I}}$ the matrix $\underline{\underline{A}}$ can be obtained as

$$\underline{\underline{A}} = [\underline{\underline{V}}^T\underline{\underline{V}}]^{-1}. \tag{4.33}$$

The matrix $[\underline{\underline{V}}^T\underline{\underline{V}}]$ represents a low-dimensional $p \times p$ matrix, that can be inverted without difficulties.

For the mode equation we take the system (4.22a) written in the following form

$$\xi_{n+1}^i = f_c(\xi_n^1, ..., \xi_n^p)(\xi_n^i - (\xi_n^i)^2) + (\xi_n^i)^2, \ i = 1, ..., p, \tag{4.34}$$

where f_c is a coupling function as the following polynomial

$$f_c = k_0 + \sum_{i=1}^{p} k_j \xi_n^j, \tag{4.35}$$

where k_0, k_i are coefficients (we use here the two-ways coupling ring). Calculating these coefficients, as shown in (Kornienko *et al.*, 2002b) and (Kornienko, 2007), we get the following coefficients

$$k_0 = 2, k_i = 1/2, k = -2, \tag{4.36}$$

where index i in k_i is equal to the number of equation, that the function (4.35) is inserted in. The rest of coefficients k is equal to one another and denoted simply as k. As a result we get the coupled system (4.34), where in long time dynamics only one of the variables is equal to one, whereas all other variables become equal to zero. This "one" variable corresponds to

(a)   (b)

Figure 4.11: **(a)** *A collective perception by six blind men of Indostan who try to learn what an elephant is (from famous Indian fable "The Blind Men and the Elephant"), image taken from (Ye et al., 2002);* **(b)** *Result of collective perception by six blind men, Elephant illustration (c)2002 Jason Hunt, www.naturalchild.org/jason.*

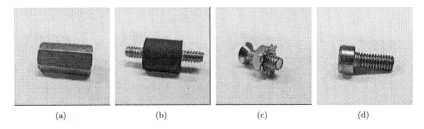

(a)   (b)   (c)   (d)

Figure 4.12: *Images used as spatial eigenvectors.*

a pattern (an image) that is recognized. The winning state variable ξ^i is defined by initial conditions, i.e. by the input image (one of images from Figure 4.10).

The system (4.34) describes a macroscopic behavior of common system in terms of variables ξ_n that correspond to global patterns (states). The winning variable determines the pattern that will be recognized at the end. However, separate agents do not observe this global pattern, they have only a segmented "view" and can work only with groups of pixels. In this way we need a system that will describe a process of pattern recognition from the agent's viewpoint, i.e. on microscopic level. Let q^i be such a pixel of a pattern. Collecting m-such fragments into a vector $\underline{q}$, we can write

$$\underline{q} = \underline{\underline{V}}_1\xi^1 + \underline{\underline{V}}_2\xi^2 + ... + \underline{\underline{V}}_p\xi^p = (\underline{\underline{V}}\,\underline{\xi}), \qquad (4.37)$$

where $\underline{\underline{V}}$ represents a stored pattern that consists of m components and p is the number of the stored patterns. Now we transform the system (4.34) from the "macroscopic" form into the "microscopic" one, using the transformation (4.37) and corresponding $\underline{\underline{V}}$, $\underline{\underline{V}}^{-1}$. Finally the system (4.34) yields

$$\underline{q}_{n+1} = \underline{\underline{V}}^{-1}[(k_0\underline{\underline{I}} + \underline{\underline{K}}\,\underline{\underline{V}}\,\underline{q}_n)(\underline{\underline{V}}\,\underline{q}_n - [\underline{\underline{V}}\,\underline{q}_n]^2)] + \underline{\underline{V}}^{-1}[\underline{\underline{V}}\,\underline{q}_n]^2, \qquad (4.38)$$

where the main diagonal of the matrix $\underline{\underline{K}}$ consists of the coefficients k_1, whereas all other elements are equal to k. In the equation (4.38) all operations in the square brackets should be performed in the component form, e.g. $[\underline{a}]^2 = (a_1^2, a_2^2, ...)$. The process of recognition in the

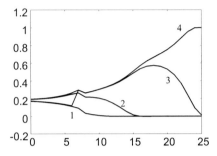

Figure 4.13: *Macroscopic selection dynamics of the system (4.34) representing competition of sensed images in collective perception. The number 1-4 correspond to the images (a)-(d) from Figure 4.12.*

"macroscopic" form as a selection dynamics is shown in Figure 4.13. The microscopic form of the recognition dynamics is shown in Figure 4.14. As initial values for recognition, i.e.

Figure 4.14: *Microscopic dynamics of collective perception. Shown are the values of q_n^i every 5 time steps ordered as 512×512 array.*

the input image, we can choose the average values of all partial images shown in Figure 4.10. In this way we can perform a collective recognition of the "most observed" object. Choosing the initial values q_0 in another way, we can correspondingly achieve other collective effect.

The presented example is of a bit idealized nature. So, we do not consider the invariance of images (e.g. the rotation and shift invariance, see (Haken, 1991)), many practical questions about implementation of communications remained outside the focus. However, this example has demonstrated that the purposeful functional self-organization with spatial eigenvectors can be very useful in many practical situations. The dynamics, determined by order parameter, can also be transferred into another coordinate basis, e.g. defined in terms of some functional constriction, like those shown in Figure 3.12. In this case we will observe completely different cooperative phenomena, however with the same principle: order parameters → coordinate transformations → collective phenomena.

4.3.7 Collective activity far away from instability

The self-organization phenomena can be determined and manipulated in many different ways. If it is viewed as a change in collective behavior, we can focus on the dynamics in the vicinity of corresponding instabilities. Applying the time scale hierarchy, the system's dynamics can be separated into "components", the slowest of which determines a local behavior. Thus, modifying this slowest component, we can influence the self-organization. More generally, self-organization represents ordered behavior of many autonomous elements (agents), where an activity of each agent is synchronized with a group activity. From this viewpoint, an emergence of ordered behavior becomes in the focus of consideration. In this case, the approaches based on the time scale hierarchy, become "less useful", because the system is far away from instability.

There are many approaches, dealing with dynamical systems in stationary states (fixed, periodical, quasi-periodical and even chaotic ones). Most of these approaches originate from the field of control theory that lies outside this work. Overview of some dedicated control mechanisms, applied to self-organization can be found in (Kornienko, 2007). Other, so-called "manifold approaches" deal with a dynamics from the viewpoint of invariant manifolds. Several earlier remarks on stable, central, unstable and central-stable, central-unstable manifold can be found in (Kelley, 1967). Further, we refer "manifold approaches" primarily to the well-known work of Carr (Carr, 1981).

In the next section we briefly demonstrate several main notions of global attracting manifolds, so-called global attractors, that can be applied to controlling self-organization. These global attractors determine a long-time dynamics of systems (with necessary and sufficient conditions for an existence of such an attractor (Yigitbasi, 1996)). Thus, the global attractor can be thought as of the order parameter that "slaves" a behavior of other components. We can use this invariant manifold in order to synchronize an activity of separated elements. In the following representation we introduce the global attracting manifolds, denoted as inertial manifold (Foias *et al.*, 1988). The inertial manifold can be introduced into system's dynamics so that to achieve a desired behavior of the whole system (this approach was first suggested by Kolesnikov (Kolesnikov, 1994)). The performed modifications (additional terms introduced into each subsystem) allow ordering a behavior of all elements and can be considered as additional macroscopic rules.

4.3.8 Global attracting manifolds

We start treatment of global attractor with two simple examples that represent a damped oscillator in linear (Arnold, 1983, p.121)

$$\dot{x} = y, \tag{4.39a}$$
$$\dot{y} = ay + bx, \tag{4.39b}$$

and nonlinear cases (Jetschke, 1989, p.105)

$$\dot{x} = y, \tag{4.40a}$$
$$\dot{y} = ay + bx - x^3, \tag{4.40b}$$

where $x, y \in N$, a and b are parameters. Eigenvalues and eigenvectors evaluated on zero stationary states $x_{st} = y_{st} = 0$ have the following form for both systems

$$\lambda_{1,2} = \frac{a \pm \sqrt{a^2 + 4b}}{2}, \quad \underline{\underline{V}} = (\underline{v}_1, \underline{v}_2) = \begin{pmatrix} 1 & 1 \\ \lambda_1 & \lambda_2 \end{pmatrix}, \tag{4.41}$$

If C_1, C_2 are arbitrary constants, the solution of the system (4.39) is given by

$$(x(t), y(t))^T = (C_1 e^{\lambda_1 t} \underline{v}_1 + C_2 e^{\lambda_2 t} \underline{v}_2) \tag{4.42}$$

At the condition $0 > \lambda_1 > \lambda_2$ the second term in rhs of (4.42) (connected with λ_2) decay faster then the first one (connected with with λ_1). It means that all solutions determined by (4.42) after some time will be attracted to the eigenvector $\underline{v}_1$. This time is determined by two factors: first, absolute value of both eigenvalues, and second a difference between eigenvalues. This statement can be exemplified by setting $a = -10/3$ and $b = -1$. Then $\lambda_1 = -1/3$, $\lambda_2 = -3$ and eigenvectors $(\underline{v}_1) = (v_{11}, v_{12}) = (-3, 1)$, $(\underline{v}_2) = (v_{21}, v_{22}) = (1, -3)$, that correspond to the lines $v_1 \rightarrow y = -1/3x$ and $v_2 \rightarrow y = -3x$. Phase diagram of the system (4.39) at these values of parameters a, b is shown in Figure 4.15(a). The behavior

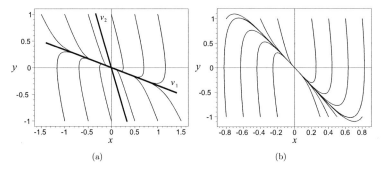

(a)   (b)

Figure 4.15: *The phase-diagram of:* **(a)** *the system (4.39), $a = -10/3$, $b = -1$;* **(b)** *the system (4.40), $a = -10$, $b = -15$;*

of nonlinear system (4.40) can be analyzed in the way shown e.g. in (Jetschke, 1989, p.105) or (Haken, 1983a, p.188). Equation (4.40b) can be solved by integration

$$y(t) = y(0)e^{at} + \int_0^t e^{a(t-\tau)}(bx(\tau) - x(\tau)^3)d\tau \tag{4.43}$$

and using partial integration $\int \dot{u}w \, d\tau = uw - \int u\dot{w} \, d\tau$ represents in the following form

$$y(t) = y(0)e^{at} - a^{-1}\left(e^{a(t-\tau)}(bx(\tau) - x(\tau)^3)|_0^t\right) + a^{-1}\int_0^t e^{a(t-\tau)}\left[\dot{x}_\tau(\tau)(b - 3x(\tau)^2)\right]d\tau \tag{4.44}$$

where $\dot{x} = y$ from (4.40a). Provided that $x(t)$ and $y(t)$ are continuously differentiable and monotone functions (as can see from Figure 4.15(b) it is true after some $t = \tilde{t}$), we can apply the mean value theorem for interval $[\tilde{t}, t]$

$$y(t) = y(0)e^{at} - a^{-1}\left(e^{a(t-\tau)}(bx(\tau) - x(\tau)^3)|_0^t\right) + a^{-1}\int_0^t e^{a(t-\tau)}\left[y(\tau)(b - 3x(\tau)^2)\right]d\tau +$$

$$+ a^{-1}\left[y(0)(b - 3x(0)^2)\right]\int_{\tilde{t}}^{\tilde{\tilde{t}}} e^{a(t-\tau)}d\tau + a^{-1}\left[y(t)(b - 3x(t)^2)\right]\int_{\tilde{t}}^t e^{a(t-\tau)}d\tau \tag{4.45}$$

and finally get

$$y(t) = y(0)e^{at} - a^{-1}\left[bx(t) - x(t)^3\right] + a^{-1}\left[bx(0) - x(0)^3\right]e^{at} +$$

$$+a^{-1}\int_0^{\tilde{t}} e^{a(t-\tau)}\left[y(\tau)(b - 3x(\tau)^2)\right]d\tau -$$

$$-a^{-2}\left[y(0)(b - 3x(0)^2)\right]\left(e^{a(t-\tilde{t})} - e^{at}\right) - a^{-2}\left[y(t)(b - 3x(t)^2)\right]\left(1 - e^{a(t-\tilde{t})}\right). \quad (4.46)$$

Now if we assume that $a \ll 0$ and $t > \tilde{t}$ the integral as well as all terms containing e^{at} in (4.46) can be neglected

$$y(t) = -a^{-1}\left[x(t)(b - x(t)^2)\right] - a^{-2}\left[y(t)(b - 3x(t)^2)\right]. \quad (4.47)$$

This expression coincides with an approximation shown in (Jetschke, 1989, p.106) for time $t \gg 1/a$. The formula (4.47) rewritten in the explicit form

$$y(t) = -a\frac{bx(t) - x(t)^3}{b - 2x(t)^2 + a^2} \quad (4.48)$$

approximately describes a dependence between variables x and y at the same time. For the parameter values $a = -10$, $b = -15$ the eigenvalues (4.41) for the system (4.40) evaluated on zero stationary states $x_{st} = y_{st} = 0$ are equal to $\lambda_{1,2} = -5 \pm \sqrt{10} \approx (-1.83, -8, 16)$. It means that the fixed point in the origin of coordinate system is stable, moreover after some $t > \tilde{t}$ a trajectory of motion to this fixed point is described by expression (4.48) as shown in Figure 4.15(b).

As shown in Figure 4.15, solutions of the systems (4.39), (4.40) are "attracted" to invariant manifolds and verge towards stable fixed points along these manifolds. Existence of these global attracting manifolds has two important consequences. Firstly, a dynamics of a high-dimensional system on this manifold is described by low-dimensional evolutional equations, i.e. a dimension of a system is reduced. This dimension reduction far away from an instability has applications not only for finite dimensional systems, but also for infinite dimensional ones.

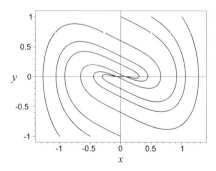

Figure 4.16: *The phase-diagram of the system (4.40), $a = -0.5$, $b = 0$.*

Secondly, when solutions land on the manifold, a relation between variables does not changes with time any more, i.e. variables became synchronized. Moreover, this synchronization can be exactly specified and used in distributed systems. The last remark concerns an existence of the invariant attracting manifold. This global attractor exists only by specific conditions. For example the system (4.40) at values $a = -0.5$, $b = 0$ (Figure 4.16) does not appear the effect shown in Figure 4.15. The necessary and sufficient conditions for existence of such an attractor are investigated by several authors (see e.g. (Eden *et al.*, 1994), (Constantin *et al.*, 1989), (Jarnik & Kurzweil, 1969)). The theory of inertial manifolds has many practical applications, for example the AKAR method, developed by A. Kolesnikov and utilized in the field of control theory (Kolesnikov, 1994).

4.4 Computational treatment of self-organization

4.4.1 Motivation

The previous sections of this chapter give a brief review of a few reductive approaches, unified by synergetic methodology. From this viewpoint, the interacting systems can be described by nonlinear equations of motion. The derived order parameter describes macroscopic changes, introduced by self-organization. The reductive modeling approach treats a dynamics of collective systems only in the dedicated regions, like instabilities or inertial manifolds. Within these regions, a dimension and complexity of these systems can be essentially reduced. This allows analyzing the dynamics, general forecasting and controlling a behavior. However, in many cases, SO phenomena do not demonstrate any observable macroscopic changes, as e.g. a behavior of cellular automata. Here *a complexity of collective phenomena cannot be reduced, because otherwise the macroscopic emergence will be lost.*

More generally, SO systems can possess such character and structures, that do not suppose a modeling and analysis in the suggested analytical way. Sometimes, the focus of investigation lies on such aspects of collective behavior, which cannot be modeled analytically. In these cases the reductive approach cannot be applied and we have to use computational techniques. *If we consider the whole dynamics of collective systems, for example from the viewpoint of emergent properties, we cannot reduce the complexity anymore. The emergent properties arise just due to high complexity of interacting systems. Therefore here, instead of predicting behavior by applying reductive techniques, we will predict it by applying computational approaches, i.e. by simulation.* Considering computational approaches, we return again to problem of modeling. Models, used in computational case, are either hybrid models, introduced in Section 2.4.3, or pure algorithmic models. Their dynamics can be determined by e.g. Petri Nets, as shown in Section 2.4.4. Thus, in a few next sections we consider computational (algorithmic) instruments, applied to creating functional self-organization. We demonstrate them, without lost of generality, on two practical examples, originated from industrial manufacturing, made in the framework of SFB 467 "Transformable Business Structures for Multiple-Variant Series Production", supported by the German Research Foundation.

4.4.2 Self-organization in autonomous systems

We consider algorithmic side of self-organization in relation to multi-agent systems as well as to more common class of autonomous systems. This generalization allows us to treat not only software systems (software agents), but also so-called hardware agents, like micro-robots from the I-SWARM project. We consider emergent properties of these systems in Section 5.7.2, whereas here we only point to some common ideas underlying an algorithmic treatment of self-organization.

The emergence in MAS has a form of "combinatorial" emergence (see e.g. (Cariani, 1997)). This point can be explained in the following way. The multi-agent system can be considered from a viewpoint of the theory of finite-state automata (Carroll & Long, 1989). Transition of m-states automaton (with or without memory, it does not change the matter) from one state to another is determined by some rules (by a program), therefore the automaton behaves in a completely deterministic way. If a control cycle is closed (see e.g. (Weiss, 1999)) the automaton is autonomous, i.e. behaves independently of environment (other automata). Now we consider a few such automata coupled into a system *in the way that keeps their autonomy*. Since each automaton behaves according to its own rules, there is no central program that determines a state transition for the whole system. As mentioned in Section 2.4.5, in the "worst case" coupling n automatons with m states, the coupled system can demonstrate m^n states.

Evidently this "worst case" has never to arise in the system, but how should the behavior of the distributed system be controlled without a central program (without a centralized mediator) ? The point is that all automata are continuously communicating in order to synchronize their own states in regard to environment, to the solving task, etc. (in this case, the notion of an automaton is replaced by the notion of an agent). The agents during communication "consider" all possible states and then "choose" such a state that is the most suitable to a current problem to be solved. This is the main difference to the "centralized programming" approach. With "centralized programming" the system can only react in such a way that was preprogrammed. For example 10 agents with 10 states can demonstrate 10^{10} different combinations. However, no programmer is able to predict all situations to use all these states. Thus, if the "centralized programming" approach is applied to a multi-agent system, it simply restricts its behavior, although there are essentially more abilities to react.

The sufficient number of degrees of freedom represents a key problem of the multi-agent technology. *On the one hand, if the system is hard restricted in the behavior, such advantages of MAS as flexibility, emergent behavior, self-organization and so on are lost. On the other hand, if the system has too many degrees of freedom it can communicate an infinitely long time without results.* In other words, in specific conditions only several combinations of agents states have a sense and the point is of how to achieve and to manage these states. This is a hard problem arising in many branches of science and engineering and correspondingly there are several ways to solve it. The solution suggested here is based on a hierarchic architecture of roles and emergencies that supports agent's autonomy.

Before starting to describe an approach, one methodological point concerning decentralization of multi-agent system needs to be mentioned, as shown in Figure 4.17. The MAS solves a problem by using some methodological basis. For example, the CSP and COP approaches basically underlie the solution of constraint problems. The point is that a methodological basis, in almost all cases, is formulated in a centralized way. It looks like a "battle plan", where all agents and their interactions are shown. Therefore this global description is often denoted an *interaction pattern*.

However, the agents do not possess such a global point of view and the interaction pattern has to be distributed among agents. This decentralization concerns global information, message transfer, synchronization, decision making and so forth. The decentralized description of the chosen method should determine an individual activity of an agent as well as its interactions with other agents. It is also important that all agents behave in the ordered way, i.e. this distributed description has to include cooperation mechanisms (protocols). In order to enable a transition from the interaction pattern to the *cooperation protocol* (see Figure 4.17), a notion of a role is introduced (Muscholl, 2001). A role is associated with a specific activity needed to be performed (according to a methodological basis). An agent can "play" one role or a sequence of roles. In this way, interactions are primarily determined between roles and an agent (with corresponding abilities) handles according to the

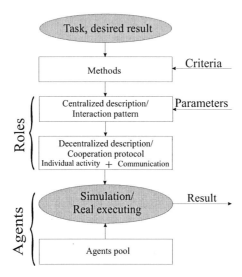

Figure 4.17: *Methodological approach towards agent-based applications.*

role being played at the moment. An advantage of this approach is that the centralized description (familiar for human thinking) is preserved, whereas the roles in the interaction pattern are "in fact" already distributed, i.e. a mapping "agent-on-role" may be performed in a formalized way by a program. Thus, an interaction pattern is a "mosaic image" that looks like a common picture (method) from afar, but considering it closely - it is a set of separate fragments (roles). Moreover, a concept of roles allows decoupling the structure of cooperation processes from agent organizations, so that any modification of agents does not affect the cooperation process and vice versa (Muscholl, 2001).

Thus, the self-organization in autonomous (MAS) system has many similarities with the "common self-organization", described e.g. by synergetics. Interaction patterns and cooperation protocols are equivalent to synergetic macroscopic and microscopic considera-tion's levels. Autonomy of an agent corresponds to the closed iterative cycle of each map in CML, interactions and communications correspond to couplings. Control parameters re-main control parameters in both cases. Therefore, general synergetic ideas (e.g. top-down, bottom-up strategies) can still be applied to the algorithmic self-organization.

Distinctive feature of algorithmic SO, emerged in autonomous systems, consists in a high degrees of freedom. This non-reductive complexity makes impossible applying the concepts of order parameter and slaving principle in more or less "direct" form. The procedure of collective decision making represents only one exception. The collective decision describes a change in collective behavior and therefore is in this sense an algorithmic "equivalent" of the order parameter (see more in (Kornienko, 2007)). Other distinctive features are sensors and actors. The famous Brooks saying "simulations are doomed to succeed" is closely related with skepticism towards simulation of real sensors and actors. These elements influence emergent properties of collective systems that are completely skipped in the analytic treat-ment of SO problems. Finally, we point to the problems of constraints as one of the hardest problems of SO in autonomous systems. This is also leaved out in analytic case. We discuss these problems more in details in Chapter 5.

4.4.3 Treatment of non-reductive complexity

The complexity of SO phenomena in algorithmic case cannot be reduced. We pointed out many time that a complexity in general represents some fundamental issue. It is closely related with our possibility of analysis. So, for example, W. Ross Ashby express this problem: "*when the complexity of the system exceeds the finite capacity of the scientist, the scientist can no longer understand the system ....*" (Ashby, 1958, p.97). This opinion also shared by M. Minsky in (Minsky, 1985). Some ideas about complexity and self-organization are expressed by e.g. F. Heylighen (Heylighen, 1996) and complexity and evolution by e.g. V. Turchin (Turchin, 1977). Aside many open theoretical questions we encounter pure practical one: how to treat non-reductive complexity in systems undergoing functional self-organization ?

As pointed out in the previous section, an emergence, and so a complexity, has a combinatorial character in multi-agent systems. The complexity appears in a high degree of freedom, that a system possesses. If the multi-agent system has to achieve an intended by designer result, it is necessary to control these degrees of freedom (especially at working in cooperation)! This is the main problem of developing the coordination and cooperation mechanisms for multi-agent systems. If the number of degrees of freedom is too high, the agents can negotiate a long time without any progress. The system becomes non-controllable in this case. Otherwise, if the number of degrees of freedom is too low, the flexibility, emergent properties and other advantages of artificial SO, mentioned in Section 3.5.4, are lost. Achieving a reasonable compromise between complexity and useful emergent properties represents one of the most important points at developing the multi-agent systems.

Performing experiments, we remarked, that a complexity of system and a complexity of problem to be solved are closely interrelated. The system (we consider here primarily planning systems) transits from one state to another. We can calculate/determine the expected next state. The disturbance (the problem to be solved) declines the system from this expected state. *We state that the complexity of system depends on a deviation from the expected state. The larger is this deviation, the more degrees of freedom have to be involved to absorb this deviation.* Depending on a deviation, we can distinguish between regular and irregular process. A regular process consists of some "stereotyped", preplanned activities with a small number of involved unknown values. In contrast, an irregular process means a deviation from a plan, where many new activities are involved and this process, as a consequence, possesses many degrees of freedom. The ideas, underlying the planed state and a deviation from this state, will be developed further in Chapter 5.

Depending on the complexity of disturbances, we can control the number of involved degrees of freedom required to adsorb this disturbance. This systematic way is shown in Figure 4.18. As mentioned in the previous section, the interaction pattern determines a *primary activity* (primary algorithm) of the multi-agent system. The primary algorithm also includes some parameters, whose modifications can be commonly associated with disturbances (expected disturbances). A variation of these parameters does not disturb the activity of agents. A reaction of the system on the expected disturbances is incorporated into the primary algorithm (forecasted and preprogrammed). However, due to specific disturbances, every agent can reach such a state that is not described by the primary algorithm and where performing the next step is not possible. As shown in Figure 4.18, the agent switches in this case to the *local emergency state* and tries to resolve the arisen situation alone or with the assistance of neighboring agents (*secondary activity*). If the abilities of

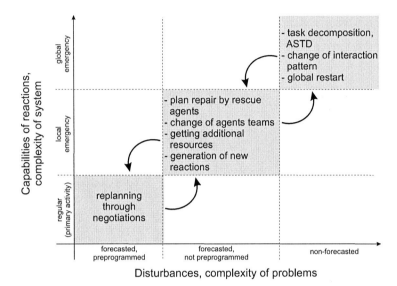

Figure 4.18: *The systematic way to control a complexity of systems.*

an agent are not sufficient or it requires additional resources, it calls a rescue agent. The rescue agent is an agent that possesses specific (usually hardware) abilities. The aim of agents in the local emergency state is to change a part of the primary algorithm so that to adapt it to disturbances. The disturbances, causing local emergency, are predicted, but their handling is not introduced into the primary algorithm (i.e. they are forecasted, but not preprogrammed).

The primary algorithm as well as its parametrization is optimal only for specific conditions (see Section 4.4.4.3) (e.g. combinatorial/heuristic methods for solutions of combinatorial problems, CSP/COP for constraints, etc.). If disturbances change these conditions, the primary algorithm may become non-optimal and it has no sense to repair it. All agents have collectively to recognize such a global change and to make a collective decision towards replacement of the primary algorithm. This change corresponds to a global emergency. The disturbances causing the global emergency are not expected (predicted), however they influence the conditions of primary algorithms and in this way can be recognized. Finally, such disturbances, that cannot be absorbed by any change of an algorithm, remain irresolvable.

The main advantage of the concept of roles and emergencies is that an interaction pattern, defined macroscopically, can involve a huge number of roles (even more than it is required for executing primary plan), that are already *consistent with each other*. The detailed, microscopic description of every role in the cooperation protocol (i.e. a program for an agent) can be generated automatically. Depending on its own conditions and abilities, an agent *can execute every role in the interaction pattern*. In this way, *the MAS's degrees of freedom become bounded, but not restricted* to only one type of activity. So, a complexity of the problem remains *tractable*. If this number of degrees of freedom is insufficient for an adaptation of the planning approach, the system stepwise increases it in different emergency states, until the disturbance will be absorbed or stated as irresolvable under existing conditions. This process enables to control emergent properties of the whole MAS in the framework of functional SO. Now we describe the mentioned primary algorithm as well as emergency states in the language of cooperative processes on the example of manufacturing planning.

4.4.4 Functional self-organization in manufacturing planning

[3] As already mentioned in Section 4.4.1, it is difficult to treat computational aspects of algorithmic SO in pure theoretical way. Therefore we introduce the example originated from manufacturing planning, developed within the framework of SFB 467 (Sonderforschungbereich) *"Transformable Business Structures for Multiple-Variant Series Production"*. The problems, demonstrated here, have a specific form and require some "non-standard" approaches to be solved. The suggested self-organizing mechanisms can be applied not only to the shown example, but also to a wide spectrum of other similar problems in autonomous systems.

The introduced example concerns manufacturing systems. In the modern world, competition among international suppliers and globalization of national markets requires production systems that can successfully operate in this global and quickly changing market (e.g. (Wiendahl, 2002)). From this viewpoint there are several requirements that should be satisfied by these systems. Firstly, the time needed from development of a product to its serial production should be essentially shortened. Secondly, manufacturing systems should become oriented to a multitude of parts and variants of customer requirements. This means a product will be fabricated in small series with different consumer properties, like color, equipment and so forth. Moreover, a product should often be fabricated on the demand of a client with a unique specification (Peeters *et al.*, 1998), achieving the aim of mass customization (Pine, 1999). All these requirements may only be satisfied by flexible, quickly reconfigurable production systems. Not only the physical fabrication should be flexible (equipped with e.g. reconfigurable machinery), but also all operational, executive and developing processes of modern production systems. For such a factory a completely new structure, new organizational principles and, correspondingly, new software and hardware instruments should be developed (Bussmann & Schild, 2000).

Taking into account a spatial distribution of manufacturing elements and the requirement of flexibility to the whole system, the concept of autonomous agents has found some applications in this field (Weiss, 1999). Moreover:

- activity of agents is a result of the group behavior that bases on different forms of negotiations among agents. Because of this specific form of "programming", the problem solving (decision making, planning, etc.) in a multi-agent system (MAS) has essentially more degrees of freedom, than in traditional centralized systems. The negotiation-based MAS planning system becomes more flexible and, in this way, more "stable" to different predicted and (sometimes unpredicted) disturbances, e.g. machine failures, technological changes etc.;

- there is a trend to equip processing elements (processing machines) with some degree of autonomy and "intelligence", allowing them to react to short-term disturbances, perform self-maintenance and integrate to autonomous manufacturing. This trend

---

[3] *This section represents the example developed in collaboration between author and O. Kornienko, J. Priese within the SFB 467, see (Kornienko et al., 2004c). Based on this example, we demonstrate in the following subsections the results, obtained by author. The external parts, whose assist to understand this example, are cited in each case separately.*

corresponds to the agent concept, in this way the processing element becomes an agent;

- in some situations (e.g. hazardous and dangerous environments) a human worker needs to be replaced in modern manufacturing. The replacement element should have a behavior similar to human, i.e. it should be autonomous, make decisions and communicate with human or non-human workers.

Application of the agents to manufacturing requires also a development of new approaches towards typical problems of multi-agent technology, such as distributed problem solving, planning or collective decision making (Sandholm, 1996). The following agent-oriented application is addressed to the lowest level of manufacturing architecture, where the low-level jobs (for example "to produce one workpiece with a defined specification") should be assigned to available machines. The aim is to generate this assignment via agents that represent different factory departments as well as processing elements.

The main point of the discussion is the flexibility of planning systems ensured by the concept of agent's "roles" and "emergencies". Depending on the state of "emergency", the system gradually receives additional degrees of freedom to adapt the planning to the changing conditions of the manufacturing floor. The distributed constraint satisfaction and optimization approaches, underlying the solution of the assignment problem, as well as activities of rescue agents, are described in the form of Petri Nets providing both the conceptual notions and main details of implementation.

The assignment problem is often encountered in manufacturing. It is a part of Operations Research / Management Science (OR/MS), where the flow-shop and job-shop problems with deterministic, stochastic, one-step or many-steps characters are distinguished (Dörrsam, 1999). Generally, the assignment problem can be classified into scheduling, resource allocation and planning of operation order (e.g. (Pinedo, 1995)). This is a classical NP-hard problem, there are known solutions by combinatorial optimization (Graves *et al.*, 1993), dynamical optimization (Haken *et al.*, 1999), evolutionary approaches (Blazewicz *et al.*, 1996), constraint satisfaction and optimization (Alicke, 1999) as well as discrete dynamic programming (Bellman & Dreyfus, 1962). However, these methods are developed as central planning approaches, the distributed or multi-agents planning for the assignment problem has in fact not been investigated (overview e.g. in (Durfee, 1999)).

The following scenario is based on a flexible manufacturing system (FMS). This kind of production system is especially suitable for implementation of the agent-based process planning as a consequence of the high level of flexibility and technological abilities of FMS. FMSs are the networks of machines with some or completely equal abilities, being able to manufacture the same production tasks. They are also able to process continuously and synchronously several workpieces in different manufacturing processes without retooling.

The typical design of a FMS is shown in Figure 4.19 which exemplifies the presented approach. The main properties are three machining centers, a transport system, clamping places, buffer places and storages for workpieces and tools. Additionally, the system possesses control and communication parts. The simulation of this flexible manufacturing system by using Delmia © Quest^{TM} is shown in Figure 4.20. In this example, all machines have partly equal abilities, but no machine is suitable to handle all production orders on its own. Figure 4.21 shows an exemplary working plan with the corresponding working steps and a drawing of the workpiece.

In the considered example the FMS has to manufacture a multitude of parts and variants of production orders (see Table 4.1). In total there are 5 types of workpieces (5-20 pieces of each type) that have to be manufactured on available machines. Table 4.2 shows the

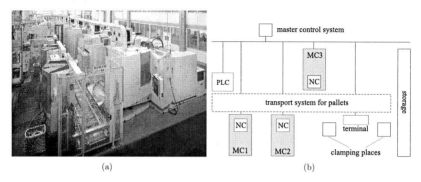

Figure 4.19: **(a)** *Example of a real flexible manufacturing system (FMS) (courtesy of Heller Maschinenfabrik GmbH);* **(b)** *Layout of FMS used in the presented work, where NC is a numerical control, PLC is a programmable logic controller, and MC is a machine center. This Figure is taken from (Kornienko et al., 2004c).*

sequence of working steps for the workpiece of type A, where all mentioned technological constraints are already considered.

piece type	N of pieces of each type	technology/ N of steps	N avail. of machines
A	5	Table A/11	3
B	15	Figure 4.21/14	3
C	10	7	4
D	20	10	2
E	5	5	3

Table 4.1: *Types, pieces and machines in the assignment problem. Technological restrictions required for workpieces of type A and B are shown in Table 4.2 and in Figure 4.21 correspondingly. This Table is taken from (Kornienko et al., 2004c).*

Processing of each workpiece consists of several working steps (defined by a technological process), all these working steps cannot be processed on one machine. Each from the working steps has different length and also cost. Moreover, each type of workpiece has its own technology, i.e. its processing consists of different working steps. For simplification it is assumed that available machines are of the same type, therefore the cost and length of the same working step do not differ on these machines (in the general case they are different). The aim is to generate a plan of how to manufacture these workpieces with minimal cost, minimal time (or other optimization criteria), taking into account the restrictions summarized in Tables 4.1 and 4.2. Because of these restrictions, this problem belongs to the so-called constraint class of problems, where, firstly, an optimization landscape is discrete (small islands on the landscape), secondly, there is no continuous gradient. As suggested by some authors, this problem can be separated into a constraints satisfaction problem (CSP) and constraints optimization problem (COP). In the given work this methodological way is used.

Let us denote a working step as WS_j^i, where i is the type of workpiece and j the number of the working step. An available machine is denoted as M_k, where k is the number of

Figure 4.20: *Simulation of the flexible manufacturing system by using Delmia © Quest^{TM}.*

machine. We also need to introduce a piece P_n^m, where m is the priority of production and n is the number of this piece. In this way $st(P_n^m(WS_j^i))$, $fn(P_n^m(WS_j^i))$ denotes the start and end positions of the corresponding working step that belongs to the corresponding piece $(st(WS_j^i), fn(WS_j^i)$ for all pieces). We start with the definition of these values

$$P_{n\in[1-20]}^{m\in[1-20]}(WS_{j\in[1,...,11]}^{i\in\{A,B,C,D,E\}}) = o \in operation, \tag{4.49}$$

$$M_{k\in\{1,2,3,4\}} = \{o \in operation\}, \tag{4.50}$$

$$st(P_n^m(WS_j^i)) = \{t \geq 0, t \in R\}, \tag{4.51}$$

$$fn(P_n^m(WS_j^i)) = \{st(P_n^m(WS_j^i)) + length(P_n^m(WS_j^i))\}. \tag{4.52}$$

The first constraint determines a correspondence between operations of working step and of the k-machine

$$C_1 = \{(o_1, o_2)|o_1 \in P_n^m(WS_j^i), o_2 \in M_k, o_1 = o_2\}. \tag{4.53}$$

The technological restrictions given by the Table 4.2 (for all workpieces of type A) can be rewritten in the following form

$$C_2 = \{(fn(WS_{[1]}^A) < st(WS_{[2-6]}^A)) \subset WS_j^A \times WS_j^A\}, \tag{4.54}$$

$$C_3 = \{(fn(WS_{[2-6]}^A) < st(WS_{[7]}^A)) \subset WS_j^A \times WS_j^A\}, \tag{4.55}$$

$$C_4 = \{(fn(WS_{[7]}^A) < st(WS_{[8-11]}^A)) \subset WS_j^A \times WS_j^A\}, \tag{4.56}$$

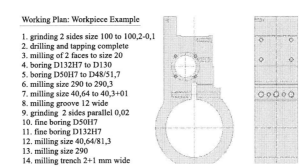

Figure 4.21: *Working steps for manufacturing the workpiece B (see Table 4.1). This Figure is taken from (Kornienko et al., 2004c).*

working step	length/mach. 1	length/mach. 2	length/mach. 3	order
1	1	0	1	1
2	2	0	2	2
3	0	1	1	2
4	3	0	3	2
5	1	1	0	2
6	2	2	2	2
7	0	1	1	3
8	3	0	3	4
9	2	0	2	4
10	1	1	0	4
11	1	1	1	4

Table 4.2: *Technological Table A for workpiece type A. Zero in a length (of a working step) at corresponding machine means that this machine cannot perform the requested operation. Order of working steps means, that e.g. the steps 2,3,4,5,6 should be produced after the step 1 and before the step 7. It is natural to assume these steps cannot be performed at the same time on different machines. This Table is taken from (Kornienko et al., 2004c).*

where $WS^A_{[2-6]}$ (for all pieces) cannot be performed at the same time

$$C_5 = \{(j \in [st(WS^A_{[w]}), ..., fn(WS^A_{[w]})] \neq j \in [st(WS^A_{[w']}), ..., fn(WS^A_{[w']})])$$
$$\subset WS^A_j \times WS^A_j; w, w' = 2, 3, 4, 5, 6; w \neq w'\}$$
$$(4.57)$$

and also $WS^A_{[8-11]}$

$$C_6 = \{(j \in [st(WS^A_{[w]}), ..., fn(WS^A_{[w]})] \neq j \in [st(WS^A_{[w']}), ..., fn(WS^A_{[w']})])$$
$$\subset WS^A_j \times WS^A_j; w, w' = 8, 9, 10, 11; w \neq w'\}.$$
$$(4.58)$$

Priority of production can be expressed by

$$C_7 = \{(m \in P^m_n > m \in P^m_{n'}|st(P^m_n(WS^A_j)) > st(P^m_{n'}(WS^A_j)))$$
$$\subset P^m_n \times P^m_n, n \neq n'\}.$$
$$(4.59)$$

As soon as the variables, the domains of values and constraints are defined, a propagation approach can be started. The aim is to restrict the values of variables (or to find such

143

values of variables) that will satisfy all constraints. This propagation can be represented in the way shown in Figure 4.22. All working steps, that belong to the same workpiece,

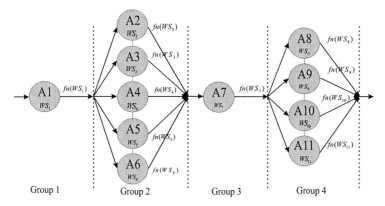

Figure 4.22: *Constraint network for the assignment problem. This Figure is taken from (Kornienko et al., 2004c).*

build a sequence. Each node in this sequence gets a "finish"-position of a working step from the previous node. Using this value, a current node looks for "start"-positions of the next working step that satisfy local constraints, calculates "finish"-positions and propagates them to the next node. If no position satisfying the local constraints can be found, the node requests another "finish"-position from the previous node. Thus, the network can determine locally consistent positions of all working steps. After that, the obtained values should be tested for a global consistence.

As mentioned, the main problem of process planning consists in often arisen disturbances (like machine malfunctions or urgent production orders). Several types of these disturbances is shown in Table 4.3. Therefore the goal of planning approach is not only to generate in

Disturbances on:	Example	Reaction
management level	aims, appointments, deadlines	long-term middle-term
organizational level	orders, lot size, urgent order	short-term
technological level	product-technology process-technology	middle-term long-term
resources level	machines, supplies	short-term

Table 4.3: *Several types of disturbances. This Table is taken from (Kornienko et al., 2004c).*

distributed way an optimized plan satisfying all restriction but also to do it in presence of different disturbances. The next section is devoted to application of multi-agent technology to this problem.

4.4.4.1 The primary activity

In the case of an assignment planning, the primary algorithm is determined by the CS approach described in Section 4.4.4 (generally usage of constraint-based approaches for MAS is not new, see e.g. (Nareyek, 2001)). Each working step in the approach is represented by a node in the constraint network, shown in Figure 4.22. These nodes are separated from one another, moreover their behavior is determined by propagations. Therefore it is natural to give a separate role to each node. However, before starting a propagation, this network has to be created and parameterized by technology, machines, number of workpieces and so on. These two steps (parametrization and propagation) will be described by interaction patterns using corresponding roles.

As already mentioned, the primary algorithm consists of two parts, parametrization and propagation, that represent a linear sequence of activities. The parametrization part, shown in Figure 4.23, has three phases p_0, p_1, p_2 whose main result consists of determining a structure, neighborhood relations and parametrization of nodes of the constraint network. The roles γ_0, γ_1 are "Initializers" of WS-order and WS-nodes correspondingly. The role γ_0

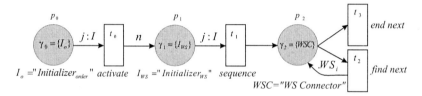

Figure 4.23: *Primary algorithm: Parametrization part.*

is activated by the first production order. This role reads resource-objects and determines how many nodes (WS-roles) are required. The transition t_0 proves, whether the result of $j.returnEND()$ is true (action is successful) and activates γ_1 with the parameter n as the number of required nodes. The γ_1 initializes each node according to all restrictions (technology, propagation rules, number of machines and so on). If this activity is also successful (transition t_1), the third role γ_2 is activated. It connects the created nodes (return a pointer to previous node), composing in this way a network. This interaction plan is finished (transition t_3) if no further nodes exist that are needed to be connected.

The propagation part, shown in Figure 4.24, consists of three blocks: local (the phases p_3, p_4, p_5) and global (the phase p_6) propagations and an activity (the phase p_7) in the case of empty sets. The roles γ_3, γ_5 determine the propagation in the first and the last nodes, whereas γ_4 does the same for all other nodes. The transition t_7 verifies, whether the local propagation was successful for all nodes and activates the global propagation in γ_6. We emphasize that the local propagation requires a sequential execution of the roles, whereas in global propagation all roles can be executed in parallel. Finally, the transition t_9 proves, whether the values set (WS-positions) of each node is empty. In the case of empty sets the role γ_7 tries to increase initial areas of values, first locally in neighbour nodes, then globally by the restart of the local propagation. Descriptions of phases and transitions from Figures 4.23, 4.24 are collected in Tables 4.4 and 4.5.

Considering these interaction patterns, we see they include several parameters (e.g. number of available machines, time slot, technology etc.), that can appear as expected disturbances. Moreover, these patterns can hierarchically include such activities, that are not directly connected with a CSP problem, e.g. control and optimization of logistical opera-

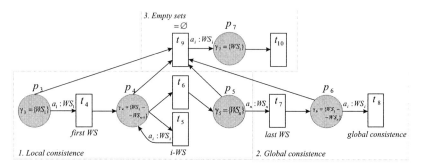

Figure 4.24: *Primary algorithm: Propagation part.*

tions. Consequently the MAS, even in the phase of primary activity, has enough degrees of freedom to behave adaptively. As followed from the experiments with the planning system, approximately 90% of all one-step, short-term disturbances and 30%-40% one-step, middle-term disturbances can be absorbed in the primary phase.

4.4.4.2 The local emergency and rescue agents

As mentioned, an agent performs some activities, whose results are tested by the transition. The local emergency arises, when the results at transitions are of such a type, which cannot be processed by this transition. The local emergency arises also when there are generally no results. In both cases an agent cannot finish a current role and execution of a common interaction pattern is stopped. The local emergency has a natural analogy in real manufacturing. The manufacturing can be disordered by failures, by absence of resources, by fire and so forth. In each case the reason of disorder is different, however, the classification enables to react on a disorder in some predicted way. In each case there is a schema of how to react, e.g. at fire alarm. The interaction patterns of local emergency are similar to these schemes, where specific resources/abilities, like a fire brigade, are represented by rescue agents.

The agent, playing a role, cannot perform recognition of an emergency. For this aim a so-called *activity guard* agent is needed, whose macroscopic interaction pattern is shown in Figure 4.25. In phase p_0 it observes an execution of agent's activities and in the case either the "wrong type of variables" or "time out" messages at transition occur the guard agent activates the phase p_1. Here, the concept of the error-return-code (ERC) is utilized, that allows identification of the arisen problem. A typical example of the basic ERC is I/O messages known in each programming language. Each activity, performed by an agent, is equipped with a set of ERCs, including resource-ERC, activity-ERC and so forth. Based on this returned code, a specific problem solving process can be started. If an ERC is returned, the phase p_2 is activated, otherwise the software-rescue agent (role γ_3) is called. The problem solving process in phase p_2 requires specific resources and abilities. If a current agent possesses these, this agent (roles γ_2, γ_4) resolves the problem. Otherwise a specialized rescue agent (role γ_5) with the required abilities will be called. The roles γ_2, γ_4 represent in turn the interaction patterns of a complex nature that are hierarchically called when the corresponding role is activated. The problem types used for the assignment of rescue agents are summarized in the Table 4.6. The interaction pattern for the problem-oriented rescue

Phase	Roles
$p_0, \gamma_0 = \{(I)Initializer_{order}\}$	$I = (D_r = \{services\}, \underline{z} = (objects),$ $act = < initialize.object,$ $technology.getNumberOfWS >)$
$p_1, \gamma_1 = \{(I)Initializer_{WS}\}$	$I = (D_r = \{services\}, \underline{z} = (objects),$ $act = < initialize.WS_i >)$
$p_2, \gamma_2 = \{(WSC)WS-$ $-Connector\}$	$WSC = (D_r = \{services\}, \underline{z} = (objects),$ $act = < find.next(a_i) >)$
$p_3, \gamma_3 = \{WS_1\}$	$WS_1 = (D_r = \{planning\}, \underline{z} = (positions),$ $act = < WS_1.sendV, WS_1.calculateL >)$
$p_4, \gamma_4 = \{WS_i\}$	$WS_i = (D_r = \{planning\}, \underline{z} = (positions),$ $act = < WS_i.sendV, WS_i.calculateL >)$
$p_5, \gamma_5 = \{WS_n\}$	$WS_n = (D_r = \{planning\}, \underline{z} = (positions),$ $act = < WS_n.sendV, WS_n.sendG, WS_n.calculateL >)$
$p_6, \gamma_6 = \{WS_1, ..., WS_n\}$	$WS_i = (D_r = \{planning\}, \underline{z} = (positions),$ $act = < WS_i.calculateG >)$
$p_7, \gamma_7 = \{WS_i\}$	$WS_i = (D_r = \{planning, services\}, \underline{z} = (positions),$ $act = < WS_i.send >)$

Table 4.4: *Description of phases in cooperation patterns shown in Figures 4.23, 4.24.*

roles is not described, because their reaction is evident and moreover they depend on the implementation details.

However, in the case of a "time out" error, an agent cannot form an error-return-code. This situation points to the case, when an agent cannot accomplish an internal activity cycle not because of the absence of resources (i.e. problem-oriented emergency), but because of internal confusion in an agent's program. In this case the software-rescue (SR) agent should be called. The first aim of the SR-agent is to prove an internal structure of an agent in relation to current data from sensors and communications. This can point to internal software errors. The second aim is to ascertain the problems in external activity that lead to the "time out" emergency.

The idea of the SR agent is based on the autonomy cycle, shown in Figure 4.26. The autonomy cycle represents the common steps that any agent cyclically executes. If there is an emergency of this kind, it means a problem has arisen on some of these steps. The SR agent simulates the distorted role (roles) first with ideal input/output data. When this simulation is successful, the SR-agent replaces stepwise each input/output with real ones, until the problem is brought to light. However, there exists one critical point concerning the reaction of the SR-agent on the detected problem. Generally, any problem on this step means, that the agent does not correspond to the environment. The adequate reaction of the SR-agent can include activity to modify the agent or its environment. Modification of the environment can be performed either by a specific rescue agent or simply by sending a message to operator, however, a modification of the internal program structure of an agent causes several problems. This step includes developing a program generator that will be briefly discussed in the next section. In the given implementation, this problem still remains unresolved and the SR-agent reacts on the problem only by sending a corresponding error-message.

T	Description
	$\sigma(p_0, t_0) = (j : I)$, $\sigma(t_0) = j.returnEND$,
t_0	$\sigma(t_0, p_1) = n \leftarrow j.numberOfWS$
	$\sigma(p_1, t_1) = (j : I, \forall a_i : WS)$, $\sigma(t_1, p_2) = a_i \leftarrow pointer(WS_i)$,
t_1	$\sigma(t_1) = j.returnEND(1) \; \& \; ... \; \& \; j.returnEND(n)$
	$\sigma(p_2, t_2) = (j : WSC, \forall a_i : WS)$, $\sigma(t_2) = j.returnNext$
t_2	$\sigma(t_2, p_3) = \{i + +, a_i \leftarrow pointer(a_{i-1})\}$
t_3	$\sigma(p_3, t_3) = (j : WSC)$, $\sigma(t_3) = !j.returnNext$
	$\sigma(p_3, t_4) = (\forall a_i : WS)$, $\sigma(t_4) = a_1.retValues \neq \emptyset$,
t_4	$\sigma(t_4, p_4) = \lambda \leftarrow a_1.retValues$
	$\sigma(p_4, t_5) = (\forall a_i : WS, \lambda : Positions)$, $\sigma(t_5) = a_i.retValues \neq \emptyset \; \& \; i < n$,
t_5	$\sigma(t_5, p_4) = \{\lambda \leftarrow a_i.retValues, i + +\}$
	$\sigma(p_4, t_6) = (\forall a_i : WS, \lambda : Positions)$, $\sigma(t_6) = a_n.retValues \neq \emptyset$,
t_6	$\sigma(t_6, p_5) = \lambda \leftarrow a_i.retValues$
	$\sigma(p_5, t_7) = (\forall a_i : WS)$, $\sigma(t_7) = a_n.retValues \neq \emptyset$,
t_7	$\sigma(t_7, p_6) = \forall a_i \leftarrow "FinishLocal"$
t_8	$\sigma(p_6, t_8) = (\forall a_i : WS)$, $\sigma(t_8) = a_i.retValues \neq \emptyset$
	$\sigma(\{p_3, p4, p5, p6\}, t_9) = (\forall a_i : WS)$, $\sigma(t_9) = a_i = \emptyset$,
t_9	$\sigma(t_9, p_7) = i \leftarrow a_i$
t_{10}	$\sigma(p_7, t_{10}) = (\forall a_i : WS)$, $\sigma(t_{10}) = a_i.returnEND$

Table 4.5: *Description of transitions in cooperation patterns shown in Figures 4.23, 4.24.*

Type of spec. rescue agent (RA)	Type of problem	Input parameter	Type of reaction
Input resource RA	absent	type of resources	to supply
Output resource RA	absent	type of resources	to supply
Object-availability RA	not available	object	to provide
Technology RA	not executable	working step,object	to replace
Software RA	not responded	agent	simulation

Table 4.6: *Types of specialized rescue agents.*

4.4.4.3 The global emergency

A global emergency arises, when the multi-agent system is no longer able to follow the primary algorithm and to react adequately on the emerged disturbances. The disturbances causing the global emergency cannot be nearly identified, however, they can be recognized by the effects left over. Firstly, they disturb the global criteria underlying methodological approach so that it is no longer valid or, secondly, a local emergency is not resolvable even by rescue agents.

In the first case the disturbances achieve some qualitative threshold that completely disturbs the primary algorithm. For example, if the technology will be changed so that most of the restrictions will disappear. This leads to an agent's state space, such that after the CS approach is equal (or almost equal) to initial space, i.e. the original methodological assumption is no longer valid. The mentioned disturbances have a global nature that influences all agents. In order to recognize this effect, all agents have to perform a negotiation and to make a collective decision (Kornienko, 2007).

The second reason, causing global emergency, is an irresolvable local emergency. Before declaring a state to be generally non-resolvable, an agent (even a rescue agent) trans-

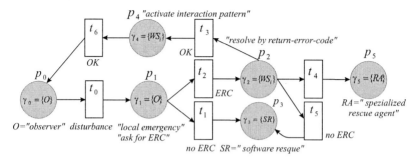

Figure 4.25: *Macroscopic interaction plan for local emergency.*

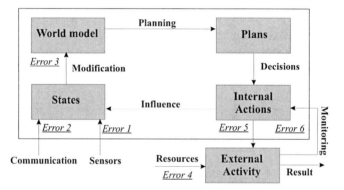

Figure 4.26: *Autonomy cycle of an agent (see Figure 2.1) with corresponding ERC. "Error 1" - wrong type of sensor data, "error 2" - this type of communication data is not expected, "error 3" - world model does not support the input data, "error 4" - wrong type of resources, "error 5" - external activity is not responded, "error 6" - wrong type of external activity.*

fers information about the problem to other agents in hoping they have the needed resources/abilities and can solve the problem. This solution may have also a local or global form. In the local case another agent takes over the solution of the problem that is equivalent to the local emergency discussed in the previous section. The global form means the mentioned global change.

Now, the point is of what kind of global change is required by a global emergency in the agent group ? If the methodological approach is no longer valid or the agents, using all current interaction pattern, are not able to resolve the arisen problem, it is natural to change this interaction pattern. However, the question is which new interaction pattern should arise (and of no lesser importance - how should it arise) ? Generally, there are two possibilities, either to use pre-formulated interaction patterns or to generate this pattern dynamically by request. The generation of an interaction pattern represents a separate topic involving software-specific questions (e.g. language semantics, parsers and so on) and treatment of more general algorithms of tasks decomposition. One such algorithm, so-called algorithm of symbolic tasks decomposition (ASTD, see Section 5.7.4) based on

149

some synergetic properties of collective systems, has been already developed and is being tested for manufacturing-specific problems (Kornienko *et al.*, 2004e). Treatment of such a generator, because of the complexity of this issue, represents the focus of a separate work.

However, several cases of global emergency in the planning approach can be covered by the reserve interaction patterns (see Table 4.7). If the measures undertaken in the case

Type of problem	Consequence	Resolving
number of technological restriction is highly reduced	state space overflow, CS approach fails	use combinatorial optimization
frequent disturbances, especially in resources	frequent replanning, irregular filling of production's queue	send corresponding message
frequently unavailable communication	propagation fails	restart of network components

Table 4.7: *Problems causing global emergency and their resolution.*

of a global emergency are insufficient and do not lead to resolution of the problem, the multi-agent system declares the current state as irresolvable.

4.4.4.4 Discussion of results

The discussion includes two main points that concern a classification of disturbances and remarks towards planning approach. Turbulences, as suggested in (SFB467, 2001), can be classified into four main groups: management, organizational, technological and resource ones. From the viewpoint of multi-agent system these disturbances can be expected and included into the primary algorithm. Disturbances represent in this case some external parameters that control a planning process. Next, disturbances can be predicted, but, however, not included into the primary algorithm, because they occurs seldom and have a specific nature. These disturbances generally causes the local emergency. The group of unexpected disturbances is also divided into two parts by their effect. If the effect of disturbances changes several global parameters, the system can absorb them by equivalent global changes. The rest of unexpected disturbances builds the last group of irresolvable disturbances. Correspondence between the disturbances and reaction of the multi-agent system is shown in Table 4.8 (additionally to Table 4.3).

Disturbances on:	Example	Type of reaction time
management level	aims, appointments, deadlines	not expected, not included expected but not included
organizational level	orders, lot size, urgency	expected and included
technological level	product-technology process-technology	expected but not included not expected, not included
resources level	machines, supplies	expected and included

Table 4.8: *Equivalence between disturbances and a reaction of multi-agent system, additionally to Table 4.3.*

In the performed simulations we have reproduced the most typical disturbances arising in real manufacturing (SFB467, 2002/2003), to test the MAS planning system. *These disturbances are introduced after the planning phase and immediately before manufacturing, as well as during the manufacturing phase.* In the last case replanning takes into account the already manufactured part of the distorted plan, and so the MAS-based planning in fact accompanies a manufacturing process. As it turned out, the system is stable to almost all one-step, short-terms disturbances (except exotic ones like "a supply is completely broken down"). The majority of one-step, middle-term disturbances can be also successfully treated, but it depends on the abilities of the rescue agents. Generally, the more abilities that are delegated to the agents, the wider the spectrum of disturbances that can be automatically absorbed. However, the great problem arises at many-steps disturbances (several disturbances simultaneously or in a short time slot, so that they nonlinearly influence each other). We suppose the complexity of such a problem oversteps, in many cases, today's possibilities of algorithmic problem solving. For the long-term disturbances the system has been not tested. A pair of obtained assignment plans are shown in Figure 4.27.

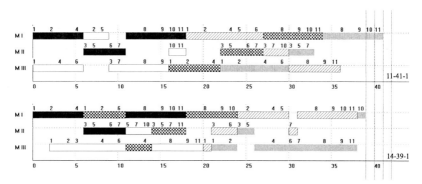

Figure 4.27: *Two assignments of with different length and transportation costs.*

The presented approach integrates a process planning and manufacturing control in the multi-agent way. On the one hand, utilizing the concept of roles and emergency states, the complexity of multi-agent system is bounded, *this makes the problem of agent-based scheduling tractable.* On the other hand, the planning system still possesses enough degrees of freedom to react reasonably and adaptively to disturbances. Thus, the fundamental problem of a relation between complexity and flexibility, known from other MAS-approaches, is solved here in this way. The approach does not require any centralized elements. That, firstly, enables a distributed implementation, secondly, essentially increases a reliability of common system. However, such problems as a treatment of irresolvable disturbances in the global emergency state still remain unsolved and require more general algorithms of tasks decomposition, that represent an open research field in modern manufacturing as well as in computer science.

4.4.5 MA-mechanisms providing scalability

[4]The example from the previous section was intended to demonstrate that emergent properties of multi-agent system can be successfully controlled by applying two mechanisms. The first one is the stepwise growth of a system's complexity, depending on a problem's complexity. The second one is the concept of roles, determines by Petri Nets, that describes

---

[4]*This section represents results obtained by author. There results are parts of the work, within the SFB 467, that has been done in collaboration between author and O. Kornienko, C. Constantinescu, U. Heinkel, see (Constantinescu et al., 2004).*

a *functionality* of collective systems. The example in this section is intended to demonstrate that not only functional but also *dynamical properties* of collective systems can be successfully treated by the mentioned mechanisms. For this example we select the problem of scalability, introduced in Section 2.6.

The problem of scalability is closely related to the changes of system's relevant parameters and to the reaction of the system on these changes. In this context we distinguish between *scaling values* (parameters) and *absorbing values* that are in charge of absorbing the changes caused by scaling. The scaling mechanisms have to provide the stable working with similar performance in some range of scaling as well as absorbing parameters.

The using of the mechanisms proving scalability brings us in following three cases of interest:

- the system is not sensitive to the variation of scaling values;

- the changes of scaling parameters can be absorbed by similar changes of absorbing parameters in linear or sub-linear proportion;

- the scaling changes require multiple modifications of absorbing parameters or even modification of system's structure.

The first case is the most relevant for the scale-invariant systems. Although this issue is of huge interest, the treatment of this problem oversteps the framework of this work.

The second case represents the standard speedup solution: a growth of scaling parameters is compensated by an equivalent growth of resources. For example, each new query (in some data processing system) is connected with a new handling process. Thus, N new queries create in parallel exactly N new processes, the total system's performance remains the same for different load N. If we can guarantee that the consumed resources by these processes grow *sub-linearly* or *linearly* with N, this scheme can underlay the mechanisms providing scalability. However, in many cases, the speedup schemes cannot assure a complete absorbance of changes.

The reasons of this deficiency consists in a nonlinear multiple dependence between scaling and absorbing values. This is the last case of our interest. In this case we cannot absorb the changes in the speedup way. As a result, we need to perform more complex modifications, even to modify the structure of the system. For example, increasing the frequency f_q of querying, we can achieve the limit, where new processes get started when already started processes are not yet finished. These N new handling processes will be added to the not-finished ones and the total number of started process N_p grows exponentially with f_q. The speedup solution is not useful here, this problem can be solved only by shorting the time required by handling process. This, in turn, requires multiple modifications of the system structure.

The speedup and the multiple modifications represent two main scaling mechanisms utilized further. We propose to employ the Multi-Agent-Systems (MAS) for implementing these mechanisms, based on two reasons. *The first reason lies in the autonomy of agent behavior.* Each agent executes cyclically a sequence of activities, like collecting of information, planning and so on. These activities can include a monitoring of scaling values to perform an adaptive speedup. An agent can continuously monitor changes in the system in order to start new processes, as well. Generally, the autonomy gives to agent-based approaches the ability to react dynamically in continuously changing environment.

The second reason consists in agent's ability to find collective solution based on negotiation. The point is that the collective solution space is essentially larger, than that of individual agents. The agents group can find (and optimize) the solution in situations where separate agents fail. This property is of essence for the mechanisms involving multiple modifications. In the performed experiments the dependence between some scaling and absorbing value continuously changes. It is very difficult to find an optimal relation (and sometimes even a non-optimal one) in advance. Therefore agents, based on negotiations, have to find this relation so that to guarantee scalability in a given range.

In the following we employ agents-based technologies to solve problems arising primarily at *diversity scalability* as well as *load and dynamic scalability* in collective information system. Our case study refers the data change propagation system *Champagne* (Rantzau *et al.*, 2002). This application allows considering, without loss of generality, the common tendencies of providing structural scalability and illustrate them by a practical example.

In the example, that we consider, there are two data structures of source and destination systems. The changes of source data structures have to be propagated to the destination system. In order to do it, these data structures (as well as containing constraints) have to be matched. The revealed dependencies between both data structures have to be written into the propagation script. The architecture of multi-agent propagation systems as well as details of the performed experiment are demonstrated in the next section.

4.4.5.1 Multi-agent architecture and details of experiment

We propose the following MAS architecture in order to implement the mentioned scaling. The architecture consists of two layers, focusing on *primary* and *secondary* activities, as presented in Figure 4.28. The *primary activity* layer implements the constraint-based matching

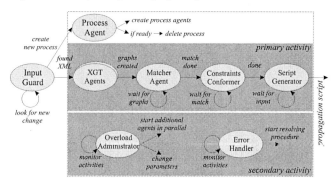

Figure 4.28: *Structure and main activities of multi-agent dependency manager.*

that underlies the dependency manager during the process of dependency creation. The **Input Guard** agent monitors the changes in a given system and triggered by a changed data starts the **Process Agent**. This also has a hierarchical structure and consists of the **XGT** (XML-Graph-Transformer), **Matching**, **Constraint Conformer** and **Script Generator** agents. XGT agent gets two XML scripts from Input Guard, describing the data structures of source and destination systems. These XML structures are converted into an internal graph representation. The matching agent receives these graphs and performs the matching. The contained XML constraints are processed by the Constraint Conformer agent. The goal of this operation is to find compromises between constraints of source data structures and destination data structures. Finally, the Script Generator agent creates the propagation scripts. The details of agents implementation as well as of the performed operation are given in the next section.

The scaling values of this architecture are represented by the frequency of querying f_q, the number of querying processes at once N_q and the diversity D_{XML} of XML data structures. These values correspond to the load and diversity scaling, mentioned in Section 2.6. The absorbing values are the number of simultaneously started processes N_p and the number of started matching agents N_m. In the speedup solution we create constant linear dependency between N_q and N_p and variable linear dependency between D_{XML} and N_m. The creation of nonlinear dependency between absorbing values N_m, N_p and the frequency of querying f_q is used in the mechanism of multiple modification. The details as well as results of experiments are discussed in Section 4.4.5.2.

The *secondary activity* layer handles the irregularities arising during the constraint-based matching. We identify two kinds of irregularities: overloads and errors in XML data structures. These are managed correspondingly by the **Overload Administrator** and the **Error Handler** agents. Since Error Handler does not affect the scaling properties of the propagation system, its activities are limited by simple generation of error messages. However, overloads are closely connected with scaling values (they cause overloads). To handle them we utilize the collective properties of multi-agent system to find such a combination of system's parameters to absorb the overload.

For the Overload Administrator agent we apply a simple evolutionary strategy of collective solution as presented in Table 4.9. The Overload Administrator agent monitors system's

agent:role(Overload Administrator)	**agent: extend agent** (*name*)
do always monitor system's *load*	:**role**(Change Absorbing Value)
activate if *load > threshold* **do iteratively**	**create** (*list* of absorbing values)
create (*list* of agents)	**do iteratively** (change *values*)
call agents (from *list*) **set role**=change	**synchronize agent** (empty)
absorbing value	**if** *load* goes down **do** further
finish iteration if *load< threshold*	**finish iteration if** *list* empty ||
endactivate	*load* goes up
endrole	**endrole**

Table 4.9: *Example of role-based evolutionary strategy for collective solution finding.*

load (number of started agents, resources consumed by agents) and, at overstepping some threshold, it calls other agents and suggests them to change the absorbing values that these agents have available. The called agents start the role *Change Absorbing Value* and try to vary the parameters. They continue the changing of parameters if the load goes down, otherwise they start to try new combination of parameters. Since the number of possible absorbing parameters in the dependency manager is small, agents do not need to synchronize explicitly the changing behavior. The changes of load allow an implicit synchronization. Although this simple strategy cannot guarantee convergency for a large number of agents, for a small number of agents it allows finding the gradient and continuous descent on the gradient.

We implemented the agent-based dependency manager in Java, by using the AnyLogic[5] simulation engine for managing agent activities. Instead of converting XML data structures, we create in our experiments the graph according the following format:

*Field*1 {*Subfield*1 (value, constraints),
      *Subfield*2 (value, constraints),...},

---

[5]www.xjtek.com

Field2 {*Subfield1* (value, constraints),
    Subfield2 (value, constraints),...},
...

The number of fields and subfields is random between 1 and *FieldMax*=[1 - 1000]. For matching, we use the approach suggested in (Rahm & Bernstein, 2001), which recommends the matching of *name similarity, position in hierarchy* and *similarity of constraints*. The constraints are given in the form of *value type* (integer, double, string) and *permissible range* (e.g. 0-1000). In the match of candidates with similar constraints (e.g. integer → integer, or integer → double) we perform transformation of constraints. The Input Guard agent can be activated 1-100 times per second (f_q) and it can start 1-1000 process agents simultaneously (N_q). The number of matching agents N_m varies between 1 per process and *number of Field* (we perform parallel matching on the subfield level only, since deeper level of parallelization brought no added benefit). The experiments are performed with a single-processor machine Pentium 2,0 Mhz with 512MB memory. Since we use a single-processor machine, the started agents are executed by the AnyLogic simulation engine in sequence. Therefore the number of simulation steps, required for *one agent* to perform all activities, can be assumed to be proportional to consumed system's resources (CPU time, memory and so on) by the whole simulation. This value is adopted as a consumption of system's resources.

4.4.5.2   Load scalability

We mainly use in our experiments the load as the *number of querying processes started at once* N_q and the *frequency of query to propagate changed data*, f_q. The Figures 4.29(a) and 4.30(a) represent the load of the system through these two parameters. Figure 4.29

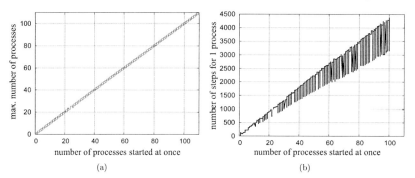

(a)   (b)

Figure 4.29: **(a)** *Load scalability as the number of querying processes started at once,* $f_q = 1$, *number of matching agents* $N_m = 1$; **(b)** *Dependency between this load and consumption of system's resources.*

highlights that the system is *Superscalable* at the growing number of parallel processes. This points to the coincidence of the results with the speedup scheme. The consumed system's resources grow linearly (in this case slightly *sublinear*) with the number of processes. In a multi-processor implementation the consumed resources by one process are expected to remain constant.

According to the experiments shown in Figure 4.30, the system has for the variable f_q the range [0 - 8], where the number of processes remains constant. However, beyond this range

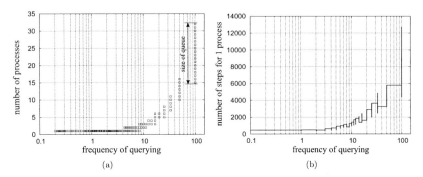

Figure 4.30: **(a)** *Load scalability as the frequency of querying, $N_m = 1$;* **(b)** *Dependency between this load and consumption of system's resources. Both dependencies are shown in logarithmic scale of the x-axis. Overload Administrator is off.*

the number of processes (Figure 4.30(a)) as well as the consumed resources (Figure 4.30(b)) grow exponentially with f_q. As already mentioned, we explain this behavior through new processes which get started when already started processes are not yet finished. The size of queue containing not-finished processes is constant for the same f_q, but grows exponentially with f_q. The size of queue depends on several other parameters, the most important is the length of process. This depends on matching parameters, on the number of matching agents, on the constraints converting procedure and so on. After discussing the meaning of these parameters for diversity scaling, we return to the frequency of querying, in trying to improve this relation.

4.4.5.3 Diversity scalability

We define and use the term of diversity scalability as the number of fields that do not coincide in source and destination data structures. The dependency between the length of matching and the maximal number of fields is reflected in our approach by defining the following parameter:

$$K = random(\frac{maxFields}{100}maxDiversity, maxFields) \qquad (4.60)$$

The difference between values of K_1 (calculated for the first graph) and K_2 (for the second graph) gives us the real diversity. The values of $maxDiversity$ (expressed in %) describes how the first graph differs from the second one (for $maxDiversity = 100\%$ they do not differ at all). The $maxFields$ is the maximal length of fields in the relation (4.60). To demonstrate the dependency between length of fields, diversity and the time of matching we adopt $maxFields$ as *the value of diversity* in the performed experiments.

We illustrate in Figure 4.31 the dependence between $maxFields$, in the range [3 - 100], and the time needed for matching. The matching time is taken as the number of matched fields multiplied on the number of steps required to match one field. Figure 4.31(a) shows this dependence in the case of one matching agent started, whereas Figure 4.31(b) presents the case where the number of started matching agents equals to the number of *Fields* in the graphs. The linear dependency between the number of matching agents working in parallel and the corresponding consumed resources is presented in Figure 4.32(a).

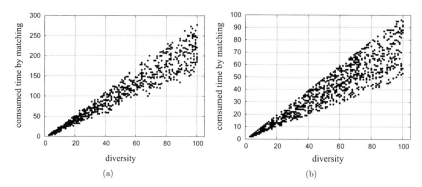

Figure 4.31: **(a)** *Diversity scalability (*maxFields*) at* $N_m = 1$, $f_q = 1$; **(b)** *Diversity scalability* *(*maxLFields*) at* $N_m = number\ of\ Fields$, $f_q = 1$.

A comparison between Figures 4.31 and 4.32(a) reveals that the load scalability (frequency of querying) has greater impact on the system than the diversity scalability. The resources consumed by agents grow *linearly* (like in Figure 4.29 slightly sublinearly) with the number of agents that points to a constant consumption in the multi-processor implementation. The time of matching is closely related to the size of the queue in the case of increasing frequency of querying. We discuss this dependence in the next section.

4.4.5.4 Improving load scalability

To improve the load scalability, we intend to short the process time. In the proposed architecture, the most time is consumed by the matching agent. Therefore, shortening the matching time, we can reduce the process time. Two parameters enables us to reduce the matching time: the number of simultaneously started matching agents N_m and the way how to perform the distributed matching (e.g. the level of distribution). Changing the level of distribution from *Fields* to *SubFields* or even deeper to *Value, Constraints*, in the performed tests, we did not achieve real increase of performance, because to collect the matched results from the deepest level agents consumes time, as well. This collecting time finally grows proportionally to the level of distribution. Therefore N_m remains the only effective parameter that can be handled.

The *Overload Administrator* agent monitors the system's load (in this case the number of processes N_p in queue) and if N_p grows considerably it calls the role *Change Absorbing Value* of other agents. Since N_m is only one effective parameter in the system, the call of this role changes only the number of simultaneously started matching agents. The dependency between the number of started processes, the consumed resources by agents and the frequency of querying is shown in Figures 4.32(b).

Comparing Figures 4.30 and 4.32(b), we conclude that the number of processes in the queue do not grow significantly if the *Overload Administrator* is on. However, we are not able to achieve the constant size of queue. Moreover, the consumption of system's resources still increases exponentially with f_q. We give to this result the following two explanations. Firstly, there is a "physical" limit imposed on the minimal time of processes. If we increase the querying frequency so that it oversteps this limit, there is no approach that can avoid increasing the queue size. Secondly, the mentioned "physical" limit depends on several

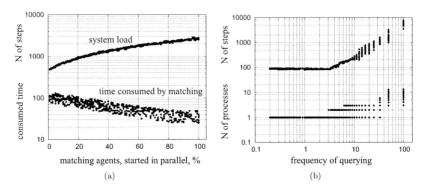

Figure 4.32: **(a)** *Dependence between the number of matching agents, working in parallel, resources consumed by agents and the time needed for matching;* **(b)** *Dependency between the number of processes, consumption of system's resources and frequency of querying if the Overload Administrator is on. Both dependencies are shown in logarithmic scale of the x,y-axis.*

parameters. Modifying these parameters, we could, in principle, reduce this limit. However, in the used simple architecture there is no enough degrees of freedom (parameters) to achieve it. Agents can modify only the number of started matching agents. This strategy leads finally to exponential consumption of system's resources. In the architectures, possessing more degrees of freedom, the more "intelligent" solutions towards improving load scalability are expected to be found.

4.4.5.5 Discussion of results

In order to employ agent-based technology for designing dynamical properties of collective systems, we performed some experiments which proved the expected benefits of our proposal. This work represents crucial steps before implementing the first prototype of the agent-based approach. As shown by experiments, the highest impact on the scalability represents the system's load. The load consists of the number of simultaneously started querying processes N_q, in our case propagated changed data, and the frequency of querying f_q for propagation. The proposed agent-based solution supports large scaling of N_q-load and restricted scaling (in the given range) in the case of f_q-load. We identified that the f_q-load is of "physical" nature and this cannot be got round. The consumed resources depend linearly on the number of started processes (in area where f_q-load is constant). We conclude that the real implementation of such an agent-based system is feasible.

Another result, that has to be mentioned, is the support of agility provided by agent-based technology. The implemented agents continuously monitor the changes in the system as well as in the environment and rapidly react to the changed load, overload, unexpected changes of system's parameters. In our first experiments we did not used the whole potential of collective solution finding for reaction on these changes. Therefore, on the one hand, the advantage is that monitoring the load and its reduction is done autonomously. However, on the other hand, the programming effort and the consumption of system's resources essentially increase in the case of agent-based implementation. *For simple architectures or if the system's behavior is known and can be preprogrammed, the benefit of agent-based implementation is minimal. Otherwise, for complex architectures with many relations among components, the agent-based technology offers agility and scalability to the system.*

4.5 Summary

In this Chapter we have demonstrated different mechanisms and approaches, which can be applied to treating artificial functional self-organization. These mechanisms have been considered from analytical and algorithmic sides. There are two differences between them: different modeling techniques and different treatment of complexity of collective phenomena. In the modeling, the main focus of reductive approaches lies on the equation-based representation, whereas the computational approaches focus primarily on the hybrid or pure algorithmic representation. These models require different approaches allowing analysis and forecasting of behavior. The equation-based dynamical models can be either directly solved (that is possible only for very simple systems), or we apply reductive approaches, like center manifold reduction, normal form reduction and so on (as well as many pure numerical approaches). The dynamical models, based on the Petri Nets (or similar approaches), can be analyzed by methods of symbolic dynamics, Kolmogorov complexity, graph-based approaches, temporal logic and so on.

The analysis of these models represent the second difference between reductive and computational treatment of artificial SO phenomena. Analytical approaches reduce the complexity of systems in trying to find some compact characteristics. These characteristics, like order parameters, eigenvalues (Lyapunov coefficients), dimension and codimension, allow us to understand the typical dynamical properties (like stability, bifurcations) of the system. Algorithmic approaches, in contrast, do not attempt to reduce a complexity. The behavior of collective system is analyzed and forecasted by means of simulation. Both approaches supplement each other.

In this Chapter we did not consider the problem of local rules and especially derivation of these local rules. The main attention was focused on a treatment of typical for functional SO-phenomena problems, consisting in many degrees of freedom. In the next Chapter we consider structural case and apply several techniques to produce local rules in the context of structural self-organization.

Chapter 5

Generation of horizontal structural emergence

5.1 Motivation

In the previous chapters we discussed about the origin of problems in collective systems, some general notions about self-organization in artificial systems and demonstrated a few instruments applied for creating SO-phenomena. We came to the conclusion that the artificial self-organization contains structural and functional components. Observable macroscopic emergence is created by the distributed transfer function, generated by functional rules. In turn, structural rules produce functional part of SO-systems. Functional self-organization occurs when this distributed function is generated by fixed functional rules, whereas structural self-organization assumes some "autonomous" generation of the sequence: *functional rules → distributed transfer function → macroscopic emergence*.

Issue of local rules is central in treating collective phenomena and includes many different aspects: hierarchies, reductionism, usability of emergent properties. The treatment of functional local rules as well as functional self-organization are demonstrated in Chapter 4. Since functional rules are of preprogrammed nature, the capabilities of functional self-organization depend primarily on the abilities of developers to forecast collective activities. As known from Chapters 2 and 3, the relation between microscopic and macroscopic behavior is highly non-trivial, therefore we cannot derive different emergent properties in functional SO-systems.

In this chapter we consider the next step in creating artificial self-organization that concerns an automatic generation of local rules. In the classification scheme shown in Figure 3.20 (Section 3.6.2) this automatic generation belongs to the 3rd-level SO-architectures, that we denoted as the structural SO-systems. As pointed out, the structural SO-systems are seldom encountered in praxis (except for grammar-based ones). The reason lies primarily in a high complexity of these collective systems. Many principles of the three-level SO-architectures are unclear and still discussed in different scientific forums.

In this chapter we give first an overview of already known 3rd-level generators. We start with the fixed rules generation by examples of L-systems in Section 5.2, Kataoka-Kaneko self-referred systems in Section 5.3 and the extension of them for the distributed case with cooperation in Section 5.4. These techniques cover the **bottom-up** approaches. The **evolutionary** approaches towards rule generation are presented in Section 5.5 by several approximation techniques and, in Section 5.6, by the famous genetic programming. The **top-down** approaches are given by the decomposition-based approach, developed by author. In Section 5.7 we introduce first the decomposition approach and then, in Section 5.8, the rule derivation procedure based on this decomposition. These approaches are first developed for re-planning problems in manufacturing environment, however their general application is rule-generation for emergent behavior in collective systems. This will be demonstrated in several experiments with real swarm robots by involving the swarm embodiment concept. Summary finishes this chapter.

5.2 Bottom-up rules generation: L-systems

We start our representation of structural generators from the case of the fixed rule generation. The common class of these systems calls grammar-based generators and is closely related with the formal language theory. We demonstrate the fixed rule generation on the example with L-systems by following the book (Prusinkiewicz & Hanan, 1980).

L-systems are proposed by Aristid Lindenmayer in 1968. The central notion of L-systems is the concept of rewriting, i.e. a successive replacing of a simple initial object using a set of rewriting rules or productions. This process can be demonstrated by the Koch curve, suggested by Koch in 1905, see Figure 5.1.

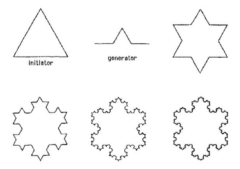

Figure 5.1: *Construction of the Koch curve. This image is taken from (Prusinkiewicz & Hanan, 1980).*

"*One begins with two shapes, an initiator and a generator. The latter is an oriented broken line made up of N equal sides of length r. Thus each stage of the construction begins with a broken line and consists in replacing each straight interval with a copy of the generator, reduced and displaced so as to have the same end points as those of the interval being displaced*" (Mandelbrot, 1982, p.39).

There are several types of L-systems. Context-free L-systems are the simplest and most common type. Context-free means that only one symbol of the current string need be matched for a substitution. To catch the environment around a symbol, context-sensitive L-systems are introduced. Context-sensitive L-systems are difficult to implement because the meaning of context-sensitive is not clearly defined. Context-free L-systems are the only special cases of the general context-sensitive L-systems.

Another kind of L-system, the stochastic model, adds randomness to producing. In this system there are several rules with the same matching condition. The choice of a specific rule is determined by a probability distribution, that is introduced as a parameter in these rules. Stochastic L-systems produce different output every time, i.e. the process is not predictable or reproducible with the same axiom and rules.

A production in L-systems consists of two strings - the predecessor and successor. When the production is applied to the string, the predecessor compares each symbol of the string. The successor replaces the symbol if it matches the predecessor. For example, the following rules

$$p_1 : m_l \rightarrow m_r e_l$$
$$p_2 : e_l \rightarrow e_r m_l$$
$$p_3 : m_r \rightarrow e_r$$
$$p_4 : e_r \rightarrow m_l e_l$$

produce the sequence

$$e_l$$
$$e_r m_l$$
$$m_l e_l m_r e_l$$
$$m_r e_l e_r m_l e_r e_r m_l$$
$$...$$

Finding a correspondence between a symbols and graphical elements, we can produce very complex graphical objects. Several examples are shown in Figure 5.2. In the process of string rewriting, we see that the string keeps growing in length, moreover all patterns of the old strings are preserved in some way. The number of times when a string is rewritten is called the depth or order. Simple axioms and rules can produce more and more complicated patterns, even complicated enough to mimic nature's growing process.

The L-systems belong to more common class of grammar-based systems. They are the most simple and perhaps most old systems, that allow modifying structures. A parser generator creates a parser for formatted data, given a rule-based description of its structure (i.e. grammar). Grammars can be used to describe the syntax of any formal languages. Parser generators are commonly used in the development of compilers and interpreters. The output of a parser generator is source code, which can then be compiled and linked. Semantics, defined within the grammar, are used to control the data processing. When a given symbol is parsed by the parser, corresponding application code gets executed. Semantic actions consist of compilable statements from the target programming language.

In this way, the fixed generation can also be applied to structural rule. In this case we have the structural rules, functional rules and finally, as an output, the generated sequences. Although the fixed rule generation can include different conditions, delays, even propagation of information, we encounter serious difficulties to apply this approach to structural generator. Firstly, L-systems and, more generally, grammar-based systems do not offer the automatization/systematization in deriving macroscopic phenomena. The L-systems represent more a collection of interesting examples than really systematic tools. The grammar-based systems have similar problem that is closely related with automatic generation of computer programs. We discuss this problem more in Section 5.6 on the example of genetic programming. Another problem consists in centralized character of grammar-based systems, that hiders applications of this approach in collective systems. We consider some possible combination between fixed rule generation and collective decision making in Section 5.4.

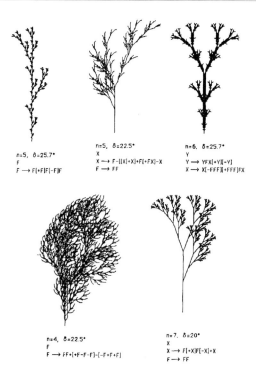

Figure 5.2: *Examples of plant-like structures, produced by L-systems. Initial elements and producing rules are shown near the corresponding structure. These images are taken from (Prusinkiewicz & Hanan, 1980).*

5.3   Bottom-up rules generation: Self-reference

The demonstrated in the previous section fixed rule generation distinguishes between producing rules and sequences that these rules are applied to. Very interesting example of fixed generation is represented in the case when the producing rules are applied to themselves. In this discussion we follow the work (Kataoka & Kaneko, 2000).

"For the study of codes, generative grammar deals with transformation of words and sentences. Given a formal system, such transformations are classified into several classes, according to computation theory. Study of generative grammar has succeeded in describing how an already described language is structured. However, this is just a one-way flow from the phones or letters to the language structure. Natural language cannot be generated only by this language structure. To produce a sentence, it is inevitably necessary to refer to the real world. If we have to refer to real world structure in order to produce sentences, the syntactic rules must be complemented by additional cognitive rules in order for a machine to be able to speak or a program to be able to write. Thus, a theory or a model of articulation of language is necessary, e.g., to construct a machine which can use language" (Kataoka & Kaneko, 2000, p.227).

Authors study the map

$$f_{n+1} = (1 - \epsilon)f_n(x) + \epsilon f_n \circ f_n(x), \tag{5.1}$$

where the term $f_n \circ f_n(x)$ changes the connections from $x \to f(x)$ to $x \to f \circ f(x)$ for all x. The term $f \circ f(x)$ represents the application of the function to itself. In the case $\epsilon = 1$ the Eq. (5.1) yields

$$f_{n+1} = f_n \circ f_n(x) \tag{5.2}$$

As a simple introduction, authors consider the discrete mesh case, where the initial function $f_0(x)$ takes only M possible values. The evolution of the network of M elements is shown in Figure 5.3. The network with the number of elements $M = 3$ has period 2, with $M = 5$ has period 4, and with $M = 7$ has period 3. Interesting that the networks with $M = 4$ and $M = 6$ are disintegrated to two more simple networks, with $M = 4$ is reduced to four disintegrated fixed points and with $M = 6$ is reduced to two disintegrated $M = 3$ networks.

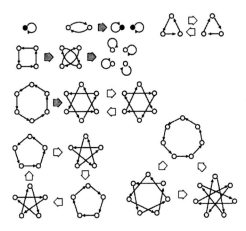

Figure 5.3: *Time self-refereed evolution of cyclic networks with $M = 1, 2, ..., 7$, see description in text. This image is taken from (Kataoka & Kaneko, 2000).*

Since the self-refereed system can be determined in analytical forms, authors can apply different reductive approaches to analyze its dynamics. Due to self-reference, the equation (5.1) can be viewed as functional as well as structural system. It is interesting, that a structural dynamics also undergoes different bifurcations, even bifurcation cascades. In our opinion the work (Kataoka & Kaneko, 2000) as well as the second part (Kataoka & Kaneko, 2001) represents one of only a few attempts to investigate the structural dynamics in the analytical way.

5.4   Bottom-up rules generation: Case of cooperation

As already mentioned, the fixed rule generation cannot be applied directly to collective systems. The main problem is to define appropriate interactions among components so that the common system behaves in the desired way. We consider two most earlier approaches intended to solve the problem of interactions. Both approaches deals with a development of interaction protocols in the bottom-up way. However, the difference between them lies primarily in the number of degrees of freedom granted to the system. The first approach originates from the domain of theoretical computer science and deals with distributed grammars applied to describe cooperating agents.

"The situation becomes more complex when we consider more than one grammar operating on one (or more) common tape(s). In this case we talk about the grammar systems. Grammar systems are symbolic devices composed of a set of elements (grammars) that interact with each other by means of the tape where they rewrite the symbols. This paradigm can be used to formally model multiagent systems. Several grammars (thought of as agents) operate on the symbolic tape (the environment) and bring about changes in it by means of rewriting rules (the behavior of agents). The grammar system then can be looked upon as a MAS with given properties" (Kubík, 2003, p.47).

Cooperating distributed (CD) grammar systems have been introduced by E. Csuhaj-Varju and J. Dassow in 1988 for describing multi-agent systems by means of formal grammars and languages (Csuhaj-Varju et al., 1994). The theory provides theoretical frameworks for describing multi-agent systems, such as distributed and cooperative systems of problem solving, collective robotics, computer networks, and other areas where set of agents work together in some well-defined manner. Known are also some works, investigating a behavior of cooperative automata based on CD grammars (ter Beek, 2003). The work of H. ter Beek is very characteristic to demonstrate the underlying idea of this approach.

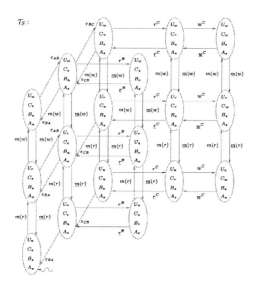

Figure 5.4: *Example of synchronized automata from the works of H. ter Beek (ter Beek, 2003, p.300).*

"A synchronized automaton over a set of automata is an automaton, determined by the way in which its constituting automata cooperate by means of synchronized transitions. Its *(initial) states are combinations - a cartesian product of (initial) states - of its constituting automata. Its actions are the actions of its constituting automata. Its transitions, finally, are synchronizations of labelled transitions of its constituting automata modelling the simultaneous execution of the same single action by several (one or more) automata. The label of a transition is the action being simultaneously executed. When the synchronized automaton changes state by executing an action, all automata which participate simultaneously change state by executing that action, while all others remain idle"* (ter Beek, 2003, p.14). One example of such a synchronization is shown in Figure 5.4. We see that the behavior not only of separate automata but also of complete systems gets completely deterministic.

Another approach towards the problem of interaction in the bottom-up rule generation appears in the domain of distributed artificial intelligence. *Multi-agent systems consisting of self-interested agents are becoming ubiquitous. Such agents cannot be coordinated by externally imposing the agent's strategies. Instead the interaction protocols have to be designed so that each agent really is motivated to follow the strategies that the protocol designer wants it to follow* (Sandholm, 1999, p.251). Instead of determining a behavior, we develop a strategy that "motivate" agent to follow the desired way. However, agent can choice another alternative, that becomes synchronized with group behavior via collective decision making. Example of this approach has been already represented in Section 4.4.4 for the assignment problem.

The collective decision making can be also applied for a generation of structural rules. The local producing rules are stored in each agent, like in CD-grammars, but the connection between them is performed by collective decisions. This approach is sketched in Figure 3.19, shown in Section 3.6.1. The main problem, that we encountered here, consists in a "surprising" behavior generated by structural rules, combined by collective decision making. It was difficult to forecast the collective behavior obtained in this way. This problem is common for all bottom-up approaches, therefore we applied evolutional approach, as shown in Figure 3.6.1, to find such a combination of rules that satisfy the imposed requirements. In the next section we consider evolutional side of rule generation.

5.5   Evolutional rules generation: Approximation

Idea of evolutional rule generation fundamentally differs from the bottom-up way. In bottom-up approaches the developer of cooperation protocol is in charge of collective phenomena. In opposite, the evolutional approaches give the main role to environment, that the system operates in. The local rules emerge automatically because the collective system adapts to its environment. There are two main approaches. In the first one, the collective system is originally unknown, therefore the local rules have to be approximated by a set of "universal rules", usually the IF-THEN algorithmic structures. This approach has some analogies with a decomposition of an analytical solution into e.g. Taylor or Fourier series. The second evolutional approach composes the behavior from known basic rules. In this way, we do not need to perform any approximations because the system, that demonstrate the desired collective behavior, is already known.

Both approaches have their own application field. The rule approximation techniques are useful when the system has specific architecture like, neural networks. *"In the last two decades artificial neural networks have been successfully applied in a broad range of problem domains. In spite of their numerous advantages, like universal approximation property, robustness and ability to learn, neural networks suffer from one significant drawback. When feeding an input to a trained neural network the user is unable to infer how a particular output is obtained. In other words, there is no possibility to come up with a meaningful interpretation of the network parameters and its response to a specific input"* (Gaweda *et al.*, 2000). Authors of the above cited work demonstrate an example of the following nonlinear system:

$$y_{k+1} = (y_k - u_k)^2 + \epsilon \tag{5.3}$$

for $y, u \in [0, 1]$, $\epsilon \sim N(0, 0.05)$ is the noise, approximated the the following set of rules:

$$R_1 : IF \ -2.6y_k + 2.5u_k - 1.0 = 0 \ AND \ -2.2y_k + 2.2u_k - 1.1 = 0 \ THEN \ y_{k+1} = 0.3$$
$$R_2 : IF \ -2.6y_k + 2.5u_k + 0.3 = 0 \ AND \ -2.2y_k + 2.2u_k + 0.1 = 0 \ THEN \ y_{k+1} = 0.0$$
$$R_3 : IF \ -2.6y_k + 2.5u_k + 1.6 = 0 \ AND \ -2.2y_k + 2.2u_k + 0.4 = 0 \ THEN \ y_{k+1} = 0.4$$

Another field, where approximation is useful, represents the systems, whose architecture and principles of functioning are ether too complex or generally unknown. The problem of approximation calls in this case the data mining and knowledge discovering. *"... in data mining we are often interested in discovering knowledge which has a certain predictive power. The basic idea is to predict the value that some attribute(s) will take on in "the future", based on previously observed data. In this context, we want the discovered knowledge to have a high predictive accuracy rate. We also want the discovered knowledge to be comprehensible for the user. This is necessary whenever the discovered knowledge is to be used for supporting a decision to be made by a human being. If the discovered "knowledge" is just a black box, which makes predictions without explaining them, the user may not trust it. Knowledge comprehensibility can be achieved by using highlevel knowledge representations"* (Freitas, 2002). Data mining and knowledge discovering are closely related with extracting the generating rules from time series. This problem calls approximating the smallest grammar (Charikar *et al.*, 2002) or estimation of Kolmogorov complexity (Li & Vitanyi, 1997). Performing an overview about evolutionary rule approximation, we have to mention a methodology based on swarm-based approaches. In this case we refer to the works of Casillas (Casillas *et al.*, 2000) within the context of learning fuzzy rules, and by Parpinelli (Parpinelli *et al.*, 2002) for learning rules using ant algorithms.

Generally, spectrum of approximating techniques is wide: from analytical time series analysis till computer grammars. In the next section we demonstrate genetic programming, also utilized in several techniques. Problems of approximation are similar to those known from analytical domain: finding the elementary blocks of approximating series and their convergence. In the algorithmic case these problems have the specific form: the representation of knowledge/semantic in rules and the length of approximating rules. In further discussion about rules approximation we refer e.g. to the book (Li & Vitanyi, 1997).

5.6 Evolutional rules generation: Genetic programming

Evolutionary algorithms represent a general notion of many techniques for a computer simulation of evolution. Evolution in this case means Darwin's principle of natural selection explaining *"the evolution of all life form on Earth"*. Using algorithmic models of organic evolution, evolutionary approaches are applied to various problems in computer science, primarily optimization and learning, that are not easy to solve by conventional methods. Being not intended to treat the whole spectrum of evolutionary algorithms, we focus the consideration on the main point of interest, namely the evolution of structures. As pointed out in the Chapter 3, the von Neumann computer architecture represents a typical structural hierarchy: - writer of program - algorithmic program - data treated by this program. The most evolutionary approaches work on the data's level (e.g. classical task of finding optimal solution), these can be denoted as the first level algorithms. There are also several methods of EA that deal with programs, i.e. on the second level. This branch of the second level EA-algorithms is named evolutionary programming, we are interested primarily in the genetic programming.

The genetic programming was first introduced by Koza in 1992 and shown on a lot of examples featuring importance of the method. In his book he formulates it in the following way: "*I claim that the process of solving these problems [problems in computer science, e.g. symbolic processing, machine learning] can be reformulated as a search for a highly fit individual computer program in the space of possible computer programs. When viewed in this way, the process of solving these problems becomes equivalent to searching a space of possible computer programs for the fittest individual computer program. In particular, the search space is the space of all possible computer programs composed of functions and terminals appropriate to the problem domain. Genetic programming provide a way to search for this fittest individual computer program*" (Koza, 1992, p.73). Starting with the initial population of randomly generated computer programs, every program in this population is measured in term of how well it solves the given task, i.e. fitness measure. In proportion to fitness, only several programs are selected from the initial population to reproduce a new population. After the operation of reproduction and crossover the whole cycle is repeated. The best individual in every population represents the result produced by genetic programming. However, we have also to mention one of the problem in genetic programming - the large amount of useless "genetic code" that requires a serious "after-process" optimization.

Dissociating from details, being specific for the genetic techniques, remark that the result of them is finally a program, that manipulates the data in the required way. Here a program consists of functions and terminals. Since there elements are arbitrary (arithmetical or logical operations, algorithmic constructions, structural operations, etc.) the produced program has a general nature. This explains a wide application field of genetic programming, e.g. from a construction of functions and symbolic manipulation, till computer programs executed in a distributed way. The considered construction *structure-function-information* can be also described in the way of function and terminals, therefore GP can successfully be applied to the rule generation. This idea will be demonstrated by the following example of emergent collective behavior, shown by Koza in (Koza, 1992, p.340).

There is a group of independent agent (in this case an ant agent), every agent can move in the plane and pick up a foots pellets which are also placed in the plane. The goal is to consolidate the food into one pile. The terminal set for this problem consists of four following functions without arguments:

$$T = \{(MOVE - RANDOM), (PICK - UP), (MOVE), (DROP - FOOD)\} \quad (5.4)$$

- *MOVE*: moves the agent one step in the direction it is currently facing if there is no agent at this location;

- *MOVE-RANDOM*: randomly changes direction in which the agent is facing;

- *PICK-UP*: picks up food at the current location if the ant is not already carrying food;

- *DROP-FOOD*: drops food provided there is no food at this location;

and function set with connective function PROGN2:

$$F = \{IF - FOOD - HERE, IF - CARRYING - FOOD, \quad (5.5)$$
$$IF - FOOD - ADJACENT, PROGN2\}$$

- *IF-FOOD-HERE*: a two argument conditional branching operator, execute the first argument if there is a food at the ant's current position and otherwise the second argument;

- *IF-CARRYING-FOOD*: a two argument conditional branching operator, execute the first argument if the ant is currently carrying food and otherwise the second argument;

- *IF-FOOD-ADJACENT*: a two argument conditional branching operator searching the positions adjacent to the agent, execute the first argument if any food is discovered and otherwise the second argument;

Since the goal of agent is a compact combination of food pellets, fitness should measure compactness of the pile. In the given example the fitness is a sum of distances over each food pellets to all other food pellets. The initial and final positions of foots pellets as well as agents are shown in Figure 5.5. This examples demonstrated:

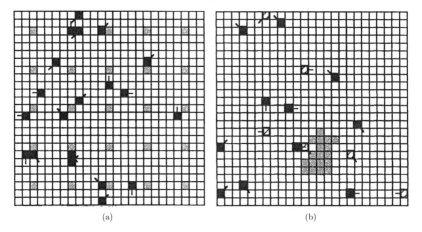

(a)   (b)

Figure 5.5: **(a)** *Initial configuration of 25 foot pallets and 20 agents;* **(b)** *Epoch 2,705 of best-of-generation individuals from generation 34, see description in text. Images are taken from the works of Koza (Koza, 1992, p.340).*

- The derivation of the second level rules can be considered as optimization problem. Applying evolutionary approach (GP), this rules can be generated by using a priori given fitness and programs construction set. Moreover in the case of the environment changes the rules can be regenerated dynamically.

- This approach is unable to generate autonomously the fitness and the programs construction set.

5.7 Top-down rules generation: tasks decomposition

5.7.1 Introduction

After a brief representation of several bottom-up and evolutionary approaches towards rules generation, we start with the top-down approach. A motivation towards the top-down strategy has been made in Section 3.6. This approach is intended to solve, at least in principle, the problem of bottom-up and evolutionary approaches, namely, how to obtain the desired macroscopic pattern.

The top-down methodology is generally not new in the domain of collective systems. As pointed out in Section 2.3.1, some origin of this approach can be found in thermodynamics. Analyzing the modern literature on the object, we encounter many top-down oriented works, as those with macroscopic and mezoscopic models, or with statistical analysis. Using appropriate macroscopic values, like a total consumption of fuel in traffic models (Helbing, 1997), the macroscopic approaches allow a purposeful modification of individual behavior. However, the almost all cases, the individual models are also of statistical (or macroscopic/mezoscopic) nature that cannot be directly used in generating local rules.

After some tries with the macroscopic methodology, we decided to use computational strategy in the top-down rules generation. The origin of this strategy lies in the domain of multi-agent systems, or, more exactly, in decomposition approaches known in this domain. These decompositions start in the top-down way with the global formulation of the problem and then step-wisely divide it into low-level pieces of information/activities/steps. Such a decomposition, formulated more generally, can represent the fist phase in the top-down rule generation. The next phase is to derive the producing rules from the sequences of low-level steps. This phase is very similar with the evolutionary approximating techniques, discussed in Section 5.5

In this way, we have three steps in the top-down rules generating approach:

1. 1. Formulation of the desired macroscopic pattern;

2. 2. Decomposition into a sequence of steps so that to achieve this pattern;

3. 3. Extraction of local rules being able to produce these steps and so the desired macroscopic pattern.

1. Formulation of macroscopic patterns. As mentioned in Chapter 3, regular patterns can be formulated as a detailed low-level description or as some variational form (by analogy with Lagrangian and Hamiltonian formulation of dynamics). However, many collective activities cannot be formalized ! In trying to describe the collective activity, we reduce the emergence to some limited descriptions and so that, finally, the emergence is lost. We made a good experience with evolutionary description of collective activity like those, mentioned in the work of Koza (Koza, 1992). We compare the evolutionary and non-evolutionary description in examples in Sections 5.8.3 and 5.8.4. However, it needs to admit that we are far away from a final generalization of this issue.

2. Decomposition approaches. We devote the complete Section 5.7 to develop such a computational approach that can be applied for rules generation. We denote this approach as the algorithm of symbolic tasks decomposition (ASTD). This approach originates from the manufacturing field (within the SFB 467). In Section 5.8 we discuss an adaptation of ASTD approach to the rules generation.

3. Rule approximation. The last step consists in extracting underlying rules from the sequence of steps, derived by the ASTD approach. This issue belongs generally to the problem of Kolmogorov complexity, mentioned in Sections 3.6 and 5.5. In Section 5.8 we discuss an approximation of derived sequences by producing rules. In this section we also discuss several examples of this approach within the I-Swarm and Collective Micro-Robotic projects.

5.7.2 Origin of decomposition approach

The decomposition approach originates from manufacturing field, or more exactly, from the short-term manufacturing planning. We have already introduced the manufacturing planning on the example of the assignment problem, discussed in Section 4.4.4. In this section we extend this problem to the short-term re-planning and introduce some decomposing formalism, needed farther for the rules generation.

As already mentioned in Section 4.4.4, modern manufacturing operates in such an environment, where almost all elements of management, organizational, planning, technological and manufacturing processes can quickly change. The reasons for that are different: competition in global markets, change of consumer properties by a demand of client, small series production with enlarged products spectrum, technological innovation, different failures and so on (e.g. (Wiendahl, 2002)). To survive in these hard conditions, enterprises are forced, among other arrangements, to react dynamically to these changes, to have flexible (transformable) structure on all levels of organization ((Peeters *et al.*, 1998), (Pine, 1999)). This work focuses on one aspect of this transformability, namely on an adaptable planning of the lowest level, denoted usually as process planning. This planning is the most sensitive element to all possible changes occurring in the production chain.

These changes, or more exactly deviations from expected states, can be of different types. We denote disturbances "predicted", if some parameters are changed, but a plan has a mechanism performing a re-planning. This re-planning often involves into a plan a huge number of states. Typical example is a failure of processing machines. In principle, this failure can be simply absorbed by rescheduling other machines. But if there are reconfigurable machines, the number of possible functional alternatives grows exponentially with a number of such machines. "Unpredicted" disturbances arise when an existing plan does not contain a mechanism of how to perform re-planning (e.g. modification of geometrical features, as shown in the next section). To repair a damaged plan in the case of unpredicted disturbances, a re-planning involves into a plan new states. Therefore the need is to develop a mechanism that is able autonomously to repair a plan damaged by predicted and unpredicted disturbances.

This mechanism is a part of MaPP (Multi-agent Process Planning) system representing a rapid prototyping system for flexible manufacturing control in turbulent environment (Kornienko *et al.*, 2004c), (Kornienko *et al.*, 2003c). The idea is to apply AI and DAI approaches (distributed CSP/COP, agent-based and knowledge based reasoning, conflict resolution and so on, see e.g. (Russell, 1995), (Weiss, 1999)) to manufacturing PPC/APC systems (e.g. (Kusiak, 1990)). In this way, firstly, Re-planning should remain in the short-term planning horizon (that reduces time and cost of re-planning), secondly, a common planning should get more reliable, especially to unpredictable disturbances (failures).

As already mentioned, modern manufacturing is a highly dynamic and complex environment. However, this environment possesses specific properties, which make the applied autonomous systems different from other kinds of autonomous systems, e.g. mobile robots (Lafrenz *et al.*, 2002), UAV (Unmanned Aerial Vehicle) (Engelson, 2000) or stationary autonomous systems (Williams & Nayak, 1996). The main difference lies in a complexity of input/output states. So, e.g. mobile robots operate in real (uncertain) environment and the main problem, that requires the most efforts of researchers, is a perception. The similar problem exists in the UAV field, where the input information has a huge state space, whereas the output state space is often limited by six till ten main activities (see e.g. description of WITAS's projects, http://www.ida.liu.se/ext/witas/). Contrary to these systems, input information in the manufacturing field has a well defined and limited character (e.g. 150-200 states), but the output space consists often of thousands states. However, the really interesting problem is that some of these states can not be defined in advance, i.e. a mechanism of dynamic generation of new states has to be developed.

To exemplify this affirmation, let us consider briefly a process planning for the workpiece shown in Figure 5.6. Manufacturing of this billet consists of 17 working steps (WS) (see

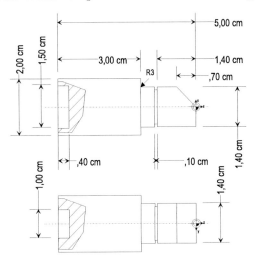

Figure 5.6: *Example of a workpiece to be manufactured.*

Step NC (ISO/DIS14649-1, 2000)). Order of these steps is defined by technological network (see Figure 5.7), however in a group way, e.g. the second group should follow after the

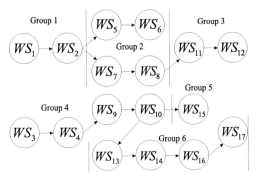

Figure 5.7: *Technological network determining the order of working steps for the workpiece in Figure 5.6.*

first group, whereas within the second groups the order of $WS5$, $WS6$ or $WS7$, $WS8$ is arbitrary. Each node in this network determines one processing operation (i.e. WS), that consists of a geometrical description of required features and technological description of how to manufacture them (Figure 5.8). Besides restrictions determined by the order of

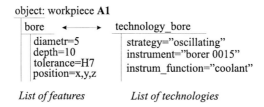

object: workpiece **A1**

bore ◄───►	technology_bore
diametr=5	strategy="oscillating"
depth=10	instrument="borer 0015"
tolerance=H7	instrum_function="coolant"
position=x,y,z	

List of features *List of technologies*

Figure 5.8: *Geometrical description of features and corresponding production technology for a node in the network in Figure 5.7;*

WS (Figure 5.7) and by technological/geometrical descriptions (Figure 5.8), there is a lot of organizational, technical and other restrictions. All these restrictions define a common producing technology, therefore this kind of problem can be formulated as the constraint-satisfaction problem (CSP), details of this approach can be found e.g. in (Kornienko *et al.*, 2004c), (Kornienko *et al.*, 2003b). The final plan after CSP-solver can be thought of as an assignment between low-level jobs and available machines, that satisfies all restrictions. As seen from Figure 4.27, this assignment can be of different length and cost, therefore a final plan has to be optimized by a chosen criterion. *In the following consideration we denote this assignment plan as a primary plan, and activities to generate it as a primary activity of the planning system.*

Modern manufacturing is a custom-oriented, demand-driven fabrication. It means, the produced in small series product can be changed in customer properties (like color or equipment), in a number of pieces, in a time given for production, in priority of different products. Change of customer properties can influence a manufacturing technology, technical basis (replacement or retooling of a machine), can require other resources. Moreover the machine can fail, an instrument can break down, a supply of resources can be interrupted and so on. Several types of these disturbance are collected in Table 4.8, shown in Chapter4.

We are mainly interested in sort-term disturbances, which occur either during execution of primary plan or between the steps of a primary plan. The problem of short-term disturbances is that they deviate the executing conditions of primary plan, so that a primary plan can not be accomplished. In this way the primary plan is getting damaged by disturbances. In several cases this problem can be solved by a total regeneration of primary plan, but in the most cases the primary plan should be repaired (e.g. at a change of geometrical features). "Reparation" means the system should generate a plan that changes the executing conditions of primary plan so that it can prolong an aborted executing. *This kind of a plan we denote as a secondary plan and activities to generate it as a secondary activity of planning system.*

There are different ways to react to each disturbance. For example, a reaction to a machine failure can be following: to reorder or to reschedule machines, to retool or to re-operate other machines, to increase a redundancy, to produce a detail externally and so on. Some examples of these reactions are collected in Table 5.1. These reactions compose sequences of alternatives, like a decision tree. We distinguish between organizational and functional alternatives. *Functional alternatives* mean different sequences of production activities (e.g. retooling or rescheduling), whereas *organizational alternatives* mean more macroscopic activities (e.g. to take from a lager, to produce externally and so on). The alternative, utilized

Type of reaction	N	Examples
time/order	1	re-scheduling
oriented	2	re-ordering
	3	re-optimization
	4	shift of deadline
technical/	5	retooling
technological	6	operation replacement
increase of	7	additional machines
redundancy	8	increase buffer
management	9	external manufacturing

Table 5.1: *Several types of reaction on disturbances.*

on the next planning steps, depends on the used alternatives on the previous steps, moreover this dependence is nonlinear. *The problem is that there is no way to know beforehand, which route in this three of alternatives will be optimal from the viewpoint of cost or time of final plan. In several cases, the number of alternatives is so huge that they can not be preprogrammed in advance.* Let us consider this point on an example of autonomous planning system.

The goal of this system is to generate, to monitor and to repair a short-term process plan. Common structure of this system is shown in Figure 5.9. This system consists of two parts:

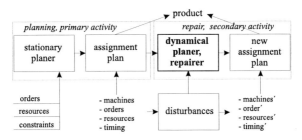

Figure 5.9: *Common structure of an autonomous planning system.*

the planning part and a part that is in charge of re-planning and repairing of primary plans. Whereas the first part is already considered in (Kornienko *et al.*, 2004c), (Kornienko *et al.*, 2003c), (Kornienko *et al.*, 2003b), here we focus on the second part of this system. In the field of mobile agents, this subsystem is also known as dynamic planner, whose structure is shown in Figure 5.10. As followed from this scheme, the functional alternatives (as a reaction to the occurred disturbance) are produced in the generator of alternative solutions, this is a main module considered further. These alternatives, after CSP-solution and optimization, are stored in buffer, this cycle is repeated until all functional alternatives are proved. The best solution from buffer goes to output as a new plan.

Let us estimate *the worst case for a number of functional alternatives*. For instance, the workpiece shown in Figure 5.6 has 17 working steps, that contain circa 130 geometrical and technological parameters that can be perturbed. Adding several management and other disturbances from Tables 4.8 and 5.1, we can estimate the number of possible disturbances as circa 200. In the worst case we assume that, firstly, each of these disturbances can be absorbed in 10 different ways, secondly, these functional alternatives are applicable to all

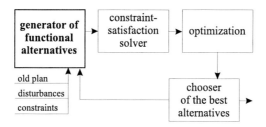

Figure 5.10: *Structure of the repair part from Figure 5.9.*

next working steps after disturbance (e.g. to avoid an arisen bottle neck/lack of resources and to retain a deadline). In this way we have circa 2000 functional alternatives for one detail and 10000 for a lot of 5 details. For the average and best cases we assume there are some heuristic approaches reducing this number.

Now we consider *the worst case for a number of planning states.* As an example, let us assume a disturbance changes a diameter of the boring hole shown in Figure 5.6. As a functional alternative the system chooses remanufacturing. However, the exact reaction depends on the exact kind of disturbance. If instead of 5 mm we have really only 1 mm, one can bore once again with a drill diameter 5 mm. However, if we get a hole 10 mm instead of 5 mm, there is no way to repair it. However, what is to do if a boring angle (or drilling temperature or something else) has been changed ? If we take into account all possible ways to disturb 130 technological and geometrical parameters of the workpiece in Figure 5.6, we achieve an enormously big number of possible reactions (output plan state) and it is obviously that *all these reactions can not be preprogrammed in advance. In this case we can assume the disturbance leads to an appearance of new states in the plan.*

Summarizing this section, we argue that a specificity of manufacturing environment consists, firstly, in a limited number of input states, but a huge number of output states, secondly, in an appearance of new states in output plan. In order to deal with output states as well as with new states *the conceptual idea is to introduce a generator into a repair part of planning system and to generate all states of the secondary plan.* This point will be evolved in the next sections. The manufacturing re-planning is quite equivalent to the problem of emergent behavior in collective systems, therefore the approach from the next section will be applied also to the experiments with the swarm robots Jasmine, described in the Section 5.9.2.

5.7.3 Multi-agent re-planning system

Consider the process planning problem more in detail. The plan P itself is a step-wise mapping S between available machines M and working steps WS in a time window T bounded by constraints C_g

$$S = \{M \times WS \rightarrow T, \{C_g\}\}, \qquad (5.6)$$

where $S \in (\mathbb{S}^{P_1} \cup \mathbb{S}^{P_2} \cup \mathbb{S}^{P_3} \cup ... \equiv \mathbb{S})$ and $\mathbb{S}$ is a state space of all plans and $\mathbb{S}^{P_i}$ are corresponding subspaces. Global constraints C_g define manufacturing technology, e.g. the order of operations (see Figure 5.7), organizational and other requirements, applied to the whole sequence of WS. The state space $\mathbb{S}$ possesses an ordered structure and can be represented as sequences of steps .., S_{i-1}^j, S_i^j, S_{i+1}^j,... where the subindex means the number of step and the superindex means the number of plan. This structure is determined by a transition Tr

that connects the state S_i with the state S_{i+1}

$$Tr = \{Tr^j : S_i^j \rightarrow S_{i+1}^j\}, \qquad (5.7)$$

where also $Tr \in \mathbb{T}r$, $\mathbb{T}r$ is a space of all transitions. As shown later, Tr is also structured into several domains. The common plan can be written as

$$Pl = \{\mathbb{T}r(\mathbb{S}) \rightarrow \mathbb{S}\}. \qquad (5.8)$$

All well-known planning approaches (e.g. MDP (Monahan, 1982)) require that $\mathbb{S}$ and $\mathbb{T}r$ are predefined. For a small number of states (even hundreds of states) it does not represent a real problem, however if the number of states becomes huge or there are new states needed to be introduced into a plan, the planning approach fails. *Therefore our idea is, firstly, to introduce a generator of new states Γ and, secondly, to transform a space $\mathbb{T}r$ so that at least a part of it can be dynamically generated by demand.*

Let us first consider the generator Γ of new states. Per definition there are no equal mappings S in $\mathbb{S}$, however the question is whether there states are really unique or they can be decomposed on some atomic constructions ? Looking at (5.6), we see that the time window T and machines M are of elementary nature, only a working step WS is composed from other terms. As followed from a definition of working step in Sec. 5.7.2, it consists of the activity A parameterized by the technology (modality) D, geometrical descriptions of features F bounded by constraints C_l

$$\mathbb{W}S = \{A(D) \rightarrow F, \{C_l\}\}, \qquad (5.9)$$

where $WS \in \mathbb{W}S$. Local constraints C_l define a manufacturing technology (see the right side of Figure 5.8), applied only to one WS. If we consider e.g. $WS5$ "mill" and $WS6$ "fine mill", the difference between them lies primarily in a manufacturing technology (the right part of Figure 5.8) and only then in geometrical descriptions of features (the left part of Figure 5.8). Manufacturing technology for WS "mill" consists of 9 steps, preparing a machine for performing this operation. In several cases, e.g. a transportation of a workpiece from one machine to another (see e.g. assignment plans shown in Figure 4.27), it requires even more steps. In this way we see each WS is composed from other activities that are of elementary nature. Specifying a complete set of these atomic activities, we suppose that in fact each arbitrary state of a process plan can be composed from them.

What kind of generator can be applied to this problem ? Analyzing the structure of this problem, we remark one interesting intersection with the problem solving in multi-agent systems. Here we refer to the underlying idea of multi-agent (MA) systems, that consists, among other aspects, in autonomy of each agent. Speaking in a combinatorial language, the MA system of m agents each with n internal states for time interval t is able to emerge n^{m^t} combinations of internal states. Transforming it to the manufacturing problem, we have 4 retooling activities (for reconfigurable machines): *set mill, set drill, set bore, set grind*; 8 basic activities: *grinding, boring, milling, drilling, shift, transport, load, upload*; 9 preparing activities (example for milling): *choose a type, prepare tools, set rate of feed, set a cutting speed, set a machine function, set depth of cut, processing strategy, set mill overlapping, set oversize* for each basic function. By different combinations of these activities is possible e.g. to mill by a normal machine function, by a retooling or by applying other operations (e.g. drilling with correspondingly prepared machine), i.e.

$$S = \{M \times (\Gamma \rightarrow F, \{C_l\}) \rightarrow T, \{C_g\}\}. \qquad (5.10)$$

For instance, if the maximal length of a repairing plan is equal to 10 steps, this MA generator Γ is able to emerge maximal 21^{10} different combinations of atomic activities (i.e. states S), it is much more than the disturbances described in Section 5.7.2 can ever cause. The point is that, firstly, not all of these combinations have a sense for manufacturing problem, secondly, how to force the agents to find to required combinations. The last question can be solved by a specifically chosen negotiation among agents (Weiss, 1999). As mentioned in the previous section, the manufacturing technology is defined in the form of different constraints. Therefore, the negotiations for MA systems can also have a form CSP-based approaches used in the generation of primary plans (see e.g. (Kornienko et al., 2004c)).

Now we rewrite (5.7), taking into account the made assumptions about the generator Γ

$$Tr = \{Tr^j : S_i^j \to (M \times (\Gamma \to F, \{C_l\})) \to T, \{C_g\})\}. \tag{5.11}$$

As seen from this expression, the S_i^j is known, but $S_{i+1}^j = \Gamma(S_i)$ is yet unknown. Therefore Tr, beside transition, has in this context a role of a decomposition algorithm that tells Γ which new state is required on the next step. The problem is that a transition (per definition) determines an order of steps and performs a parameterizations of WS by geometry. Changing Tr, we change in this way a global technology and as a result a final product. Therefore, it makes sense to divide the space $\mathbb{T}r$ into two subspaces of primary $\mathbb{T}r_p$ and of secondary $\mathbb{T}r_s$ activities. The first one defines a manufacturing technology for a product and the second one is directed to repair a primary activity. $\mathbb{T}r_p$ is predefined and may not be changed, whereas $\mathbb{T}r_s$ is in charge of reactions to disturbances, includes a functional decomposition and should be so flexible as possible. Rewriting finally (5.8), we get

$$Pl = \begin{cases} prim. : Tr_p(M \times WS \to T, \{C_g\}), \\ sec. : Tr_s(M \times (\Gamma \to F, \{C_l\}) \to T, \{C_g\}). \end{cases} \tag{5.12}$$

Transforming this functional expression into graphical form, we obtain the following structure of the MA generator of functional alternatives for damaged process plans, shown in Figure 5.11. Basic element of the primary structure in this figure is a WS-planning agent,

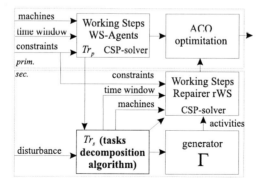

Figure 5.11: *Structure of MA generator.*

described e.g. in (Kornienko et al., 2004c). The kernel of the secondary structure is a task decomposition algorithm, described in the next section.

5.7.4 Algorithm of symbolic tasks decomposition (ASTD)

As stated in the previous section, Tr_s has a nature of tasks decomposition algorithm, more-over it is closely related with the generator Γ, that, based on a negotiation among agents, creates new states in the plan. Generally, the algorithm of task decomposition is perhaps the most challenging problem not only in the distributed planning approaches, but also in domain of distributed problem solving, coordination and so on. There is a lot of known solutions (see e.g. (Weiss, 1999)), however these approaches are applicable only to a limited number of specific problems and can not be generalized even to common problem-oriented domain.

Our idea of task decomposition originates from nonlinear dynamics and synergetics (see e.g. (Haken, 1983a)). It is known that a motion of a system is defined by a vector field and if this field contains an attracting manifold, the system from arbitrary initial state (in attracting area) will land on this attractor. Among many applications in bifurcation analysis, in systems's control, there are applications to robot navigation and agent coordination (e.g. (Levi *et al.*, 1999), (Kornienko *et al.*, 2001)). However, performing experiments, we have encountered one interesting effect, shown in Figure 3.31 in Section 3.7.2. If we perturb nonlinear field (by putting some obstacle on a motion trajectory), a system finds a bypass by all alone. It is especially evident in time-discrete systems, e.g. the way L from the point "A" to "B" will be automatically decomposed on small parts L_1, L_2, L_3, L_4 approximating a bypass. The question is whether this analytical approach can be applied by analogy to algorithmic problems ?

We start from several basic thoughts, being motivated by the example with a motion in a vector field. Creating a bypass consists of three phases: a detection of obstacle and an interaction with it, and, finally, a motion in the field so that to achieve the final goal. Consider these phases from the viewpoint of MA systems.

I. Detection of disturbance. This is a complex problem that is widely discussed in the corresponding communities. However, in the manufacturing environment this problem is simplified, firstly, by certain and limited sensor input, secondly, by a construction of the system, where the agent, that performs an activity, performs also a monitoring of this activity. Since each disturbance perturbs a formalized primary plan, a detection of this deviation does not represent, at least in principle, a problem (see more about this point in the next sections).

II. Reaction on disturbance. Intuitively, if the disturbance changes some feature, to change this feature backwards, we need an activity that is able to change this feature. For instance, if the feature "position" has been modified by a disturbance, we need an agent "transporter" that is able to modify a position of objects. Speaking more strongly, we suppose that a reaction to disturbance is determined by some equivalent to vector field, which is a media for a propagation of interactions. The most simple way to create this media is to connect source and receiver of activities (agents and objects), so that each perturbation can be propagated further (modifying attributes and activities), till this perturbation will be absorbed. More exactly, the features of objects have to be connected with corresponding activities of agents, e.g. feature "position" has to be connected with activity "to move" of an agent "transporter" (see Figure 5.12). We denote a network of coupled features-activities as the FA-network N_{FA}.

III. Achievement of a final goal. This is the most important question that is closely related with a reversibility of processes. This point corresponds to creating the sequences of activities that repair a damaged primary plan. This point can be reformulated in the following way: Can each arbitrary disturbance be absorbed ? or Can each arbitrarily damaged plan be repaired ? Intuitively we so answer this question: if disturbance breaks

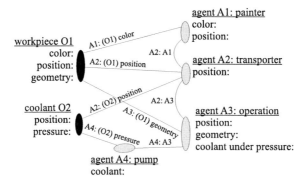

Figure 5.12: *Simple example of FA-network with two objects and four agents.*

one of technological or other restrictions, the primary plan cannot be repaired (e.g. if instead of 5 mm drill hole, we get 10 mm, there is no operation that can drill -5 mm). However, this point needs more detailed investigation. By analogy, a motion in the vector field is an equivalent to executing a primary plan, where the FA-network is applied to each disturbance to absorb it, as shown in Figure 5.13. Moreover, if all constraints are satisfied, the system

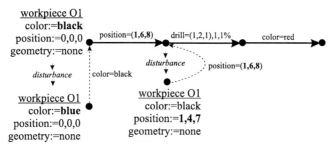

Figure 5.13: *Executing of primary plan (bold), where the FA-network is applied to each disturbance (dotted) to absorb it.*

can accomplish this plan, i.e. achieve a final goal.

Now we formalize these intuitive propositions. As stated in the previous section, a planning system is a transition system, where the states are mappings between machines, working steps into a time windows. Let us introduce a new transition Tr_{dam}, representing a disturbance

$$Tr_{dam} = \{Tr_{dam}^j : S_i^j \to S_{i+1}'^j\}, \tag{5.13}$$

where the state $S_{i+1}'^j$ is a new perturbed state, deviating from the desired state S_{i+1}^j. If the transition Tr_{dam} perturbs only one feature of an object, we speak about single Tr_{dam}^s, if Tr_{dam} perturbs simultaneously several features of one or more objects, we speak about multiple Tr_{dam}^m. In this work we generally focus only on Tr_{dam}^s. The aim of the planning system is to create a repairing plan Pl_{sec} that returns the system into the state S^j_{i+1}

$$Pl_{sec} = \{Tr^j_s(S'^j_{i+1}) \to S^j_{i+1}\} \tag{5.14}$$

Considering this expression, we claim there are one-step plans and many-step plans satisfying (5.14).

Statement 1 *Let N_{FA} be a FA-network and Tr^s_{dam} is a single perturbing transition. If Pl_{sec} is defined as one-step plan, there is always Tr_s in sense of (5.14), if and only if the corresponding C_l are satisfied.*

By construction of the N_{FA} network there is always an activity that is able to modify the perturbed attribute in S'^j_{i+1}. Limitation of this activity is determined by the local constraints C_l. Therefore if all C_l are satisfied by Tr_s, the system can achieve the state S^j_{i+1}.

Statement 2 *Let N_{FA} be a FA-network and Tr^s_{dam} is a single perturbing transition. If Pl_{sec} is defined as a many-step plan, there is always a sequence of Tr_s in sense of (5.14) if and only if*

- *(1) all local constraints C_l are satisfied;*
- *(2) all global constraints C_g are satisfied;*
- *(3) Tr^s_{dam} and Tr_s never intersects.*

In this case we follow the previous statement. If Tr^s_{dam} perturbs only one feature, we have a global technology (determined by C_g) of how to change it. If these conditions are satisfied, then we can apply step-by-step the statement 1. Important is that Tr_{dam} does not cause an additional perturbation during an executing of Pl_{sec}, because an accumulation of several Tr_{dam} may have a nonlinear influence on one another and lead to multiple Tr^m_{dam}. Therefore we require that Tr_{dam} and Tr_s never intersects in this sense. If (1)-(3) are satisfied, and N_{FA} is closed (all features are connected with activities), any arisen perturbations will be propagated in this network, till it will be absorbed.

Now the question is of how to derive Tr_s. From (5.6) we have

$$S = \{M \times WS \to T, \{C_g\}\}, \quad S' = \{M' \times WS' \to T', \{C_g\}\}. \tag{5.15}$$

Let us define a difference between S and S' as $\triangle S'$. We assume that modifications of machines M and time T can be absorbed by rescheduling. Therefore functional decompositions from $\triangle S'$ concern only working steps (denoted as $\triangle WS'$). The goal of Tr_s is to minimize $\triangle S'$, i.e. we can write

$$Tr_s(M \times WS' \to T, \{C_g\}) = \triangle S' \tag{5.16}$$

or with generator Γ:

$$Tr_s(M \times (\Gamma \to F, \{C_l\}) \to T, \{C_g\}) = \triangle S', \tag{5.17}$$

where

$$(\Gamma \to F, \{C_l\}) = \triangle WS'. \tag{5.18}$$

Expressions (5.16) and (5.18) give us a practical way to derive Tr_s. Thus, a *task decomposition represents a systematic way to find a difference between real state and desired state in a form of working steps, generated by Γ. For many-step plans this rule should be applied on each step of executing, moreover this sequence of generated working states converges in sense of (5.14).* So far as the problem, before decomposition, should be first formulated in a symbolic form (as FA-network), we call this algorithm as the symbolic tasks decomposition.

agent:role (monitoring)
    do always monitor *attributes* of the plan
    activate if not equal **do** call FA-connected agent
                  role=change attribute
        finish if receive cost
    endactivate
    endrole

agent:role (change attribute)
    do always monitor *attributes* of the plan
    activate if not equal **do** take role=monitoring
        finish if receive cost
    endactivate
    activate if equal **do** change attribute
        finish if calculate cost
    endactivate
    endrole

Table 5.2: *The simple algorithm that implements (5.16), (5.18) in the agent-based way.*

The most simple algorithm, that implements (5.16), (5.18) in the agent-based way, has the form, shown in Table 5.2. This algorithm assumes the FA-network is already constructed, moreover, there is only Tr_{dam}^s. The role "monitoring" detects a deviation from a plan and calls the role "change attribute" of a connected agent. The connected agent (from FA-network) compares the executing conditions, in case of mismatch, it calls the role "monitoring", otherwise it changes an attribute, calculates cost and returns this cost to a parent activity.

5.7.5 Experiments in TMS-scenario

The ideas, described above, have been implemented in the TMS-scenario (Transformable Manufacturing Systems). Part of this scenario has been already demonstrated in Section 4.4.4. In this scenario there are three machine shops, each of them contains three-five reconfigurable and non-reconfigurable processing machines. Each of non-reconfigurable machines is able to perform two different (of four required) processing operations. These machines are connected by a kind of conveyer belt, so that details can be transported from one machine to another within one machine shop (see Figure 5.14). There is also a transporter being able to transport details from one shop to another. One shop consists completely of reconfigurable machines, one shop has only one reconfigurable machine and the last shop consists only of non-reconfigurable machines. This scenario is a part of rapid prototyping demonstrator for a manufacturing control in turbulent environment. The planning system uses Agent-Based Scheduling Engine ABSE (Kornienko *et al.*, 2003b), with CSP-solver and MAS optimization module based on ACO algorithm (Kornienko *et al.*, 2003c). For programming this systems the RoPE (Role-oriented Programming Environment (Muscholl, 2001) has been partly used, where agent-management system has been reimplemented in C++ (because of optimization speed), the rest is written on Java. The ASTD module as well as the generator Γ are implemented by OpenCybele (see http://www.opencybele.org) on Java. Coupling between ABSE, CSP-ACO structures and ASTD-Γ modules is shown

Figure 5.14: *Example of a reconfigurable machine (taken from www.hueller-hille.com).*

in Figure 5.9, 5.10, 5.11. The main idea is following: as soon as a disturbance perturbs a plan (generated by RoPE engine in the form of modified Petri-networks, see Figure 5.15), the ASTD-Γ makes a functional decomposition and using CSP-solver generates sequences of activities. These sequences are optimized by MAS-ACO engine, where the best ones are stored in a buffer. Example of this sequence is shown in Figure 5.15. Finally, the optimized plans for different functional alternatives are compared by the cost or time criterion.

Different disturbances are also composed into several scenarios, including management, organizational, technological, technical and resources levels. Development of these scenarios has been motivated to find the worst case for a planning system, where the human assistance can lead to better solution, than the solution suggested by the planning system. As shown by experiments, ABSE-ASTD-Γ engine is able to deal with huge sequences of activities, to perform functional decomposition and to find the best sequence from them. However, the ASTD is not able to perform an organizational decomposition completely autonomous, therefore the human assistance for organizational decomposition can essentially improve the plan and lead to better solution.

5.7.6   Application of ASTD to other environments

The application of ASTD can of interest in other environments (e.g. mobile robots, UAV) for the goal of plan repair and maintenance. However, here there are several points needed to be discussed. The first problem is a plan monitoring. In manufacturing environment this function can be performed by the processing agent immediately after a processing operation (e.g. by laser scanner). However, in several other applications, the need is to introduce a special agent that will recognize an intentions of other agents and in this way a failure. The uncertainty of this recognition as well as generally an uncertainty in planning is the second problem of ASTD approach. The classical probabilistic methods, like MDP (Monahan, 1982) (and its different modifications) require to know probabilistic relations between nodes in the plan. Without these relations none of new nodes can be introduced into a plan. In this way one of the priority developments is to apply ASTD for MDP planning methods. In a certain environment, like the software agent in internet, assistant agents, the ASTD approach can be applied without any great modifications.

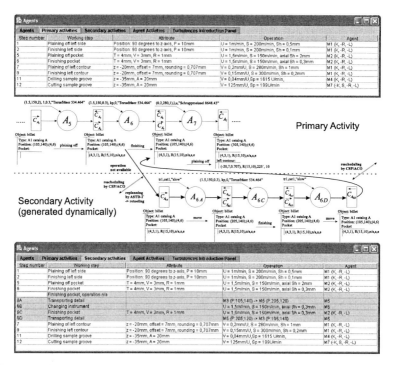

Figure 5.15: *Example of activities in primary plan (above) and generated sequences in secondary plan (below) as a screenshot and in the form of Petri net. The chosen functional alternative is a retooling.*

5.8 Top-down rules generation: decomposition-based approach

The demonstrated in the previous section ASTD-approach allows obtaining a sequence of steps that can solve the problem of irregular behavior. In this section we demonstrate some modifications of this approach to apply it to a derivation of local rules.

5.8.1 Introduction into micro-swarms

Some descriptions of micro-swarms have been already made in Sections 2.5 and 3.5. Generally, a manipulation of organic and anorganic matter on micro- and nano-scales becomes a new paradigm of modern science. This paradigm appears from two sides: firstly, technologies from material science, biology and other disciplines dealing traditionally on these scales, secondly, a development of fully functional molecular-scale devices and robots. Micro-robots of the projects MINIMAN, MiCRoN and I-Swarm (MINIMAN *et al.*, n.d.) represent the second trend. A problem of these robots is that they have very limited computational and communicating resources on board, but have a broad spectra of tasks (cleaning, micro-assembling, transportation, collective perception) to be solved. There is no central instance being in charge of coordination.

183

An approach to control micro-robots consists in creating desired collective behavior (like insect swarm-behavior). If the number of robots is large enough (several hundreds "I-Swarm" robots), they collectively accomplish the common goal. Swarm-like behavior is an emergent property of the system that cannot be directly preprogrammed. It is created by specific interactions among micro-robots. These, in turn, are determined by local rules, governing behavior of every robot.

For "insect-standard" problems, like foraging, route optimization, collective defense and so forth we can find and adopt the rules from the insect-world (Bonabeau *et al.*, 1999). But for technical activities, like assembling of micro-constructions, we have to derive artificial rules, leading to desired emergent behavior.

Another problem, that we encounter here, consists in regularity and irregularity of desired collective behavioral pattern. We can derive some compact optimization principles or fitness criteria for evolutionary generation (like genetic programming) of regular behavioral patterns. However, for generating irregular patterns, the irregularities have to be completely described (the Kolmogorov complexity of generating grammar is much higher, than the generated pattern itself). Unfortunately, the most of technically useful behavioral patterns are irregular.

5.8.2 Top-Down rule generation

Several methodological notions of the top-down approach towards a generation of local rules has been already discussed in Section 3.6. Here, we briefly repeat some of these methodological ideas and introduce a formalism.

As already mentioned, the general problem of bottom-up approach is that we cannot say in advance, which emergent behavior will be generated by the chosen rules. Therefore we suggest deriving local rules from emergent behavior in the top-down way. The idea behind the top-down approach originates from the distributed AI field. Assume, we have an algorithm, that can decompose the common task Ω into n-subtasks Ω_i. We also have a set of agents $\{Ag\}$ with corresponding elementary activities, however so, that they can collectively solve each of Ω_i. The decomposition algorithm splits up each of Ω_i further, up to elementary agent's activities. Thus, we have $\{\Omega_{i=1...n}^{j=1...m}\}$ sequences of activities, where an agent Ag_k needs m steps to solve Ω_i. Since this algorithm decomposes systematically, we can assume that all agents can solve Ω by executing $\{\Omega_i^j\}$. Remark, that a cooperation between agents arises naturally as the top-down decomposition of common task.

From agent's viewpoint, each agent Ag_k has a sequence of activities $S_k = \{\Omega_1, \Omega_2, ..., \Omega_m\}$. Now, calculating the Kolmogorov complexity of the sequence S_k (finding the smallest grammar (Charikar *et al.*, 2002)), we can derive local rules R_k that can generate S_k. The set of these rules $\{R\}$ defines a cooperation between agents that allows the agent's group cooperatively to solve the common task Ω. Thus, the task decomposition algorithm, demonstrated in the Section 5.7.4 is the kern of the top-down rule generator.

The rule generating machine Rg is a triple (Pl, Ag, Ob) consisting of a planning system Pl, agents $\{Ag\}$, each with activities $\{A_i\}$ and agent-features $\{F_A\}$ and, finally, objects $\{Ob\}$, each with object-features $\{F_O\}$. We say that an activity A and a feature $F_{A,O}$ are of the same type if A can modify $F_{A,O}$ ($F_{A,O} = F_A$ or F_O). For example, the activity "move" modifies the feature "position". More formally, an activity A, parameterized by a technology (modality) D, by technological descriptions of feature $F_{A,O}$, bounded by constraints C_l composes a construction that we denote as the working step WS of an agent $WS = \{A(D) \rightarrow F_{A,O}, \{C_l\}\}$, where $WS \in \mathbb{WS}$. C_l defines local constraints of agents activities, applied only to WS. Now we connect activities with features of the same type. Moreover we require that all feature are connected with corresponding activities (closeness condition). We denote a network of coupled **Features-Activities** as the FA-network, $N_{FA} = (\{A \times F_{A,O}\})$. Pl is a transition system $Pl = \{\mathbb{T}r(\mathbb{S}) \to \mathbb{S}\}$ and

$$Tr = \{Tr^j : S_i^j \to S_{i+1}^j\}, \quad S = \{Ob \times WS \to T, \{C_g\}\}, \tag{5.19}$$

where $S \in (\mathbb{S}^{P_1} \cup \mathbb{S}^{P_2} \cup \mathbb{S}^{P_3} \cup ... \equiv \mathbb{S})$ and $\mathbb{S}$ is a state space of all plans, $\mathbb{S}^{P_i}$ are corresponding subspaces, and $Tr \in \mathbb{T}r$, $\mathbb{T}r$ is a space of all transitions. State of this plan is a mapping between a working step WS and an object Ob into a time window T, bounded by constraints C_g. A technology (modality) D used in WS is defined in the state S. Here we point to difference of global constraints C_g originating from the plan and local ones C_l, originating from activities of an agent.

Remember, that WS consists of different quantities, being of elementary nature. Specifying a complete set of these atomic quantities, we suppose that each state of a plan can be composed from them by a generator Γ. Now we rewrite (5.19) with the generator Γ

$$Tr = \{Tr^j : S_i^j \to (Ob \times (\Gamma \to F_{A,O}, \{C_l\}) \to T, \{C_g\})\},$$
$$S = \{Ob \times (\Gamma \to F_{A,O}, \{C_l\}) \to T, \{C_g\}\}. \tag{5.20}$$

The meaning of S, Tr is like those represented in Section 5.7.4. Now introducing a new disturbing transition Tr_{dam} and a disturbed state S'^j_{i+1}, we yield a planning system that has to return the original system into the expected state S_{i+1}^j

$$Pl_{sec} = \{Tr_s^j(S'^j_{i+1}) \to S_{i+1}^j\} \tag{5.21}$$

In Section 5.7.4 we discussed a convergence of this procedure as well as derived the expressions (5.16) and (5.18) that gives us the way to implement Eq. (5.21). In application to the generation of rules, the perturbed state S'^j_{i+1} represents the initial state of the agents' system. The state S_{i+1}^j represent a desired state, where a common task Ω is solved. Decomposition algorithm produces a sequence of $\{Tr_s\}$ for each agent, so that to achieve S_{i+1}^j from S'^j_{i+1}. From an agent's viewpoint, each agent Ag_k has a sequence of activities S_k allowing the common group to accomplish Ω. Note, that all constraints as well as communication are implicitly contained in S_k.

We assume that the sequences $\{Tr_s\}$ **have an internal structure, that can be reproduced by a set of generating (local) rules.** In several cases, these rules are very obvious. More generally, to derive the local rules R_k, we can calculate the Kolmogorov complexity of sequence S_k (finding the smallest grammar ((Charikar *et al.*, 2002))). There are known several approaches - Bisection algorithm, the scheme LZ77 (see e.g. (Charikar *et al.*, 2002)). In this way, we can formally derive the set of these rules that defines a cooperation between agents and allows the agents' group jointly to solve the common task Ω. We point once again that the top-down approach does not try to find any solutions from knowing (or determining) all interactions among agents. We utilize a **computational approach** to approximate such a solution. **The local rules generate only a specific behavioral pattern, but do not preprogram each step of an agent.** Note, that the set of local rules $\{R\}$ generates not only one desired pattern but a cluster of such patterns that can be then parameterized. We illustrate this idea in the next section.

5.8.3 Emergent spatial behavior

In this section we demonstrate an example of using the decomposition approach, mentioned before, for deriving emergent spatial behavior. This will be first applied for simulation environment and later for real robotic swarm. In simulation we used discrete 8-directional DOFs motion systems, motivated by the embodiment concept and real robots Jasmine, explained in Section 5.9. Since the agents possess several specific motion properties, we can consider them as microscopic restrictions. In this section, we intend to show that the local rules for this specific motion system can be obtained in the mentioned top-down way by using a computational approach. We demonstrate also a construction of the generator Γ and a difference between a formation of spatially regular and irregular configuration. Moreover, we compare an efficiency of the "bottom-up" and "top-down" local rules. The macroscopic patterns Ω are the simple n-polygonal shapes (triangle, square and so on) determined by distances D between corresponding corners of these shapes. The group of robots has to reproduce these shapes (to build the same spatial construction).

Construction of FA-network. We have n agents that have activities of type "move" and feature "position", $Ag_i = (A = \{M\}, F_A = (x, y))$. All positions are calculated in local agent's coordinates, where own position of an agent represents the origin of coordinates. "Move" consists if 9 activities: 8 one-step movements in each compass direction of the 8-neighborhood, as shown in Figure 5.16(c), and one activity "do nothing", $M = (1, 2, 3, ..., 9)$. In the FA-network we connect a position of one agent with activity "move" of other agent, $N_{FA} = (A(move) \times F_A(x, y))$. It means, *if an agent has to change a position of another agent, it has to "move" itself.* The very simple action system is chosen by the reason of presentation's clearness. Disadvantage consists in a set of initial deadlocks (e.g. all agents are placed on the diagonal line), where agents cannot make any progress.

Construction of the planning system. States of a planer are global spatial positions (x, y) of corresponding corners of spatial shapes. Transitions are distance-relations between these corners. The state S_{i+1}^j is a final constellation of all corner-points, representing this shape, see Figures 5.16(a)-(c).

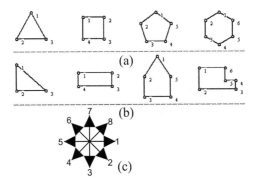

Figure 5.16: **(a)** *The first row: regular spatial formations;* **(b)** *The second row: irregular spatial formations;* **(c)** *Sensor's compass directions of target, the same directions are used for actors.*

Perturbation. Perturbed state of system $S_{i+1}'^j$ is a set of agents' random initial positions. Therefore, agents' initial positions are random with one restriction: they cannot be positioned on one line.

Construction of generator Γ. The generator Γ composes each agent's working step WS so that to minimize $\triangle S'$, i.e. deviation between $S_{i+1}'^j$ and S_{i+1}^j in terms of available activities. It reads a target and a distance from the planning system (the corresponding

spatial pattern) and tries to minimize distance between itself and the chosen target
D=distance(itself and target[from plan]);

```
for (int i=1; i<=9; i++) {
do (virtual Activity i);
D[i]=distance(itself and target[from plan]);}
```

j=find minimal(delta=D-D[j]); do (Activity j);

Executing. In the executing (see Figure 5.17), the algorithm produces a sequence of
agents step ("evolutional" rules). In this derived S_k we analyzed a dependence between

$$t=0 \qquad t=100 \qquad t=200 \qquad t=300$$

Figure 5.17: *Dynamics of forming spatial groups, $t = 0$ - initial formation, $t = 300$ - final formation
(in each section links - original shape, right - reproduced shape).*

agent's movement i_{actors} and sensor data $i_{sensors}$. Since the actor's system consists only
of 8 movements of the same type, for analysis we do not need complex approaches. In
Figure 5.18 we plot $i_{sensors} - i_{actors}$ for the cases increasing and decreasing a distance.

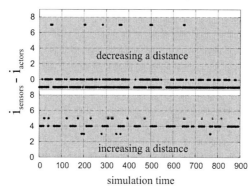

simulation time

Figure 5.18: *Difference between agents' movement i_{actors} and sensor data $i_{sensors}$ for the cases
increasing and decreasing a distance.*

The rules, generating these sequences, have the following form (Ds - distance between
agent and target from sensors, i - direction of target, Dp - distance between agent and target
from plan (patterns in figures 5.16):

```
if (Ds<Dp) {for even i -> do (Activity i-4);
            for odd i  -> do (Activity i-3);}
if (Ds>Dp) {for even i -> do (Activity i);
            for odd i -> do (Activity i-1);}
```

This is very surprising result. For even sensor's directions (2,4,6,8), see Figure 5.16(c), agent moves directly towards or directly backwards a target. However, for odd sensor's directions (1,3,5,7) it does not use direct movement, it moves sideways! To prove this unexpected result we compare these "top-down" rules with the following ones

```
if (Ds<Dp)  for i -> do (Activity i-4);
if (Ds>Dp)  for i -> do (Activity i);
```

obtained by a "common sense logic" in the "bottom-up" way. Here we use only direct movement towards or backwards a target. Comparison between the number of steps, needed to reproduce the given pattern, with different sets of local rules is shown in Figure 5.19.

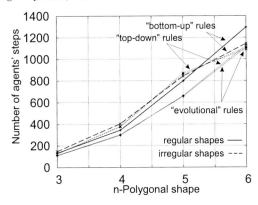

Figure 5.19: *Comparison between the number of steps, needed to reproduce the shapes from Figures 5.16(a), 5.16(b). Agents start from random initial conditions, 100×100 square, shown is the average result of 100 000 simulation's cycles.*

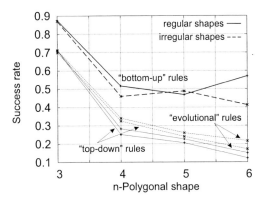

Figure 5.20: *The reproduction rate for random initial conditions.*

As shown in this figure, the "bottom-up" rules require the most numbers of steps to reproduce the corresponding shape. The "evolutional" and "top-down" rules differs in ≈

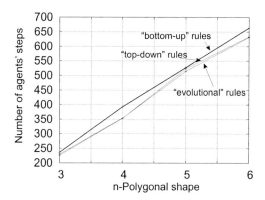

Figure 5.21: *Comparison between the number of steps, needed to reproduce the shapes from Figure 5.16. Agents start in natural order from random initial conditions in a circle of radius 100, $Tresh = 50$, shown is the average result of 100 000 simulation's cycles.*

1%, that point to a good quality of approximating rules. By increasing the number of simulation's cycles, they are expected to be coincided. The "top-down" and the "bottom-up" sets differ in 5-20%. Another interesting result is that the **more regular and less regular shapes with the same area** requires different number of steps. Less regular shapes from Figure 5.16(b) require more steps.

As already mentioned, the "rudimentary" actor system has some initial deadlocks. As turned out, the "bottom-up" rules are more stable to different initial conditions, as shown in Figure 5.20. To compare the rules in "ideal" conditions, we place agent in natural order (but also randomly) on the circle. Moreover, we require that a difference between the pattern and the reproduced shape is less then the threshold $Tresh$. In this way the reproduction rate is of ≈99% for all rules for all shapes. In these conditions we compare again the number of steps required to reproduce the shapes for three sets of rules, as shown in Figure 5.21. We see, that although the difference between "bottom-up" rules and others gets smaller, they anyway remain less efficient, than "evolutionary" and "top-down" rules.

Can the shapes from Figure 5.16(a)-(b) be generated without reading distances from the pattern ? For equilateral triangle in Figure 5.16(a) it is possible (for large number of agents it appears in hexagonal structures). However, can the shape from Figure 3.10 be generated in "evolutional" way ? As mentioned, we know only one type of evolution that can reproduce it - namely, the evolution of human civilization ! If we need more "compact" generator, we need to describe all irregularities in the shape. *Remark, that local rules do not predetermine the behavior of agent, they create a specific group's behavioral pattern, that can reproduce any of shapes from Figure 5.16.*

5.8.4   Emergent functional behavior: assembling

In the previous example we have shown, that the rules for emergent spatial behavior can be derived in the top-down way, and they are more efficient, than the bottom-up rules. However, in the micro-robotic scenario, as well as in the industrial manufacturing scenario, we need also different types of **functional behavior**. We consider such a functional behavior on the example of assembling of micro-objects. This example is already introduced in Section 3.5.1.

Here we only introduce some formalism, according to the ASTD approach.

Construction of FA-network. The first type of agents, Ag^1 can rotate an object, $Ag^1 = (A = \{move, rotate\}, F_A = (x, y))$, where as the second one can transport an object $Ag^2 = (A = \{move, transport\}, F_A = (x, y))$. Both agents have a feature "position" (x, y) in the agent's local coordinate system and have a movement system like the agents from the previous section. Objects have features "position" (x, y), "rotation angle" α and "geometry" (h, l), $Ob^1 = (F_O = \{(x, y), \alpha, (h_1, l_1)\})$, $Ob^2 = (F_O = \{(x, y), \alpha, (h_2, l_2)\})$. The FA-network N_{FA} connects "rotation" with "angle", "transport" with "position" of objects, and "move" with "position" of agents, $N_{FA} = (A(rotate) \times F_O(\alpha); A(transport) \times F_O(x, y); A(move) \times F_A(x, y))$. Each agent observes neighbors in some radius R_{vis} and within this radius can recognize a distance to target and a rotational angle of target. In order to simplify the FA-network, we do not consider collisions between agents and an agent takes an object by placing itself in the geometric origin of an object (x_0, y_0). Activity of each agent can be represented in the form of Petri-nodes. In order to start an activity, a lot of local restrictions C_l (shown in Figure 3.3 in Section 3.5.1) has to be fulfilled.

Construction of the planning system. A plan of an assembling has a form of the 7th-nodes Petri net, shown in Figure 3.2 in Section 3.5.1. The restrictions from this plan are the global restrictions C_g. Agents read from plan only relative distances between objects (position of assembling place is marked by a mark). If an agent starts some activity with an object, it marks this object by putting a number of current phase on the mark (e.g. in the electromagnetic way).

Perturbation S'_{n+1}. Agents and objects are placed randomly, but without intersections between objects.

Construction of generator Γ. The generator Γ composes activities so that to minimize $\Delta S'$. However we see, that activities of agents are bounded by constraints C_l and C_g so that they can not be generated in the way, shown in Section 5.8.3 (generally we solve this problem as the constraint satisfaction problem (CPS) (Kornienko *et al.*, 2004c)). In this case the generator Γ minimizes $\Delta S'$ simply by choosing different order of allowed phases p_i (here we do not consider other group's strategies):

```
i=take random phase; do (planning activities);
choice i so that to minimize common time;
```

Executing. Each agent looks for objects within R_{vis} and reads the objects' marks. It takes C_g and the modality D from the plan. The agent's local rules consist of C_l from Figure 3.3 and the rule "do close phase(Activity)", obtained from the generator Γ:

```
Ob=look for (visible objects); read mark (Ob);
if (constraints(Ob)) do close phase (Activity);
```

This additional rule optimizes cooperation between agents and means, if an agent has a choice, it chooses an activity most closely to the first phase. The generated agent-agent cooperation is shown in Figure 5.22. Now we can "improve" this cooperation by putting the additional "bottom-up" cooperation rule:

```
I'm Ag_i; if ($Ag_j$=take the same Ob as I){
Ob belongs to Ag with smaller distance to it;}
```

In Figure 5.23 we show the comparison between the "bottom-up" and "top-down" rules. For small n, the "top-down" rules are more efficient. However, if n grows, new group's strategies appear and we have correspondingly to modify the generator Γ.

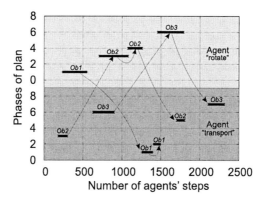

Figure 5.22: *The agent-agent cooperation, generated by the "top-down" rules.*

5.8.5 Scalability of emergent behavior

As known from natural systems, emergent behavior is scalable, the number of participants can be increased and decreased without essential change of behavior's features. However, investigating scalability in technical systems we encounter two following issues.

Appearance of rules hierarchy.

If the desired emergent behavior is regular, the scaling does not represent any problems. However, if the desired pattern contains irregularities, we need additional rules that describe scalability of irregularities. These irregularities are nonsymmetric form of shapes, specific connections between basic elements (see Figure 5.24) and so on. As a result, a hierarchy of rules appears (see Figure 5.25). The more irregularities will be inserted into the scaled pattern, the more hierarchical rules need to be introduced into each agent. There are two main problems of such a rules' hierarchy. The first one consists in a close connection with a size of a group. At really large groups there arises a large hierarchy of rules, so that a hardware abilities of real micro-robots can be quickly exhausted. The second problem is rules' preconditions. Each behavioral rule has a precondition and a post-condition, as shown in Figure 3.3. If there arise many hierarchical rules, then there arise also many hierarchical pre-conditions. At each step, an agent tries to calculate all these preconditions in order to choose the next rule. It consumes time and computational resources. Generally, this problem is also known in other robotic scenarios, e.g. soccer-playing robots in RoboCup. However, for micro-robots, this can have essentially more grievous consequences. Therefore irregularities of emergent behavioral patterns represents a serious obstacle, especially in large groups. A strategy to get round this problem consists in finding a compromise between "useful" and "useless" emergency, as mentioned in Section 3.5.1.

Change of collective strategy.

By scaling, the group can undergo a change of collective strategy. This effect was demonstrated by putting the additional "bottom-up" cooperation rule into assembling rules, discussed in the previous section. For a small number of agents, the "top-down" rules are more efficient. However, if this number grows, the "top-down" rules becomes less efficient. At some turn-over-threshold, the group changes the collective strategy and the "old" rules can not guarantee any longer the achievement of desired emergence. Therefore this effect, and especially a drift of the turn-over-threshold, has to be taken into account at the top-

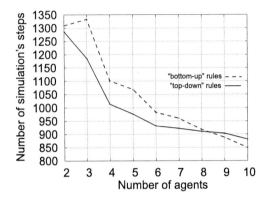

Figure 5.23: *Comparison between the "bottom-up" and "top-down" rules. Agents start from random initial conditions,100×100 square,R_{vis} = 400, shown is the average result of 100000 simulation's cycles.*

down design of local rules.

5.9 Structural emergence and embodiment in real micro-robotic swarm

In this section we consider the next step in creating structural phenomena: a few practical examples of artificial self-organization applied to a micro-robotic swarm based on the robot Jasmine. This robot has been developed by author (robot's concept, electronics, modularity, BIOS/autonomy cycle software) within the framework of open-hardware project, where he was a coordinator. The robot was developed by taking into account the capabilities of collective work in a swarm. Formulated more formally, these capabilities are embodied microscopic and macroscopic constraints, which are also represented here.

5.9.1 Embodiment and self-organization

As already mentioned in Section 5.8, miniaturization represents now a very important trend in many areas of research. Molecular-scale or nanotechnological devices jumped from science-fiction novels to research papers. Even the today's technology allows creating complete autonomous systems, such as robots, in the size of 1 mm^3. As demonstrated by a progress in the I-Swarm project (I-Swarm, 2003-2007), the swarm of thousand such micro-robots gets reality as well as come into the reality impressive applications of this technology.

The scaling down of the hardware influences almost all important parameters of micro-robots, as e.g. running time, communication distance and channel capacity, computational power, movement and so on. However, we ask ourselves about *"intelligence" of such a micro-robot; is it also scaled down so that we get finally some "stupid moving thing"* (Kornienko et al., 2004d) ? Since many years there exists in the scientific literature the opinion that "artificial intelligence" for very small systems drifts towards "collective artificial intelligence", like those in social insects (Bonabeau et al., 1999). For collective systems the "individual intelligence" gets some pre-intelligence form. The question is *which minimal degree of individual intelligence does allow growing "collective intelligence"* ?

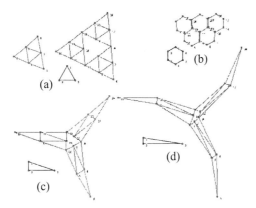

Figure 5.24: *Examples of scaled spatial formations, built dynamically by agents. Small shapes represent basic structural elements of corresponding formations.*

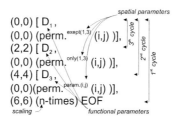

Figure 5.25: *Appearance of rules' hierarchy at the scaling, shown is the schematic output of LZ77 algorithm.*

For answering these questions we designed and prototyped our own micro-robot, calls Jasmine. This is is actually larger as envisioned in I-Swarm project however is very cheap and easy to reproduce without specific equipment. The size of the robot is $26 \times 26 \times 20$mm. It uses the two Atmel AVR Mega microcontrollers, the details of robot construction will be given in the Section 5.9.2. Based on this robot we can investigate questions about "individual/collective intelligence". However, the real micro-robotic system allows us not only to look for inspiration of "individual/collective intelligence", but also to demonstrate the following idea: real artificial emergence has additional degree of freedom, we call it *embodiment*.

The point is that micro-robots, due to small size, are very restricted in hardware capabilities. The most important constraints are the communication and perception radius, type of sensors, time of autonomous work and so on. We can say, that the microscopic constrains originate mainly from a construction of a robot (see e.g. the micro-robot Jasmine in Figure 5.26(r)). These individual capabilities essentially impact a group behavior.

Macroscopic constraints arise if the collective systems have to emerge the technically useful behavior. The appearance of these constraints has been demonstrated in Section 3.5.1 on a simple assembling example, where robots push three different objects into one defined construction. The microscopic and macroscopic constraints as well as parameterization and optimization of the emergent behavior appear on the swarm level. All these constraints are closely related with each other and hardly limit the emergent properties of collective systems. In trying to derive the desired emergence, we permanently confront with these constraints so that we identify *the problem of constrained emergent behavior as one of the main problems in artificial swarms* (from the viewpoint of controlling). Without systematic procedure, that allows involving constraints into the collective behavior, the derivation of desired emergence is performed mostly "by trial and error". How to put all these, often conflicting requirements, into one robust system ? In this section we demonstrate that one successful way may consist in a specific system development, where the requirements are implemented in hardware and software by using the top-down methodology.

To exemplify this idea, let us consider again the rule generation approaches, described in the sections 4.2 and 5.8.2-5.8.4. These top-down obtained rules R_k produce a sequence of agents steps S_k allowing building different spatial or functional behavioral types. However, during derivation of these local rules R_k we assume some basic functionality F_b, like message transmission or environmental sensing. However, the perfectly working simulative sensors essentially differ from real ones. In this way the swarm behavior, generated by R_k, often diverges from our expectations. To get round this problem, we involved the embodiment concept. This says that the same functionality can be implemented in many different ways: Rolf Pfeiffer demonstrated that an "intelligent behavior" can even be implemented when using only some properties of materials (Pfeifer & Iida, 2004). Embodied functionally is also often implemented in some "unusual" way. For example a robot can get a distance to neighbors by sending an IR-impulse and measuring a reflected light. However, distances can also be obtaining during communication by measuring a signal intensity. This simple trick saves time and energy: such an unusual functionality is a typical sight of embodiment.

More generally, embodiment means that the system possesses the desired functionality F_b, but this functionality is in a latent form, "it is not appeared". This offers a way of how to get a basic functionality for the local rules R_k: the local rules have to influence the hardware development of a robot. The swarm embodiment takes then the following form: definition of the macroscopic pattern Ω and the corresponding microscopic/macroscopic constraints; derivation of the local rules R_k; trade off between required functionality and adjustment of hardware; change of the hardware. The local rules have always been considered as a pure software components, however now they are a combination between software and hardware. We can say that in this way *the local rules for the whole swarm behavior are embodied into each individual robot*. In the following sections we demonstrate how the embodiment influence the hardware and software development of the micro-robot Jasmine and show the real swarm experiments with these robots.

5.9.2 Microscopic constrains: micro-robot Jasmine

The development of the micro-robot Jasmine started in October 2004. It was originally a joint development of University of Stuttgart (all electronic parts) and University of Karlsruhe (mechanic pars). Idea of making a robot originated from the I-Swarm project, where this robot has been applied for tests of algorithms (and mostly BIOS system) before a development of the I-Swarm robot. However, later Jasmine followed its own way as public open-hardware development in **www.swarmrobot.org**, where many persons, companies and research institutions contributed to further development. The presented here version Jasmine-III (finish of development December 2005) is developed by author. The choice of the name "Jasmine" was influenced by the personage from the Disney's "Alladin" during the first development and tests (see Figure 5.26(c)).

On the development, one of our goals was to create a simple micro-robot, that could be easy reproduced without special equipment. Therefore, the communication and sensing components should be cheap and available on micro-components market. They should consume as less energy as possible so that to be directly powered by I/O port of microcontrollers, as such from Microchip or Atmel (20-25 mA each port, totally up to 300-400 mA). They should be also of a small size so that to be placed in the chassis *less than 30mm-cube*. Finally, the same sensors have to be used, as far as possible, for communication, proximity sensing and perception. The time of autonomous work should be at least of 1-2 hours with Li-Po accumulators and voltage supply 3 or 5 volt.

The first development was based on the megabitty (Megabitty, 2005) board (see Figures 5.26(a)-(e)), however from the third version we switch to own microcontroller board. From the beginning we developed a few different versions of the robot, shown in Figure 5.26. In the version III, the robot has two microcontrollers: Atmel Mega88 (motor control, odometry, touch and internal sensing) and Mega168 (communication, sensing, perception, remote control and user defined tasks), 6 (60 degree opening angle) communication channels (they are also used for proximity sensing) and one perception channel (15 degree opening angle) based on the IR receivers and transmitters. Both microcontrollers communicate through high-speed two-wired TWI (I2C) interface. It has also remote control and robot-host communication (uplink and downlink), which is isolated from all other channels (through modulation). The robot uses two DC motors with internal gears, two differentially driven wheels on one axis with a geared motor-wheels coupling. Jasmine III uses 3V power supply (from 3,7V Li-Po accumulator) with internal IC-stabilization of voltage. Power consumption during motion is about 200mA, in stand - 10-30mA, in stand-by mode less 1 mA.

Because we need a swarm robot, and not a stand-alone robot, we put into development many ideas from the previous chanters of this PhD work. It concerns mainly communication, working on top-down derived rules and cooperative actuation. These steps, denoted as Embodiment I, II and III are described in the next sections.

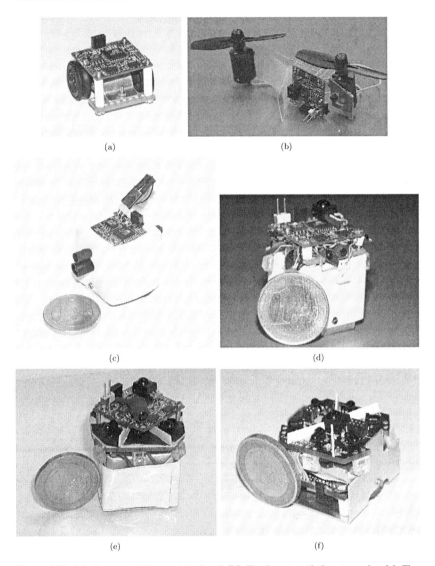

(a)   (b)

(c)   (d)

(e)   (f)

Figure 5.26: (a) *Chassis with the megabitty board;* (b) *The fly-tests with the micro-robot;* (c) *The first test development for testing of sensors;* (d) *The first version of micro-robot Jasmine;* (e) *The second version of micro-robot Jasmine;* (f) *The third version of micro-robot Jasmine;*

5.9.3 Embodiment I: information diffusion and swarm density

The communication is the most important component for real swarm system. It plays the role like nervous system in human body. Since micro-robots in a swarm can communicate only locally with their neighbors, such a "swarm nervous system" can be produced only by a mechanism that propagates information through multiple robot-robot connections. Parameters of a global circulation of information (like global propagation speed or global propagation time) depend on characteristics of local communication (communication radius R_c, the number of robots within R_c). In this section we demonstrate the embodiment of swarm communication into hardware and software. We start with a derivation of theoretical relations, which are necessary for further development of the robot's communication hardware, after that we show the hardware and software development.

Parameters of local communication between robots depend on their behavior, therefore we differentiate three following behavioral cases:

1. Robots move only in small areas, so called clusters. In this case robots are situated more or less closely to each other, so that swarm peer-to-peer network (SPPN) is created "automatically". The main problem is a communication between such clusters.

2. Robots move in large areas (typical swarm scenario). Robots exchange information only when they meet each other. The inter-cluster communication belongs to this case.

3. Part of robotic swarm purposely creates and supports the SPPN. This is the most interesting case, that provide stable communication in swarm .

In the further calculation we consider the most hardest case of a large-area swarm. We can intuitively assume that the communication radius R_c, the swarm density D_{sw}, the robots motion velocity v and the time t are closely related in propagating the information. For deriving a relation between them, we take several analogies to molecular-kinetic theory of ideal gas, more exactly diffusion in ideal gas (by these analogies we denote also a "diffusion of information"). We introduce the following notions: the sensor radius R_s, where a collision-avoiding procedure is started; l_c the length of free path from the start of motion till the first communication contact; l_s the length of free path from the start of motion till the first collision-avoiding contact; n_c and n_s are correspondingly the number of communication and collision-avoiding contacts; S_c and S_s are the area of the "broken" rectangles built by a motion in some time interval t with R_c and R_s. In Figure 5.27(a) we sketch our consideration. Firstly, we are interested in the number of communication contacts n_c happen during the motion. This value is equal to the average number of robots in the area S_c,

$$n_c = S_c D_{sw}, \tag{5.22}$$

where D_{sw} is the swarm density. We assume that the collision avoiding radius and the robot's rotation radius are small so that we can neglect the area of fractures. In this case $S_c = 2R_c vt$. D_{sw} can be calculated as the number of robots N in swarm divided by the area available for the whole swarm S_{sw}:

$$D_{sw} = \frac{N}{S_{sw}} \quad \rightarrow \quad n_c = \frac{2R_c vt N}{S_{sw}}. \tag{5.23}$$

In the relation (5.23) we assume only one robot moves whereas other are motionless. More exact relation, when all robots move, differs from (5.23) only by the numeric coefficient $\sqrt{2}$ (as proved by Maxwell for a diffusion in ideal gas). For the further calculation we use

$$n_c = \frac{2\sqrt{2} R_c vt N}{S_{sw}}. \tag{5.24}$$

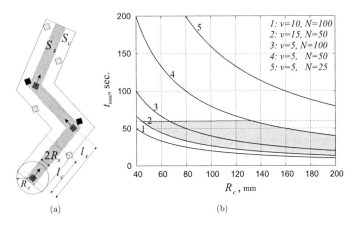

(a)   (b)

Figure 5.27: **(a)** *Motion path of a robot with communication and collision-avoiding contacts;* **(b)** *Total propagation time t_{total} as a function of communication distance R_c with different values of velocity v and the number of robots N.*

Now we have to estimate how the information will be propagated after the first communication contact. This propagation dynamics is similar to "epidemic infection" dynamics, estimated as the series:

$$[n_c + 1] + n_c[n_c + 1] + n_c[n_c + 1 + n_c(n_c + 1)] + ... \quad (5.25)$$

and written iteratively as

$$k_n = n_c k_{n-1} + k_{n-1} = k_{n-1}(n_c + 1), \qquad k_0 = 1. \quad (5.26)$$

that is the "standard" exponential form $(n_c + 1)^n$. We are interested in the case when all robots are "infected" $(n_c + 1)^n \geq N$ or $n = log_{(n_c+1)}N$. From real experiments we know that for establishing a communication contact and transmitting messages, robots need some time p_t, that can be measured experimentally. The information transfer starts when the first robot "infects" one additional robot($n_c = 1$); the time till the first infection t_{first} and the total time $t_{total} = n \ t_{first} + N p_t$ for infecting the whole swarm can be obtained as:

$$t_{first} = \frac{S_{sw}}{2\sqrt{2}R_c v N}, \quad t_{total} = N p_t + \frac{S_{sw}}{2\sqrt{2}R_c v N} log_2(N). \quad (5.27)$$

In the performed simulations ($p_t = 0$), the swarm areal is $800 \times 650 \ pixels^2$, $N = 50$ with $D_{sw} \approx 10 \ pix./sec.$, $R_c = 40 \ pix.$ Formula (5.27) gives us $t_{total} \approx 52 \ sec..$ In many performed simulation cycles we observed t_{total} between 30 and 90 sec. Formula (5.27) is also useful in estimating the energy needed for each robot. For example, swarm during the running time has to propagate 100 different messages; it takes about 2 hours in the mentioned example. So the power supply should provide energy at least for 2 hours.

For developing a real micro-robotic swarm we can take $S_{sw} = 1000 \times 1000 \ mm^2$, $N = 50$ and assume first $p_t = 0$ (see Section 5.9.6 for the real p_t). In Figure 5.27(b) we plot t_{total} depending of R_c with different values of N and v. We see, that for the average propagation time 1 min, the R_c for $N = 50$ lies between 50 mm and 140 mm. Thus, for the targeted robots body of 25-30 mm, the communication radius R_c is of 4-5 times larger then the size of the robot.

At the end of this section we discuss such an important point as the critical swarm density D_{sw}^{crit}. The critical swarm density and the "coefficient of swarm efficiency" (the relation between the number of robots with useful/desired and useless/undesired activities) determine the minimal number of robots N_{min} in some areal S_{ws} required to perform some operation successfully. For the considered example with the given $S_{sw} = 1000 \times 1000\ mm^2$, $t_{total} = 30\ sec.$, $R_c = 100\ mm$ and $v = 20mm/sec.$ (related to the random motion), the minimal number $N_{min} \approx 29$ and the critical swarm density $D_{sw}^{crit} = 28.46^{-6}$. This relation is not exact, because it does not involve the size of a robot into this calculation, however in the micro-robotic case with $S_{robot} \ll S_{sw}$, it can serve as a good approximation.

Hardware requirements

The requirements concern choosing the transmission equipment, the number of directional communication channels, communication radius and the hardware reduction of communication deadlocks. The communication equipment of a micro-robot should consume as less energy as possible and be of a small size. Finally, the communication equipment should include, as far as possible, other functions, like proximity or distance measurement. The communication radius $R_c = 50 - 140\ mm$ can be implemented in the radio-frequency (RF) and infrared (IR) way.

The *RF* provides duplex communication within several meters and modern one-chip RF modules, even 802.11b/802.11g modules, consume energy in mW area. However, we have a serious objection against RF in a swarm. Firstly, simultaneous transmissions of many (80-150) micro-robots lead to massive RF-interferences. Secondly, RF-systems with a large communication radius transmit local information (exchange between neighbor robots) globally in a swarm. This local information does not have too much sense for all robots, so that we have high communication overhead in this case. RF-communication is still useful for a global host-robot communication.

Wire communication takes place when one robot touches another one. In this moment they have high-speed connection, where essential amount of information can be exchanged within milliseconds. Although transmission speed is high, the communication radius is of robot's body (20-30 mm), therefore the time required for global propagation of information is very large (we do not consider collision avoiding issues of wired communication).

The *IR communication* is recently dominant in so-called small-distance-domain, as e.g. for communication between laptops, hand-held devices, remote control and others. In IR domain we can choose between several different technologies, like IrDA[1], 34-38 Khz PCM-based devices and so on. Additional advantage of IR solution consists in performing communication and proximity/distance sensing with the same sensors. IR emitter-receiver provides half-duplex communication, they are compact and energy consumption corresponds to I/O ports of microcontrollers. The IR solution is not new in robotic domain, see e.g. (Kube, 1996), (Suzuki *et al.*, 1995), however there are almost no solutions that combine perception, proximity sensing and communication.

The IR-equipment has also the problem of interferences. They appear, like in RF case, when several neighbor robots transmit simultaneously. The problem of IR-interferences can be avoided by restricting an opening angle of a pair IR-receiver-transmitter. For four communication channels, the opening angle of each channel is $90°$. In this case we have 2- and

---

[1]IrDA requires additional chips, and if we think about 4-6 channels communication, this solution is not really suitable for the implementation in micro-robots.

3-robots IR-interferences even in the "closest" radius (50 mm). Reducing the opening angle to 60° or to 40° allows avoiding IR-interferences in the "close" and "near" radius (100 mm) (Figure 5.28(a)). Since many microcontrollers have 8-channel ADC (one ADC input is used by the distance sensor), we choose 6-channel directional communication (Figure 5.28(b)).

Directional communication is extremely important in a swarm also from another reason. The point is that a robot has to know not only a message itself, but also the context of this message (e.g. the direction from which the message is received, intensity of signal, communicating neighbor and so on). Without directional communication hardware, we cannot implement algorithms providing a spatial context. From many software requirements the communication radius R_c and the number of directional communication channels are the most important ones. From this viewpoint, the IR is more suitable for robot-robot communication than the RF. The host-robot communication can also be implemented with IR (a sensor with PCM-filter for receiving global modulated signal). Such a signal can be thought as of a remote control or a global information exchange between robots and host.

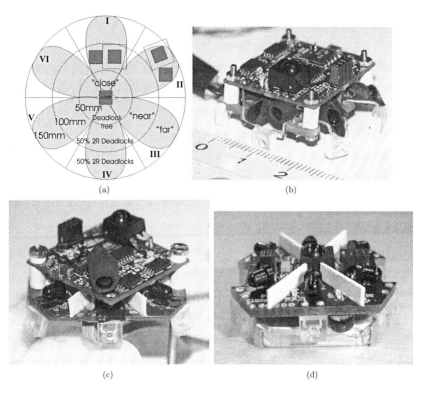

Figure 5.28: **(a)** *Problem of IR-interferences in the "close", "near" and "far" communication zones;* **(b)** *The first version of the sensors board (with Megabitty board) that supports 6-x directional robot-robot and host-robot communication proximity sensing and perception of surfaces geometry;* **(c)** *The second version of the sensors board;* **(c)** *The third version of the sensors board.*

Influence of ambient light on communication/reflextion

Speaking about IR communication, we have to mention the problem of ambient light. Ambient light represents generally very critical issue, because it can essentially distort or even completely break IR communication/sensing. The experiments are performed with luminescent lamp, filament lamp and daylight. We can estimate three different components of a distortion introduced by ambient light. The direct light saturates photoelectric transistor so that it gets "blind". Secondly, ambient light reduces sensor sensitivity, even when it does not fail directly on sensor. Finally, indirect ambient light reduces contrasts between object and background, so that results of measurement are no more reliable and reproducible. In Table 5.3 we collect some qualitative results. As followed from this table, a **swarm has**

IR device	Filament lamp	Daylight	Luminescent lamp
IR sensors without ambient light filter $\lambda \approx 300...1100\ nm$	completely "blind"	"blind" or sensitivity very reduced	R_c reduced on 20%-50%
IR sensors with ambient light filter $\lambda \approx 880...1000\ nm$	R_c reduced on 80%-90%	R_c reduced on 20%-50%	small "dark" current
IR sensors based on modulated IR radiation	it works, but not always stable	OK for small R_c, not stable for large R_c	no remarkable enfluence

Table 5.3: *Some qualitative results by testing different IR devices with ambient light.*

to be protected against a light of filament lamps. As far as possible, the direct daylight should be also avoided. Use of modulated light can essentially improve communication against ambient light, however this solution is not always feasible/acceptable.

The filament lamps can be used as a global pheromone to control a swarm (Bonabeau *et al.*, 1999). When it is emitted simultaneously with luminescent light, the robot reacts more intensively on filament light. This effect can be utilized in many purposes, like finding the food source, navigation or even a quick message about some global event. This communication way does not require any additional sensors, however should be used only as an exception, because it essentially distorts a regular communication.

Implementation

In the following, we briefly describe the developed hardware solution for the directional IR-communication and sensing. More details for hardware can be found in (Kornienko *et al.*, 2005c). In the hardware we do not use such popular sensors as IS471F or Sharp's GP2Dxxx with binary output, because they do not assume active control needed for communication. We encountered that small integrated transistor-diode pairs like SFH9201, TCNT1000, TCRT 1000/1010, GP2D120, QRB1134 are not suitable as distance, proximity and communicating sensors for R_c of 130-150 mm. There are also several problems with spectral matching of some receiver-emitter pairs, despite they use the same wavelength. In the tested phototransistors with 60° angle, we choose TEFT4300 (60°, collector light current 3,2 mA, 875...1000 nm), TSKS5400-FSZ as IR-emitter for proximity measurement and communication (60°, 950 nm, 2-7 mW/sr) and GaAs/GaAlAs IR-emitter TSAL6100 (20°, 950 nm, >80 mW/sr) for distance measurement. This pair is very small (emitter 5x5x2.65

mm and receiver 4,5xϕ3 mm) so that they can easily be integrated in the sensors board. In experiments the current I_F of IR-emitters was limited to 20 mA, that corresponds to I/O port of the microcontroller. The developed sensors boards are shown in Figure 5.28.

In experiments we used the following pairs TEST2600:TSSS2600, TEFT4300: (IRL80A, TSKS5400-FSZ, LD271L), integrated sensors SFH9201, TCNT1000, TCRT1000, QRB1134, QRD1113. Generally we tested also IR emitters with small opening angles like SFH409, but they do not satisfy the requirements. We also have several problems to isolate TEST2600:TSSS2600 optically one from another. This pair has wide vertical opening angle 120°, so that to remove completely a leak of IR radiation in sensor was not really possible. In Fig. 5.29(a) we demonstrate the emitter voltage of IR receiver in dependence of distances in the "near" and "close" zones for some tested pairs. In Fig. 5.29(b) we plot a degradation of IR radiation V_{0grad}/V_{i-grad}, depending on a deviation from the cental line (V_{0grad} was measured on the central line and V_{i-grad} voltage with corresponding angular displacement, the referent distance 100mm).

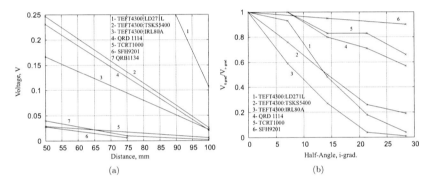

Figure 5.29: **(a)** *Dependence between output emitter voltage V_o of IR reflective pairs and distance to the object on the central line;* **(b)** *Degradation of V_o at shifting an object from the central line in the distance of 100 mm.*

Analyzing the results of experiments, we came to the conclusion that the integrated sensors are not really suitable for this application, although they have good coverage in 60° sector. The measured distances is only of 40-50 mm (on the brink of recognizability), and communication radius R_c is about 60-70 mm (also on the brink of recognizability). The IR emitters with opening angle of 40 and less degree do not provide a good coverage in 60° sector. From the tested IR emitters only one TSKS5400-FSZ demonstrated acceptable coverage that can be approximated in the algorithmic way. The sensor QRD1113 shows really good results, however it was extremely sensitive even to the luminescent light, so that its further calibration represents essential difficulties. **Receiver and emitter should be optically isolated so that to provide only 60° opening angle** (they can perceive and send till 80-90°).

Tests of communication was performed by sending small packages with PCM modulation. The duration of "T"-pulses was chosen to 1-0,5 ms, so that at least the rate 1000 bit/sec can be provided with low error rate, so that an application of error-correction approaches is not required. The communication signal from 150 mm distance on the direct line was of 0.7-0.8 V, in different directions within 60° not less than 0.1 V. The signal outside of 60° was less than 0.1 V for sensors with optical isolation. In this way robots can receive very exact information about a spatial origin of signal. Communication distance can be easy reduced (or even increased) in the algorithmic way by putting some threshold on the ADC values of IR-receivers or by modulating a signal on IR-emitters with a sub-frequency to reduce amount of emitted energy.

Software aspects of communication

After describing the IR hardware solution, we focus on the "software support" of communication and perception. As already mentioned, a propagation of information through a swarm represents the main problem (see for details (Kornienko *et al.*, 2005b)). We suggest to solve this by using directional communication with specific logical protocol. In Table 5.4 we collect some points of logical communication in swarm.

On the level of physical transmission the problem of communication is related to a choice of modulation/transmission approach suitable for the IR based signal transmission. In experiments we choose pulse code modulation (PCM) approach for remote control and inter-robot communication with half-duplex data exchange. In remote control scheme, the input of PCM sensor (TSOP4836, 36kH sub-frequency) is connected with the external interruption input of the microcontroller. Activating the interruption on the failing or rising edges we can differentiate between T and information impulses. Timer counts during information impulses so that we can easily recognize logical "0" and "1". Inter-robot communication utilizes similar principle, however does not modulate the signal with sub-frequency.

Level of logical communication	Known solution	Problems in swarm application
IR based signal transmission	Simple impulses PCM, PWM IrDA	Small channel capacity Problems with encoding Specific hardware
Comm. protocols, propagation of information	Package-based Pheromone-based	Problem of routing Small infom. capacity
Subsystems that require communication	Collective perception Coordination Decision making	—
Creating and supporting SPPN	Small-area swarms Inter-clusters exchange Active SPPN	Not realistic Req. too much energy Robots overhead

Table 5.4: *Levels of logical communication in swarm.*

Level of logical communication protocols concerns the propagation of information in swarm. We investigated several approaches like package- and pheromone-based communication, some indirect communication mechanisms. The main problem of package-based logical communication is a routing of messages through a swarm and providing a context of messages. In (Kornienko *et al.*, 2005b) we suggest to use a context diffusion approach, that is similar to "spreading a virtual pheromone". As demonstrated by experiments, in this way we can solve at least a part of problems related to global propagation of information. Propagation of information can essentially be improved when at least a part of robots is contained within the communication radius of each other (so-called the swarm peer-to-peer network (SPPN) or "communication street"). More generally, by creating and supporting SPPN, the robots are able for quick communication, global navigation, spatial over-swarm perception and so on. Therefore this point is open for further research.

After a description of the communication protocols, we return to our original question about Collective Intelligence. The question is *"which degree of collective intelligence is still feasible in the group of micro-robots ?"* and *"How to implement it ?"* In Table 5.5 we collect some "swarm activities" that micro-robots can collectively perform. These collective

Context	N	Swarm Capability
Spatial	1	Spatial orientation
	2	Building spatial structures
	3	Collective movement
Information	4	Building informational structures
	5	Collective decision making
	6	Collective information processing
	7	Collective perception/recognition
Functional	8	Building functional structures
	9	Collective task decomposition
	10	Collective planning
	11	Group-based specialization

Table 5.5: *Some collective activities performed by the whole swarm.*

activities build a basis of swarm intelligence. We take the most simple example of spatial orientation. Let us assume, a robot has found a "food source" being relevant for the whole swarm. It sends the message "I, robot X, found Y, come to me". When this message is propagated through a swarm, each robot knows there is a resource Y at the robot X. However, robots cannot find it because they do not know a coordinate of this "food source". The robot X cannot provide these coordinates because it does not know its own position. Therefore even for the simple collective feature of spatial orientation, a **local context of messages determines a global capability of the whole group**. Collective systems often have many different contexts, so that we have a context hierarchy.

The main point here is that the required context can be processed/provided by communication. However, which level of communication can do it ? After hardware level, there are four such levels: level of physical signal transmission, level of communication protocols and level of informational structures, that require communication. In swarm-based systems we have the additional level concerned to the robot's behavior for creating and supporting required communication.

1. On the level of physical transmission, the problem of communication is related to a choice of modulation/transmission approaches suitable for the IR-based signal transmission. On this level such properties of signals as strength, IR-interferences, directions can be extracted and incorporated into high-level protocols (it is closely related with the robot embodiment).

2. Level of communication protocols concerns the propagation of information in a swarm. Generally, there are only two main ways of such a propagation:

- each robot routes communication packages from other robots without any changes (package-based communication);

- each robot processes the information from other low-level packages and sends only its own messages further.

In the package-based communication each package consists of a header with IDs of sender and receiver, routing information and the package content. The package ID can be coded by 10 bits, IDs of sender/receiver by 12 bits (6 bit each), so the header is of 22 bits, the package content is only of 8 bits. For recording the package history each robot needs about 900 bytes RAM only for routing 300-600 packages within a few minutes ($N = 50$ robots, each sends max. 1-2 messages each 10 sec, propagation time of 1 min.). In order to use the (spatial) context of message (e.g. the spatial location of the sender), the robots can follow the propagation way by using ID-history. However, since all robots are continuously moving, the propagation way does not exist a long time. In the simulation, when a particular robot tries to achieve the source of a message by following the propagation way, it fails in 80-90% ! After many experiments we came at the conclusion, that pure routing is not really suitable for propagating information thought a swarm (however package-based communication is used for local communication between neighbor robots). Thus, the second approach represents the main way of incorporating the information context into communication.

3,4. Levels of informational structures and specific collective behavior belong to the high level of information processing in a swarm. These levels deal with optimal representation of information, a minimization of communication flow, availability of information and supporting multiple peer-to-peer connections for a large-distance information transmission.

As already mentioned, the context of message cannot be extracted from the message itself. This point has been discussed many time in collective AI community. In "AI world" there exist some approaches to retrieve the required context, however the micro-robots are too limited to use them. Our proposal is that robots work with communication context during communication.

There are many different approaches to work with messages context. One of them is to incorporate the embodied information (signal intensity, direction, neighbors) into non-routed packages. The robots during "normal" communication process this context, so that it diffuses over a swarm. In this way a specific collective activity can be coordinated/created/controlled.

Another approach is a pheromone-based communication, well-known in natural (Bonabeau *et al.*, 1999) as well as in technical/robotic systems (Payton *et al.*, 2001). Pheromone-based communication can be divided into two main groups: with pheromone leaved on immovable objects (ground, floor and so on) and pheromone leaved on moving objects like robots. Whereas the first type of pheromone assumes usually real (physical) pheromone, like chemical substances or electromagnetic marks, the second type of pheromone can also have some virtual nature. For instance, robots exchange the values of some variables, these variables are "located" on a robot and we can speak about "virtual pheromone".

Basic idea of pheromone-based communication is quite simple. Let assume that the information source, robot X, sends a message, say "I found Y". This message is binary, however the robot X represents it by some integer value. This value is maximal at the origin. Any other robot, when getting this value, subtracts some constant and sends it further. In this way, the far away from the source the value is propagated, the less is its intensity. Based on this gradient every robot can conclude about the source Y and its origin (Figure 5.30). In this way not only a content of information ("something is found") is propagated, but also a spatial context (spatial origin of this "something"). More generally, different temporary, spatial or functional context can be provided by this "field".

Independently of the implemented mechanism, the "diffusion field" can be of four different types: non-gradient (used simply for transmitting some signals), gradient (to provide spatial context of a message), oriented (some specific direction) and functional (e.g. repelling or attracting). The values of this field can be calculated as a function of connectivity (the number of neighbors, see (Nembrini *et al.*, 2002)), time, specific input (e.g. only robots that see something transmit a pheromone), embodied information. Diffusion field can consist of

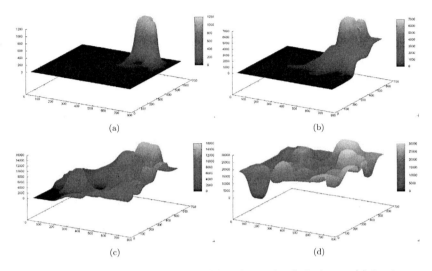

Figure 5.30: *Propagation of the pheromone field from the initial to the final states.* **(a)** *Initial state of pheromone field;* **(b,c)** *Intermediate states where propagation of field is not finished;* **(d)** *Final state of pheromone field, where all robots get the message and know its spatial origin.*

many different subfields, i.e. with hierarchical structure.

1. Diffusion of the size context. The diffusion field is a function of the connectivity degree:

$$\Phi_{n+1} = f(\textstyle\sum_i \Phi_n^i) \tag{5.28}$$

where i goes over all local neighbors. The more large is the group of robots, the more higher is the value, so that a context is the size of the whole group.

2. Diffusion of the spatial context. The source emits a constant value. All other robots subtract some constants C_i from this value (see Figure 5.30):

$$\Phi_{n+1}^{source} = C_1, \Phi_{n+1} = f(\textstyle\sum_i \Phi_n^i) - C_2 \tag{5.29}$$

and transmit it further. Disadvantage of this relation is that robots can move in clusters, so that we can have local maximums of the diffusion field. Instead we can use

$$\Phi_{n+1} = f(\max(\Phi_n^1, ..., \Phi_n^i,)) - C_2. \tag{5.30}$$

In this case the clusterization effect is removed (however it cannot be completely removed from a swarm).

3. Diffusion of the directional context. As already mentioned, robots support directional communication. The source emits a specific signal only in one direction. All other robots transmit this signal also only in one direction, as opposite to a receiving direction (received on "north", send to "south"). In this way, "communication streets" appear, that can be used for e.g. navigation.

4. Diffusion of the temporal context. The diffusion field is a function of time:

$$\Phi_{n+1} = f(\max(\Phi_n^1, ..., \Phi_n^i,)) - f(t). \qquad (5.31)$$

This can be useful for coordinating some temporary event (activities) in a swarm.

5. Diffusion of the activity context. This kind of field transmits a stimulus for a specific activity. Since all robots are heterogenous, a robot can need an assistance of only specific robots (with some specific functionality). Field can have a gradient and non-gradient character.

6. Multiple diffusion. The context, especially spatial one, can be useful not only for

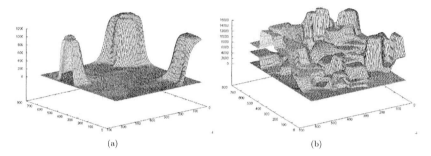

(a)   (b)

Figure 5.31: **(a)** *Initial location of 3 different field sources;* **(b)** *Final distribution of 3-fields.*

information transfer, but also for many other spatial operations like navigation, localization and so on. In the most simple form there are two or three field sources that are propagated in a swarm (Figure 5.31). Three fields are more preferable, because in this case robots can perform triangulation, like GPS.

5.9.4 Embodiment II: sensing and perception

Sensing and perception is the second important aspect for swarm systems. We mean here not only capability of individual perception, but also collective perception (that is based on individual one). In this section we show the application of the embodiment concept for achieving collective perception capabilities.

We expect to have proximity sensors in each of motion directions, that can estimate a distance to an obstacle as "far", "near" and "close" (Fig. 5.27(b)). In the most Scenarios, imposed on a micro-robotic swarm, robots have to perform different spatial operation, like building spatial formation, recognition of object's size and so on. For these tasks robots need a sensor that can measure the distance between itself and an obstacle. Measuring distances, geometrical features and visible size of surfaces are expected to be obtained. Based on them the robot can perform first the individual surface recognition, that can later be expanded on collective perception of large objects.

In the distance measurement the following parameters are the most important: max. measuring distance R_{max}, optimal recognition distance R_{rec}, opening angle of radiation/reflection ray α on R_{rec}, degradation of the IR radiation outsize opening angle $D_{dist}^{in}/D_{dist}^{out}$, object and geometry resolution O_{res}, D_{res} in R_{rec}, dependency of reflection on color/slope of an object, as shown in Fig. 5.32. We expect that distances are provided, at least, within R_c and a section of the IR radiation cone is less than the size of robot's body.

The general problem of distance and proximity sensing is so-called indiscernible distance (Fig. 5.32(a,b)). The sensor cannot differentiate whether the object is on the central line

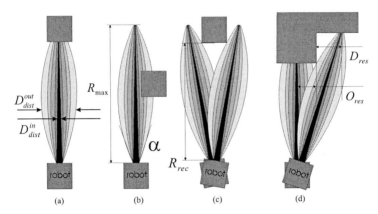

Figure 5.32: *Perception of geometries by IR beam.* (a),(b) *Example of indiscernible distance;* (c) *Active perception of the robot;* (d) *Recognition of geometries.*

IR device	Number	Opening angle	Reflection/ communic. distance
Proximity sensors	min. 4, max. 6	90-60	"large" 100-150 mm "near" 50-100 mm "close" 0-50 mm
Distance sensor	1	10-15	max. 150mm
Touch sensor	1	10-15	0mm(touch)
Color sensor	1	—	—
Communication transmitter-receiver	6-8	60-40	max. 140 mm
PCM-receiver	1(compos. 3)	90-120	max. 1000 mm
PCM-emitter	1(compos. 3)	90-120	max. 1000 mm

Table 5.6: *Required IR devices for a micro-robot.*

but in a large distance, or the real distance is smaller but the object is displaced from the central line. This problem still remains open (can be solve when a robot undertakes several measurements in different directions).

Finally, robots should have some touch sensor, that is required for transporting operations. Sensors, that can perceive a color of objects, are also useful in many scenarios. We collect the required IR devices in Table 5.6.

Although the IR can be used for *sensing*, a small LCD camera (or faceted camera) is also feasible and could be also very useful for a micro-robot. We tested some low-resolution (10×10-20×20 pixel, omnidirectional and directional) images for navigation and perception. Based on region and edge extraction approaches, they can be applied for object detection, however we have serious problems with collective perception in this case. The geometry of surfaces, scanned by IR beam, provides much more information for collective perception, than edges and regions from grey-scale images. Taking into account the functionality, energy consumption, size and price of all solutions, we decided to use only IR both for communication and proximity/distance sensing.

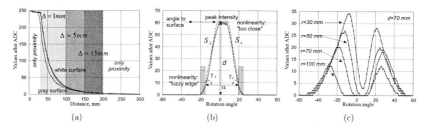

(a)   (b)   (c)

Figure 5.33: *IR-diagrams and the used objects features.* **(a)** *Dependency between ADC values of emitter voltage on phototransistor and the distance to reflecting object. Shown are values for the white reflecting object (white paper) and the grey reflecting object (grey cardboard);* **(b)** *The used features of IR-diagrams relevant for identifying the surfaces;* **(c)** *The "thickness effect" of radiation beam by scanning a gap with different size r. The distance between a micro-robot and the gap is 70 mm.*

As mentioned before, the recognition of large objects by small micro-robots is primarily performed in a collective way. This approach is described in (Kornienko *et al.*, 2005a). However, the prerequisite for collective perception is the surface identification and classification that is performed by each micro-obot. We name further this process as individual perception. From the collective perception point of view the following types of surfaces are required to be identified:

1. *Infinite-size surfaces* (from a robot's viewpoint), as huge objects or borders;

2. *Finite-size surfaces* (a micro-robot has to calculate the visible size of a surface) which are classified, at least, into small, medium and large;

3. *Convex and concave corners;*

4. *2-side and 3-side concave surfaces;*

5. *One-surface/many-surfaces geometry.*

Additionally, the micro-robots have to be able to perform the following activities:

1. *Detection of holes (gangways) in surfaces;*

2. *Classification of the perceived surfaces into defined classes and providing a probability of correct classification;*

3. *Recognition of robot's own position in relation to a corner* (left/right from a corner) or even its own slope to a surface;

When each robot identifies the surface in its own sensing areal (all robots exchange such possible identifications that have the probability over 30%), further collective processing consists in fusing individual observations into many hypotheses and collective identification of most probable hypothesis about the observed object (see also (Ye *et al.*, 2002)).

Returning to the issue of individual perception, we identified the following implementation possibilities:

1. **Vision-based** way by e.g. using some small micro(faced)-cameras;

2. **Reflection-based** way by using laser or infra-red light, ultra-sound etc.;

3. **Wavelength-based** way such as color sensing;

4. By using **specific** chemical, temperature, vibration, magnetic and so on sensors (we do not consider them here).

The vision-based way represents the most information intensive mode. However, its application in micro-robotics has several difficulties caused by very limited computational capabilities and small memory. Algorithms of image processing are challenging for implementation in this hardware. Moreover, due to very small size we prefer to use the same sensors for navigation (proximity sensing and obstacle detection) and communication (robot-robot and host-robot) purposes as well. Finally, the geometrical features from deep images are essentially more useful for collective perception than edges and regions from camera's grey-value images. Thus, the vision-based as well as wavelength-based ways, although they have found a large application in mini- and usual robotics, unfortunately are less useful here. The reflection-based perception uses the principle of sending and receiving a signal, that can be also used for navigation and communication.

Considering different alternatives for reflection-based perception, we focus primarily on laser, electro-magnetic/inductive and infra-red systems. Ultra-sound systems do not satisfy the size limitation. Though the laser provides the most exact measurement and long range and even the cheap VSEL lasers consume energy in mW area, it is difficult to measure the flying time/reflection of laser by a "slow" microcontroller. So, choosing between electro-magnetic/inductive and infra-red systems, we prefer the last ones due to their simplicity, relative long working range and small energy consumption.

Generally, the IR-systems are recently dominant in so-called small-distance-domain, as e.g. for communication between laptops, hand-held devices, remote control and others. The IR-solution is not new in robotic domain, see e.g. (Kube, 1996), (Suzuki *et al.*, 1995). There are many approved schemes or even industrial sensors for IR-communication. However the fusion of perception and communication using IR-devices does not find too many applications, perhaps because of a high nonlinearity of IR-based perception and availability of more appropriate solutions in the domain of usual robotics. Therefore the micro-robotic domain of integrated IR-solution (perception, communication, navigation) is more or less unexploited.

The IR-based perception consists in sending an IR radiation beam and receiving the reflected light. The intensity of this light contains information about the geometry of reflecting surface (primarily a distance between IR-receiver/emitter and surface). As mentioned, the IR-based perception is highly nonlinear. The most large influence on accuracy of perception exerts the resolution of the distance sensor. In the center of radiation ray, the intensity of IR radiation is highest. Closely to the bounds of this ray, this intensity becomes gradually degraded (Figure 5.33). The main component of a reflecting light consists of the energy of central radiation stream. However, low-intensity "secondary streams" spread the reflecting light so that object's edges and gaps between objects get non-recognizable. With a poor resolution of distance sensor, small geometrical elements cannot be perceived and so cannot be used as features for recognition. Therefore for perception are suitable only such IR-emitters that have an as small as possible opening angle of the beam.

Secondly, the accuracy of measurement depends on the distance to a reflecting surface[2]. In Figure 5.33(a) we demonstrate this effect for the developed sensor system. Nonlinear

---

[2]The dependence between reflecting light and distance is also nonlinear however this problem can be easily solved by a look-up table or some approximation functions.

accuracy essentially influences the further recognition of features. The reflecting light is also very sensitive to the color of reflection object. In Figure 5.33(a) we show the distance measuring values for white and gray objects. Further in experiments we use only white color for objects. The distance measuring also depends on the object's slope to a radiation ray. In the next sections we discuss these nonlinearities and suggest some approaches to absorb them.

Development of the IR-based perception system

The main requirement on the IR-perception is given by a small opening angle of the radiation ray. Additionally, IR-emitter has to provide a high energy beam, being able to get good deep images. Finally, IR-emitter and receiver should be able to work in a communication mode. The perception system of the micro-robot is a part of IR-system used for proximity sensing, obstacle detection, distance measurement and communication, as well (Figure 5.34).

For the perception and objects recognition we use only the distance measuring sensor, so that only this sensor is further considered. This sensor consists of a receiver with a wide opening angle (used also for communication and proximity sensing) and an emitter with as small as possible beam angle (used for perception and long-range communication).

In experiments we firstly looked at IR devices datasheets of many manufacturer, like Vishay, Sharp, Osram, Siemens and others. The problem is that such an important parameter as the reflection/communication distance for separate optical diodes and transistor was not specified there. The suggested spectrally matched pairs diode/transistor usually do not satisfy the requirements on opening angle. Moreover, many desired IR devices are not available on micro-component market (or require large order). Finally, we decided to purchase all suitable and available IR devices (they are not expensive, usual price is of cents) and to perform experiments with them. In the purchasing we select different groups of sensors so that results of experiments can be applied not only to the chosen sensor, but also to the whole group of sensors. In experiments we investigated the following parameters:

- Influence of ambient light on communication/reflextion;
- Reflection distance/reflection angle;
- Communication distance/communication angle;
- Communication speed;
- Size and energy consumption.

The current I_F of IR emitters was limited to 20 mA, that corresponds to I/O ports of the microcontroller. Experiments have been done by measuring a voltage V_o on the emitter of phototransistor. The emitter resistance are chosen so that at a maximal reflection the max. voltage equals $V_o \approx 5V$. Measurements have been done with the digital voltmeter "Voltcraft M-3850". We purchased also only such devices that provide analog output signal, therefore such popular sensors as IS471F or Sharp's GP2Dxxx with binary output are not considered. In Fig. 5.34 we show some tested sensors (from over 30 pairs).

For sensing, we choice IR emitters only with small opening angles, as e.g. TSAL6100, TSTS7100, LD274, SFH484 and SFH4510. Moreover, we also tested distance sensors, that combines emitter and receiver, such as GP2D120, QRB1134 and QRB1113. For experiments we use a plastic cube with the edge 25 mm. Sides of this cube are painted in different colors so that we can compare reflectivity depending on object's color.

The distance sensor GP2D120. As stated in its datasheet, this sensor can measure distances between 40 and 300 mm, $R_{max} = 300mm$ (within this range it delivers the values, that are independent from a color of the object, slope, and the light). The sensor is really

Figure 5.34: *Some sensors used in experiments.*

insensitive to ambient light, however for open distances (over 300-500 mm), it produces some "background" voltage, that depends on illumination. This sensor, perhaps because of non-symmetrical construction, has completely different values on left and right part regarding the central line (symmetry of the robot).

Separated IR emitters and receivers with ambient light filter. We are going to use the same receiver for distance measurement and communication, therefore we prefer sensors wide opening angle, e.g. TEFT4300, TEST2600 ($\alpha = 60$), in the "control group" we have SFH3100F with $\alpha = 30$. Some distance measurements are shown in Fig. 5.35(a).

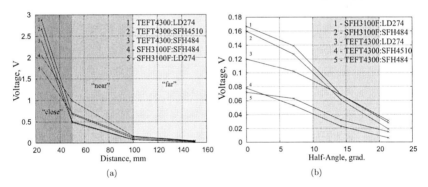

(a) (b)

Figure 5.35: **(a)** *Dependence between output emitter voltage V_o of IR reflective pairs and distance to the object on the central line;* **(b)** *Degradation of V_o at shifting an object from the central line in the distance of 100 mm.*

In the Fig. 5.35(b) we plot for some tested pairs the degradation of V_o in dependance on a deviation from the central line in the distance 100 mm. We see that in fact all values disappear only at the angle 30-35 grad. For 30° radiation ray, the geometrical resolution G_{res} from Fig. 5.32(d) is 25-30 mm for the distance of 100 mm. The slope of degradation corves is too small to provide "abrupt boundary" of the radiation ray, needed for a good object resolution. Ambiguity in 5-10° leads to the minimal resolution of 15-20 mm in 100 mm distance. The geometrical resolution depends also on the accuracy of robot's rotation.

The minimal recognizable distance is about 5 - 10 mm and depends on a construction of the sensor and optical isolation. Generally, a detection of the touch (contact with an object) is not possible with reflective IR sensor. In a small distance the voltage V_o in fact does not depend on the slope of objects, however highly sensitive to the color. For the black color, the V_o was reduced in 5-10 times in comparison to the white color. Therefore, for calibration of the distance sensor, all objects have to be of white or, at least, light (grey) color.

Proximity sensors underlie less requirements than the distance sensor. Primarily, they have to provide the wide 60° opening angle with an uniform distribution of IR radiation in this sector. Desired coverage zones are "close", "near" and, if possible, "far". The delivered values have to enable a detection of obstacles in these zones. The sensors, chosen for communication, satisfy these requirement.

We utilize the Si phototransistor TEFT4300 (60°, peak sensitivity 950 nm) and the high power GaAs/GaAlAs emitter TSAL6100 (radiant intensity >80 mW/sr, 20°, the real opening angle is of 18-22°, 950 nm). This combination is a result of many experiments with different sensors (over 30 pairs), with integrated receiver/emitter like SFH9201, as well as non-integrated ones. The TEFT4300-TSAL6100 pair demonstrated the best spectral coupling, the longest sensing distance and the acceptable nonlinearity of sensing. Although the IR-emitter is relatively large for the micro-robot ($8x\phi5$ mm), the specific construction of the chassis allows to hide it inside the robot.

For color sensing we tested TSLB257, TSLG257, TSLR257 color-light-to-voltage convertors. The main problem we encountered is that the color perception as well as a communication by color LEDs cannot be done in a presence of any ambient light. The sensor cannot differentiate whether the light comes from color emitter (or reflected light from colored object) or it is an ambient light. Therefore the color perception is performed in another way: emitting light of three different colors and measurement of a difference in a reflected intensity (it depends on surface color). This solution is testing in version III.

Since IR-emitter and receiver are non-integrated and are placed side by side in the chassis, they have to be optically isolated. The optical isolation of the emitter allows also reducing the opening angle of the beam up to 10-15° (it reduces also a perception distance). However, the main problem here is to provide similar optical characteristics of isolation for a large number of different micro-robots in a swarm (to avoid later the problem of individual calibration of each micro-robot). This problem is solved in version III.

Features extraction from IR-deep images

The principle of object recognition is the following. As soon as a robot detects (by means of proximity sensors) an obstacle in front of itself, it switches on the high power IR-emitter and after 1ms delay (needed to get reliable reflecting light) measures voltage on the emitter of phototransistor. The dependence between emitter voltage (after ADC) and the distance to an object is shown in Figure 5.33(a). Generally, this sensor perceives distances up to 300mm. However, accuracy of measurement is different. For the pair *distance-accuracy* where Δ is the accuracy, we obtained the following values: 30-100mm - Δ=1mm, 100-150 mm - Δ=3-5mm, 150-200mm - Δ=10-15mm and after 200mm - Δ=30-50mm. Therefore, the reasonable measuring distance for object recognition lies within 30mm-100mm (with the accuracy of 1-2mm).

Not only the resolution of the IR-sensor is important for scanning the objects. During scanning, a micro-robot rotates on some degrees. The more exact is this rotation, the more precise is the spatial resolution of sensor data. Micro-robot does not possess any devices allowing to measure positions and orientation of chassis or wheels. Therefore there is only one way to rotate a robot, namely to turn the motors on and after some delay turn them off. This delay has to be so chosen, that a robot rotates on some fixed degree. The motors are controlled through the H-bridge SI9988, that can change a polarity of supplying current.

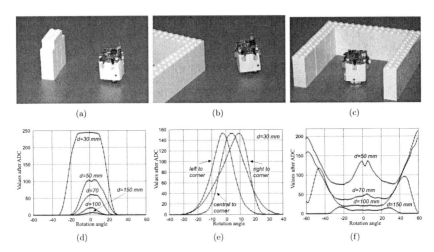

Figure 5.36: *Jasmine, the prototype of the micro-robot, scans different surfaces, where d is the distance to surfaces.* **(a)** *Scanning of the finite-size surface, object 48 mm;* **(b)** *Scanning of the convex surface;* **(c)** *Scanning of the 3-concave surface;* **(d)** *The IR-diagram for finite-size surface;* **(e)** *The IR-diagram for convex surface;* **(f)** *The IR-diagram for 3-concave sides surface of 95×95×95 mm;*

Choosing normal polarity for one motor and inverse polarity for the second motor, the robot can rotate without changing its own position. In this way we get relatively shift-errorless deep images. With odometrical system we achieved a good angular resolution and accuracy of rotation. However, due to different friction between weels/chassis and floor surface there is always some rotation inaccuracy or "rotation noise" that has to be taken into consideration during recognition phase.

In our experiments, when a robot detects an obstacle on the distance of 70mm ± 10mm, it stops and then rotates 60° left. After that, it scans the obstacle with the distance sensor by rotating 120 ^{o} right. During this scanning it writes the obtained values of distances each 1 degree into an integer array. In this way we have 120 values describing a visible geometry of the encountered obstacle. In Figure 5.36 and 5.37 we demonstrate some geometries of encountered obstacles and the scanned surfaces.

After performing the first experiments, we faced the following challenge: which features of the obtained IR-diagrams are relevant for identifying the geometry of the surfaces ? By analyzing the IR-diagrams in Figure 5.36 and 5.37, we find the following features as representative and useful in the IR-based individual perception (Figure 5.33(b)):

1. *The angle* α, which represents the scanning angle between the first visible edge and the last visible edge of the surface;

2. *The peak intensity of the diagram,* I_{max}. This corresponds to the maximal intensity of reflecting light and, in turn, to the minimal distance d between the surface and the micro-robot. For the most types of surfaces (beside convex corners) this minimal distance is measured as a perpendicular to a surface. This feature allows calculating the visible size of a surface by using trigonometric relations;

3. *The left and right slopes,* denoted as γ_l and γ_r are useful for identifying the size-type of the

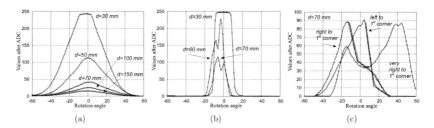

Figure 5.37: *IR-diagrams for different types of surfaces, d is a distance to surfaces.* **(a)** *"Infinite-size" surfaces with flat geometry;* **(b)** *Convex round (external diameter 125 mm) surface;* **(c)** *Many-surfaces geometry (1ˢᵗ convex corner 122×60 mm and 2ⁿᵈ concave corner 60×95 mm), robot positioned 70 mm before the middle part.*

surface (unlimited, big, medium, small). They are calculated as slopes of the approximation lines S_l, S_r. The slope denotes also the "degree of a distance decreasing" and enable us to identify the so-called "convex surfaces" that cannot be recognized in the trigonometric way;

4. *The position of the "center" of the IR-diagram,* P_{imax} in relation to the scanning angle ("0", origin point on the X axis). Displacement of the center points to a slope between the front of robot and surface. In this way we can identify a directional orientation of the micro-robot.

Now we formalize the mentioned nonlinearities and present their impact on the corresponding features:

1. *Nonlinear thickness* of the IR radiation ray and so different distribution between high-energy beam and low-energy beam. The first effect of this nonlinearity consists in spread edges (Figure 5.33(b)). This nonlinear effect can be absorbed by calibration. The second effect is shown in Figure 5.33(c). At scanning many-surfaces geometry (a gap between objects) a robot cannot reliable differentiate between 2-concave surfaces and surfaces that belong to different objects;

2. *Nonlinear measurement for small distances.* As known from other IR-distance measurement systems (e.g. (Caprari & Siegwart, 2003)), the maximal intensity of measurement lies in 10-25% before the front of IR-receiver, after that the intensity goes down (therefore small distances cannot be measured by these systems at all). Due to the specific restriction and the application of high-power GaAs/GaAlAs emitter, we removed this effect. However, the surfaces that lie less then 40 mm away from a robot are represented only by values 245-250. In this way, for close measurement (30 mm) we get a flat horizontal diagram. Another undesired effect in small-average distances (40-70 mm) consists in a spontaneous decreasing of peak intensity (this is observable in all IR-diagrams in Figures 5.36 and 5.37). We cannot identify the nature of this nonlinearity and assume multiple IR-reflections as a reason for them;

3. *Nonlinear accuracy* of distance measurement. This requires nonlinear correction (it is done as a look-up table) of trigonometric relation in dependence of distance. However, this nonlinearity is very "tricky". Even when a robot starts a measurement in the "good" area of 40-120 mm, a part of geometry can lie over 150 or 200 mm away. The effect of this nonlinearity appears in unreliable identification of many-surfaces geometry (Figure 5.37(c) "left to 1st. corner");

4. *Nonlinear rotation* of the robot. This can lead to different left γ_l and right γ_r slopes even

215

for symmetric surfaces. The most easiest solution here is to calibrate γ_l and γ_r;

5. *Nonlinearity in measuring convex surfaces.* The identification of all types of convex geometries is performed by γ_l and γ_r. The difference between slopes for e.g. round objects (Figure 5.37(b)), convex corners (Figure 5.36(b)) and finite-size flat objects (Figure 5.36(a)) is small, moreover due to a nonlinear intensity diagram, these slopes change with distances. This problem has some basic character and we hardly belief that with all nonlinearities of IR-perception we are able to reliable identify the type of convex surfaces.

The main problem of these nonlinearities represents the necessity to maintain many look-up tables for corrections. This, in turn, is limited by a small memory of Atmel microcontroller. The assumption is that this problem can be solved in collective way. We can reduce the accuracy of individual recognition (so that to satisfy all hardware constraints) till such a degree which still allows a reliable collective recognition. Now, based on the discussed features and nonlinearities, we can briefly analyze the types of surfaces.

1. Surfaces with flat geometry. The flat type of geometry is primarily characterized by only one peak value on the IR-diagram. Finite-size surfaces are also characterized by large left and right slopes and scanning angle $\alpha \ll 120°$, Figure 5.36(a). The size L_{vis} can be calculated as $2d\tan(\alpha/2)$, taking into account the "fuzzi edge" nonlinearity.

"Infinite-size" surfaces (Figure 5.37(a)) have small slopes of IR-diagrams and $\alpha \sim 120°$. To absorb the nonlinearity of slopes for small and large distance, we apply the polygonal approximation (Pitas, 1993) and use in calculation the relation $\gamma_{\{r,l\}}/S_{\{r,l\}}$ instead of simple $\gamma_{\{r,l\}}$, where $S_{\{r,l\}}$ is the length of approximating line. In the performed experiments the probability of correct identification is very high and the accuracy of size calculation is of 5 mm (15 mm in the worst case).

2. Surfaces with convex geometry.

Surfaces with convex geometry possess also only one peak value, but with larger slopes then flat geometries. This type of geometry has to be identified before the calculation of size, which has no sense in this case. There are several types of convex geometry: convex corners and convex round surfaces (Figure 5.36(b)), convex many-surface geometry (can be recognized only collectively)(Figure 5.36(f)). We identify this geometry by $\gamma_{\{r,l\}}/S_{\{r,l\}}$ in the IR-diagrams. The difference between them points to a position in relation to a corner (left to a corner, right to a corner). The probability of correct identification of convex round geometry is very high, however convex corners are often classified as flat geometry. One approach to avoid this problem is the so-called "active exploration" (simple move towards the surface and scan again induces the appearance of a large "flat region" in the peak intensity which points to the flat type of geometry).

3. Many-surfaces and concave geometries. Concave geometries manifest primarily as multiple peaks in IR-diagrams. Based on the number of peaks we can differentiate between 2-concave (concave corners) and 3-concave sides geometry (Figure 5.36(c)). Concave many-surfaces geometries (Figure 5.36(b)) can be also classified by one robot. They have one peak value, however multiple left or right slopes. Many-surfaces geometry can also be composed from surfaces that belong to different objects. Generally, concave geometries can be identified with high reliability, however some fine differentiation between them is not always possible.

4. Estimation of probability. Since the robot cannot reliable classify the type of surfaces, it calculates a probability of correct classification. The calculation is done in the following way. We measure the possible values of α, d, $\gamma_{\{r,l\}}/S_{\{r,l\}}$, P_{imax} and estimate L_{vis} for all types of surfaces. The robot uses last square metrics to calculate the relation between the measured values and these presaved types. For collective perception a robot sends all possible classifications that have the probability over 30%. Through the presented features of the IR-deep image we tried to classify several surfaces and to identify the classification probability as well, as base steps or components required for the individual perception.

The developed algorithms, based on the discussed features and nonlinearities, allow classifying surfaces. For all types of geometry, the robot estimates also a probability of correct recognition for further multi-hypotheses classification and collective perception. In (Kornienko *et al.*, 2005a) we describe the collective perception based on the Dampster-Shafer evidential reasoning.

5.9.5 Embodiment III: cooperative actuation

In the previous section we considered two important capabilities of collective systems: communication (cooperative information processing) and perception (collective perception). In this section we deal with the last collective capability of cooperative actuation in a swarm. All these capabilities form a basis for artificial self-organization in robotic groups.

As already mentioned, we also use for cooperative actuation the embodiment concept. The capability of cooperative actuation means primarily the following:

1. Acquiring a relative position of a robot in a swarm;

2. Acquiring a relative position of an object of interest;

3. Having a tool being able to manipulate objects of interest and to sense the changes of objects position, orientation or others;

4. Capabilities of tracking objects and robot positions.

From all of them the most principal is a capability of position estimation applied to the robot itself and the object of interest. Knowing the positions, robots can coordinate the collective behavior and actuate cooperatively with other robots (equipped with corresponding tools). Positioning system can be divided into:

Absolute Positioning. Absolute positioning can be divided into two categories: global localization and local tracking. Global localization is used to find the mobile robot's position without any prior position information. There are several ways to achieve the mobile robot localization: map matching, GPS, landmarks, probabilistic models, etc. Generally they can be divided into matching methods and probabilistic methods. Local tracking is used to track the mobile robots position over time given the initial position of mobile robot.

Biology-motivated positioning. Biology-motivated approaches are relatively new in the robotics. The main concept is a stigmergy that is used in biology to describe the influence of the persisting environmental effects on behavior. For instance, pheromone trails is an example of how stigmergy works: when one ant places pheromone along the way to a food source it is changing the path that the next ant would follow, because the second ant will follow the pheromone path to the food source instead of wandering around. Many localization algorithms based on pheromone have been developed, multi-pheromone systems (**?**), chain formation (**?**). The necessity of storing the pheromone, the extra hardware needed to place them and sense them have lead to other localization algorithms based on pheromone, but without the extra hardware requirements, the virtual pheromone.

Relative Positioning. In this approach every robot updates its own position from time to time using dead reckoning sensors and without any global positioning capabilities. Odometrical method uses encoders to measure wheel rotation and/or steering orientation. Odometry has the advantage that it is totally self-contained, and it is always capable of providing the vehicle with an estimate of its position. The disadvantage of odometry is that the position error grows without bound unless an independent reference is used periodically to reduce the error (?). The method Inertial Navigation uses gyroscopes and sometimes accelerometers to measure rate of rotation and acceleration. Measurements are integrated once (or twice) to yield position.

After analyzing the hardware possibilities of the already existed prototypes of Jasmine-I and II we decided to integrate odometric system into the robot. The odometric method uses encoders to measure wheel rotation and/or steering orientation. This method uses a simple mathematical procedure for determining the present position of the robot by advancing some previous position through known course and velocity information over a given length of time called Dead reckoning (derived from "deduced reckoning of sailing days).

Suppose, that at sampling interval, the left and right encoders show a pulse increment of N_L on the left wheel and N_R on the right wheel. Suppose further that $c_m = \frac{\pi D_n}{nC_e}$, where c_m is the conversion factor that translates encoder pulses into linear wheel displacement D_n is the nominal wheel diameter (in mm) C_e is the encoder resolution (in pulses per revolution) and n is the gear ratio of the reduction gear between the motor (where the encoder is attached) and the drive wheel. We can compute the incremental travel distance for the left and right wheel, $\Delta U_{L,i}$ and $\Delta U_{R,i}$ according to $\Delta U_{L/R,i} = c_m N_{L/R,i}$ and the incremental linear displacement of the robot's center point C, denoted ΔU_i, according to $\Delta U_i = \frac{(\Delta U_L + \Delta U_R)}{2}$. Next, we compute the robot's incremental change of orientation $\Delta \Phi_i = \frac{(\Delta U_R - \Delta U_L)}{b}$, where b is the wheelbase of the vehicle, ideally measured as the distance between the two contact points between the wheels and the floor.

The robot's new relative orientation Φ_i can be computed from $\Phi_i = \Phi_{i-I} + \Delta \Phi_i$ and the relative position of the center point is:

$$x_i = x_{i-I} + \Delta U_i cos \Phi_i \tag{5.32}$$

$$y_i = y_{i-I} + \Delta U_i sin \Phi_i \tag{5.33}$$

where x_i, y_i are the relative position of the robot's center point c at instant i. With these equations two main things can be done: the design of the sensor and surface over the wheel as well as the programming of the positioning system.

We have to determine the encoder resolution (in pulses per revolution), but this parameter depends only on the precision of the sensor. A small SMD-sensor of 2,5 mm of length can be used. It is required to be completely covered with the color to be sensed, so this establishes the minimum sector size of one color in the surface to cover the wheel, and consequently establishes the maximum number of sectors in a wheel. We can obtain the resolution (or number of sectors in the wheel) by $Perimeter = 2\pi r = \pi D_n$ $C_e \leq \frac{Perimeter}{d_{min}}, where, d_{min} = 2, 5mm$. Then $C_e \leq 12, 56$ (12 sectors are needed in the wheel). Then the next calculations can be done $c_m = 2, 6179$ $\Delta U_{L/R,i} = 2, 6179 N_{L/R,i}$ $\Delta \Phi_i = 0, 11(N_R - N_L)$

There are two fundamental types of errors in odometrical systems: systematic errors and non-systematic errors. The clear distinction between systematic and non-systematic errors is of great importance for the effective reduction of odometry errors. For example, systematic errors are particularly grave because they accumulate constantly, but in our case, only the last systematic error (finite encoder resolution) have importance. We suppose the physical errors (as measures of the robots) has minimal importance considering the size of the robot and the precision of fabrication process. The non-systematic errors are minimal since we can control the medium surrounding the robot (e.g. floor). Two or more robots can measure their positions mutually. When one of the robots moves to another place, the other observes this motion and determines new position of the first robot. In other words, at any time one robot localizes itself with reference to a fixed object: the standing robot or landmark. Robots can transmit information about the mutual references to one another. This way the swarm can autocorrect the errors in the position information.

Implementation

The first version of the wheel encoder was pained in black and white colors (see Figure 5.38(a)). The black and white areas needs to cover the whole wheel to generate the maximum or minimum voltage at the output. The chosen sensor is TCNT1000 with integrated phototransistor and an emitting IR-LED. Depending on the position of the sensor respect the wheels, the area below the sensor is different. In the first case the part of the sensor closest to the wheel's center must contain an arc of $arc = 4.4mm$ just below (3.4mm plus 1mm of margin), and the lowest part of the sensor is at a distance $d = 2.3mm$. In the second case $arc' = 3.7mm$ and $d = 1.6mm$. This gives a maximum number of division of:

$$r cld \cdot \theta = arc, \tag{5.34}$$
$$\theta = arc/d, \tag{5.35}$$
$$\theta = 1.913 \ [rad], \tag{5.36}$$
$$\theta' = 2.3125 \ [rad], \tag{5.37}$$
$$\lfloor 2\pi/\theta \rfloor = 3 \ divisions, \tag{5.38}$$
$$\lfloor 2\pi/\theta' \rfloor = 2 \ divisions. \tag{5.39}$$

In the first version of the odometrical system, only six divisions were used, the difference between black and white was about $2V$. The number of divisions can be increased even more if a high variation in the output is not needed. With six divisions per wheel the output voltage will have a variation close to the feeding voltage. The number of divisions can be doubled, at a cost of smaller variation in the output which leads to a more difficult peak detection.

For the second generation of odometrical system we used geared coupling between wheel and motors instead of painted strips (see Figure 5.38(b)). It is more precise, however brought new problems. Now a big cog is directly attached to the wheels, making impossible to place the sensor close to them. The first idea was to use the cog's teeth as divisions, but the difference in reflection was rather poor and only noise was detected by the ADC. To improve reflection the cog's teeth were painted, the cog has twelve teeth (six black and six unpainted), so the TCNT1000 must be able to detect, with enough difference, twelve divisions and, to make things worse, the sensor could not be placed at the optimum distance of 1mm from the reflecting surface due to space problems. Several test were performed with different position of the sensor. The Figure 5.38(c) shows that twelve divisions can be recognized. The limit in the maximum wheel division can be calculated with the Nyquist theorem. The encoder produces a sinusoidal output when moving, which frequency depends on the rotational velocity of the wheel. The sampling rate should be twice the maximum frequency of the encoder signal (reached at maximum speed). The sampling rate needed depending on the number of divisions can be calculated for the maximum speed of the robot.

$$F_s \geq 2F_n = 2\frac{v_{max}}{2\pi R}N. \tag{5.40}$$

In which v_{max} is the maximum speed of the robot ($10cm/s$), R is the wheel's radius ($0.5cm$) and N is the number of divisions per wheel. Depending on the number of divisions the sampling rate is:

$$rccN = 12 \rightarrow F_S \geq 76.392\ Hz \equiv 13.1\ ms, \tag{5.41}$$

$$N = 24 \rightarrow F_S \geq 152.784\ Hz \equiv 6.54\ ms, \tag{5.42}$$

$$N = 48 \rightarrow F_S \geq 305.568\ Hz \equiv 3.27\ ms, \tag{5.43}$$

$$N = 64 \rightarrow F_S \geq 407.424\ Hz \equiv 2.45\ ms. \tag{5.44}$$

With twelve divisions the uncertainty is about $2\pi R/12 = 2.61mm$. We need 64 divisions to keep the uncertainty below $0.5mm$.

Due to external noise from the motors and microcontroller the signal is not clean and this makes the threshold recognition rather difficult. By using a simple lowpass filter (a simple averaging) the signal can be improved.

After having the encoder sensors properly configured, the spoke count can start. While twelve divisions per wheel cycle were used, the uncertainty is about $\pi/12 = 2.61cm$. It is important to note there are twice as many spoke edges as there are spokes. Therefore, by sensing the edges of the spokes, rather than the spokes themselves, the program can sense the wheel position with twice the accuracy, measuring the wheel position to $1/24$ of a revolution. Spoke edges can easily be sensed by detecting the sensor signal transitions from low to high and high to low.

Furthermore, if the encoder signal is approximately linear, theoretically any voltage change can be directly translated to actual motion. With this the accuracy can be improved, to reduce the uncertainty to $0.5mm$, 64 divisions are needed. Which means that any pulse must be divided into $\lceil 64/12 \rceil = 6$ voltage changes. This will increase the accuracy but also the noise, the computational efforts and the sampling rate.

5.9.6   Artificial self-organization: a few swarm experiments

We performed several experiments with a small group of micro-robots Jasmine-I and Jasmine-III in our robotic lab as well as in other Universities (generally, during 2005 we performed with MT-students about 20 different tests in out lab, that are described in details in the corresponding master theses). The goal was to test the collective capabilities of the developed robot and to prove the concept of the "embodied top-down" collective intelligence. Summarizing, we can say a few very limited individual capabilities of a robot, but designed especially to speed-up collective performance, allow the whole robotic group to perform many "advanced" collective activities (collective navigation and coordination, cooperative actuation and perception, spatial information processing). The development of collective behavior involved a definition of macroscopic patterns, derivation of local rules and redesigning of hardware components. As demonstrated by these experiments, the proposed approach allows creating a specific group's behavioral pattern, whereas robotic behavior still remained flexible (not predetermined). In the following we describe two series of experiment intended for collective perception and spatial information processing.

In this section I thank all my students for helping in preparation and making experiments: collective information processing Xuan Chen (Chen, 2004), Frank Mletzko (Mletzko, 2006), Roland Geider (Geider, 2006); self-organization Omer Warraich (Warraich, 2005), Zheng Fu

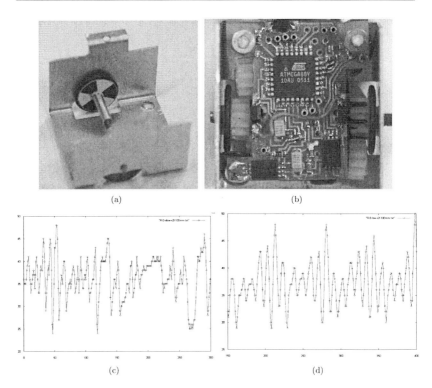

Figure 5.38: *The first odometry configuration, black and white paper divided the wheel in six; ADC signal with twelve divisions and the highest sampling rate achieved; ADC signal with twelve divisions and the highest sampling rate achieved after a lowpass filter. Images (c) and (d) are from (Jiménez, 2005).*

(Fu, 2005); collective perception Mauricio Pradier (Pradier, 2005), embodiment and odometry Manuel Jimenez (Jiménez, 2005) and Juan Caselles (Caselles, 2005), power management and energetic homeostasis Kristof Jebens (Jebens, 2006) and Afshin Attarzadeh (Attarzadeh, 2006). In the cases, when a joint publication with these students was done, I make reference on this. For all other cases, I refer to the corresponding master thesis.

Functional self-organization

The first series of experiments was intended to the functional self-organization with local rules in the form of *if ... then* conditions, as described in Chapters 4 and 5. We remarked, that when robots possess good individual capabilities of communication, perception and navigation, the functional self-organization can be performed with a low number of relatively simple rules. For example, in Figure 5.39 we demonstrate a few images (extracted from video clip), where robots look for specific geometrical objects (in this case concave corners) in the whole arena and clusterize themselves around such an object. The rules

221

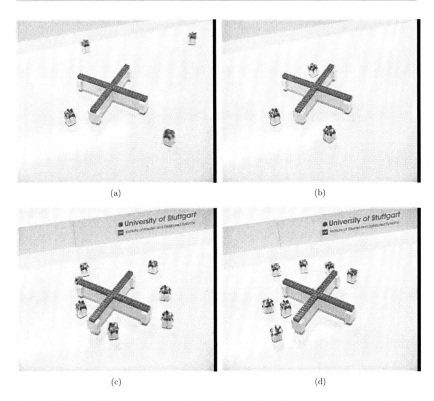

(a)   (b)

(c)   (d)

Figure 5.39: **(a)-(d)** *Example of functional self-organization "look for ... and surround" in the group of micro-robots with the rules in the form of if...then conditions.*

are *if (geometryFound) sendCommand(comeToMe)* and *if (commandReceived(comeToMe) moveTo(signalOrigin).* Even with such simple rules, all robots are able to demonstrate interesting collective behavior without being preprogrammed.

Other series of experiments are devoted to collective navigation in a swarm. As known, swarm navigation represents a serious problem for robots, because they have very limited perception radius and cannot "see" the whole arena to navigate. Therefore we made the following experiments: robots dynamically build a "communication street", as mentioned in Section 5.9.3. Such a communication street can serve as a quick communication link and a navigation guide, e.g. between two points in arena. Dynamical building of a "communication street" is shown in Figure 5.40. The robots have a few connection rules in the form of commands *moveTo(directionOfSignal)*, which allows them to make a directional spatial constructions. Usually the first point represents a mark (robot that marks a resource). Navigation along a communication street is shown in Figure 5.41. Here, the moving robot asks the robots in the "communication street" about their and neighbor IDs and can decide about direction towards the mark. Making a proximity sensing or by using communication as proximity sensing, the moving can easily move along the "street" in a defined distance.

(a)   (b)

(c)   (d)

Figure 5.40: **(a)-(d)** *Micro-robots Jasmine dynamically build a communication street without fixed programming.*

"Vertical" structural self-organization in collective information processing

In many cases only *if ... then* rules, like those in the functional SO, cannot are not enough to generate the desired emergence in robotic group. In this we have to combine a few structural rules on the high level of system hierarchy with low-level functional rules. In this case we obtain SO-system with vertical operational principle, described in Section 3.7.1. The example of that can be given by collective spatial information processing. The micro-robots possess limited perception radius, however in many simulations robots have to calculate the distance between several robots, e.g. in a "communication street". Among distances over a swarm, robots have to calculate the center of gravity, estimate the number of robots in a specific direction and so on. This spatial information processing, performed in a collective way, is an important capability of any collective system.

Calculation of distances between a few robots is based on simple geometrical relations, e.g.

$$AC = \sqrt{AB^2 + BC^2 - 2AB \times BC \times \cos(ABC)} \qquad (5.45)$$

223

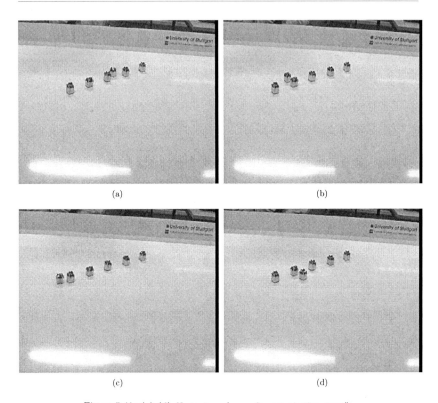

Figure 5.41: **(a)-(d)** *Navigation along a "communication street".*

for Figure 5.42(a). Obviously, that this kind of relation can be expanded to more robots, as shown in Figures 5.42(b),(c). When the robots are displaced in a regular "line-similar" structure, this approach works quite good. However, when the structures connect a few short lines (like in Figure 5.40(d)), or there is a line with a few interconnections (like in Figure 5.42(d)) the relation (5.45) is no longer applicable, because there is no corresponding geometrical structure. Therefore, a particular robot first recognizes the spatial structure (by collecting IDs and connectivity of neighbor robots in a sequence) and then generates the corresponding geometrical relations for this structure (this approach generally correspond to the described in the Section 3.7.1).

Horizontal structural self-organization in collective perception

These experiments with collective perception differ from the described in Section 4.3.6. The main idea here is to show that "embodied perception intelligence" together with a few structural horizontal rules allow a robotic group to recognize large object. Due to high complexity of this task we limit ourselves only to the problem of *collective classification* (Pradier, 2005), where the robots possess the objects models and have only to order the

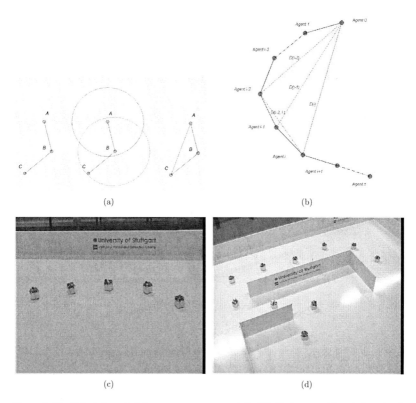

(a)   (b)

(c)   (d)

Figure 5.42: *Calculation of distances over a swarm.* **(a)**, **(b)** *Basic geometric relations for the calculation. Images are from (Fu, 2005);* **(c)** *Ideal communication line for spatial calculation;* **(c)** *Communication line for spatial calculation with a few interconnections in corner areas where robots perceive several neighbors.*

collective sensor input to one of the presaved model. Material of this section is originating from (Kornienko *et al.*, 2005a).

In the robotic group there is no privileged agent with a special role: all robots perform the same operations. The suggested method is homogeneous, i.e. all robots act the same and there is no need for a leader. Due to the homogeneous architecture the approach is robust, scalable, moreover new robots can join the team dynamically without any need to readjust any task assignment. Figure 5.43(a) shows how robots are deployed during collective observation. The whole approach is based on embodied perception capabilities, described in the Section 5.9.4 and two self-organizing actions: functional emergent clusterization around an object (described in the Section 4.2) and horizontally self-organized hypotheses fusion, based on probabilistic reasoning procedure, described further.

Figure 5.43(b) shows the 2D geometries of the four object classes which will be used subsequently. Once robots are clustered around the object, they can estimate the local properties of the object as seen from their current positions called *viewpoints*. The actual

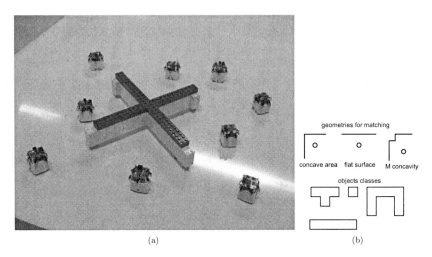

(a) (b)

Figure 5.43: *Horizontal structural self-organization in collective perception.* (a) *Spatial distribution of the robots around the observed object;* (b) *Geometries for matching and objects classes, see (Kornienko et al., 2005a).*

measurement obtained from a viewpoint v can be noted as $S(v)$; $S : V \mapsto$ feature vector and represents the output of the distance sensors. Given an object class, it is possible to establish the expected sensor outputs for a number of views. A number of viewpoints $n_V^{K_i}$ for each object class K_i are chosen, along a trajectory situated in the center of the measurement domain, and noted as $\mathfrak{V}^{\mathfrak{K}_i} = \left(v_n^{K_i}\right)$. The corresponding expected measurements for objects of class K_i are $S\left(\mathfrak{V}^{\mathfrak{K}_i}\right) = \left(S\left(v_1^{K_i}\right), \ldots, S\left(v_{n_V}^{K_i}\right)\right)$. Therefore, the object model for a class K_i incorporates an ordered sequence of views for different *successive* positions around objects of that class. Additionally, object models include information about the reachability of different viewpoints, taking into account both geometrical constraints and the limitations imposed by the communication capabilities of the robots. It is noted as $W^{K_i} = \left\{ \left.\left(v_j^{K_i}, v_k^{K_i}\right)\right| v_k^{K_i} \text{ reachable from } v_j^{K_i} \right\}$. Finally, the corresponding distances between viewpoints in W^{K_i} are added to the object model, as $d_{\mathfrak{V}} : \mathfrak{V}^{\mathfrak{K}_i} \times \mathfrak{V}^{\mathfrak{K}_i} \to \mathbb{R}$.

The set of all canonical measurements — corresponding to sets of observable features, called *aspects* — in the model is noted $A = \left\{ S\left(v_i^{K_j}\right) \right\}$ and its cardinality can be reduced by clustering the expected measurements. In that case, a sequence of canonical views could match several *(identity, position)* pairs.

The goal of collective classification in a swarm of robots is to estimate that class K_i the object being observed belongs to. When n_r robots are situated in an area surrounding the object (measurement domain) in positions $w_1, \ldots, w_{n_r}$, they are ordered implicitly depending on their position around the object as the perimeter of the latter is explored in a given trigonometric direction. Given these positions, the robots will measure $(S(w_1), \ldots, S(w_{n_r}))$. The proposed collaborative classification method will try to estimate the corresponding canonical viewpoints $\left(v_{n(1)}^{K_n}, \ldots, v_{n(n_r)}^{K_n}\right)$ given the above measurements; the end result, namely the class K_n the object belongs to, is implicit. *This means that not* only the class of the object, but also the relative positioning of each robot can be obtained.

Structural self-organization for hypotheses fusion. By observing the object from a given position, a robot can only generate local, basic hypotheses. Generally this is not enough to determine the class the object belongs to. The information obtained from different measurements should be fused via exchange of hypotheses between different robots. This fusion should be performed in a self-organizing way (i.e. be not predetermined). We already mentioned that structural self-organization works in the following way: **structural rules** → **functions** → **behavior**. *Behavior* in this case is the final classification of the object. *Functions* are the capabilities of the large-object-recognition. This function is generated by set of structural rules. However which rules ? In this chapter we demonstrated that structural rules are a few "simple" constructions in a proper level of system's organization, they can be generated dynamically, by evolutional approach, by decomposition approach etc. In this experiment we also demonstrated that structural rules can be generated by a *reasoning system*.

For application for a generation system we chose Dempster-Shafer (DS) evidential reasoning (Shafer, 1976). It is an extension to Bayesian inference that allows each source of information to contribute only to the evidence it has gathered, without overcommitting or trying to make hasty choices based on incomplete information. The Dempster-Shafer approach allows to express the lack of information by separating belief for a proposition from its mere plausibility, assigning probability masses to sets of propositions in such a way that the latter is free to move to any subset. This approach is described in details in (Kornienko *et al.*, 2005a) and (Pradier, 2005), in the following we given a few explanation and demonstrate the results of experiments.

Information sources can distribute probability masses among subsets of Θ, where Θ is the set of all statements about the possible outcomes of a random experiment. It is represented by the *frame of discernment* (FOD). The FOD is a set of mutually exclusive and exhaustive statements named *singletons*. When a probability mass is assigned to a set of singletons, it is free to move to any subset. Consequently, assignment of probability mass to Θ represents ignorance, since the probability mass can move to any element of Θ. When a source of evidence cannot differentiate between two propositions, it can assign a probability mass to a set including both.

The *probability mass assignment* function associates a probability mass to the sets in the power-set 2^Θ of Θ; it is therefore a function $m : 2^\Theta \longrightarrow \mathbb{R}$ verifying the following properties $m(\emptyset) = 0$, $0 \leq m(X) \leq 1$, $\sum_{x \in 2^\Theta} m(x) = 1$. The subsets $\{x_i\}$ of Θ such that $m(x_i) > 0$ are called *focal elements*; the union of those subsets is termed *core* of the probability assignment m.

Dempster's orthogonal sum. Two different sources of information will yield different mass distributions m_1 and m_2. Dempster's *rule of combination*, or *orthogonal sum*, can combine them if they are relative to the same FOD Θ, according to $m = m_1 \oplus m_2$, $m(X) = K \sum_{X_1 \cap X_2 = X} m_1(X_1) m_2(X_2)$. K is a normalization term defined as

$$K = \frac{1}{1 - \sum_{X_1 \cap X_2 = \emptyset} m_1(X_1) m_2(X_2)}, \qquad (5.46)$$

which normalizes the new probability masses so that their sum is still unity. It can be seen as a measure of the degree of conflict between the two sources of information. When $\sum_{X_1 \cap X_2 = \emptyset} m_1(X_1) m_2(X_2) = 1$, the information is completely inconsistent and it is impossible to integrate it: the orthogonal sum is then undefined.

Hypothesis refinement. General, non-basic hypotheses are noted

$$H^{level} = \{(a_k, \ldots) | a_k \in A\}. \qquad (5.47)$$

It is important to note that a_k could correspond to the output from several canonical viewpoints. The set of all possible hypotheses is noted H. Clearly the sequences of canonical measurements can only correspond to valid view sequences in some object model; impossible sequences, such as those having views that cannot belong to the same object, will not be generated.

In general, a robot will propagate its current beliefs about the object to the "next" neighboring robot along the perimeter of the object — initially $m\left(H^0\right)$. When this information is sent, the receiving robot can access the following:
- belief of the previous robot $m_1\left(H^n\right)$;
- distance to the robot whose message is being received d_{pre};
- its own beliefs about the observing part of the object $m_2\left(H^0\right)$.

The Dempster-Shafer combination rule for two hypothesis sets in a compatible frame of discernment

$$m\left(H_n\right) = \frac{\sum_{H_i \cap H_j = H_n} m\left(H_i\right) m\left(H_j\right)}{1 - \sum_{H_i \cap H_j = \varnothing} m\left(H_i\right) m\left(H_j\right)} \tag{5.48}$$

is slightly modified to use the information about the relative positions of the robots as follows. Given an hypothesis set H^n, the refined hypotheses will be

$$H^{n+1} = \left\{ U\left(h \oplus a\right) \mid h \in H^n, a \in A, h \oplus a \in H \right\}, \tag{5.49}$$

where the last condition means that the new view sequence must be possible for at least one object class. The operation $\oplus : H \times A \longmapsto H$ is defined as $h \oplus x = \left(h_1, \ldots, h_n, \ldots, a_{m_1}, \ldots, a_{m_p}, x\right)$, where the views $a_{m_1}, \ldots, a_{m_n}$ are a "filler", and x is the view that is to be added to the sequence. An additional restriction can be imposed to the $\oplus$ operation, namely that the filler has to be no longer than some arbitrary number of viewpoints k with $p < k$ in the above expression. The output of the function $U(h)$ is defined as the shortest hypothesis equivalent to h, that is, an hypothesis that corresponds to the same (object, offset) matches.

The new probability mass assignment is calculated with

$$m'\left(h_i^{n+1}\right) = \sum_{h^n \oplus x = h_i^{n+1}} m_1\left(h^n\right) m_2\left(x\right) \xi\left(d_{pre}, d_{model}\right), \tag{5.50}$$

$$m\left(h_i^{n+1}\right) = \frac{m'\left(h_i^{n+1}\right)}{\sum_k m'\left(h_k^{n+1}\right)}, \tag{5.51}$$

where an additional normalization is required due to the usage of the distance term $\xi\left(d_{pre}, d_{model}\right)$. The latter reuses the known distances between the last canonical viewpoint of h^n and the viewpoint that is chosen to match x. ξ is taken as the normal distribution $\xi\left(d_{pre}, d_{model}\right) = \frac{1}{\sqrt{2\pi}\gamma d_{model}} e^{-\frac{\left(d_{pre} - d_{model}\right)^2}{2\gamma^2 d_{model}^2}}$ whose standard deviation depends on the expected distance, to cope with the increasing inaccuracy as the latter grows; in practice, values around $\gamma \sim 0.5$ yield good results.

Hypothesis encoding and compression Once a number of robots have acquired information about the object they are observing, hypotheses can be refined through exchanges. The associated communication cost is proportional to the volume of data being communicated. It is possible to bound the cost of the communication associated to collective classification as follows. It can be seen that there can only be at most $n_V = \sum_i n_V^{K_i}$ hypotheses being considered at any point in time, representing the number of differentiable object identities and poses. The information about the hypothesis to be transmitted can be encoded either by explicit encoding on a per-hypothesis basis, or by factoring out information common to multiple hypotheses and using implicit information (like ordering) across message fragments.

Experiments Preliminary experiments have been performed with 10 prototypes of the

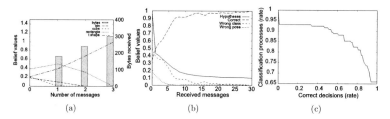

(a)   (b)   (c)

Figure 5.44: **(a)** *Evolution of the classifying estimations of a robot. The belief value evolves as the robot obtains information from its peers, while observing an object of class "T shape";* **(b)** *Convergence in successful collective classification processes (T);* **(c)** *Success rate for different convergence thresholds.*

micro-robots Jasmine-I. In experiments we measured the feature extraction and surface's recognition and collective hypothesis refinement. The robots are placed in the situations like those depicted in Figures 5.36, 5.37. Table 5.7 contains the probability mass assignments for the three stored patterns "flat surface", "concave area" and "M concavity", represented in Figure 5.43 (b). The calculated probabilities from experimental scans confirm the results predicted by the simulation. Figure 5.44(a) shows the belief of a robot after its initial

Feature	Distances			Probability masses		
	Flat	Concv.	M	Flat	Concv.	M
Conca-	1020	543	1096	0.26	0.49	0.24
vity	765	872	1359	0.41	0.36	0.23
	664	764	1251	0.42	0.36	0.22
	1275	861	995	0.27	0.39	0.34
	702	215	1105	0.20	0.67	0.13
	1020	1020	1418	0.37	0.37	0.26
Flat	258	812	1864	0.69	0.22	0.10
surface	259	954	1846	0.71	0.19	0.10
	510	872	1862	0.54	0.31	0.15
M	1785	1785	1646	0.32	0.32	0.25
conca-	1530	1343	789	0.25	0.28	0.48
vity	1436	1288	1190	0.30	0.34	0.36
	1444	1331	895	0.27	0.29	0.44
	1530	1376	1053	0.28	0.31	0.41
	1624	1570	1312	0.31	0.32	0.38
	1457	1294	861	0.26	0.29	0.44
	1275	1061	559	0.22	0.27	0.51

Table 5.7: Probability mass assignments according to Jasmine's scan data.

estimation, which is based only on the information obtained via distance sensors, and after reception of messages from other robots. The belief values converge quickly towards the correct value.

Figure 5.44(b) illustrates the evolution of robots placed around a "T shaped" object. The curves "correct", "wrong class" and "wrong pose" indicate respectively the fraction of robots that took the correct decision, those which made a mistake in the class of the object, and finally those which were able to determine the class of the object correctly but could not estimate their relative positions accurately. The graphs corresponds to an average value for several successful processes.

Figure 5.44(c) shows the success rate for different convergence rates. It can be interpreted as follows: a pair $\left(\frac{x}{100}, \frac{y}{100}\right)$ in the curve means that in y percent of the runs the rate of correct decisions remained stable at x percent or higher after thirty message exchanges. We can therefore see that in around 66% of the processes all robots took the right decision regarding the object identity and their relative position (the rate for a convergence equals to or greater than 80% exceeds 82%), more than one half of the robots reached correct decisions regarding both object identity and position in over 90% of the classification operations. The group of micro-robots converged towards a wrong decision regarding the identity of the object in around 5% of the classification processes. Around 10% of the classification processes end up with less than one robot out of ten with correct identity but wrong positional decisions. Around 15% of the classification processes failed to converge to either a correct decision within a 20% rate or to an erroneous decision.

5.10 Summary

In this chapter we represented several approaches towards a generation of structural rules and application of structural self-organization in manufacturing and swarm robotics. Bottom-up and evolutionary rules generation are overviewed, whereas the main contribution has been made in the field of the top-down derivation.

Top-down decomposition approach. We have presented a part of the autonomous system applied to the process planning in a turbulent manufacturing environment. The main aim of this part is to recognize a turbulence (failure) and to generate a sequence of activities so that to absorb this disturbance and to repair a damaged primary plan. The kernel of this approach is an algorithm of symbolic task decomposition. ASTD is able to perform a functional decomposition of the difference between a current and the desired state into a sequence of activities, so that to drive the system from current state to desired one. Application of ASTD allows solving the problem of huge state space in manufacturing planning systems: instead of reprogramming all possible reactions to disturbances, ASTD generates these reactions dynamically. ASTD approach can also be applied in generating emergent behavior by working together with a rule-extracting approach, like estimation of Kolmogorov-complexity.

Top-down derivation of rules. We have also shown the top-down derivation of rules that generate the desired emergent behavior. As shown in spatial and functional cases, these rules lead to more efficient behavior, than the corresponding bottom-up derived rules. The obtained local rules are very compact and can be implemented as chip-built-functions in each micro-robot.

Scalability. The system based on the top-down derived rules is scaled-free (tested up to 1000 agents). However, if the number of agents grows, the system can change collective strategy, as shown in Figure 5.23. An appearance of rules hierarchy is also possible.

Irregularities. Technically useful emergence differs from natural emergence in several points, the most important is an appearance of irregularities. The treatment of irregularities concerns a coalition formation, constructions of spatial and functional groups, planning and so on. Especially serious problem arises at scaling emergent behavior. Generally, a treatment of irregularities represents a point of further research.

Embodiment. The real technical systems behave much more complex then ones in simulative environments. Therefore the top-down generated rules need a "support" of basic functionality, originally designed for working in collective systems. This functionality is often implemented in "unusual way", so that we denoted it as embodiment. For real experiments in swarm applications we developed the micro-robotic platform which is extremely cheap and whose parts are available in micro-component market. The expended collective capabilities of the Jasmine allow exploring a phenomenon of swarm intelligence in real experiments.

Chapter 6

Conclusion

The main topic of this work was devoted to the investigation of a relation between structures, functions and emergent behavior of self-organizing processes in collective systems as such multi-agents and multi-robotic systems. We intended to achieve three following research goals:

1. to specify a relation between functional, structural and emergent properties of collective systems;

2. to demonstrate the methodological way of how to deal with a high complexity of emergent phenomena;

3. to investigate structural self-organization in artificial (multi-agent) systems and to develop an approach to generate local rules.

The general goal of the thesis has been achieved. We demonstrated that desired emergent properties of collective systems can be designed on different levels. On the functional level it takes a form of fixed local rules, whereas on the structural level we introduced several generators. The desired self-organization has been demonstrated in real experiments with micro-robotic swarm.

1. Relation between functional, structural and emergent properties of collective systems.

We demonstrated that functions and structures in artificial emergent phenomena are closely related. This relation has a form of hierarchical production. We introduced a horizontal and vertical rules production. This double separation maps a relation between structures, functions and macroscopic properties in real collective systems. We considered also some complementary questions, like the benefit of SO-phenomena, the origin of collective problems, a circulation of information, swarm embodiment and so on.

2. Methodological way of treating a high complexity of emergent phenomena.

Complexity is one of the most hardest issues in collective systems. However, it takes different forms in functional and structural cases as well as in reductive and computational approaches. In the functional case a complexity appears as the ambiguity problem and consists in many degrees of freedom. This combinatorial complexity can be treated in step-wise way: to give only so much degrees of freedom how the system requires to solve a task. In the structural case a complexity appears as the microscopic-macroscopic problem: there is no explicit relation between structural rules and generated emergence. We suggested to solve this problem in the top-down way: to start a production of rules from the emergent phenomena. From a methodological side, reductive approaches reduce a complexity to several descriptors/order parameters, whereas computational approaches consider complexity as non-reductive value and profit from simulations.

3. Investigation of structural self-organization in artificial (multi-agent and multi-robotic) systems and generation of local rules.

We suggested top-down rules production. For that we developed decomposing approach, that divide an achievement of a goal into a set of simple steps. Rules can be extracted form these steps by approximating approaches, like estimation of Kolmogorov complexity. We tested this approach on several quite simple problems.

Open problems.

This work demonstrated several problems that essentially outstep the framework of the thesis. The first and most difficult problem concerns the notion of evolution, mentioned in Chapter 1. We revealed some mechanisms *structure* → *functions* and *functions* → *emergence*, additionally to those, suggested e.g. in (Kornienko, 2007) or in other works. However the mechanisms *emergence* → *structures* remained unclear. Without this part the evolutional cycle cannot be closed and investigated. The problems of the *self-replication* and the *collective evolution* have been also mentioned, however their detailed treatment, especially a relation to the co-evolution, remained outside.

Other serious problems touch the issue of local rules. Parametrization of local rules represents the first of them. It defines the degree of irregularity. Should the technically useful behavior be totally predetermined by the parametrization ? The derivation of non-parameterized rules for technical swarms represent an open research point. The second problem concerns an approximation of structural rules. This problem involves a huge number of approaches from computer languages, symbolic grounding, time series analysis and others. This requires a collaboration between corresponding scientific domains. The swarm embodiment is closely connected with the problem of local rules. We demonstrated a few examples of successful embodiment in micro-robots Jasmine. These examples demonstrate challenges of making real artificial self-organizing systems. These challenges are related not only to the low-level problems (e.g. hardware), but also to absence of any systematic re-embodiment procedures for real systems. These problems represent, generally, the research points of further works.

Appendix A

Electrical schemes of Jasmine-III

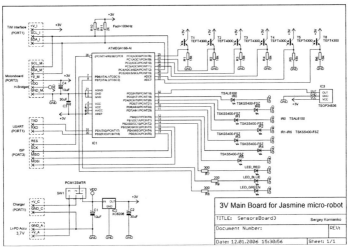

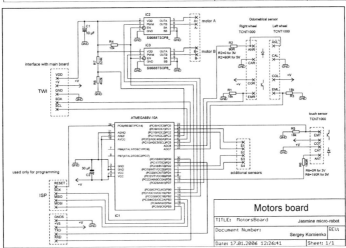

References

Ackley, D., Hinton, G., & Sejnowski, T. 1985. A learning algorithm for Boltzmann Machines. *Cognitive Science*, **9**, 147–169.

Alicke, K. 1999. *Modellierung und Optimierung von mehrstufigen Umschlagsystemen.* PhD thesis, University of Karlsruhe, Karlsruhe.

Alvarenz-Ramírez, J. 1993. Using nonlinear saturated feedback to control chaos: Hénon map. *Physical Review*, **E48**(6), 3165–3167.

Aristotle. 1989. *Metaphysics.* London, William Heinemann Ltd., translated by H. Tredennick, G. Cyril Armstrong. 1933: Cambridge, MA, Harvard University Press.

Arnold, V.I. 1983. *Geometrical methods in the theory of ordinary differential equations.* Berlin: Springer Verlag.

Arnold(Ed.), V.I. 1988. *Dynamical systems III.* Berlin, Heidelberg, New York: Springer Verlag.

Arrowsmith, D.K. 1990. *An introduction to dynamical systems.* Cambridge: Cambridge University Press.

Ashby, W.R. 1957. *An introduction to cybernetics.* London: Chapman & Hall LTD.

Ashby, W.R. 1958. Requisite variety and its implications for the control of complex systems. *Cybernetica*, **1**, 83–99.

Ashby, W.R. 1962. Principles of the self-organizing system. *In: Principles of Self-Organizatin.* Oxford: Pergamon.

Attarzadeh, A. 2006. *Development of advanced power management for autonomous microrobots.* Germany: Master Thesis, University of Stuttgart.

Back, R. J. R., & Kurki-Suonio, F. 1988. Distributed cooperation with action systems. *ACM Trans. Program. Lang. Syst.*, **10**(4), 513–554.

Back, R. J. R., & Sere, K. 1991. Stepwise refinement of action systems. *Structured Programming*, **12**, 17–30.

Balzani, V., Vetturi, M., & Credi, A. 2003. *Molecular Devices and Machines. A Journey into Nanoworld.* Weinhaim, Germany: Wiley-VCH.

Banzhaf, W., Dittrich, P., & Eller, B. 1999. Self-organization in a system of binary strings with spatial interactions. *Physica D*, **125**, 85–104.

Barabási, A.-L., & Albert, R. 1999. Emergence of scaling in random networks. *Science*, **286**, 509–512.

Basso, M., Evangelisti, A., Genesio, R., & Tesi, A. 1998. On bifurcation control in time delay feedback systems. *Int. J. Bifurcation and Chaos*, **8**(4), 713–721.

Bellman, R., & Dreyfus, S.E. 1962. *Applied dynamic programming*. Princeton, New Jersey.

Berg, L. 1986. *Lineare Gleichungssysteme mit Bandstruktur und ihr asymptotisches Verhalten*. München: Hanser Verlag.

Bertelle, C., Flouret, M., Jay, V., Olivier, D., & Ponty., J.-L. 2001. Automata with multiplicities as behaviour model in multi-agent simulations. *In: Proceeding of SCI'2001*. Orlando, Florida, USA.

Birkhoff, G.D. 1927a. *Dynamical Systems*. AMS.

Birkhoff, G.D. 1927b. On the periodic motions of dynamical systems. *Acta Math. (reprinted in MacKay and Meiss 1987)*, **50**, 359.

Blazewicz, J., Domschke, W., & Pesch, E. 1996. The Job Shop Scheduling Problem: Conventional and New Solution Techniques. *European Journal of Operational Research*, **93**, 1–33.

Bonabeau, E., Dorigo, M., & Theraulaz, G. 1999. *Swarm intelligence: from natural to artificial systems*. New York: Oxford University Press.

Bondi, A.B. 2000. Characteristics of scalability and their impact on performance. *Pages 195–203 of: Proc. of the second international workshop on Software and performance*. ACM Press.

Böttcher, A., & Silbermann, B. 1990. *Analysis of Toeplitz operators*. Berlin, Heidelberg: Springer Verlag.

Böttcher, A., & Silbermann, B. 1999. *Introduction to large truncated Toeplitz matrices*. New York: Springer-Verlag.

Boutet de Monvel, L., & Guillemin, V. 1981. *The spectral theory of Toeplitz operators*. Princeton, NJ: Princeton Univ. Press.

Bradie, M., & Duncan, C. 1997. *The evolution of the concepts of space and time*. http://chandra.bgsu.edu/ gcd/titlepage.tableofcontents.html: not published, available online.

Brataas, G., & Hughes, P. 2004. Exploring architectural scalability. *Pages 125–129 of: Proc. of the fourth international workshop on Software and performance*. ACM Press.

Bushev, M. 1994. *Synergetics: chaos, order, self-organization*. World Scientific Publisher.

Bussmann, S., & Schild, K. 2000. Self-Organizing Manufacturing Control: An Industrial Application of Agent Technology. *In: Proc. of ICMAS'2000*. Boston: MA.

Camazine, S., Deneubourg, J-L., Franks, N.R., Sneyd, J., Theraulaz, G., & Bonabeau, E. 2003. *Self-Organization in Biological Systems*. Princeton, NJ, USA: Princeton University Press.

Campbell, N.A. 1990. *Biology, 2nd ed.* Benjamin/Cummings.

Caprari, G., & Siegwart, R. 2003. Design and Control of the Mobile Micro Robot Alice. *Pages 23–32 of: Proc. of the 2nd Int. Symposium on Autonomous Minirobots for Research and Edutainment, AMiRE'2003.*

Cariani, P. 1997. Emergence of new signal-primitives in neural networks. *Intellectica*, **2**, 95–143.

Carr, J. 1981. *Applications of Centre Manifold Theory.* New York, Heidelberg, Berlin: Springer-Verlag.

Carrillo, L., Marzo, J.L., Harle, D., & Vilà, P. 2003. A Review of Scalability and its Application in the Evaluation of the Scalability Measure of AntNet Routing. *In: Proc. of the IASTED-CSN 2003.*

Carroll, J., & Long, D. 1989. *Theory of finite automata.* Englewood Cliffs, NJ : Prentice Hall.

Caselles, J.F. 2005. *Exploration of embodiment in real microrobotic swarm.* Germany: Master Thesis, University of Stuttgart.

Casillas, J., Cordon, O., & Herrera, F. 2000. Learning fuzzy rules using ant colony algorithms. *Pages 13–21 of: Proc. of the 2nd Int. Workshop on Ant Algorithms (ANTS 2000), Brussels, Belgium.*

Chantemargue, F., & Hirsbrunner, B. 1999. A collective robotics application based on emergence and self-organization. *In: Proceedings of ICYCS'99.*

Charikar, M., Lehman, E., Liu, D., Panigrahy, R., Prabhakaran, M., Rasala, A., Sahai, A., & Shelat, A. 2002. Approximating the smallest grammar: Kolmogorov complexity in natural models. *Pages 792–801 of: Proc. of the 34th ACM symposium on Theory of computing.* ACM Press.

Chen, X. 2004. *Optimization of communication in a swarm of micro-robots.* Germany: Master Thesis, University of Stuttgart.

Chou, H.-H., & Reggia, J.A. 1997. Emergence of self-replicating structures in a cellular automata space. *Physica D*, **110**, 252–276.

Clausius, R. 1865. (english translate see in *W.F. Magie, A Source Book in Physics; McGraw-Hill: New York, 1935).* Annalen der Physik und Chemie, **125**, *353.*

Codd, E.F. 1968. Cellular Automata. *New York: Academic Press.*

Cohen, S.M., Curd, P., & Reeve, C.D.C. 2000. Readings in Ancient Greek Philosophy: From Thales to Aristotle. *Hackett Pub. Co. Inc.*

Conant, R. 1974. W. Ross Ashby (1903-1972). International Journal of General Systems, **1**, *4–7.*

Constantin, P., Foias, C., Nicolaenko, B., & Temam, R. 1989. Integral manifolds and inertial manifolds for dissipative partial differential equations. *New York, Heidelberg, Berlin: Springer-Verlag.*

Constantinescu, C., Kornienko, S., Kornienko, O., & Heinkel, U. 2004. An agent-based approach to support the scalability of change propagation. Pages 157–164 of: Proc. of ISCA04.

Cooper, G.F. 1990. The computational complexity of probabilistic inferences. Artificial Intelligence, **42**, 393–405.

Coulouris, G., Dollimore, J., & Kindberg, T. 2001. Distributed Systems. Addison-Wesley Longman, Amsterdam.

Csuhaj-Varju, E., Kelemen, J., Paun, G., & Dassow, J. 1994. Grammar Systems: A Grammatical Approach to Distribution and Cooperation. Gordon and Breach Science Publishers, Inc.

Darley, V. 1994. Emergent Phenomena and Complexity. In: Proc. of Alive IV Workshop.

Davis, P. 1979. Circulant matrices. John Willey & Sons.

Dorogovtsev, S.N., & Mendes, J.F.F. 2001. Scaling properties of scale-free evolving networks: Continuous approach. Phys. Rev. E, **63**, 056125 1–19.

Dörrsam, V. 1999. Materialflussrientierte Leistungsanalyse einstufiger Produktionssysteme. PhD thesis, University of Karlsruhe, Karlsruhe.

Durfee, E.H. 1999. Distributed Problem Solving and Planning. Pages 121–164 of: Weiss, G. (ed), Multiagent Systems: A Modern Introduction to Distributed Artificial Intelligence. MIT Press.

Ebeling, W., & Feistel, R. 1986. Physik der Selbstorganisation und Evolution. Akademie-Verlag.

Ebeling, W., Freund, J., & Schweitzer, F. 1998. Komplexe Structuren: Entropie und Information. B.G. Teubner.

Eden, A., Foias, C., Nicolaenko, B., & Temam, R. 1994. Exponential attractors for dissipative evolution equations. John Willey & Sons.

Eigen, M., & Schuster, P. 1978. The hypercycle - Part B: The abstract hypercycle. Die Naturwissenschaften, **65**, 7–41.

Eigen, M., McCasill, J., & Schuster, P. 1988. Molecular quasi-species. Journal of Physical Chemistry, **92**(24), 6881–6891.

Engelson, V. 2000. Simulation and Visualization of Autonomous Helicopter and Service Robots. Linköping Electronic Articles in Computer and Information Science, ISSN 1401-9841, **5**(013).

Foias, C., Sell, G., & Temam, R. 1988. Inertial manifolds for nonlinear evolution equations. Jornal of differential equation, **73**, 309–353.

Freitas, A.A. 2002. A survey of evolutionary algorithms for data mining and knowledge discovery. In: Ghosh, A., & Tsutsui(Eds.), S. (eds), Advances in Evolutionary Computation. Springer-Verlag.

Fu, Zh. 2005. Swarm-based computation and spatial decision making. Germany: Master Thesis, University of Stuttgart.

Fukuda, T. 1997. Controlling spatial groups of mobile robots. *Presentation of T. Fukuda and privat discussion at the university of Heidelberg.*

Fukuda, T., & Ueyama, T. 1994. Cellular robotics and micro robotic systems. *World Scientific Publishing Co. Pte. Ltd.*

Futuyma, D.J. 1986. Evolutionary Biology. *Sinauer Associates, Inc.*

Gaweda, A.E., Setiono, R., & Zurada, J.M. 2000. Rule Extraction from Feedforward Neural Network for Function Approximation. Pages 311–316 of: Proc. of the 5th Conf. Neural Networks And Soft Computing, Zakopane, Poland.

Geider, R. 2006. Development of context-based communication protocols for the microrobot 'Jasmine'. *Germany: Studienarbeit, University of Stuttgart.*

Girko, V.L. 1974. On the distribution of solutions of systems of linear equations with random coefficients. Theory of probability and mathematical statistics, **2**, *41–44.*

Golubitsky, M., & Schaeffer, D.G. 1985. Singularities and groups in bifurcation theory, Vol. I. *New York: Springer-Verlag.*

Golubitsky, M., Stewart, I., & Schaeffer, D.G. 1988. Singularities and groups in bifurcation theory Vol.II. *New York: Springer-Verlag.*

Goss, S., Deneubourg, S. Aron J.L., & Pasteels, J.M. 1989. Selforganized Shortcuts in the Argentine Ant. Naturwissenschaften, **76**, *579–581.*

Graves, S., Kan, A.H.G. Rinnooy, & Zipkin, P. 1993. Logistics of Production and Inventory. *Volume 4 of Handbooks in Operations Research and Management Science, North Holland.*

Green, D. 1994. Emergent behavior in biological systems. Complexity International, **1**, *1–12.*

Grenander, U., & Szegö, G. 1958. Toeplitz forms and their applications. *Berkeley: Univ. of California Press.*

Greuter, W. 2002. The ancient Greek roots of biological science. In. VI International Congress of Systematic and Evolutionary Biology.

Grigoriev, R.O., Cross, M.C., & Schuster, H.G. 1997. Pinning control of spatiotemporal chaos. Phys. Rev. Letters, **79**(15), *2795–2798.*

Grigorieva, E.V., Haken, H., Kashchenko, S.A., & Pelster, A. 1999. Travelling wave dynamics in a nonlinear interferometer with spatial field transformer in feedback. Physica D, **125**(1-2), *123–141.*

Gu, Y., Tung, M., Yuan, J.-M., Feng, D.H., & Narducci, L.M. 1984. Crises and Hysteresis in coupled logistic map. Phys. Rev. Letters, **25**(9), *701–704.*

Guckenheimer, J., & Holmes, P.J. 1983. Nonlinear oscillations, dynamical systems, and bifurcations of vector fields. *Berlin: Springer-Verlag.*

Haken, H. 1977. Synergetics: An introduction. *Berlin, Heidelberg: Springer-Verlag.*

Haken, H. 1983a. Advanced synergetics. *Berlin: Springer-Verlag.*

Haken, H. 1983b. Synergetics: An introduction, third edition. *New York: Springer-Verlag.*

Haken, H. 1984. Laser theory. *Berlin: Springer-Verlag.*

Haken, H. 1988. Information and Self-Organisation. *Berlin, Heidelberg, New York, Tokyo: Springer-Verlag.*

Haken, H. 1991. Synergetic computers and congnition. *Berlin: Springer-Verlag.*

Haken, H. 1996. Principles of brain functioning. *Berlin: Springer-Verlag.*

Haken, H., Schanz, M., & Starke, J. 1999. Treatment of combinatorial optimization problems using selection equations with cost terms. Part I. Two-dimensional assignment problems. Physica D, **134**, *227–241.*

Halpern, J.Y., & Mosesi, Y. 1990. Knowledge and common knowledge in a distributed environment. J. of the Association for Computer Machinery, **37***(3), 549–587.*

Hassard, B.D., Kazarinoff, N.D., & Wan, Y.-H. 1981. Theory and Applications of Hopf Bifurcation. *London, NY, Melbourne, Sydney: Cambridge University Press.*

Hejl, P. 1981. The Definition of System and the Problem of the Observer: The Example of the Theory of Society. Pages 170–185 of: *und H. Schwegler, G. Roth (ed),* Self-organizing Systems. An interdisciplinary Approach. *Frankfurt a.M., New York: Campus.*

Helbing, D. 1997. Verkehrsdynamik. *Berlin, Heidelberg: Springer-Verlag.*

Helbing, D. 2001. Traffic and related self-driven many-particle systems. Reviews of Modern Physics, **73**, *1067–1141.*

Helbing, D., & Vicsek, T. 1999. Optimal self-organization. New Journal of Physics, **1**, *13.1–13.16.*

Heylighen, F. 1996. The Growth of Structural and Functional Complexity during Evolution. In: *Heylighen, F., & (eds.), D. Aerts (eds),* The Evolution of Complexity. *(taken from http://pespmc1.vub.ac.be/papers/): Kluwer Academic Publishers.*

Hirschman, I., & Hughes, D. 1977. Extreme eigen values of Toeplitz operators. *Berlin: Springer-Verlag.*

Hodson, G. 1990. Concealed Wisdom in World Mythology. *Natl Book Network.*

Hu, G., Xiao, J., Yang, J., Xie, F., & Qu, Z. 1997. Synchronization of spatiotemporal chaos and its applications. Phys. Rev. E, **56***(3), 2738–2746.*

I-Swarm. 2003-2007. I-Swarm: Intelligent Small World Autonomous Robots for Micromanipulation, 6th Framework Programme Project No FP6-2002-IST-1. *European Communities.*

ISO/DIS14649-1. 2000. Part 1: Overview and fundamental principles. *Genf Final DIS.*

Jarnik, J., & Kurzweil, J. 1969. On invariant sets and invariant manifolds of differential systems. Jornal of differential equation, **6**, *247–263.*

Jebens, K. 2006. Development of a docking approach for autonomous recharging system for micro-robot 'Jasmine'. *Germany: Studienarbeit, University of Stuttgart.*

Jetschke, G. 1989. Mathematik der Selbstorganisation. *Braunschweig, Wiesbaden: Friedr. Vieweg & Sohn.*

Jiménez, M.G. 2005. Cooperative actuation in a large robotic swarm. *Germany: Master Thesis, University of Stuttgart.*

Jogalekar, P., & Woodside, M. 2000. Evaluating the Scalability of Distributed Systems. IEEE Transactions on Parallel and Distributed Systems, **11***(6), 589 – 603.*

Jongbloet, P.H., Zielhuis, G.A., Groenewoud, H.M.M., & de Jong, P.C.M. Pasker. 2001. The Secular Trends in Male:Female Ratio at Birth in Postwar Industrialized Countries. Environmental Health Perspectives, **109***(7), 749–752.*

Jost, J., & Joy, M.P. 2002. Spectral properties and synchronization in coupled map lattices. Phys. Rev. E, **65***, 016201:1–9.*

Kaneko, K. 1993. Theory and application of coupled map lattices. *Chichester, New York, Brisbane, Toronto, Singapore: John Willey & Sons.*

Kaneko, K. 1994. Relevance of dynamic clustering to biological networks. Physica D, **75**, *55–73.*

Kataoka, N., & Kaneko, K. 2000. Functional dynamics I: Articulation process. Physica D, **138***, 255–250.*

Kataoka, N., & Kaneko, K. 2001. Functional dynamics II: Syntactic structure. Physica D, **149***, 174196.*

Kauffman, S.A. 1993. The Origins of Order: Self-Organization and Selection in Evolution. *New York: Oxford University Press.*

Kelley, A. 1967. The stable, center-stable, center, center-unstable, unstable manifolds. Jornal of differential equation, **3***, 546–570.*

Kelley, W.G., & Peterson, A C. 1991. Difference equations. An introduction with Applications. *Academic Press: B.G. Teubner Stuttgart.*

Kishine, Takuro. 1997. Eastern Sunrise, Western Sunset: The Cycle of Civilizations. *Coarsegold: Oughten House Publications.*

Klimontovich, Y. 1995. Statistical theory of open systems. *Dordrecht, Kluwer.*

Kocarev, L., & Parlitz, U. 1995. General Approach for Chaotic Synchronization with Applications to Communication. Physical Review Letters, **74***, 5028–5031.*

Kolesnikov, A. 1994. Synergetic control theory, in russian (А. А. Колесников, Синергетическая теория управления). *Taganrog: Taganrog state university.*

Kolmogorov, A.N. 1963. Three approaches to the definition of the concept quantity of information. IEEE Transactions Inform., **14***, 14.*

Konishi, K., & Kokame, H. 1999. Decentralized delayed-feedback control of a one-way coupled ring lattice. Physica D, **127***, 1–12.*

Kornienko, O. 2007. The synergetic approach towards analysing and controlling the collective phenomena in multi-agents systems, PhD thesis. *University of Stuttgart: to be published.*

Kornienko, O., Kornienko, S., & Levi, P. 2001. Collective decision making using natural self-organization in distributed systems. Pages 460–471 of: Proc. of Int. Conf. on Computational Intelligence for Modelling, Control and Automation (CIMCA'2001), Las Vegas, USA.

Kornienko, O., Kornienko, S., & Levi, P. 2003a. Behandlung von Turbulenzen in der Produktion durch intelligente Agentensysteme. Lebendige Wissenschaft, *2, 41–46.*

Kornienko, O., Kornienko, S., & Levi, P. 2004a. Dynamische Prozessplanung auf der Basis der Multi-Agenten Technologie. Industrie Management, **20***(2), 35–38.*

Kornienko, S., & Kornienko, O. 1999. Control of periodical motion using the synergetic concept. *not published yet.*

Kornienko, S., & Kornienko, O. 2000. Methods of synergetic analysis applied to time discrete dynamical systems. *not published yet.*

Kornienko, S., & Kornienko, O. 2002. Contribution of coupling modifications to functional dynamics of distributed systems. *submitted to Physica D.*

Kornienko, S., Thenius, R., Kornienko, O., & Schmickl, T. Re-Embodiment of Honeybee Aggregation Behavior in Artificial Micro-Robotic System. Adaptive Behavior (accepted for publication).

Kornienko, S., Kornienko, O., & Levi, P. 2002a. Synergetic mechanisms of distributed coordination in technical multi-agent systems. Part I. *not published yet.*

Kornienko, S., Kornienko, O., & Levi, P. 2002b. Synergetic mechanisms of distributed coordination in technical multi-agent systems. Part II. *not published yet.*

Kornienko, S., Kornienko, O., & Levi, P. 2003b. Application of distributed constraint satisfaction problem to the agent-based planning in manufacturing systems. Pages 124–140 of: Proc. of IEEE Int. Conf. on AI Systems (AIS'03), Divnomorsk, Russia.

Kornienko, S., Kornienko, O., & Levi, P. 2003c. Flexible manufacturing process planning based on the multi-agent technology. Pages 156–161 of: Proc. of the 21st IASTED Int. Conf. on AI and Applications (AIA '2003), Innsbruck, Austria.

Kornienko, S., Kornienko, O., & Levi, P. 2004b. About nature of emergent behavior in micro-systems. Pages 33–40 of: Proc. of the Int. Conf. on Informatics in Control, Automation and Robotics (ICINCO 2004), Setubal, Portugal.

Kornienko, S., Kornienko, O., & Priese, J. 2004c. Application of multi-agent planning to the assignment problem. Computers in Industry, **54***(3), 273–290.*

Kornienko, S., Kornienko, O., & Levi, P. 2004d. Generation of desired emergent behavior in swarm of micro-robots. In: Proc. of the 16th European Conf. on AI (ECAI 2004), Valencia, Spain.

Kornienko, S., Kornienko, O., & Levi, P. 2004e. Multi-agent repairer of damaged process plans in manufacturing environment. Pages 485–494 of: Proc. of the 8th Conf. on Intelligent Autonomous Systems (IAS-8), Amsterdam, NL.

Kornienko, S., Kornienko, O., Constantinescu, C., Pradier, M., & Levi, P. 2005a. Cognitive micro-Agents: individual and collective perception in microrobotic swarm. In: Proc. of the IJCAI-05 Workshop on Agents in real-time and dynamic environments, Edinburgh, UK.

Kornienko, S., Kornienko, O., & Levi, P. 2005b. Collective AI: context awareness via communication. In: Proc. of the IJCAI 2005, Edinburgh, UK.

Kornienko, S., Kornienko, O., & Levi, P. 2005c. IR-based communication and perception in microrobotic swarms. In: Proc. of the IROS 2005, Edmonton, Canada.

Koza, J. 1992. Genetic programming: on the programming of computers by means of natural selection. *MIT Press, Cambridge, Massacgusetts, London, England.*

Kube, C.R. 1996. A Minimal Infrared Obstacle Detection Scheme. The Journal for Robot Builders, **2***(2), 15–20.*

Kubík, A. 2003. Toward a Formalization of Emergence. Artificial Life, **9**, *4165.*

Kusiak, A. 1990. Intelligent manufacturing systems. *Englewood Cliffs, NJ: Prentice-Hall.*

Kuzmina, L. K. 2001. General modelling problem. *private communication.*

Kuznetsov, Yu. A. 1995. Elements of applied bifurcation theory. *New York, Berlin, Heidelberg, Tokyo: Springer-Verlag.*

Lafrenz, R., Becht, M., Buchheim, T., Burger, P., Hetzel, G., Kindermann, G., Schanz, M., Schulé, M., & Levi, P. 2002. CoPS-Team description. Pages 616–619 of: *Birk, A., Coradeschi, S., & Tadokoro, S. (eds),* RoboCup-01: Robot Soccer World Cup V. *Springer Verlag.*

Lakshmikantham, V., & Rao, M. Rama Mohana. 1995. Theory of Integro-Differential Equations (Stability and Control: Theory, Methods and Applications). *Lausanne, Switzerland: Gordon and Breach Science.*

Landau, L.D., & Lifshitz, E.M. 1976. Course of theoretical physics. Volume 1. Mechanics. *Oxford: Butterworth-Heinemann.*

Landau, L.D., & Lifshitz, E.M. 1981. Course of theoretical physics. Volume 3. Quantum Mechanics: Non-Relativistic Theory. *Oxford: Butterworth-Heinemann.*

Lehn, J.-M. 2002. Toward complex matter: Supramolecular chemistry and self-organization. Proc. of National Academy of Sciences, **99***(8), 4763–4768.*

Levi, P. 1989. Architectures of individual and distributed autonomous agents. IAS, **2**, *315–324.*

Levi, P., Schanz, M., Kornienko, S., & Kornienko, O. 1999. Application of order parameter equation for the analysis and the control of nonlinear time discrete dynamical systems. Int. J. Bifurcation and Chaos, **9***(8), 1619–1634.*

Levine, J.R., Mason, T., & Brown, D. 1992. Lex & yacc. O'Reilly & Associates.

Li, M., & Vitanyi, P.M.B. 1997. An Introduction to Kolmogorov Complexity and Its Applications (Graduate Texts in Computer Science). Springer-Verlag.

Liebherr, K. 1995. Workshop on Adaptable and Adaptiv Software. Pages 149–154 of: Austin, TX (ed), Addendium to the proceedings of OOPSLA'05.

Luna, F., & Stefannson, B. 2000. Economic Simulations in Swarm: Agent-Based Modelling and Object Oriented Programming. Kluwer Academic Publishers.

Maistrenko, Yu.L., Maistrenko, V.L., & Popovich, A. 1998. Transverse instability and riddled basin in a system of two coupled logistic maps. Phys. Rev. E, **57**(3), 2713–2724.

Malone, Th. W. 1987. Modeling coordination in organizations and markets. Manage. Sci., **33**(10), 1317–1332.

Mandelbrot, B.B. 1982. The fractal geometry of nature. San Francisco: W.H. Freeman.

Mann, R., Jepson, A., & Siskind, J. 1997. The computational perception of scene dynamics. Computer Vision and Image Understanding, **65**(2), 113128.

Marchal, C. 1990. The Three-Body Problem. Amsterdam: Elsevier.

Mataric, M.J. 1992. Designing Emergent Behaviors: From Local Interactions to Collective Intelligence. Pages 432–441 of: J-A. Meyer, H. Roitblat, & S. Wilson, eds. (eds), Proc. of the 2nd Int. Conference on Simulation of Adaptive Behavior (SAB-92). MIT Press.

Megabitty. 2005. see http://groups.yahoo.com/group/megabitty/.

Meier, C.A., Enz, C.P., Roscoe, D., Fierz, M., & Pauli, W. 2001. Atom and Archetype : The Pauli/Jung Letters, 1932-1958. Princeton, NJ: Princeton Univ. Press.

Miller, D. 2002. SPHERES - Synchronized Position Hold, Engage, Reorient, Experimental Satellites, Critical Design Review. Tech. rept. Space Systems Laboratory, MIT, Massachusetts, USA.

MINIMAN, MiCRoN, & I-Swarm. (MINIMAN) ESPRIT-Project-33915, (MiCRON) IST-2001-33567, (I-Swarm) IST FET-open Project 507006. EU Projects.

Minsky, M. 1985. Communication with Alien Intelligence. In: Regis, E. (ed), Extraterrestrials: Science and Alien Intelligence. Cambridge University Press.

MIT, SSL. 2004a. DSS - Distributed Satellite System. http://ssl.mit.edu/ground/dss.html. Space Systems Laboratory, MIT,USA.

MIT, SSL. 2004b. SPHERES - Synchronized Position Hold Engage and Reorient Experimental Satellites. http://ssl.mit.edu/spheres/. Space Systems Laboratory, MIT,USA.

Mletzko, F.U. 2006. Testing and Re-Implementation of Communication Protocols for the Microrobot Jasmine. Germany: Studienarbeit, University of Stuttgart.

Mobus, G.E., & Fisher, P.S. 1999. Foraging Search at the Edge of Chaos. In: Levine, D., Brown, V.R., & (eds.), V.T. Shirey (eds), Oscillations in Neural Networks. Lawerence Erlbaum & Associates, Mahwah, NJ.

Monahan, G.E. 1982. A survey of partially observable Markov decision processes: Theory, models, and algorithms. Management Science, **28**(1), 1–16.

Morris, C.W. 1938. Foundations of the theory of signss. In: et al. (edt.), O. Neurath (ed), Internat. Encyclopedia of Unified Science I. Chicago.

Murray, J.D. 1977. Lecture on Nonlinear-differential-equation models in biology. Oxford: Clarendon Press.

Muscholl, M. 2001. Interaction und Kooperation in Multiagentsystemen. PhD thesis, University of Stuttgart, Stuttgart.

Nareyek, A. 2001. Constraint-Based Agents. Lecture Notes in Computer Science, vol. 2062. Springer-Verlag.

Nayfeh, A. 1993. Method of normal forms. New York: John Wiley & Sohn.

Nembrini, J., Winfield, A., & Melhuish, C. 2002. Minimalist Coherent Swarming of Wireless Connected Autonomous Mobile Robots. In: Proc. of Int. Conf. on Simulation of Artificial Behaviour.

Newton, I. 1687. Philosophiae Naturalis Principia Mathematica, (Eng. transl: Mathematical Principles of Natural Philosophy). New York: Translated by Andrew Motte 1729.

Nicolis, G., & Prigogine, I. 1977. Self-organization nonequilibrium systems. New York: Wiley-Interscience.

Nolfi, S., & Floreano, D. 2004. Evolutionary Robotics: The Biology, Intelligence, and Technology of Self-Organizing Machines. Massachusetts: MIT Press/Bradford Book.

Oswald, N., Becht, M., Buchheim, T., Burger, P., Hetzel, G., Kindermann, G., Lafrenz, R., Schanz, M., Schulé, M., & Levi, P. 2000. CoPS-Team description. RoboCup 2000. Tech. rept. University of Stuttgart, Melbourne.

Parpinelli, R.S., Lopes, H.S., & Freitas, A.A. 2002. An Ant Colony Algorithm for Classification Rule Discovery. Pages 190–208 of: Abbas, H.A., & RA, R.A. Sarker (eds), Data Mining. A Heurlstlc Approach. London: Idea Group Publishing.

Pasteels, J.M., Deneubourg, J., & Goss, S. 1987. Selforganization mechanisms in ant societies. Pages 155–175 of: Pasteels, J.M., & Deneubourg, J. (eds), From individual to collective behaviour in social insects. Basel: Birkhauser.

Payton, D.W., Daily, M., Estowski, R., Howard, M., & Lee, C. 2001. Pheromone Robotic. Auton. Robots, **11**(3), 319–324.

Peeters, P., Heikkilä, T., Bussman, S., Wyns, J., Jo, Valckenaers, P., & van Brussel, H. 1998. Novel manufacturing system requirements in automated, line-oriented discrete assembly. Page 10 of: Proc. of 4th IMS-WG - Workshop. Nancy: University of Nancy.

Pfeifer, R., & Iida, F. 2004. Embodied artificial intelligence: Trends and challenges. Pages 1–26 of: et al. (Eds), Iida (ed), Embodied artificial intelligence. Springer.

Pine, B. J. 1999. Mass Customization. The New Frontier in Business Competition. Boston, Mass: Harvard Business School Press.

Pinedo, M. 1995. Scheduling: Theory, Algorithms and Systems. *Prentice Hall.*

Pinto, J. 2003. *Distributed & Grid Computing.* AutomationTechies.com, *http://www.automationtechies.com/sitepages/pid1218.php.*

Pitas, I. 1993. Digital Image Processing Algorithms. *Prentice Hall.*

Poincaré, H. 1899. Les méthodes nouvelles de la mécanique céleste. *Vol. 3. Paris: Gauthier-Villars.*

Pradier, M. 2005. Collective Classification in a Swarm of Microrobots. *Germany: Master Thesis, University of Stuttgart.*

Prigogine, I. 1996. The End of Certainty: Time, Chaos, and the New Laws of Nature. *New York,NY: The Free Press.*

Prigogine, I., & Nicolis, G. 1977. Self-Organization in Non-Equilibrium Systems: From Dissipative Structures to Order Through Fluctuations. *New York: J. Wiley & Sons.*

Prigogine, I., & Stengers, I. 1984. Order out of chaos. *London: Heinemann.*

Prusinkiewicz, P., & Hanan, J. 1980. Lindenmayer Systems, Fractals, and Plants. *Berlin, Heidelberg, New York: Springer-Verlag.*

Rahm, E., & Bernstein, P. 2001. A survey of approaches to automatic schema matching. VLDB Journal: Very Large Data Bases, **10**(4), 334–350.

Rana, O.F., & Stout, K. 2000. What is scalability in multi-agent systems? Pages 56–63 of: Proc. of the fourth international conference on Autonomous agents. *ACM Press.*

Rantzau, R., Constantinescu, C., Heinkel, U., & Meinecke, H. 2002. Champagne: Data Change Propagation for Heterogeneous Information Systems. Pages 1099–1102 of: Proceedings of the 28th VLDB Conference, Hong Kong.

Reese, William L. 1996. Dictionary of Philosophy and Religion : Eastern and Western Thought. *New-York: Humanity Books.*

Robinson, C. 1995. Dynamical systems: stability, symbolic dynamics, and chaos. *Boca Raton, FL: CRC Press.*

Roma, G.-C., Gamble, R. F., & Ball, W. E. 1993. Formal Derivation of Rule-Based Programs. IEEE Trans. Softw. Eng., **19**(3), 277–296.

Russell, S.J. 1995. Artificial intelligence: a modern approach. *Prentice-Hall.*

Salomaa, A. 1973. Formal Languages. *Academic Press (ACM Monograph Series).*

Sanchez, E., & Tomassin, M. 1996. Towards Evolvable Hardware. The Evolutionary Engineering Approach. *Lecture Notes in Computer Science, Vol. 1062, Springer-Verlag, Berlin, Heidelberg.*

Sandefur, J.T. 1990. Discrete dynamical systems. Theory and Application. *Calarendon Press, Oxford.*

Sandholm, T. 1996. Negotiation among self-interested computationally limited agents. *Amherst: PhD thesis, University of Massachusetts.*

Sandholm, T. 1999. Distributed Rational Decision Making. Pages 201–258 of: *Weiss, G. (ed),* Multiagent Systems: A Modern Introduction to Distributed Artificial Intelligence. *MIT Press.*

Schaff, A. 1968. Die Sprache und das menschliche Handeln. In: *Schaff, Adam (ed),* Essays über die Philosophie der Sprache. *Wien,Frankfurt,Zürich.*

Sedgewick, R. 1998. Algorithms in C++. *Massachusetts: Addison-Wesley.*

Sedgewick, R., & Flajolet, P. 1996. An introduction to the analysis of algorithms. *Reading MA: Addison-Wesley.*

Sedwick, R.J., Miller, D.W., & Kong, E.M.C. 1999. Mitigation of Differential Perturbations in Clusters of Formation Flying Satellites. Journal of the Astronautical Sciences, **47***(3,4).*

SFB467. 2001. Report of SFB 467 on 05.12.2001. *Preprint. University of Stuttgart.*

SFB467. 2002/2003. Studie Turbulenz und Wandlungsfähigkeit, 2002 - 2003. *Preprint. Fraunhofer IPA, IFF Universität Stuttgart 2002/2003.*

Shafer, G. 1976. A Mathematical Theory of Evidence. *Princeton University Press.*

Shannon, C.E. 1948. A mathematical theory of communication. Bell System Technical Jornal, **27**, *379.*

Simon, H.A. 1962. The Architecture of Complexity. Pages 467–482 of: Proc. of the American Philosophical Society, *vol. 106.*

Sipper, M., Mange, D., & Stauffer, A. 1997a. Ontogenetic Hardware. BioSystems, **44***(3), 193–207.*

Sipper, M., Sanchez, E., Mange, D., Tomassini, M., Pérez-Uribe, A., & Stauffer, A. 1997b. A Phylogenetic, Ontogenetic, and Epigenetic View of Bio-Inspired Hardware Systems. IEEE Transactions on Evolutionary Computation, **1***(1), 83–97.*

Smith, C.U. 1990. Performance Engineering of Software Systems. *Addison-Wesley.*

Stauffer, A., & Sipper, M. 1998. On the relationship between cellular automata and L-systems:The self-replication case. Physica D, **116**, *71–80.*

Stöcker(Ed.), H. 1997. Taschenbuch der Physik. *Frankfurt am Main: Verlags Harri Deutsch.*

Suzuki, S., Asama, H., Uegaki, A., Kotosaka, S., Fujita, T., Matsumoto, A., Kaetsu, H., & Endo, I. 1995. An infra-red sensory system with local communication for cooperative multiple mobile robots. Pages 220–225 of: Proc. of International Conference on Intelligent Robots.

ter Beek, M.H. 2003. Team Automata - A Formal Approach to the Modeling of Collaboration Between System Components, Ph.D. thesis. *Leiden Institute of Advanced Computer Science, Leiden University.*

Thompson, A. 1997. Artificial Evolution in the Physical World. Pages 101–125 of: *(Ed.),* T. Gomi (ed), Evolutionary Robotics: From Intelligent Robots to Artificial Life. *AAI Books.*

Thompson, J.R. 1989. Empirical Model Building. *Wiley.*

Thompson, J.R. 1999. Simulation: A Modeler's Approach. *Wiley.*

Thompson, W.J. 1992. Computing for Scientists and Engineers: A Workbook of Analysis, Numerics, and Applications. *Wiley-Interscience.*

Turchin, V.F. 1977. The Phenomenon of Science, a cybernetic approach to human evolution. *Columbia University Press, New York.*

Uhl, C., Friedrich, R., & Haken, H. 1995. Analysis of spatiotemporal signals of complex systems. Phys. Rew. E, **51**(5), 3890–3900.

Vinter, R. 2000. Optimal Control. *Birkhauser Boston.*

von Neumann, J. 1966. Theory of Self-Reproducing Automata. *Illinois: University of Illinois Press, Edited and completed by A. W. Burks.*

Wall, B. 2002. Glimpses of Reality: Episodes in the History of Science. *Wall & Emerson.*

Warraich, Omer Amin. 2005. Mechanism of cooperation and functional self-organization in a swarm of micro-robots. *Germany: Master Thesis, University of Stuttgart.*

Weiss, G. 1999. Multiagent systems. A modern approach to distributed artificial intelligence. *MIT Press.*

Wiendahl, H.-P. 2002. Wandlungsfähigkeit. wt Werkstattstechnik, **92**(4), 122–127.

Wiener, N. 1948. Cybernetics, Or Control and Communication in the Animal and the Machine. *New York: Wiley.*

Wiggins, S. 1990. Introduction to applied nonlinear dynamical systems and chaos. *New York, Berlin, Heidelberg, Tokyo: Springer Verlag.*

Wilkinson, Ph., & Charing, Rabbi Douglas. 2004. Encyclopedia of Religion. *Dorling Kindersley.*

Williams, B.C., & Nayak, P. 1996. A Model-based Approach to Reactive Self-Configuring Systems. Pages 971–978 of: Proc. of 13th AAAI'96 / 8th IAAI'96, vol. 2.

Williamson, M.M. 1998. Rhythmic robot arm control using oscillators. In: Proceedings IROS'98.

Witting, L. 1997. General Theory of Evolution. *Aarhus: Peregrine Publisher.*

Wolfram, S. 1985. Undecidability and Intractability in Theoretical Physics. Physical Review Letters, **54**, 735–738.

Woodside, M. 2000. Scalability metrics and analysis of mobile agent systems. In: Proc. Workshop on Infrastructure for Scalable Mobile Agent Systems, at Autonomous Agents 2000.

Yang, J., Peng, W., Ward, M.O., & Rundensteiner, E.A. 2003. Interactive Hierarchical Dimension Ordering, Spacing and Filtering for Exploration of High Dimensional Datasets. Pages 105 – 112 of: IEEE Symposium on Information Visualization 2003 (InfoVis 2003).

Ye, Y., Boies, S., Liu, J., & Yi, X. 2002. *Collective Perception in Massive, Open, and Heterogeneous Multi-agent Environment.* Pages 1175–1182 of: Proc. of the AAMAS'02.

Yigitbasi, S. 1996. *Theorie inertialer Mannigfaltigkeiten und ihre Anwendung auf den Laser.* PhD Thesis, Stuttgart. *Aachen: Shaker Verlag,.*

Zaslavsky, G.M., & Sagdeev, R.Z. 1988. Introduction into nonlinear physics: from pendulum to turbulence and chaos, in rissian (Г.М. Заславский, Р.З. Сагдеев, Введение в нелинейную физику: от маятника до турбулентности и хаоса, Москва, Наука, 1988). *Moscow: Nauka.*

Zhabotinsky, A.M., & Zaikin, A.N. 1973. *Autowave processes in a distributed chemical system.* J. Theor. Biol, **40**, 45–61.

Zhang, H., & Wu, J. 2002. *A statistical thermodynamic model of the organizational order of vegetation.* Ecological Modelling, **153**, 6980.

Ziv, J., & Lempel, A. 1977. *A Universal Algorithm for Sequential Data Compression.* IEEE Transactions on Information Theory, **23**(3), 337–343.